PATONS

Book of
Knitting and Crochet

by Patience Horne
and Stephen Bowden

Heinemann: London

William Heinemann Ltd
15 Queen St, Mayfair, London WIX 8BE

LONDON MELBOURNE TORONTO
JOHANNESBURG AUCKLAND

Designed and printed by Lund Humphries, Bradford and London

Preface

In today's atmosphere of speed and quick-change fashion the old handcrafts would seem out of place yet the opposite is true and many crafts are having a great revival with young and old alike. This book deals with two of them, knitting and crochet. Knitting has always been popular but crafts such as crochet seemed out of touch during the twenties and thirties until it became rare to see anyone with a piece of crochet work in hand.

Victorian ladies were never idle, they painted or sang songs at the pianoforte or sat and worked at a variety of needlecrafts making novelties and articles for the home – many of which were purely decorative and often rather useless. Crochet was a favourite at this time and it is this intrinsic Victorian look which is part of its appeal today when the nostalgia for anything Victorian is so widespread. At the same time crochet is quickly learned and quick and easy to do so that an up-to-the-minute look can be speedily transposed into something to wear – thus it has special appeal to the young.

At the same time, knitting lost its long association with poverty and the struggle to supplement the family earnings through its use as a cottage craft, and became another ladylike accomplishment. Before long, knitting took its place as the leading handcraft as crochet fell away, probably because its image of delicate lacy effects, such as used for doilies and table-mats, seemed out of step with the changing pace of living.

In the fifties, the knitted look, sparked off by Dior's Aran-style coat, brought new thinking to handknitting which now keeps abreast of all the latest fashion trends, and today there is a high standard of good fashion design to be found in all aspects of the handknitted wardrobe. A well made handknitted garment has a beauty which can never be copied and the pleasure of making something to wear for yourself or for the family and home is not only personally rewarding and creatively satisfying but the gentle rhythms of knitting and crochet are soothing and relaxing, thus they are often recommended for their therapeutic qualities.

With the development of manufacturing techniques, the selection of yarns is now so interesting and varied that limitless combinations of texture and colour can be used for a wide range of designs from fabulous glamour fashions which reflect the trends from the world's couture centres, through exciting and way-out topical styles which capture instant fashion to practical family garments for the day-to-day scene.

Our aim has been to produce a really comprehensive book covering the basic principles of knitting and crochet, with simple articles to make which give practice at each stage, ending with a comprehensive selection of fashion and family designs and popular novelties for gifts and bazaars. Introductory chapters outline the social history of the crafts, the nature of the materials used and the correct after-care of finished pieces of work.

Undertaking a project of this character inevitably involves receiving a great deal of assistance which is thankfully acknowledged. Mrs. Essie Page prepared all the knitting instructions for press and checked the proofs: Tom Steel drew all the diagrams: Carlton Studios took the great majority of the photographs. We salute the memories of James Norbury, a close colleague for many years, whose files and collections of knitting books and sheaths were so readily made available and of William J. Lee whose notes were helpful. The International Wool Secretariat provided information in their publications and film strips: Michael Harvey, information on knitting in Norfolk. The support of Patons & Baldwins Limited, Stitchcraft Limited, and Woolcraft Limited has been vital: without their technical and administrative resources and their files of publications stretching back for more than eighty years, it would indeed have been difficult to complete our work.

Patience Horne
Stephen Bowden

Contents

Chapter 1

Knitting and Crochet–
The Social Background

'That this Book may prove beneficial to that numerous and useful class of Females, whose pecuniary means are limited, but whose minds and pursuits are well regulated and directed, will be the greatest reward my labours claim.'
Mrs. Jane Gaugain, 1846

Although it is not so ancient a craft as weaving, knitting comes to us from before the Christian era out of a past not only shadowy but verging on the shady at times. The picture of knitting as a quiet accomplishment designed to help genteel ladies to occupy the long hours of a Victorian afternoon is far from typical; it has not always been quite respectable or commended itself to the Establishment of the day. Immensely popular but subject to crazes, with strong local and regional styles, barely recognized by orthodox craftsmen, condemned as unoriginal and repetitive and its devotees as lazy, lacking a written tradition, the occasion of unseemly gatherings and rowdiness, knitting has many of the attributes of pop culture, including its essential vitality and contact with society's grassroots. There is even a revolutionary element represented by the tricoteuses at the foot of the guillotine. Knitting survives and flourishes as woman's principal leisure pastime because of its inherent fascination and practical character.

Knitted sandal socks and doll's cap from the fourth and fifth centuries A.D. found in Egypt. Note division of socks to allow for big toe and sandal thong. Victoria and Albert Museum. Crown Copyright.

Knitting produces fabric row by row on two or more needles from one continuous length of yarn. *Crochet* uses a hook and one continuous length of yarn to create fabric from a chain of stitches. By contrast, *weaving* involves a web of parallel longitudinal threads (the warp) which is converted into cloth by passing a crosswise thread (the weft) over and under the warp threads. Woven cloth is inelastic and is usually shaped by cutting and sewing. Knitted fabric is elastic, conforms more readily to body contours and can be shaped during knitting. Crochet fabric is less elastic than knitting and is not so easily shaped while working.

FABULOUS BEGINNINGS

Legend and conjecture obscure the early history of knitting. An ingenious author has suggested that fabrics referred to in the Iliad and the Odyssey could only have been produced by knitting and not by weaving as the Homeric texts imply; crafts akin to knitting have been dated as far back as 1500 B.C. to 1000 B.C.; we are told that, in the period immediately before the birth of Christ, the women of Thebes wore a kind of netted snood or turban as part of their hair dressing.

The earliest finds of actual knitted fabric were made at Dura-Europas in Syria and date back to the second or third century A.D. By an almost eerie coincidence, finds of knitted fabric dating back to this period, or a little later, have been made across the Atlantic in Peru, although it is difficult to say with certainty exactly how the fabric was produced. The Coptic Christians transmitted knowledge of the craft outwards from the Arabic lands and caps of the fourth century A.D. have been preserved. Arabic colour knitting of the seventh to ninth centuries A.D. has been found in Egypt.

Handknitted in red silk and gold thread, this ecclesiastical glove is one of a pair probably made in Spain for a bishop's liturgical use in the sixteenth century. Victoria and Albert Museum. Crown Copyright.

Little or nothing is known about knitting during the troublous times of the early Middle Ages, but the craft survived and must have achieved a high degree of technical sophistication. Knitted gloves for ceremonial religious use survive from mediaeval Spain; knowledge of the craft is thought to have been brought westwards from the Near East to Spain following the Moorish conquests. Knitted silk gloves used by William of Wykeham at his New College at Oxford in 1386 are thought to have come from Spain, too.

TUDOR CAPS AND STOCKINGS

In England, references to knitting became more frequent towards the end of the fifteenth century as the country settled down to Tudor rule after the Wars of the Roses. It was regarded, not as a feminine domestic accomplishment, but as an industrial craft to be practised by men; a Knitters Gild was founded in Paris in 1527. In 1571 knitters were listed as one of the fifteen crafts involved in capping in England. The Cappers Gild was established in London, Monmouth, Coventry, York, and other towns; in an Act of Henry VII the price of knitted woollen caps was fixed at 2s. 8d. in 1488, and it is reasonable to suppose that knitted caps must have been produced for a considerable time before legislation to control their price was considered necessary.

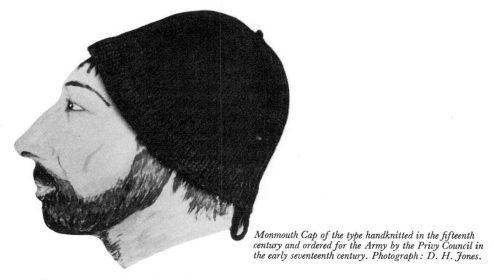

Monmouth Cap of the type handknitted in the fifteenth century and ordered for the Army by the Privy Council in the early seventeenth century. Photograph: D. H. Jones.

Gloves, caps and stockings feature prominently in knitting history – perhaps it is that human extremities are so intricately shaped and flexible that the elastic fabric of knitting offers the most satisfactory means of covering them. According to John Stow, under Henry VIII 'the youthfull Citizens also took them to the new fashion of flatte caps, knit of woollen yearne blacke . . .'. Later, the Aldermen and even the Lord Mayor succumbed to the fashion. In 1529, citizens of Bristol complained to the Court of Star Chamber that Bristol cappers were being ruined by cappers from London and other places who were coming to Redcliffe Fair and taking away the livelihood of three or four hundred Bristol carders, spinners, and knitters. The substantial extent of the trade in knitted caps is indicated by the fact that when the fashion for them seems to have flagged later in the sixteenth century, legislation was enacted to compel certain classes to wear them, under penalty of a fine. In 1575 the Council of the Marches ordered that such fines should be conscientiously collected and distributed among the poor cappers of London, Exeter, Bristol, Monmouth, Hereford, Gloucester, Worcester, and many other towns. In *The Worthies of England* Thomas Fuller drew attention to 'the tenderness of our kings to preserve the trade of cap making . . . so many thousands of people being maintained thereby in the land . . .'.

Knitted stockings with their trickily turned heels and shaped feet demanded great skill; in the sixteenth century, when knitted in silk, they became status symbols for monarchs. Henry VIII is said to have received silk stockings from Spain; Sir Thomas Gresham presented Edward VI with a pair and in 1561 Queen Elizabeth's silk woman Mrs. Montague gave the Queen a pair of knitted black silk stockings. Elizabeth liked them so well and Mrs. Montague's young serving women are said 'to have quickly become so dextrous in knitting that from henceforth Elizabeth never wore cloth hose any more'. A pair of Elizabeth's silk stockings is still preserved at Hatfield House. In 1577 George Gascoigne the poet declared that the greatest ornaments of dress were knit silk stockings and Spanish leather shoes.

At the same time the production of knitted stockings in more generally available yarns developed extensively. Sir Thomas L'Estrange of Hunstanton paid eight shillings for four pairs of knitted hose in 1533; five years later he paid a shilling for two pairs for his children. An Act of 1552 refers to 'knitte hose, knitte peticotes, knitte gloves and knitte slieves'. In 1577 it was said that the bark of alder trees was used by peasants' wives for dyeing the stockings they had knitted. When Queen

Elizabeth visited Norwich in 1579, children are said to have appeared before her, some spinning worsted yarn and some knitting hose. A school of knitting was established in Lincoln in 1591.

THE SAD STORY OF WILLIAM LEE

The Elizabethan period saw the first developments towards an industrial society in England. New raw materials were mined, collieries were expanded and new industries in metal-working were started, making cutlery, farm implements, and harness furniture. It is not surprising, then, that in an age which was so universally creative, somebody should have sought to make hand-knitting more productive. Very little is known with certainty about the life of William Lee, but he merits remembrance as the first of the great textile innovators, whose work preceded that of Arkwright, Hargreaves, and Crompton by some 180 years. Born at Woodborough in Nottinghamshire, he graduated at Cambridge in 1582/3 and in due course became curate of Calverton, some five miles from Nottingham. There, in 1589, he made his prototype of the stocking frame. Several legends surround the origin of his interest in knitting – that expulsion from a university fellowship for an imprudent marriage led to his wife knitting to support them, that a girl he was courting paid more attention to her knitting than to him and he invented the frame to spite her – but these are all apocryphal.

The facts of Lee's later life are grim. After two years of mixed fortunes at Calverton he moved to London with his brother James, who had helped his work. The frame attracted local interest and Lee approached the Queen for the grant of a monopoly. The Queen refused; she wanted a machine for fine silk stockings, fearing that Lee's coarse-mesh frame would ruin 'my poor people who obtain their bread by the employment of knitting' (an indication of the extent to which the handcraft had developed). Lee made a frame for fine silk by 1598 but Elizabeth still said no to a monopoly. Lee left England for Rouen and Paris, but the murder of Henri IV stopped any hope of French royal patronage for an English Protestant. Oppressed by melancholy, Lee died alone in Paris in 1610. His brother returned to England and established the framework knitting industry in Nottingham. By 1664, 200 men were employed there on Lee frames and by 1700 the number had increased to 1,000. That indefatigable traveller Celia Fiennes commented in 1697 that 'the manufacture of the town (Nottingham) mostly consists in weaving of stockings, which is a very ingenious art'. Framework knitting spread to other towns and Lee's invention became the basis of a national industry, which unfortunately acquired a reputation for poor pay and oppressive labour relations.

FAIR ISLE, ARAN, AND FOLK KNITTING

One of the great events of Elizabeth's reign, the defeat of the Spanish Armada in 1588, also left its mark on the history of knitting. It is said, perhaps with truth, that one of the Spanish ships was wrecked on Fair Isle and that the inhabitants copied knitting patterns, including those known as the Armada Cross and the Rose of Sharon, from the clothes of Spanish survivors or the corpses of the drowned. These patterns became the basis of the traditional Fair Isle garments which have enjoyed varying popularity, particularly after World Wars I and II. It is not unreasonable to infer that the Fair Islanders could already knit before the rich new source of inspiration struck their shores. In any event, the episode illustrates vividly the tendency for hand knitting to establish itself in marginal areas where it is difficult to make a regular living and a supplementary source of income must be found. Other island groups adopted the craft, notably the Shetland Isles, the Aran Isles off the west coast of Ireland and, of course, the Channel Islands which took to knitting when the fishing industry was declining and farming was unprofitable, during the sixteenth century. By the end of that century knitting was established in Dentdale and Garsdale in West Yorkshire, probably because the local custom of dividing land equally between a testator's sons made holdings so small that a secondary occupation was imperative. At the same period there are records of knitting in Norfolk, particularly around Great Yarmouth.

A HUMBLE CRAFT

Hand knitters were hardly considered respectable. They were poor; their craft occupied their hands but left their legs free to wander and their tongues able to chatter and sing. Because their homes would be dark and cheerless they knitted out of doors in fine weather. They enjoyed company and, in the darkness of night or winter, gathered at each others' homes to knit by firelight. These characteristics frequently brought them into conflict with the authorities who were naturally suspicious of unofficial gatherings of 'rude mechanicals'. In 1605 an Assembly (or town council) in Great Yarmouth agreed that 'all knitters which doe wander knitting in the streate shall be taken by the Aldermen, Constables or any other Free Men and immediately shall be carried to Brydewell . . .'. A biography dated 1669 of Lady Frances Hobart of Blickling Hall, Norfolk, tells how she was chastized for her visits to see the poor knitting. Celia Fiennes in 1698 tells how 'I went to Windham (Wymondham) . . . thence we went mostly through lanes where you meete the ordinary people knitting 4 or 5 in a company under the hedges; to Attleborough . . . then over an open down like Salisbery Plaine . . . still finding the country full of spinners and knitters . . .'. An Act of Court in the Channel Islands in 1606 ordered that people should not knit during the harvest or seaweed-cutting seasons under penalty of imprisonment with bread and water. Dumaresq, a local author, complained that country people were abandoning farming in favour of knitting. Jurat Poingdestre of Jersey referred to knitting as the 'lazy industry'. Nocturnal parties, called *veilles*, when songs were sung and stories told, created trouble when dispersing knitters made too much noise in the streets going home. Vivid accounts have been left of similar parties called *sittings* as they were held in Dentdale at a later date. In *The Rural Life of England* (1844) William Howitt describes how 'the whole troup of neighbours being collected, they sit and knit, sing knitting songs and tell knitting stories . . . they often get so excited that they say "Neighbours, we'll not part to-night", that is, till after twelve o'clock. All this time their knitting goes on with unremitting speed. They sit rocking to and fro like so many weird wizards'.

It may be the rapid movement of the needles, or the constant repetition of similar stitches, but the continual practice of knitting seems always to have produced in its devotees a hypnotic effect, almost like that of a drug, combined with a sort of suppressed excitement. Perhaps that accounts for the craft's fascination down the years and its liability to sudden crazes. The Rev. Andrew Dishington, Minister of Mid and South Yell in the Shetlands from 1791 to 1799, was not charmed. 'Women of every rank and distinction are employed in spinning wool and knitting coarse and fine stockings' he grumbled, 'to their great loss and miserable mis-spending of their time.'

THE GROWTH OF THE INDUSTRY

In the middle of the seventeenth century the development of hand knitting as a cottage industry producing goods for sale at home and abroad to France – and even America – was interrupted by the Civil Wars, although the production of comforts for Roundhead and Cavalier troops may have been stimulated. Knitted Monmouth caps had been ordered by the Privy Council in 1627 as part of an Army contract for 6,000 suits. After the Restoration of Charles II in 1660, the Channel Islanders had to contend with intense competition from France when seeking to revive their trade there; they met it by giving their chief types of long stocking, available in a variety of colours, such modern-sounding names as Rejoicing Widow, Mortal Sin, and Amorous Desire. Their industry grew and continued prosperous up to the period of the Napoleonic Wars, in the process adding to the English language the words jersey and guernsey. In England, the growth of the industry is demonstrated by the petition submitted to the Mayor and Burgesses of Leicester in 1674 by the stocking middlemen, begging them not to grant a knitting monopoly as this would endanger the livelihood of 2,000 poor people in Leicester and adjacent villages.

As well as a source of income and profit as a trade, knitting was regarded as a domestic skill which, like baking, spinning, brewing, and home doctoring was to be expected from a normally accomplished woman – or man. The technique was passed by word of mouth; there was little point in written or printed instructions in an age when the literacy of working people was very low. The earliest known knitting patterns are probably those published in 1655 in *Natura Exenterata*, a collection of medical hints which included, at the back, a few knitting patterns and 'the order how to knit a Hose'. Daniel Defoe's piratical novel *Captain Singleton*, published in 1720, describes the fictional adventures of one Robert Knox, a sailor who was captured with his father in 1659 and held prisoner in Ceylon for twenty years. During his captivity he acquired a Bible in exchange for a knit cap and during his eventual escape in 1679 his party used the act of knitting and the possession, for trading purposes, of 'a good parcel of cotton yarn to knit caps with' as a cover story during his journey across a wilderness. Defoe, a stickler for authentic detail, would not have made his sailors knit if such a circumstance were in any way unusual.

GEORGIAN PROSPERITY

That Defoe understood perfectly the significant growth of the knitting industry is demonstrated in *A Tour Through the Whole Island of Great Britain*, published in 1724/26. He finds knitting established in East Anglia, Tewkesbury, Nottingham, Doncaster, and Richmond, Yorkshire, where 'very coarse and ordinary' stockings in the smallest size for children are 'sold for eighteen pence per dozen or three half pence a pair, sometimes less'. Defoe also refers to the trade radiating from Westmorland – Kendal and Kirkby Stephen – into the neighbouring Yorkshire Dales. Reference has already been made to the establishment of the craft in Dentdale and Garsdale some hundred or more years earlier; Defoe comments that 'it is indeed a very considerable manufacture in it self and of late mightily encreased too'. Indeed, from a knitting point of view the middle of the eighteenth century was a golden age. Stockings were wanted for the Army, particularly during the Seven Years' War from 1756 to 1763 and the knitters of the West Yorkshire Dales provided them. They were kept so busy and paid so comparatively well that savings accumulated in the form of George III guineas. Despite desperately hard times later, some of these hoards remained intact a century or more later when *wide boys* of the period were offering dales-people prices which, though well above face value, were substantially less than collectors would pay.

Trade further north was brisk at this time, too. In 1733 Thomas Gifford of Shetland shipped to Lisbon a cargo including 800 pairs of coarse stockings. The captain of the ship sold them as directed but, unfortunately for Gifford, decamped with the proceeds. In 1773, Sir Alexander Gordon told Dr. Johnson that the value of stockings exported from Aberdeen was, in peace, a hundred thousand pounds but, in war, a hundred and seventy thousand pounds. Dr. Johnson, says Boswell, asked what made the difference? Sir Alexander answered, 'Because there is more occasion for them in war'. Another professor who was present said, 'Because the Germans, who are our great rivals in the manufacture of stockings, are otherwise employed in time of war'. Dr. Johnson replied, 'Sir, you have given a very good

solution'. The Great Cham himself was no knitter (or knotter), as Boswell relates:
'Dr. Johnson: I once tried knotting; Dempster's sister undertook to teach me, but
I could not learn it.
Boswell: So, sir; it will be related in pompous narrative "once for his amusement
he tried knotting, nor did this Hercules disdain the distaff".
Dr. Johnson: Knitting of stockings is a good amusement. As a freeman of Aberdeen,
I should be a knitter of stockings.'

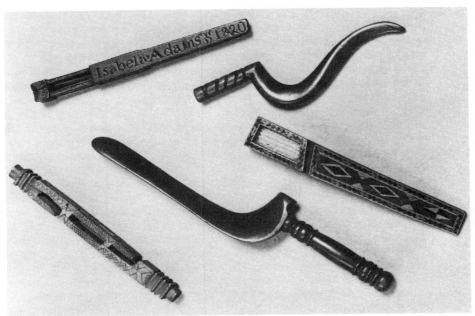

*Carved wooden sheaths as used by working knitters in the eighteenth and nineteenth centuries to anchor one
needle firmly.*

It is difficult to imagine Dr. Johnson acquiring the manual dexterity and speed
which were essential if worthwhile earnings from the craft were to be achieved.
Apart from the *sittings* or *veilles* to which reference has been made, every spare
moment had to be filled with high-speed knitting. Younger men knitted in
intervals from ploughing; old men knitted round the fire with shinguards to
prevent burning; children knitted with several skeins wound on to the same ball so
that all had to work at the same speed; women knitted as they walked to and from
the neighbouring market town to dispose of their work or obtain fresh supplies of
yarn. Greater speed can be achieved if one needle is anchored firmly and various
devices were employed for this purpose. In West Yorkshire, knitting sheaths were
common and were made in a variety of styles. Some were shaped pieces of wood
curved to the body, with a socket at the top end. The shaped part was stuck into a
belt or cowband, and one knitting needle was inserted into the socket. The
cowband often carried a hook over which the long end of the knitting was
suspended to prevent it from dangling. The sheaths were often made for the girls
by their boy-friends and were elaborately carved as tokens of affection. Today
these are collectors' pieces. In the Shetlands, knitting belts took the place of
sheaths; these took the form of leather pads stuffed with horsehair, punched with
holes and mounted on a strap. One needle was pushed into one of the holes and
anchored. Anchors with a different purpose were *worsted pots*, now very rare. They
were designed to hold a ball of wool and prevent it rolling about the floor during

knitting. They stood about twelve inches high and were solidly made. A large opening at the side allowed one or more balls of wool to be inserted and the threads were drawn out through smaller holes at the top. Worsted pots were made at the Rockingham factory during the second half of the eighteenth century.

HARD TIMES

Speed was imperative to West Yorkshire knitters at the end of the eighteenth century as they often worked with poor materials for low rates of pay. Kendal supplied a very coarse worsted yarn called *bump*. Prices could go as low as a penny for a pair of gloves and four pence for a pair of stockings. The status of the ultimate consumer was low, too. A clergyman's diary of 1818 commented that the blue woollen caps knitted by the women and children of Sedbergh, which made them look as if they came out of a dyeing factory, 'must be worn by convicts and prisoners'. Another writer in 1838 refers to 'a kind of caps worn by the negroes, called bump caps' which were a yard in length and doubled over; the knitter was paid three pence for knitting one.

Meanwhile, the early nineteenth century framework knitters had no reason to be grateful for William Lee's invention. By 1782 there were 20,000 hand frames in existence; the number had risen to 30,000 in 1812 and to a peak of 48,000 in 1844. The industry was concentrated in the counties of Leicester, Nottingham, and Derby where the framework knitters led a miserable life. Usually they owned neither the yarn they used nor the frames on which it was knitted but worked at piece rates on yarn supplied to them. Frames were hired from local tradesmen, often ignorant of the industry, who had money to spare. This system encouraged novices, including children and inexperienced women, to enter the industry and depress wage levels. Payment in kind – the notorious truck or *tommy* system – was rife. Wage rates went down whilst rates in other trades kept steady or rose. Finally, a change in fashion was replacing knee breeches, which demanded long stockings, by trousers. It was not surprising that the framework knitters' physique was reported as 'much below the average of even the manufacturing districts of the North'. Ironically this, the first textile industry to be mechanized, was among the last to feel the impact of steam power which was not widely introduced into it until after the middle of the nineteenth century.

KNITTING TURNS FASHIONABLE

Against this background – both for hand and frame knitters – of relentless effort for low pay, poor materials, poverty-stricken living conditions, catering for the lowest classes of society, and combating adverse changes of fashion, an astonishing transformation took place. During the years following the victory of Waterloo in 1815, England began to settle down to a peace-time economy. Alongside the rigours of working-class life, the industrial revolution was creating new wealth for the rapidly expanding middle classes. Leisure became available to an increasing number of women and knitting started to become a fashionable leisure pastime. The fourth volume of Beckmann's *History of Inventions* published in 1814 commends knitting in these words: 'It may be so easily acquired, even by children, as to be considered almost an amusement. It does not interrupt discourse, distract the attention, or check the powers of imagination. It forms a ready resource when a vacuity occurs in conversation; or when a circumstance occurs which ought to be heard or seen but not treated with too much seriousness; the prudent knitter then hears and sees what she does not wish to seem to hear or see. Knitting does no injury either to the body or the mind . . . the whole apparatus for knitting, which is cheap, needs so little room and is so light that it can be kept and gracefully carried about in a work-basket, the beauty of which displays the expertness, or at any rate the taste, of the fair artist.' After thus anticipating the gossipy scandal-mongering of Victorian drawing-rooms, Beckmann remembers that life is earnest and adds, 'servants, soldiers, shepherds, and the male children of the peasants who are unfit for hard labour should learn to knit . . .'.

Nineteenth-century knitting books: (bottom) Lady's Knitting, Netting and Crochet Book *by Mrs. Gaugain, 1844, 5s. 6d; (centre)* The Knitter's Friend *by Mrs. Gaugain, 1846, 2s.6d.; (top)* Knitting & Crocheting Book *by M. Elliot Scrivenor, 1896, 1s.*

Knitting was the most widely practised of a number of crafts which were introduced at this time. Embroidery on canvas was brought over from Germany and the bright skeins of Berlin wool were also used for knitting. Crochet (sometimes referred to as Tambour) came in during the 1830s and netting was popular too. By the 1870s a dizzying variety of handicrafts was available – crewel work, painting on silk, appliqué lace, spray work (using a scent or similar spray), straw work, paper plaiting, rug making, daisy mat making, and many others. The strictures on knitting by the *Magazine of Domestic Economy* in 1838 applied equally to these crafts: 'Time was, when the knitting needles were restricted to the farmhouse and the servants' hall; of late years, fashion . . . has allowed their introduction in to the drawing-room, in furtherance of those schemes miscalled charitable, which require a constant supply of pretty articles, useless for every purpose except to get rid of the hours which, but for their aid, might not be so innocently disposed of.'

VICTORIAN KNITTING BOOKS OF THE 1840s
Knowledge of 'farmhouse and the servants' hall' knitting was transmitted by word of mouth from mother to daughter or by more senior servants to their juniors. Such tuition was inappropriate to the knitting practised in boudoir and drawing-room. Books of knitting technique and patterns were called for – and readily supplied. By the middle of the 1840s the sale of elegantly produced knitting books was booming. *The Ladies' Knitting and Netting Book* appeared anonymously in 1837. It

was followed in 1840 by *The Lady's Assistant For Executing Useful and Fancy Designs in Knitting, Netting and Crochet Work* by Mrs. Gaugain who kept a fancy needlework depot at 63 George Street, Edinburgh (where tuition in various crafts was available) and was undoubtedly the most enterprising of all the early knitting pattern producers. This cloth bound volume of 250 small pages sold at 5*s.* 6*d.* a copy and by 1844 the work was in its seventh thousand. It was followed in 1842 by a second volume of 422 pages at 10*s.* 6*d.* which went into its third thousand by 1844. By comparison with today's values such prices were far from cheap; Jane Gaugain aimed high. *The List of Patronesses* printed in her first volume included the Queen Dowager, three H.R.H.s, ten Duchesses and seven Countesses. The lower orders were not neglected; Mrs. Gaugain soon issued a miniature edition at a shilling and in 1846 a 2*s.* 6*d* selection of reprints from the earlier books under the title of *The Knitter's Friend*. This aimed to provide the means of 'a genteel and easy source of livelihood to many industrious Females, both in the humble and middle ranks of life'. Contemporary Dentdale knitters turning out bump caps a yard long for threepence each may have thought her optimistic. Mrs. Gaugain must also have been one of the earliest exponents of mail order trading; she undertook to send materials for the largest item on her list for 6*s.* 3*d.*, postage included, to any post town in Great Britain. In rivalry with Mrs. Gaugain's productions Miss Lambert, authoress of *The Hand-Book of Needlework, Church Needlework, My Crochet Sampler*, etc. published an eighteen-penny work *My Knitting Book, First Series* which reached its thirty-third thousand by 1846. In the same year, Cornelia Mee (who, by permission, had dedicated her *Manual of Knitting, Netting and Crochet Work* to the Duchess of Beaufort) published *Mee's Exercises in Knitting*, also at eighteen pence.

Some designers had names which proclaimed their aristocratic connections. Mlle. Eleanore Riego de la Branchardière's span of authorship exceeded forty years. Her first manuals appeared in 1846 and she was still going strong in 1887 when she published *The Royal Jubilee Crochet Book*. In between, her *Comforts for the Crimea* of 1854 included instructions for the original Balaclava helmet. Mlle. Rigolette de la Hamelin conducted *The Royal Magazine of Knitting, Netting, Crochet and Fancy Needlework* in the 1860s. Apart from knitting, netting, and crochet instructions, which recommended Raworth's Crochet Thread with suspicious unanimity, each issue included verse or romantic serials such as *The Embroidered Ottoman; or the Effects of Pride* or *The Rival Lovers; or, The Field of Worcester*. Mrs. Wititterly would certainly have been a subscriber.

COVERING THINGS UP

The contents of the knitting books of the 1840s differed greatly from those of today. Well over half the items in 1840 comprised repeating stitch-patterns which the knitter was left to incorporate into specific articles as best she might. Although Cornelia Mee included a bodice and a spencer there were few garments to wear and the proportion of baby items was surprisingly low. What clothing items there were mainly consisted of accessories: purses, bags, comforters, shawls, chest protectors, neckerchiefs, neck tippets, frileuses, pelisses, gloves, mittens, cuffs, muffs, muffatees, and gaiters. The majority of designs catered for the Victorian passion for putting covers on their abundant furnishings. Doilies and doily patterns abounded along with mats, dressing-table sets, hair tidies, edgings, table covers, toilet covers, Stilton cheese frills, candlestick covers, tippis de pied, hassocks, foot baskets, etc. A satirical popular song, *The Knitting Mania*, declared:
'They are all knitting at our house at home.
Macassars for the sofa, where I lay my aching head,
And our beautiful work'd quilt for the extra best bed,
The Tea-pot, Cream Jug, Coffee Pot each have a little mat,
With a budding rose and bunch of grapes and a cushion for the cat.'

The fashion for knitting became so widespread at this time that general magazines dealing with women's interests started to include regular features dealing with knitting. *The Magazine of Domestic Economy* which ran from 1836 to 1844 published an occasional knitting pattern; other magazines were *The Lady's Newspaper and Pictorial Times* (which later amalgamated with *The Queen*) and *The Ladies' Treasury*. With occasional vicissitudes, women's magazines have continued to find knitting and crochet patterns good circulation builders to this day.

Beaded Bonnet – an example of decorative nineteenth-century knitting. Victoria and Albert Museum. Crown Copyright.

For almost a hundred years, notwithstanding the development of man-made fibres, the word *knitting* has been so closely associated with wool that it is appropriate to recall that the knitters of the 1840s and '50s used a wide variety of materials as well as wool, such as cotton, silk, and linen. Cotton was referred to as *fine* or *very fine* or by number according to the weight – *White No. 6, Taylor's Persian Cotton No. 4*, or *Taylor's No. 18 Cotton*. Silk included *purse twist, ardoise silk*, or *netting silk*; linen was specified by number. Wool varieties included *fleecy* in a range of weights from *2-ply Super fleecy* to 9-ply and 12-ply fleecy, the last being used for rugs and mats. *Berlin Wool* was often specified in penny skeins and there was *double German*, too. *English embroidery wool* was sometimes recommended for knitting because it washed so well. *Zephyr* and *Shetland* are also mentioned along with *Lady Betty* which dates back at least to 1820 and survived until World War II. James Baldwin of Halifax, who founded in 1785 the firm which later became Patons & Baldwins Ltd., had a daughter called Betty and the yarn, of particularly fine quality, was named as a compliment to her. It soon became a general trade description.

DECLINE AND REVIVAL – THE 1870 EDUCATION ACT

The making of comforts for the soldiers in the Crimea, the pioneer work of Florence Nightingale and the beginnings of women's higher education and emancipation may all have contributed to the reaction during the 1860s against the more frivolous types of knitting. Certainly there was a decline in popularity for twelve to fifteen years. Fittingly, interest on a more soberly practical scale was revived by an historic piece of social reform – the establishment of universal education by the Act of 1870. An important provision of the Act made it compulsory to teach all girls the rudiments of knitting, including the use of four needles for socks and stockings. This may have upheld the Victorian belief that a woman's place is in the home, but experience soon demonstrated that school managers and teaching staff regarded knitting instruction as a troublesome waste of time. Nevertheless, the legislation stimulated interest in the craft and instruction books designed to help the teaching of knitting were produced by, amongst others, the Society for Promoting Christian Knowledge which re-issued in 1883 *Directions for Knitting Socks and Stockings – For Use in Elementary Schools* by Mrs. Lewis of Meopham Vicarage, Kent. She had very forthright ideas. 'The needlework afternoon is the hardest part of the teacher's work . . . sometimes she gives up in despair . . . . There are many ladies with abundant leisure who might do a work of real practical usefulness by undertaking the knitting in the village school. One great difficulty is the wool . . . . If the lady who looks after the knitting would also procure the wool, she will have done much towards success. I do not mean that she is to *give* the wool . . . but buy a spindle (6 lbs) of a good useful wool and let the children have it in small quantities at cost price . . . . When it is known that good knitting is done at the school, orders will come in – 6 pairs Gentlemen's Socks here, Boy's Knickerbocker Stockings etc. etc. These are, of course, paid for . . . ; part of the money is given to the girl who knits them . . . besides the work itself the lady obtains great influence over the girls, she learns their characters more intimately . . . can recommend them for domestic service . . . .' Regrettably there is no evidence how many village schools benefited from the unofficial knitting lady's order-taking and employment activities!

SPINNERS' PUBLICATIONS

As the universal teaching of reading after 1870 resulted in the eventual production of a popular national halfpenny newspaper, so the more widespread knowledge of knitting led to the intensification of publicity by knitting-yarn spinners. During the 1880s and early '90s inexpensive knitting books were issued which carried spinners' advertisements; in return the editorial instructions recommended the spinners' brands. *The Knitting and Crochet Work Book* series by C. and W. Thomson cost 6*d.* each; the first series carried two pages of advertisements for J. & J. Baldwin's Bee Hive Wools and specified them editorially throughout. In 1884 Mrs. Lewis of Meopham issued *Wools and How to Use Them* with a pronounced editorial bias towards Baldwin & Walker; in 1887 Wood & Burtt advertised their Cocoon Wool in *The Young Ladies' Journal Complete Guide to the Work Table* and offered to send free knitting patterns on receipt of a stamped, addressed envelope.

One of the first, if not the first, knitting books for which the spinner took full responsibility is probably the *Knitting & Crocheting Book; John Paton Son & Co. Alloa, N.B.* This was compiled by M. Elliot Scrivenor and published in 1896. With its *art nouveau* limp cloth cover and photographic half-tone illustrations it must have seemed very advanced when it first appeared. It was priced at a shilling and included some 125 designs – 84 in knitting, 38 in crochet and 3 in netting. A revised and enlarged edition was issued in 1899 and the fourth edition of 1908 appears to have remained current until World War I. It is significant that the first edition includes a chapter on *Garments Suitable for Charitable Purposes*; this is omitted from the 1908 edition which features motor and golf jackets instead. To cater for the lower income groups Patons issued their *Universal Knitting Book* in 1899 at one penny a copy for some 60 pages of instructions for baby clothes, underwear, hats, shawls, etc. including an edifying quotation from Spenser, Milton, or other classic authors at the head of each page. This book continued on the market for a number of years in competition with similar penny knitting books from other spinners.

KNITTING MACHINES – THE EDWARDIAN AGE

During the 1880s advertisements appeared for home knitting machines, which were thought by some designers to have a promising future despite their high cost. The machines were of the circular type and their price restricted their use to large institutions and the 'upper classes'. For these reasons it was suggested that 'the better class of servants' should be required to understand a knitting machine just as they were required to understand and use a sewing machine. The analogy with the sewing machine did not prove valid and despite periodic publicity campaigns it was not until the 1950s that a really substantial sale of home knitting machines was achieved.

Edwardian knitting, encouraged by magazine features, specialized periodicals, and spinners' publications remained essentially practical. Designers seemed to concentrate on socks and stockings, vests, drawers, gloves and mittens, headgear, jerseys, sweaters and waistcoats for men and boys, baby things, and women's underclothes. Only in the years immediately preceding World War I was there much attempt to cater for women's outerwear or to pay attention to fashion. Double-breasted coats, like long-line cardigans, bodices, and jackets for motoring or golf were among the first patterns to reflect some fashion influence.

WORLD WAR I AND AFTER

The outbreak of World War I in 1914 and the attrition of bloody trench warfare resulted in the never-ending flood of knitted comforts for the troops – Balaclava helmets, scarves, socks, and waistcoats for the fighting men, hospital wear for the wounded and leisure garments for convalescence. Women had knitted for the soldiers of the Seven Years' War in the eighteenth century and the Crimean War in the nineteenth century but these were professional troops, usually unknown to those who knitted for them. The twentieth century soldiers of World War I were amateurs from every social level and the women who knitted did so for their own husbands, brothers, or the boys next door.

The Armistice of 1918 brought its inevitable reaction. Interest in knitting flagged for a time; spinners and designers alike were spurred to revise their ideas. The spinners issued more and better-styled leaflets of the type that still remain popular and designers began to think in terms of women's fashions. New sixpenny monthly magazines devoted to the interests of the modern woman began to appear and these naturally included coverage of handicrafts, particularly knitting. In revolt against the drabness of uniform, multi-coloured Fair Isle patterns swept into popularity – worn as pull-overs with plus-fours by men (whose stockings often added further pattern and colour) or as sleeveless jumpers with a costume coat and skirt by women. The word *jumper* itself is redolent of the 1920s and recalls the vogue for lacy creations knitted or crocheted in shiny viscose rayon, known at the time as *art. silk*. Later, as the 1920s passed into the 1930s and the design of hand-knits reflected an even greater influence of contemporary women's fashions, a certain consistency of style developed which seems now to characterize those years between the two wars. Time and again the little shirtwaister-style jumper in 3-ply or 4-ply crops up with its short sleeves and soft tailored fit. Sometimes the neckline is fussed up a little but more often than not it remains perfectly simple. This was a golden age for plain classics whether in jumpers, suits, or coats. Knitted dresses were much less popular.

CRAZES

Inevitably, the overall trend was punctuated from time to time by *crazes* which are such an essential part of the knitting scene over the years. There were crazes for little close-fitting caps knitted in a decorative knop yarn called Woodpecker; for knitted one-piece swim suits in *non-shrink* wool which sometimes subjected knitters with slack tension to full frontal embarrassment; for Highland spatees, which linked up with the fashion for Russian boots; for angora boleros which became popular after film prodigy Deanna Durbin had worn one.

Crazes were a reflection of public interest in knitting which increased progressively up to the outbreak of war in 1939. Some held the view that industrial depression helped the craft because it was cheaper to knit clothes than buy them ready made. This was only a half-truth. The fashion atmosphere of the 1930s was congenial to knitting; the public responded to occasions associated with it. The *Daily Mail* organized a series of annual Knitting Competitions, one of which attracted over 80,000 entries (all of which had to be returned) and nearly overwhelmed the organizers and the local post office arrangements. The Duchess of York appealed for knitters to make and donate warm garments for the unemployed. An increased number of specialist wool and art-needlework shops opened in the suburbs and centres of smaller towns; the great majority of them prospered.

WORLD WAR II AND AFTER

Vast quantities of hand-knits for the armed forces and civil defence workers were produced during World War II but knitting for normal domestic purposes was soon curtailed by the imposition of clothes rationing. Wartime controls and the need to economize in coupons led to a concentration on 3-ply yarns which many knitters eventually found to be monotonous; nevertheless, the public snapped up as many knitting magazines and leaflets as controlled supplies of paper would permit to be published. Clothes rationing continued until 1949 and post-war knitters resorted to ingenious stratagems to eke out their coupons. As after World War I, Fair Isle patterns again became enormously popular but this time not only the satisfaction of a war-starved craving for colour was involved. Darning wool skeins in a wide range of colours could be purchased free of coupon so knitters used them to provide the multicolour effects in Fair Isle patterns; coupons need only be surrendered for the background! A special Fair Isle Fingering wool was produced in the form of a 2-ply which knitted up as a 3-ply and was very economical in yardage. Even after the abolition of rationing wool supplies remained limited and demand outran supply.

Eventually the supply situation eased and growing competition in the industry stimulated developments. The packaging of knitting yarns in ready-wound balls instead of skeins became general in the early 1950s and so robbed men of their age-old chore of irritably holding skeins of wool on outstretched arms while their womenfolk wound the thread into balls. The use of double-knitting yarns increased sharply, not only because they were quicker to knit but because bulkier garments were becoming increasingly fashionable. From this time onwards knitting began to move in the circle of *haute couture* and such awe-inspiring designers as Christian Dior and Cardin began to include hand-knitted effects in their collections.

The Coronation in 1953 speeded up the spread of television and those concerned with knitting were soon asking 'Will television kill the craft?' They need not have worried; the new bulky styles were easy to knit while watching and they were so loose in fitting that the problem of accurate tension was less acute. Cinema-going declined and the women who stayed at home knitted more than ever. Double-breasted blazers with brass buttons which were fashionable in 1954 were succeeded by bulkier *fisherman's rib* designs. As fabric grew bulkier, fittings grew ever more easy until new, pencil-thick yarns such as *Big Ben* were launched in 1960 and created for a year or two the ultimate in *Sloppy Joe* styling with men's sweaters often requiring up to three pounds of wool. By 1964 the inevitable reaction had set in and for a time men and women forsook hand-knit sloppiness for the Leather Look. The natural resilience of the craft soon asserted itself and it was Ireland's turn to conquer Britain with the Aran style. From one end of Europe to the other men, women, and children were to be seen in their thousands shopping and strolling in the bobbly, off-white jackets and sweaters which owed their inspiration, however distantly, to those bleak, windswept islands off the coast of County Galway.

As the popularity of the Aran style levelled off, knitting began to acquire a Mexican flavour, although it was again in Ireland that knitted and crocheted ponchos were first seen in wear to any great extent. Women and children of widely different social types, ranging from trim little nine-year-olds at birthday parties to footloose supporters of pop festivals found the poncho style acceptable. It was still in steady favour as the 1970s began, which is as far as this survey can be taken.

KNITTING MACHINES – THE REVIVAL OF CROCHET
Two aspects of the craft itself have been noteworthy during the last twenty years. The 1950s saw an astonishing increase in the sales of home knitting machines, of which new and improved types were available, many being imported from Switzerland, Germany and, later, Japan. It is doubtful whether the majority of those bought then were ever very much used; as in the 1880s the analogy with the sewing machine as an essential item of household equipment was drawn, but it did not prove valid. Knitting machines were admirable for mothers and fathers (it was often father who bought the machine) with large families to clothe; many women sought to use them as a supplementary source of income but found it difficult unless they used very low-priced yarn. Machines could consume quickly formidable quantities of yarn. In passing, they also tended to make a tearing noise which offended other members of the family. After a period of intense activity, demand settled down to a steady level and is now tending to increase again. The latest machines show remarkable technical improvements and it is now possible to produce easily multi-coloured designs and intricate fabrics.

Of the associated crafts of knitting and crochet, knitting has usually been much more widely practised over the years. From about 1964 onwards a remarkable revival in the popularity of crochet began and still continues. It was not confined to Britain but covered the whole of Western Europe. A surprising aspect of the revival was that, in the beginning, knowledge of crochet technique was extremely limited, even among expert knitters, and there was an acute shortage of instructors. Shopkeepers organized classes for their sales assistants and publications which explained the stitches and gave instructions for simple garments were at a premium. The open, lacy fabric of crochet appealed to contemporary taste in dresses, cardigans, and wrap-around styles such as shawls and ponchos. Afghan rugs built up out of many separate crochet units joined together were used as covers for sofas or divans.

NEW MATERIALS – NEW IDEAS
The raw materials used for knitting and crochet were changing in relative importance, too. Up to the mid-1950s, wool had always been the foundation of

everyday knitted garments. The Victorian fripperies and the shiny blouses of the 1920s might have occasioned deviations to other fibres but for babies' and children's things, classic sweaters and cardigans, socks and stockings, and hats it was unthinkable to use anything but wool. Now, the influence of man-made fibres began to make itself felt. Nylon was the first to appear; introduced as a blend with wool for knitting socks and stockings, it was soon available in one hundred per cent form. To the traditional expert knitter it had many drawbacks: it handled unpleasantly, did not recover its shape like wool and was difficult to knit evenly. To the harassed mother with small babies it had two supreme merits: it could be washed in a washing-machine without fear of shrinking or felting and, at least when new, it was a dazzling blue-white. Nylon yarns soon established a small but significant share of the market which grew substantially as they improved their handle. When other fibres such as Courtelle, Orlon, and Tricel appeared the old supremacy of wool was seriously threatened.

Against the struggle for the mass market, occasional crazes continued to enliven the knitting world and keep the marginal knitter interested. Hats and headgear were frequently involved. One little cap, fitting close to the back of the head, was originally designed in Scandinavia to be knitted on an *Alice-band* from one quarter-ounce ball of Angora. It was so popular in the 1950s that, for a period, supplies of Alice-bands in chain stores completely disappeared. The pattern was consequently withdrawn, but was pirated on the Glasgow black market because it had become the accepted uniform in which to dance the *creep* in local halls. Another design, consisting of a strip of lacy fabric with a big bobble at each end, was so popular for women to wear going to and from their work that for a time one or two of these hat-scarves were to be seen in every bus queue. Finally, there was the astonishing episode of the American welfare worker who sought to interest handicapped children in knitting by using cut-down broom handles for knitting needles and several thicknesses of heavy yarn for thread. Spinners looking for a new promotion idea thought the experiment had commercial possibilities. One-inch diameter needles of wood and plastic, associated with appropriate knitting patterns, were marketed in the U.S.A., Britain, and Europe. Maxi-Pins, as they were christened in Britain, were a nine days' wonder. In America a press announcement attracted the highest reader response ever recorded and everywhere hundreds of thousands of pins and patterns were sold. Although many women tried out Maxi-Pins as directed, few garments seem ever to have been completed, let alone worn, and the craze was soon over. Laughable as the project may seem in retrospect, it does serve to illustrate the vitality and adaptability of the twin needle crafts. High fashion; down-to-earth everyday wear; bits of nonsense; baby things to grow sentimental over; comforts for the sick and elderly; knitting and crochet play a part in them all and will continue to do so as long as designers retain their freshness of outlook, their readiness to try anything once – and the common touch.

Chapter 2

Shopping Guide for Knitting and Crochet

The opening paragraphs of all knitting and crochet patterns include an item like this: 'Materials required: 8 × 50g balls XYZ Double Knitting'. It would seem an easy matter to go to a retailer, buy the material specified and start knitting, but problems often crop up: the retailer may stock XYZ but not in a suitable colour; ABC Double Knitting in exactly the desired shade may be offered in place of XYZ; a bargain line at a special price may prove tempting. Would it be safe to change? Is the alternative made up in 50g balls or in ounces? Would a greater or less weight of the alternative be needed? Would it wash and wear as well? This chapter provides background information so that knitting and crochet enthusiasts may shop with greater confidence and avoid many of the difficulties and disappointments they might otherwise experience.

THE WORD 'YARN'

Knitting and crochet use *yarn* as their material, and that word simply means any kind of thread, no matter what it was made from or how it was made: soft baby wools for knitting, cottons for sewing, and jute for carpets are all equally yarns. The word carries no implication of quality and can be applied both to superlative excellence and the lowest grade.

RAW MATERIALS

The raw materials used in the production of knitting and crochet yarns may be divided roughly into two main categories (although the distinction between them is sometimes blurred): natural fibres and man-made fibres.

Natural Fibres

These can be divided into fibres from vegetable and animal sources:

(i) **Vegetable.** Cotton and linen are the main vegetable fibres. Cotton yarns are used more for crochet than for knitting and are often made into mats, edgings for cloths, bedspreads, and table decorations as well as into clothing. Linen is frequently blended with other fibres to make summer garments.

(ii) **Animal.** Wool from sheep is the animal fibre most widely used for spinning knitting yarns although small quantities of the rarer varieties such as angora, mohair, cashmere, and camelhair are occasionally spun, particularly when mixed with other less expensive fibres. There are two main categories of raw wool:

(a) Merino or botany (from Botany Bay, Australia). These wools are soft and fine and are particularly suitable for baby wear and garments with a premium on softness. The merino breed originally came from Spain and was introduced into South Africa in 1724; in 1797 it reached Australia from the Cape. The main producers now are Australia, South Africa, and the U.S.A. Patons Beehive Baby Wool is a typical botany yarn.

(b) Crossbred. This term relates to wools which are coarser than merino, but does not necessarily denote wool from crossbred sheep. Most English pure breeds produce crossbred wools! These are crisper and more robust than botanies and knit into harder-wearing garments. Patons Purple Heather contains crossbred wools.

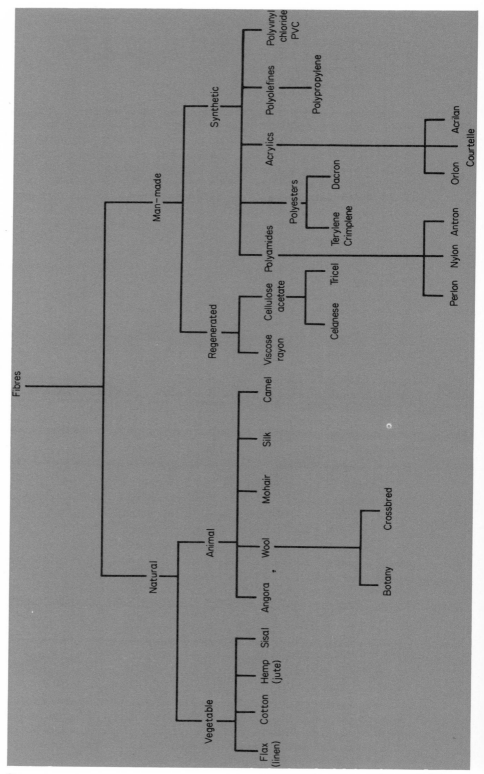

Man-made Fibres

It will help in finding the way amongst an often confusing collection of technical terms and brand names if it is understood how man-made fibres are classified and if this classification is kept available for future reference.

Basically, man-made fibres are produced by forcing a chemical solution through a block of metal pierced by a number of holes (a spinnerette). The solution coming out of the spinnerette solidifies into a long continuous thread; the diameter of the spinnerette hole determines the thickness or *denier* of the thread. The heavier the thread the higher the denier number. If the thread is used as yarn in the unbroken form it is called a *filament yarn*. Nylon stockings are made from filament yarn. For most hand-knitting yarns, however, the continuous filaments are cut or broken into shorter lengths, or *staple*, which are then made into yarn by methods similar to those used for spinning wool. These are called staple yarns.

(i) **Regenerated Fibres.** The early history of man-made fibres was chiefly concerned with the development of *regenerated* fibres, which derive from materials occurring in nature such as very short cotton fibres (*linters*) or soft wood. The chief fibres produced in this way are:

(a) Viscose rayon, invented in 1892, which used to be known as *art. silk*. This is not widely used for hand-knitting yarns except for one or two old-established specialities.

(b) Cellulose acetate. One form of this became widely known after World War I as *Celanese*. During the 1950s another version was marketed as *Tricel* which includes hand-knitting yarns.

(ii) **Synthetic Fibres.** Genuinely synthetic fibres, produced from entirely chemical sources, date back only to the late 1930s. The main chemical groups are:

(a) Polyamides. This group is better known as *Nylon* which was discovered by Du Pont chemists just before World War II. One form of it is known in Europe as *Perlon*. Originally used for women's stockings, nylon filament yarn is used for many kinds of ready-made under- and outer-wear. Nylon is used in 100 per cent form for staple yarns for hand-knitting and in blends with wool for both hand- and machine-knitting. It can be dyed to brilliant white and pastel shades. Another form of polyamide is *Antron* which uses spinnerettes of roughly triangular cross-section instead of the circular type used for conventional nylon. The resultant filament is tri-lobal instead of round.

(b) Polyesters. These were discovered in Britain in the early 1940s by chemists of the Calico Printers' Association Limited and are marketed as *Terylene* by I.C.I. and as *Dacron* by Du Pont. Textured filament polyester yarns are important for ready-made knitted garments and woven cloths, particularly in association with the name *Crimplene*. Some hand-knitting yarns of this type have been marketed but neither they nor hand-knittings spun from polyester staple have achieved any significant share of the market.

(c) Acrylics. A most important group. Although some acrylic fibres were made in Germany during the 1940s, the first commercially successful acrylic – *Orlon 42* – was marketed in 1954 by Du Pont. Other brands followed, notably *Courtelle* from Courtaulds and *Acrilan* from Monsanto Textiles. Acrylic fibres are almost entirely used as staple yarns because they can be made into excellent high-bulk yarns which are light in weight. Although they have a much lower tenacity than the polyamides and the polyesters, they are still twice as strong as wool. Bi-component acrylic fibres have also been developed; solutions of two different chemical constituents are extruded through each hole of the spinnerette so that, in effect, two fibres are fused together longitudinally in the same thread. During subsequent processing, one of the components shrinks, causing the other to buckle and coil itself around the first, so creating a much greater bulk.

(d) Polyolefines. This group includes *polyethylene*, used in large weights for moulding and as *polythene* foil, and *polypropylene*. At present polypropylene fibre is not significant for knitting yarns, chiefly because it is difficult to dye, but the material is low in cost and, with improved technology, it might become important in the future.

(e) Polyvinyl Chloride – PVC. The technical problems involved in processing 100 per cent PVC fibres are such that it is unlikely to be of interest either for knitting or weaving yarns in the near future.

Taken as a whole, the technology of man-made fibres is still progressing rapidly and the growth of their importance in the textile field shows no sign of diminishing. Amongst their advantages can be included, in greater or lesser degree according to type, brilliance, and purity of colour, high tensile strength, high bulk with light weight, and excellent washing performance, especially in washing machines.

TYPES OF HAND-KNITTING YARN

Many different kinds of hand-knitting yarn can be produced from the raw materials described in the preceding section.

Worsted and Woollen

Reference has already been made to filament yarns. Staple yarns can be produced by either of two main systems: *worsted* or *woollen* spinning. These terms refer to processes, not to the raw materials used. In worsted spinning the fibres are combed to remove short fibres and the long fibres remaining are made to lie parallel to each other as far as possible. This results in smooth, sleek yarns which knit up well into plain classic fabrics with good stitch definition. The majority of hand-knittings are worsted-spun. By contrast, no attempt is made in woollen spinning to remove the short fibres or to make the fibres lie parallel. Consequently a great variety of fibres can be used – virgin materials, either wool or synthetics, by-products of worsted spinning, and re-used textiles. Woollen-spun yarns have greater bulk and body than worsteds and, when knitted, they provide fabrics with excellent *cover*. Typical woollen-spun yarns are Patons Capstan and Turkey Rug.

The Significance of Ply

Yarns are never spun directly to the weight, or thickness, in which they are used for hand-knitting. The spinning operation results in what is known as *single yarn*; two, three, or four of these singles are then twisted together to form 2-, 3-, or 4-ply weights although the ply of a yarn may not always be stated on the label. This system provides the knitter with the same basic material in a selection of thicknesses and makes for greater flexibility in production. It should be remembered that all yarns of the same ply are not necessarily of the same thickness; a knitter cannot indiscriminately substitute one 4-ply yarn for another. In fact the difference in thickness between two singles will be accentuated in the final yarn.

Composition

Knitting yarns can be made from the materials described in the preceding section in the form of 100 per cent natural or 100 per cent man-made fibres, or in blends of the two kinds in varying proportions. The composition of a yarn is printed on the ball band or label and it is a useful precaution to check it before buying because such a wide variety of blends are available today.

Construction

Apart from their composition, the majority of hand-knitting yarns can be classified into the following groups, according to their physical construction:
(i) **Baby yarns.** These are plain, straightforward yarns which are essentially soft in wear and remain so after repeated washings. They are usually available in

3- and 4-ply weights; there is also a softly twisted, bulky *Quickerknit* form, which knits to 4-ply tension.

(ii) **Knittings** are plain classic threads for general purpose use, usually available in 2-, 3-, and 4-ply weights which, as already mentioned, are not necessarily the same thickness from one brand to another. In the past, these yarns were widely known as *fingerings*. They are sometimes marketed in the form of *crêpes* which are specially, and more tightly, twisted to produce, when knitted, a smooth fabric with a characteristic pebbled surface.

(iii) **Double Knittings.** These are the most popular of all hand-knittings because they knit up quickly into robust, serviceable fabrics. They are so called because, although normally of 4-ply construction, they are approximately double the thickness of 4-ply knittings. It should be constantly remembered that all brands of double knitting are not of the same thickness or yardage for a given weight. One brand may be thinner and provide greater yardage, but fabric knitted from it may be limper and less satisfactory than fabric knitted from another brand which has a fuller thread but less yardage. Double knittings are usually worsted-spun but some woollen-spun brands are available. They may not feel so soft as worsted-spun makes but may yield a greater yardage whilst still retaining a crisp, substantial *handle*. The crêpe version of double knitting is usually referred to as *double crêpe*.

(iv) **Double double knittings.** As the name implies, these yarns are double the thickness of double knittings and are chiefly used for sports and outdoor wear. Although thick they can be knitted into well-fitting, tailored designs.

(v) **Speciality**, or **Fancy** yarns. These are designed to provide knitted fabrics with a specially decorative appearance, such as hairy surfaces, crinkly or bouclé threads, flecks, and tweed-like effects.

Colour

Market research has demonstrated repeatedly that knitters are more influenced by colour than by any other aspect of a knitting yarn. However well it may knit, feel, wear, and wash, however reasonable its price may be, a yarn will not be acceptable if the would-be purchaser does not like the colour. A good yarn will therefore be available in a range of colours appropriate to its purpose and sufficiently fast to light and washing.

(i) **White.** When virtually all knitting yarns were spun from wool, the rich creamy white obtained by bleaching was taken as a generally accepted standard of whiteness. Later, the use of man-made fibres in conjunction with fluorescent brightening agents (or optical bleaches) made possible the introduction of brilliant blue-whites which soon established a new standard of whiteness. Equally brilliant whites in wool were demanded. Unfortunately, fluorescent brighteners which were reasonably fast on other fibres were not nearly as fast on wool. In particular, optically bleached white wool exposed to bright light *when wet* quickly deteriorated to a flat yellowish tint. It is therefore important to remember that wool which derives its whiteness from fluorescent brighteners should be dried in subdued light.

(ii) **Self shades.** Most knitting yarn colours are self shades and are acceptably fast to light and washing, with one or two exceptions. Man-made fibres can be dyed satisfactorily in bright clear pastel shades but baby pinks on wool do not have a high degree of fastness.

(iii) **Mixtures.** Colours such as clerical greys and lovats which comprise more than one shade are achieved by blending fibres dyed at an early stage of manufacture and are known as *mixtures*.

(iv) **Marls** (Twists). When single yarns of different colours are twisted together the result is called a *marl* and a wide range of colour effects can be obtained in this way.

The dyeing of knitting yarns is normally not a continuous process but is carried out in *batches* or *lots* of a certain weight. As a general rule, technical limitations make it impracticable to guarantee that yarns from two different dye lots will match each other exactly. For this reason, the ball bands or labels of a hand-knitting yarn normally carry a *lot number* in addition to the colour or shade number. When buying knitting yarn, it is most important to check that all the balls or units in the purchase carry the same lot number and to obtain, all at once, the full quantity required to finish the article to be knitted. If insufficient yarn is bought, difficulties in obtaining the correct dye lot may arise and if this is not possible a patch of uneven colour in the knitted fabric may result.

From time to time yarns with guaranteed matchability have been introduced but these have usually been restricted in their colour ranges and have not so far established themselves as a permanent feature of the market. Acrylic hand-knittings are now available, however, in Neochrome colours which are dyed during the manufacture of the fibre. Consequently, very big dye lots can be processed; this results in the establishment of fewer dye lot numbers and the increased possibility of securing a perfect match.

Finish

Wool has a natural tendency to felt if it is squeezed and relaxed when wet and slightly warm. In other words, it is apt to shrink when washed; this is particularly true of botany yarns. In the past special care was necessary in washing 100 per cent botany yarns or blends of botany with man-made fibres. Shrink-resist finishes, such as Patonising, have been available for such yarns for many years now; consequently, they can be washed with perfect safety using just normal attention. Good crossbred wools, which have a more robust character and crisper style than botanies, seldom require treatment with a shrink-resist finish.

Packaging

(i) **Type of ball.** Hand-knitting yarn is usually sold in balls which unwind from the outside. It is occasionally suggested that they should be made to unwind from the inside, but this would result in the outer layers being knitted up last with a consequent risk of soiling marks on the knitted fabric, particularly in the case of whites and pastel colours. Partly-used balls unwound from inside also collapse more readily.

(ii) **Unit of weight.** It is advisable to check the unit of weight in which the ball is made up, particularly when comparing prices. Formerly, the great majority of yarns was sold in one-ounce balls, except for some heavier weights of yarn which were made up in two-ounce units. After the introduction of high-bulk acrylic yarns some manufacturers began to sell in three-quarter-ounce balls and other fractions of an ounce were also used. The adoption of metric weight and the introduction of decimal currency have led to the making of balls in multiples of a gram – 10, 20, 25, 40, 50, and multiples of 50 thereafter. Now that there are so many units of weights on the market it is prudent to confirm what weight is being bought and that it is sufficient!

(iii) **Moisture content.** Most textile fibres and particularly wool can absorb moisture from the surrounding atmosphere and equally this will evaporate in warm or dry conditions; a ball of yarn may not weigh exactly the declared weight (e.g. 25g, 50g) at the time of purchase or use. It may weigh slightly more or less than that amount according to the temperature and/or humidity of the place in which it has been stored or kept. This variation is taken into account when specifying the quantity of yarn required in knitting instructions.

(iv) **Ball band.** As normally sold, a ball of yarn is encircled by a paper ball band which must be removed before knitting can begin. Ball bands should not be thrown away when removed but should be kept until the article has been finished. The ball band positively identifies the brand of yarn and the exact quantity used. It confirms the weight, composition, colour, and dye-lot number; usually special washing instructions or after-care symbols are included. If any query or complaint concerning a yarn should arise, the ball bands provide the manufacturer with invaluable evidence.

(v) **Price.** Suitability for the article to be made rather than price should be the guiding principle when buying knitting and crochet yarns. For sportswear or hand-knits for growing children a yarn may be best on account of its toughness and crisp handle. On the other hand, where softness, subtle colours, intricacy of stitch, and fashion are involved, it is well worth spending a little extra if the time and skill employed are to be fully rewarded. In fact, it is a good general rule always to buy the best yarn in its particular class.

Chapter 3

Knitting and Crochet Equipment and Language

NEEDLES AND HOOKS

Like all crafts, knitting and crochet have their own special tools. Knitting uses needles which are made in pairs or sets; crochet uses a single hooked pin. Today, both are easy to work with as they are usually made from lightweight materials such as coated metal, plastic, or wood. Knitting needles are also known as knitting pins.

Pairs of knitting needles are used for flat knitting which is worked backwards and forwards in rows, so they have a point at one end (the working end) and a knob at the other to prevent the work slipping off.

Sets of needles (usually four) are for working in rounds so they are pointed at both ends. A single circular needle is also made for seamless knitting.

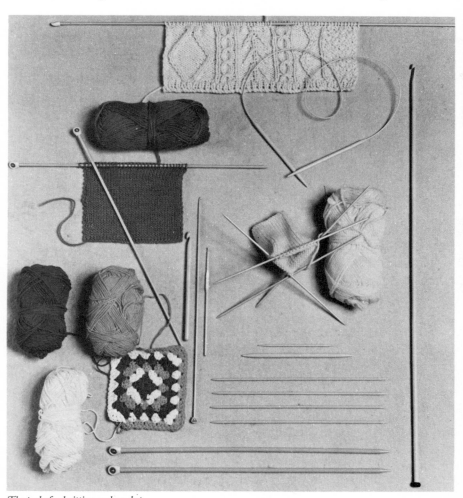

The tools for knitting and crochet

Sizes Knitting needles and crochet hooks are made in a range of thicknesses (sizes) to work with thick or thin yarns. Pairs of needles in English sizing range from extra thick sizes 000, 00, and 0 down to very fine sizes such as 14s. The higher the number the finer the size. Most flat knitting makes use of needles between 4s and 12s. Thick needles are for heavy, chunky outdoor garments, rugs, and blankets. Sets of needles usually range from 6s to 14s and are used for articles such as socks and gloves. The finest sizes are used for speciality work such as lace knitting in cotton.

English, American, and Continental knitting needle sizes are different and this difference should be particularly remembered when working from knitting instructions in American or Continental knitting publications. So far as crochet hooks are concerned, there is now a single International Table of Sizes, based on measurement in millimetres. The following tables show the position quite clearly.

Crochet Hook Size Comparison
Steel Hooks

Present Range Disc	6	5	4	3	$2\frac{1}{2}$	2
New Range International (mm)	0·60	0·75	1·00	1·25	1·50	1·75

Aluminium Hooks

Present Range Disc	14	12	11	9	8	7	6	5	4	2
New Range International (mm)	2·00	2·50	3·00	3·50	4·00	4·50	5·00	5·50	6·00	7·00

Knitting Pin Size Comparison

English	000	00	0	1	2	3	4	5	6
American	15	13	12	11	$10\frac{1}{2}$	10	9	8	7
European (metric)	9	$8\frac{1}{2}$	8	$7\frac{1}{2}$	7	$6\frac{1}{2}$	6	$5\frac{1}{2}$	5
English	7	8	9	10	11	12	13	14	
American	6	5	4	3	2	1	0	00	
European (metric)	$4\frac{1}{2}$	4	$3\frac{1}{2}$	$3\frac{1}{4}$	3 or $2\frac{3}{4}$	$2\frac{1}{2}$	$2\frac{1}{4}$	2	

Today, most needles and hooks are marked with their size, but it is useful to keep a needle-gauge available in case a pair of unmarked needles turns up.

Needle length Knitting needles vary in length from 7 to 15 inches according to type. Originally, long needles were much used by paid knitters and traditionalists would maintain that these still produce the best results for flat knitting. As described in Chapter 1, these long needles were pointed at both ends, one end being pushed into a knitting holder, sheath or stick which was held by a belt worn round the waist. Long needles are still used, particularly in the North of England and Scotland, but these are usually the conventional type with the knob end tucked under the armpit.

On the whole, it is safe to say that shorter lengths are becoming the most widely used today with the hands alone controlling the movement of the needles. Most beginners now learn with shorter needles and these are perhaps the most convenient for ease of working to suit the modern way of life. A vast amount of knitting is produced in this way with perfectly satisfactory results.

THE WELL-FITTED WORKBAG

Needles should be kept neatly in sets and pairs together to avoid frantic searches for the odd needle of a particular size to make up a pair. If there should be any odd needles, they should be kept separately and used for finishing touches, such as picking up stitches.

The other tools in a well-equipped workbag should include:

tape-measure	sewing needles	stitch-holder
scissors	darning needles	cable needle
rustless pins	tapestry needles	row-counter
large safety-pins	bodkin	needle-gauge

TOWARDS A TRIUMPHANT FINISH

Work in progress should be kept in a bag or wrapped in a clean cloth. It should never be put away with a row part completed; the row should be finished and the work folded around the needle. The needle should never be pushed through the knitting. When really expert knitters continue a piece of knitting which has been laid aside for some time, they pull back one row so that any stretching or distortion of the stitches by the needle, which would cause unevenness in the fabric, can be eliminated. A knitter's hands should always be clean and smooth so that there is no risk of soiling or catching threads with roughened skin.

The success of a knitted or crocheted article largely depends on good making up and finishing off; completing the fabric is only the first stage and it is vital to avoid the temptation of dashing quickly through the remaining steps. As pressing is most important, an iron will be needed together with a blanket, a covering cloth, and a damping cloth. General making up instructions are given in Chapter 8 and finishing off materials together with special making up details are given in the individual design instructions. Trimming accessories include such items as buttons, zips, facing ribbon, braid, and other decorative trims. A daisy-wheel and one of the newer type of plastic flower-wheel are useful for making flower trims.

THE LANGUAGE OF KNITTING AND CROCHET

As well as special equipment, knitting and crochet have their own technical terms and special language. Without them, the instructions for making even the simplest article would be far too long and the knitter would find them tedious to follow. The system of 'knitter's shorthand' which has been developed over the years enables the instructions for a large and complex piece of knitting to be conveyed simply and concisely. The uninitiated may poke fun at 'P1, K2tog' but an accurate set of knitting instructions can give a satisfaction akin to that of a musical score or a mathematical equation as is shown by the word-of-mouth reputation a particular design can acquire amongst knitters when it is known that the instructions are easy to follow and work out well. Knitting notation is based on abbreviations;

those most generally used are listed below and these apply throughout the instructions in this book.

There are other abbreviations with a more specialized application which are explained at the beginning of the individual instructions under the heading 'Additional Abbreviations' when they are used for a particular design. These abbreviations are universally understood with the exception of certain crochet terms which differ between Britain and the U.S.A. The following table includes the crochet terms as understood in Britain; the terms as used in the U.S.A. are given separately at the end of the table.

ABBREVIATIONS

* = sign of repetition
( ) = round brackets enclose a group of stitches to be repeated
/–/–/ = oblique strokes indicate stitches for alternative sizes, but where only one set of figures is given, this applies to all sizes
alt = alternate
b = back
beg = beginning
bl = block
C = cable
ch = chain
cl = cluster
cm = centimetre
cont = continue
dbl = double
d c = double crochet
dec = decrease
dtr or dbl tr = double treble
f = forward or front
foll = following
g = gram(s)
gr = group
htr or hlf tr = half treble
in = inch(es)
inc = increase
K = Knit
ltr = long treble

M1 = make one
n = needle
No = number
o = no stitches to be worked: this reference is used where instructions are given for more than one size
oz = ounce(s)
P = Purl
patt = pattern
prec = preceding
psso = pass slip stitch over
r = round
rem = remaining
rep = repeat
sc = single crochet ⎫ The actual work-
ss = slip stitch ⎬ ing is the same
sl = slip ⎭
sp(s) = space(s)
st(s) = stitch(es)
st st = stocking stitch
tbl = through back(s) of loop(s)
tog = together
tr = treble
tr tr = triple treble
tw = twist
y = yarn
yf (or yft) = yarn front or forward
yon = yarn on or over needle
yrn = yarn round needle

American Crochet Terminology

U.S.A.	BRITAIN	BRITISH ABBREVIATIONS
slip stitch	single crochet	sc
	or slip stitch	ss
single crochet	double crochet	dc
half double crochet	half treble	htr or hlf tr
double crochet	treble	tr
treble crochet	double treble	dtr or dbl tr
	or long treble	ltr
double treble	triple treble	tr tr

Chapter 4

First Steps in Knitting

Knitting is a fabric formed by making rows of chain loops with each new loop causing the preceding loop to drop down one so that the work (piece of fabric) gets longer, row by row.

Knitting is known by two methods, English and Continental. The majority of instruction patterns written in English refer to the English method. The basic principles are the same for both methods, but the working steps vary: in the English method the right hand (except for left-handed workers) holds and controls the yarn, but in the Continental method the left hand holds the yarn. The English method is explained in this chapter: the Continental method is discussed in Chapter 7. The following instructions are for right-handed knitters: hints for left-handed workers are given in Chapter 9.

HOLDING THE WORK AND CASTING ON

These must be learnt together, dealing first with knitting on two needles worked in rows (flat knitting). There are several methods of casting on using either two needles or the thumb (one needle) method. In the following instructions the parts of the hand are referred to as thumb, index, middle, fourth, and little fingers.

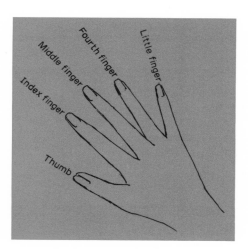

The Two-Needle Method. Casting On through the Stitch. Make a slip loop as in diagrams, put this on one needle and tighten the knot. This counts as the first stitch. Hold first needle in the left hand close up to knot of loop and second needle in right hand between thumb and index finger, as for holding a pencil. Insert point of right needle through this loop and grip both needles for the moment between index finger and thumb of left hand. Take up yarn as shown in diagram below: ball of yarn lies to the right. Let yarn run from ball and catch it round the little finger of right hand, take yarn under fourth and middle fingers and bring it to front between middle and index fingers so that it lies over index finger. Curl little finger and fourth finger as required to control yarn so that it is fairly taut between index finger and knot of loop (stitch) on left needle. This play of yarn controls the

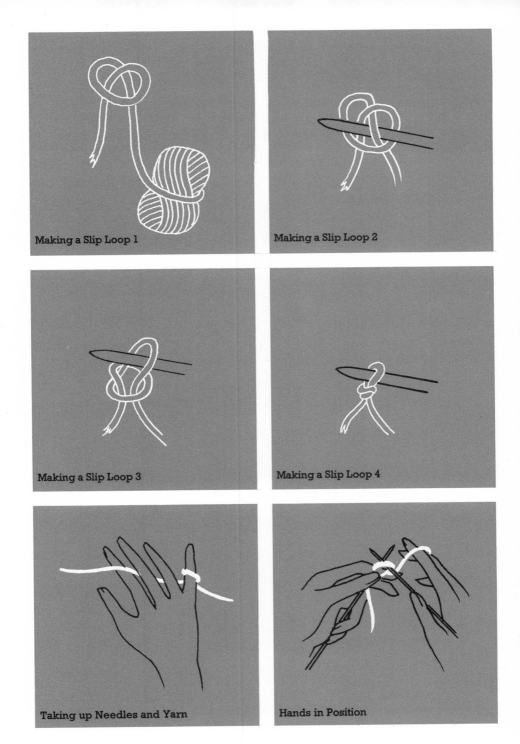

Making a Slip Loop 1

Making a Slip Loop 2

Making a Slip Loop 3

Making a Slip Loop 4

Taking up Needles and Yarn

Hands in Position

tension of the work. Beginners tend to knit loosely, but learn to control this as they gain experience.

Now take second needle in right hand and hold it between thumb and index finger and comfortably close up to knot of loop on left needle: thus second (right) needle and yarn are both held in right hand, and first (left) needle is held in left hand with cast-on stitch. This is an accepted way of taking up the yarn: knitters adapt this to suit their own way of working as they gain experience.

To Cast On More Stitches. Yarn lies at back of work whilst casting on. Insert right needle point through first loop (stitch) on left needle from front to back. With the fingers of right hand controlling the yarn, pass yarn round point of right needle, turn point of needle and pull a loop through and put this on left needle turning loop so that it lies on needle as illustrated. There are now two loops (stitches) on left needle.

Casting on more Stitches 1

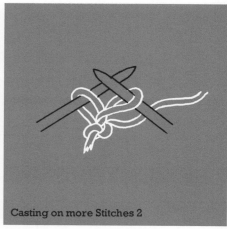

Casting on more Stitches 2

Casting on more Stitches 3

Insert right needle point through this second stitch and cast on a third stitch in the same way.

Repeat this method until the required number of stitches has been cast on: it is not necessary to withdraw the right needle each time, thus the casting on is a continuous smooth movement.

This method of casting on is through the stitch and gives a loose chain loop edge. This is the method used when a loose edge is specially required, such as picking up loops to make a hem, or if the article has a decorative (or crocheted) finishing edge which involves picking up the loops.

This loose cast-on edge can be tightened to give a firmer and more elastic edge by knitting (or purling) into the backs of the stitches on the next row (i.e. the first row of actual knitting). Knitting into the backs of stitches is explained later in twisted, or Continental, stocking stitch.

Casting On Between the Stitches. A variation on the preceding method is the cable edge, which is worked between the stitches: this is very widely used and gives a firm elastic edge which is suitable for most articles.

To do this, the working principle is the same but instead of inserting the right needle point through the stitch on the left needle, insert it through the space *between* two stitches each time after the first two stitches have been cast on through the stitches as described in the preceding method.

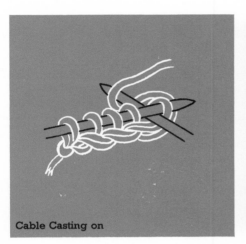

Cable Casting on

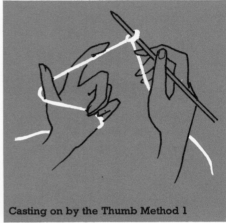

Casting on by the Thumb Method 1

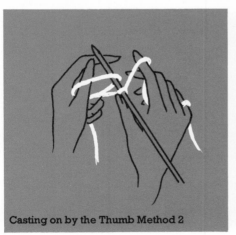

Casting on by the Thumb Method 2

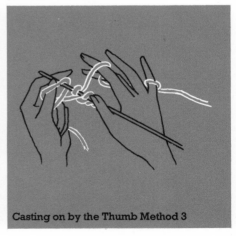

Casting on by the Thumb Method 3

The Thumb Method. The principle is the same as the two-needle method except that only one needle is used which is held in the right hand and the thumb acts as the left needle. Allow a long length of yarn from the cut end as the cast-on stitches are made by taking up this length and looping it round the thumb, and the stitches are cast on to the right needle. A guide to the length of yarn required is one inch for one stitch. Make a slip loop.

Take up yarn at the required length from cut end and loop yarn round left

33

thumb. Let ball of yarn run from right. Take up needle and hold yarn in right hand as described for two-needle method.

Insert right needle point through loop on thumb from front to back, pass yarn round right needle point and pull a loop through at the same time slipping loop off thumb, thus leaving a loop on right needle which is the second stitch (starting loop is first stitch).

Loop yarn round thumb again and repeat the action. Continue thus gradually taking up the length of yarn towards the cut end until the required number of stitches has been cast on.

This method gives a firm but elastic edge and is widely used: be careful not to pull the yarn too tightly round thumb as this makes the edge too rigid.

These are the three principal methods of casting on. There are many variations which can be learnt as experience is gained. For example, to strengthen a cast-on edge using fine yarn, cast on with two lengths of yarn. For two-colour casting on, work with two different coloured balls of yarn, casting on a stitch alternately in each colour.

In the foregoing descriptions of casting on, the stitches are actually cast on and knitted at the same time, thus the cast-on edge is, strictly speaking, the first row of knitting. This used to be known as 'knitting on' but this term has largely disappeared today, and it is generally accepted that the casting-on row is not counted.

It is possible to cast on without 'knitting on' and this method is known as **single casting on**: this is worked as follows by the thumb method.

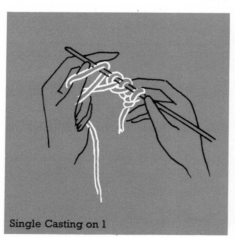

Single Casting on 1

Single Casting on 2

Allow required length of yarn from cut end and loop yarn round left thumb as for thumb method. Take one needle in right hand; insert right needle point through loop and slip loop off thumb and on to needle. Loop yarn round thumb again and repeat the action, thus forming a row of single loops (stitches) on right needle. This casting on gives a very flat elastic edge and is recommended for baby garments. The first stitch should be a slip loop, as described on page 30 to close the end.

Having learnt casting on, the next step is to learn to knit.

THE KNIT STITCH

Cast-on stitches are on the left needle and yarn runs from ball to stitch at back of work. Insert point of right needle through first stitch on left needle from front to

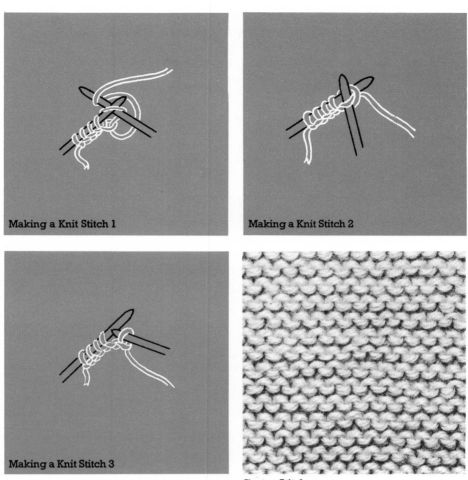

Making a Knit Stitch 1

Making a Knit Stitch 2

Making a Knit Stitch 3

Garter Stitch

back. Pass yarn round right needle point, turn needle point so that yarn can be pulled through to form a loop on right needle point, slipping left loop off left needle at the same time. This completes the first stitch.

Continue thus into each stitch on left needle until all these stitches have been knitted off on to the right needle and one row has been knitted. This is the *1st Row*. Transfer needles to opposite hands. *2nd Row*: Knit across exactly as 1st row.

Continue knitting each row until the fabric is the required length. A piece of fabric formed by knitting each row is called garter stitch.

Before going any further casting off must be learnt.

CASTING OFF KNITWAYS

Casting off knitways produces a chain edge. It is most widely used and an instruction to cast off usually implies this method.

Knit the first two stitches in the usual way then insert left needle point through first stitch (second stitch from needle point) and lift it up and over second stitch and off right needle, so that it forms a holding loop round the base of the second stitch: the first stitch has now been cast off. Knit the next stitch to give two stitches again on the right needle, and cast off first stitch as before. Continue working thus with pairs of stitches right across the row until one stitch remains on right needle. To finish off, cut yarn leaving an end a few inches long, pass this through last stitch, slip stitch off needle and pull end tight to secure last stitch: the end will be darned into work or taken in with the seam in making up.

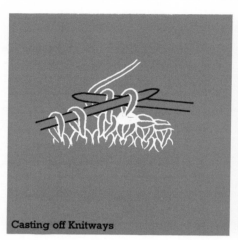

Casting off Knitways

Making a Purl Stitch 1

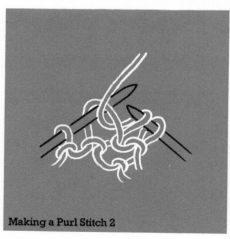

Making a Purl Stitch 2

Making a Purl Stitch 3

THE PURL STITCH

Needle with cast-on stitches is in left hand and empty needle and yarn are in right hand exactly as for knit stitch, but for purl, bring yarn to front of work, and yarn lies to the front throughout.

Insert right needle through the front of first stitch on left needle from back to front. Pass yarn round point of right needle and take a loop through to back,

36

slipping off stitch on left needle and leaving a loop (stitch) on right needle. This is the first purl stitch.

CASTING OFF PURLWAYS
The method is the same as for knitways except that the stitches are purled instead of knitted.

These are the two basic stitches of knitting and all fancy stitches and hand-knitted fabrics are formed by mixing these two stitches in various ways. Thus, as all fancy effects are developments of knit and purl stitches, they are known by their stitch name, e.g. stocking stitch, moss stitch, cable stitch. Following are some basic fabrics which use simple constructions of knit and purl stitches. They are all very easy to do, are widely used and form the basis for knitting knowledge. Practise squares of these stitches, then go on to make the simple articles.

Stocking Stitch got its name originally from knitted stockings, and is the most widely used fabric. It is formed by working one row knit and one row purl alternately for the length required.

Stocking Stitch

Double Moss Stitch Multiple of 4
1st and 2nd rows: * K2, P2; rep from * to end. 3rd and 4th rows: * P2, K2; rep from * to end. These 4 rows form patt.

Moss Stitch Multiple of 2 + 1
1st and every row: * K1, P1; rep from * to last st, K1.

37

Basket Stitch Multiple of 8
1st to 4th row: * K4, P4; rep from * to
end. 5th to 8th row: * P4, K4; rep from
* to end. These 8 rows form patt.

Broken Rib Stitch Multiple of 2
1st row: K. 2nd row: * K1, P1; rep
from * to end. These 2 rows form patt.

Tile Stitch Multiple of 3
1st and 3rd rows: * K2, P1; rep from *
to end. 2nd row: * K1, P2; rep from * to
end. 4th row: K. These 4 rows form
patt.

KNITTING WITH FOUR NEEDLES

This is for working round and round to form a tube of seamless fabric such as for
socks. Round knitting uses a set of four needles of equal length and each needle is
pointed at both ends. In round knitting the work is never turned as with two
needles: the knit (right) side of the fabric is usually facing all the time. The
principle is the same as for two-needle casting on except that the stitches are
divided equally and cast on to three needles (corresponding to the left needle) and
the fourth needle is the working (right) needle.

The diagrams show how the stitches are cast on in groups of three and it is
essential to see that they do not get twisted. When all the stitches are cast on,

arrange the needles in a triangle ready to join up the stitches to start the tube of work. Take the fourth (spare) needle and insert it in the first cast-on stitch at the beginning of the first needle: it is helpful to loop a short contrast thread at this point to mark division of rounds. Now take up yarn coming from last cast-on stitch on third needle, and knit the first cast-on stitch: thus the triangle is joined. Continue knitting off stitches on third needle on to fourth needle until the third needle becomes free: this needle now becomes the working needle. Continue working round in this way, keeping the gap between needle ends as close as possible: practice makes this easier.

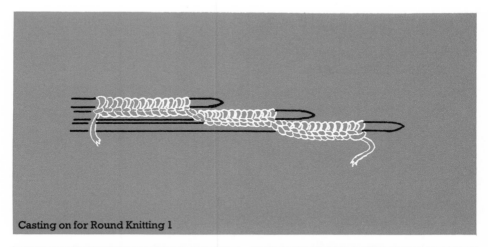

Casting on for Round Knitting 1

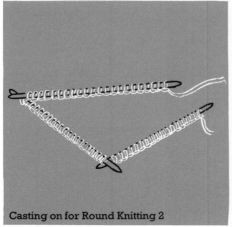

Casting on for Round Knitting 2

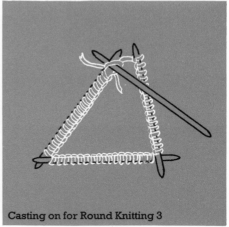

Casting on for Round Knitting 3

Four Simple Things for the Beginner to Make

Now the beginner is ready to tackle some simple accessories for the home: a cushion in garter stitch, pot holder with garter stitch border, a tea cosy in stocking stitch with moss stitch gusset, and pram cover in a diamond stitch.

Cushion

This can be knitted in one colour or in simple stripes as photographed. See page 48 for colour knitting.

Materials: 2 (50g) balls Dark, 1 (50g) ball Light and oddment Medium shades in Patons Double Knitting. Pair No 9 needles.

Measurement: 13½in square approx.

Additional Abbreviations (see page 29): D=Dark; L=Light; M=Medium.

With D, cast on 72 sts and work in garter st (every row K throughout).
Work 26 rows in D, then change to stripe patt as follows:
* 8 rows L; 2 rows D; 4 rows M; 2 rows D.* The 16 rows from * to * form stripe patt. Work from * to * 3 times more, then work 8 rows L and 27 rows D.

Cast off. Work another piece the same.

TO MAKE UP
Observing general method on page 81, block and press. With wrong side facing, join the 2 pieces round 3 sides. Turn right side out, insert cushion pad and neatly stitch up remaining side.

Pot Holder

These can be decorated with simple embroidery as photographed or left plain.

Materials: 1 (50g) ball Patons Double Knitting. Oddments in two contrasting colours for embroidery if required. Pair No 5 needles. Felt for backing.

Measurements: 7 × 6 in.

Using thumb method cast on 27 sts and work 5 rows garter st (every row K).
1st row: (wrong side), K3, P to last 3 sts, K3. 2nd row: K4, * P1, K1; rep from * to last 3 sts, K3. 3rd row: K3, P to last 3 sts, K.3. 4th, 5th and 6th rows: K. Rep last 6 rows 5 times more. K 2 rows. Cast off knitways.

TO MAKE UP

Observing general method on page 81, block and press. Decorate, if required, by working lines of darning in alternating colours going under the purl stitches. Cut a small length of felt for hanger and stitch to one corner on wrong side of work. Cut felt to same size as holder and stitch to wrong side.

Tea Cosy

Materials: 3 (50g) balls Patons Double Knitting, 2 (50g) balls White and 1 (50g) ball Green. Small amounts of Pink and Blue yarns for embroidery, if required. Pair No 9 needles. Foam rubber cut to shape and stitched together for pad.

Measurements: 9 × 14 in.

Additional Abbreviations (see page 29): W = White; G = Green.

With W, cast on 65 sts.
1st row: K. 2nd row: K1, P to last st, K1. 3rd to 9th row: Rep 1st and 2nd rows 3 times, then 1st row once. 10th row: K1, P7, (K1, P11) 4 times, K1, P7, K1. 11th to 17th row: Rep 1st and 2nd rows 3 times, then 1st row once. 18th row: K1, P13, (K1, P11) 4 times, P2, K1. Rep 3rd to 18th row incl twice.

Shape top: 1st row: K1, K2tog, K to last 3 sts, K2togtbl, K1. 2nd row: K1, P2togtbl, P to last 3 sts, P2tog, K1. 3rd row: As 1st: 59 sts. 4th row: K1, P to last st, K1. 5th to 7th row: Rep 1st to 3rd row once: 53 sts.
8th row: K1, P13, (K1, P11) 3 times, P2, K1. 9th and 10th rows: As 1st and 2nd: 49 sts. 11th to 16th row: Rep 3rd and 4th rows once, then 1st to 4th row incl once: 41 sts.
Slip sts on a length of yarn and leave. Work another piece the same.

Bands: With G, cast on 7 sts. Work in moss st (every row K1, P1 alt to last st, K1) for 9 in. Break yarn. Sl sts on a length of yarn and leave. Work another length the same but do not break yarn.

Top Band: With needle holding the 7 Band sts just worked and using G, K across 41 W sts of one half of Cosy then work across rem 7 Band sts in moss st: 55 sts.
1st row: K1, K2tog, * P1, K1; rep from * to last 4 sts, P1, K2tog, K1. 2nd row: K2, * P1, K1; rep from * to last st, K1. 3rd row: K1, P2tog, * K1, P1; rep from * to last 4 sts, K1, P2tog, K1. 4th row: * K1, P1; rep from * to last st, K1. 5th to 9th row: Rep 1st to 4th row incl once, then 1st row once. Cast off.
Work Bands on other side to match.

TO MAKE UP

Observing general method on page 81, press. Stitch side borders in position. Join back and front together. Make pad to fit and slip inside. For simple embroidery stitches see Chapter 9.

Pram Cover

Materials: 8 (50g) balls Patons Doublet. Pair No 4 (14 in) needles. $3\frac{1}{4}$ yds blanket ribbon.

Measurements: Width 20 in; length 27 in.

Tension: 8 sts and 10 rows to 2 in over st st on No 4 needles.

Cast on 73 sts. Work 6 rows in st st.
Work in patt with st st borders: 1st row: K4, * K4, P1, K3; rep from * to last 5 sts, K5. 2nd row: P4, * P3, K1, P1, K1, P2; rep from * to last 5 sts, P5. 3rd row: K4, * K2, P1, K3, P1, K1; rep from * to last 5 sts, K5.
4th row: P4, * P1, K1, P5, K1; rep from * to last 5 sts, P5. 5th row: K4, * P1, K7; rep from * to last 5 sts, P1, K4. 6th row: As 4th. 7th row: As 3rd. 8th row: As 2nd. These 8 rows form patt.
Rep rows 1 to 8 incl 15 times more, then 1st row once. Work 6 rows in st st. Cast off.

TO MAKE UP

Observing general method on page 81, block and press. Bind edges placing ribbon over st st border, mitring corners.

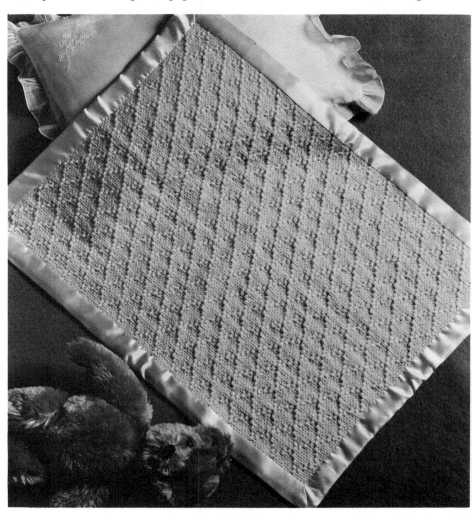

Chapter 5

Making Progress

Once the first steps in knitting explained in the preceding chapter have been grasped, the next stage is to learn how to make holes and twists in knitting to produce more elaborate fabrics. There is nothing difficult about this – many beautiful lacy and embossed effects can be achieved by using variations of the basic knit and purl movements.

For lacy and openwork effects, it is necessary to produce holes in the fabric. This is the 'over' principle, so called because the yarn is looped over or round the needle in such a way that an extra stitch is made. It follows that to keep the number of stitches correct, for every extra stitch that is made a corresponding stitch must be decreased unless, of course, the number of stitches is being increased in the actual shaping of a garment. Therefore, before you tackle these more elaborate effects, you must learn simple decreasing, that is, taking two stitches together to lose one, and increasing, which is making an extra stitch. There are different ways of doing these but most of them are variations of the following simple movements.

BASIC KNIT AND PURL INCREASE

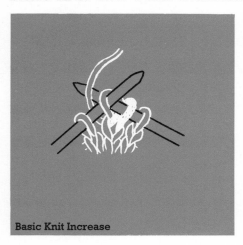

Basic Knit Increase

Knit twice into next stitch, that is, knit into front of stitch on left needle in the usual way (shaded stitch in diagram) but do not slip stitch off needle, then knit again through back of stitch so that two loops are on right needle, then slip stitch off left needle.

The principle is the same for a purl increase, purling first into the front of the stitch, then manipulating the right needle point behind and into the back of the stitch for the increase. A simple way of doing this is to slip the stitch off the needle, twist it and put it back on the needle again then purl through the front in the usual way.

MAKING AN EXTRA STITCH BY THE OVER PRINCIPLE

On knit rows, bring yarn between needles to front of work and take it *over* the right needle to knit the next stitch, thus giving an extra loop (stitch) on the right needle. This is abbreviated to 'y o n' (yarn over, or yarn on, needle) or 'y f' (yarn forward) or 'yft' (yarn front).

On purl rows, the yarn is at the front of the work, take it *over* and round the right needle and bring it to the front again ready to purl the next stitch – this is called 'y r n' (yarn round needle) and an extra stitch has been made.

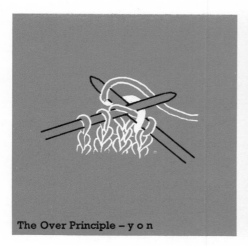

The Over Principle – y o n

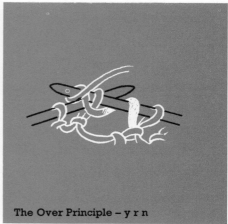

The Over Principle – y r n

These methods of using the 'over' principle will produce holes for lacy and open effects in fabrics, or small buttonholes or ribbon holes in baby garments.

INVISIBLE INCREASES

These give very neat increases and are ideal for stocking stitch or for making a stitch in the middle of a row. The two most widely used are:

Increase Through Stitch Below. With right needle point pick up loop of stitch (shaded in diagram) just below next stitch on left needle, slip it on to left needle and knit into back of it, then knit the next stitch in the usual way.

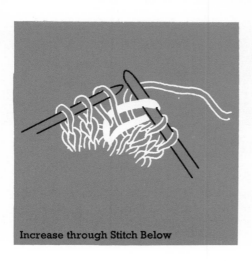

Increase through Stitch Below

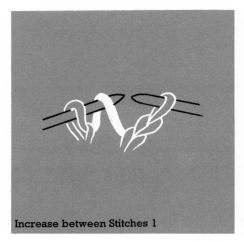

Increase between Stitches 1

Increase between Stitches 2

Increase Between Stitches. Insert right needle point under yarn lying between the two needles. Pick up this loop, put it on to right needle and knit or purl it in the usual way, or into the back which twists the 'made' loop and closes the gap.

SINGLE DECREASING IN ONE STAGE

The simplest decrease of all is to knit (or purl) two stitches together, represented by K2tog (or P2tog). To do this, insert right needle point through front of second stitch on left needle then through first stitch, and knit in the usual way drawing loop through both stitches and slipping both stitches off left needle. For P2tog, insert left needle through first and second stitches on left needle and purl them together as one stitch.

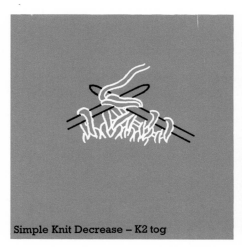

Simple Knit Decrease – K2 tog

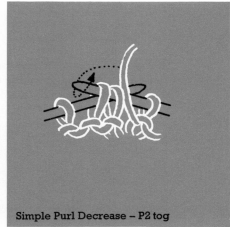

Simple Purl Decrease – P2 tog

DECREASING TWO STITCHES IN ONE STAGE

Work K3tog (or P3tog) in the same way as K2tog (or P2tog).

These simple ways of increasing and decreasing give sufficient knowledge to enable more fancy stitches to be tackled. More variations and extensions of decreasing are given in Chapter 6, and in individual design instructions where appropriate.

46

SLIP STITCHES

Pattern effects often use slip stitches. This simply means that the stitch is slipped from left needle to right needle without actually working it. The stitch can be slipped knitways or purlways, and these actions are abbreviated to Sl 1 K and Sl 1 P. A stitch can be slipped through the back (Sl1 Ktbl).

EASY-TO-KNIT FANCY EFFECTS

Twisted Effects. These can be achieved in many ways such as by working into the backs of stitches to give an all-over crossed effect as in Continental stocking stitch, described in Chapter 7, or by crossing stitches as in cabling, described later in this chapter.

Knitting into the Back

Ribbed Effects. These are vertical effects formed by alternately knitting and purling groups of stitches. Fine ribbing is generally used for welts and cuffs, and broad ribs for main fabrics.

K1 P1 Rib Multiple of 2
1st row: * K1, P1; rep from * to end.
2nd row: * P1, K1; rep from * to end.
These 2 rows form rib.

K4 P2 Rib Multiple of 6
1st row: * K4, P2, rep from * to end.
2nd row: * P2, K4, rep from * to end.
These 2 rows form patt.

Ridged Effects. Horizontal bands formed by alternating groups of knit and purl rows.

Mesh Effects. Attractive effects can be made by using one thick and one thin needle, or by incorporating rows of long stitches made by putting the yarn twice round the needle to give a long loop on the following row.

Ridged Pattern Any number
1st row: K. 2nd row: P. 3rd and 4th rows: K. 5th row: P. 6th row: K. These 6 rows form patt.

Garter Mesh Any number
1st to 4th row: K. 5th row: * K1 winding yarn twice round needle; rep from * to end. 6th row: * K every stitch dropping extra loop.

INTRODUCING COLOUR

Limitless effects in knitting can be produced from simple two-colour stripes and checks through to heavily patterned fabrics using several colours. Everyone knows the beautiful designs of traditional Fair Isle knitting: today this is so loosely applied to describe almost any type of colour work that it is more accurate to try and place some aspects of colour knitting within the context of their individual folk origins. This is dealt with in Chapter 7: for the moment here are some simple effects for the beginner.

The easiest way of introducing colour is in stripes formed by working an equal number of rows in alternating colours, for example, 2 rows dark and 2 rows light, with the yarns carried loosely up the right edge of the work. In one-row stripes, two balls of each colour are required with one of each joined in at both ends of the work: this avoids breaking off a colour at the finished row end and joining it in again at the beginning of the next working row, thus the yarns are carried loosely up both ends of the work.

When working colour stripes in ribbing on the right side of work it is usual to knit the first row when changing colour to avoid the two colours showing on the row (work a purl row when changing colour on wrong side of work). Sometimes, this two-colour effect on a row can be a feature of the design.

How to do Colour Pattern Knitting. The simplest and most widely used method is to follow the design from a chart: the method of writing out the pattern in detail row by row has largely gone out of practice. The chart is a design drawn up on a piece of squared paper: the lines of squares reading up the chart represent rows, and the lines of squares reading across represent stitches. In black and white

Stranding

Stranding – Hands position for K Row

illustrations the colours of yarns are represented by different symbols. The fabric is usually stocking stitch and the chart is followed by reading the rows alternately from right to left for knit rows and left to right for purl rows. The yarns are carried across the back (wrong side) of the work.

Stranding. The accepted method, called *Stranding*, is the simplest and most widely used. The diagram shows how the stranding is formed on the wrong side of the work.

One colour of yarn is held in each hand. The colour follows the usual knitting movement, but the second colour is held out over the index finger of the left hand and instead of looping the yarn round the right needle, the needle pulls the colour through the stitch on the principle of Continental knitting described in Chapter 7.

The following diagram shows the hands in position for a knit row.
At first glance this looks complicated but it becomes quite easy after only a few stitches. The colour to be used over the next stitch, or stitches, is the working colour, and the colour not in use for the moment is the stranding colour.

The next diagram shows the knit stitch for the first colour in right hand with the stranding colour held clear in the left hand: in the diagram following, the right colour is held clear for stranding and the second colour is being knitted.

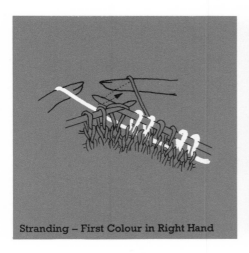

Stranding – First Colour in Right Hand

Stranding – Second Colour in Left Hand

The next two diagrams show the two purl movements.

It is not advisable to strand over more than 5 stitches, so where this occurs, weave the stranding colour over and under the centre stitch to avoid a long carrying thread.

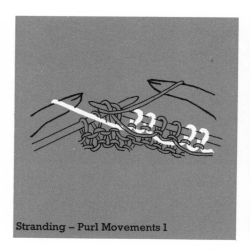

Stranding – Purl Movements 1

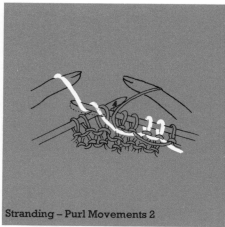

Stranding – Purl Movements 2

Although not difficult, there are some important points to note: do not drag the strands as this will tighten the tension and lose the elasticity of the knitting. The first stranding diagram on p.49 gives the correct appearance of finished work on the wrong side: the carried threads must follow the regular under and over look in the diagram, and the threads must not be twisted.

Working Blocks of Colour. Colour work sometimes involves joining in separate balls of yarn to work blocks of colour or large motifs. Where this occurs, the two colours must be woven round each other to prevent the sections separating and leaving gaps. A bobbin is helpful for this type of colour work: see Chapter 9.

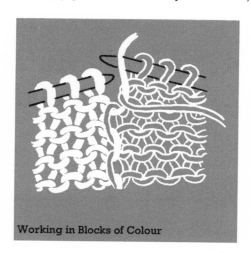

Working in Blocks of Colour

CABLED EFFECTS

These require the use of a short needle pointed at both ends, called a cable needle. Cabling produces rope-like effects on the front of a fabric. They can be very simple or extremely decorative and elaborate: they form a vital part of traditional knitting such as is used for work of the Aran type and fishermens jerseys (or guernseys). Nevertheless, no matter how complicated they may appear, in themselves they are quite simple to do.

The cabling principle is to cross one group of stitches over another by placing a stated number of stitches on a cable needle and leaving them whilst another group of stitches is worked first.

Simple cables are worked in stocking stitch and they show to best advantage with one or more purl stitches on either side so that the cable is in relief. Decorative cables are made by working fancy stitches and bobbles on the cable itself. The beginner will progress quickly from simple cable ribs to elaborate Aran-type stitches.

Practise the following colour patterns and fancy stitches.

Simple Stripe

Simple Stripe Any number
1st row: Using Main Shade, K. 2nd row: P. 3rd to 6th row: Rep 1st and 2nd rows twice. 7th row: Using Dark, K. 8th row: P.
9th and 10th rows: As 7th and 8th. 11th row: Using Main Shade, K. 12th row: K.
13th to 16th row: Rep 7th and 8th rows twice.

Check Pattern

Check Pattern Multiple of 8
1st row: * K4D, 4L, rep from * to end.
2nd row: * P4L, 4D, rep from * to end.
3rd and 4th rows: As 1st and 2nd. 5th row: * K4L, 4D, rep from * to end.
6th row: * P4D, 4L, rep from * to end.
7th and 8th rows: As 5th and 6th.
These 8 rows form patt.

Simple Cable

Simple Cable Multiple of 9 + 3
1st and 3rd rows: * P3, K6; rep from * to last 3 sts, P3. 2nd and 4th rows: * K3, P6; rep from * to last 3 sts, K3. 5th row: * P3, sl next 3 sts on to cable needle and leave at front of work, K3 sts, K3 from cable needle; rep from * to last 3 sts, P3. 6th row: As 2nd. These 6 rows form patt.

Wheatear Cable

Wheatear Cable Multiple of 11 + 3
1st and 3rd rows: * P3, K8; rep from * to last 3 sts, P3. 2nd and 4th rows: * K3, P8; rep from * to last 3 sts, K.3. 5th row: * P3, sl next 2 sts on to cable needle and leave at back of work, K2, K 2 sts from cable needle, sl next 2 sts on to cable needle, and leave at front of work, K2, K 2 sts from cable needle; rep from * to last 3 sts, P3. 6th row: As 2nd. These 6 rows form patt.

Trellis Stitch

Trellis Stitch Multiple of 4 + 1
1st row: * K1, yft, sl 3P, taking yarn across the 3 sl sts, wind yarn round right-hand needle once; rep from * to last st, K1. 2nd and 6th rows: P letting the extra loop fall to right side of work. 3rd and 7th rows: K. 4th and 8th rows: P.
5th row: K2, * with point of right-hand needle take up long thread and K with next st, yft, sl 3P, taking yarn across 3 sl sts, wind once round right-hand needle, rep from * to last 3 sts, with point of needle pick up long thread and K with next st, K2. 9th row: K1, * yft, sl 3P, taking yarn across the 3 sl sts, wind once round right-hand needle, with

point of right-hand needle take up long thread and K with next st; rep from * to last st, K1.

2nd to 9th rows form patt.

Open Rib

Open Rib Multiple of 5+3

1st row: * P1, K1tbl, P1, K2; rep from * to last 3 sts, P1, K1tbl, P1. 2nd row: K1, P1tbl, K1, * P2, K1, P1tbl, K1; rep from * to end.

3rd row: * P1, K1tbl, P1, K1, yf, K1; rep from * to last 3 sts, P1, K1tbl, P1. 4th row: K1, P1tbl, K1, * P3, K1, P1tbl, K1; rep from * to end. 5th row: * P1, K1tbl, P1, K3, pass 3rd st on right-hand needle over first 2 sts; rep from * to last 3 sts, P1, K1tbl, P1. 2nd to 5th rows form patt.

Chevron Lace

Chevron Lace Multiple of 8+1

1st row: * K1, yf, K2, sl 1, K2tog, psso, K2, yf; rep from * to last st, K1. 2nd and 4th rows: P. 3rd row: * K1, yf, K2, K3togtbl, K2, yf; rep from * to last st, K1.

Doll's Bed Set to delight a Little Girl

and to provide practice in some of the stages learned so far

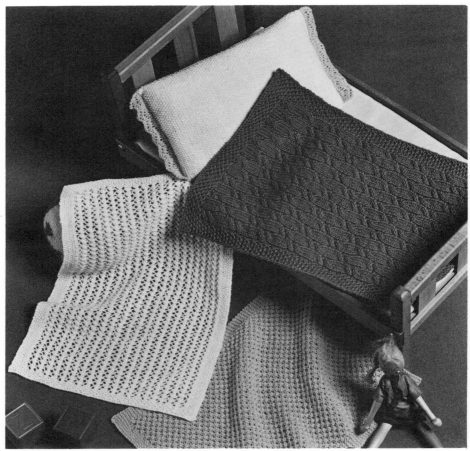

COT COVER

Materials: 2 (50g) balls Patons Double Knitting. Pair No 9 needles. Cable needle.

Measurements: 12 × 16½ in.

Additional Abbreviations (see page 29): C4=Cable 4 by slipping next 2 sts on to cable needle, leave at back of work, K next 2 sts then K 2 sts from cable needle.

Cast on 67 sts. Work sl st patt for borders as follows:

1st row: * P1, yft, sl 1; rep from * to last st, P1. 2nd row: P. 3rd row: P1, * P1, yft, sl 1; rep from * to last 2 sts, P2. 4th row: P.

Rep 1st to 4th row incl once, then 1st to 3rd row once. Next row: (Inc row), P9, * inc in next st, P3; rep from * to last 6 sts, P to end: 80 sts.

Now introduce Cable patt for centre part: 1st row: (P1, yft, sl 1) 3 times, P2, * K4, P1; rep from * to last 7 sts, (P1, yft, sl 1) 3 times, P1. 2nd row: P7, * K1, P4; rep from * to last 8 sts, K1, P7. 3rd

54

row: P1, (P1, yft, sl 1) 3 times, P1, * C4, P1, K4, P1; rep from * to last 12 sts, C4, P1, (yft, sl 1, P1) 3 times, P1. 4th row: As 2nd. 5th to 8th row: Rep rows 1 to 4 incl once.
9th row: (P1, yft, sl 1) 3 times, P2, * K4, P1; rep from * to last 7 sts, (P1, yft, sl 1) 3 times, P1. 10th row: As 2nd. 11th row: P1, (P1, yft, sl 1) 3 times, P1, * K4, P1, C4, P1; rep from * to last 12 sts, K4, P1, (yft, sl 1, P1) 3 times, P1. 12th row: As 2nd. 13th to 16th row: Rep rows 9 to 10 incl once. These 16 rows form Cable patt.
Cont in patt until work measures approx $15\frac{1}{2}$ in from start, ending with a 7th or 15th row of patt. Next row: (Dec row), P9, * P2tog, P3; rep from * to last 6 sts, P to end: 67 sts. Rep 1st to 4th row incl of border patt twice, then 1st to 3rd row once. Cast off.

BLANKET

Materials: 2 (50g) balls Patons Purple Heather 4-ply. Pair No 10 needles.

Measurements: 12 × 16 in.

Cast on 84 sts: K 9 rows for garter st border. Next row: (Inc row), K9, * inc in next st, K4; rep from * to last 5 sts, K to end: 98 sts.
Now introduce Blackberry patt for centre part as follows: 1st row: K7, * P3tog, (P1, K1, P1) into next st; rep from * to last 7 sts, K7. 2nd row: K. 3rd row: K7, * (P1, K1, P1) into next st, P3tog; rep from * to last 7 sts, K7. 4th row: K. These 4 rows form patt.
Cont in patt until work measures 15 in from start, ending with a 2nd or 4th row of patt. Next row: (Dec row) K9, * K2tog, K4; rep from * to last 5 sts, K to end: 84 sts. K8 rows. Cast off.

SHEET

Materials: 1 (50g) ball Patons Purple Heather 4-ply. Pair No 11 needles.

Measurements: 12 × 16 in.

Cast on 89 sts. Work 5 rows in moss st (every row * K1, P1; rep from * to last st, K1) for border. Next row: (Dec row) (K1, P1) 4 times, (K1, P1, K2tog) 18 times, (K1, P1) 4 times, K1: 71 sts.

Now introduce Lace Rib patt as follows: 1st row: (K1, P1) twice, K1, K2tog, * yf, K3, yf, sl 1, K2tog, psso; rep from * to last 10 sts, yf, K3, yf, K2tog, (K1, P1) twice, K1. 2nd row: (K1, P1) twice, K1, P to last 5 sts, (K1, P1) twice, K1. 3rd row: (K1, P1) twice, * K3, yf, sl 1, K2tog, psso, yf; rep from * to last 7 sts, K3, (P1, K1) twice. 4th row: As 2nd.
These 4 rows form patt. Cont in patt until work measures $15\frac{1}{2}$ in from start, ending with a 3rd row of patt. Next row: (Inc row), (K1, P1) twice, K1, P3, (P2, inc in next st) 18 times, P4, (K1, P1) twice, K1: 89 sts. Work 5 rows in moss st. Cast off.

PILLOW SLIP

Materials: 1 (50g) ball Patons Purple Heather 4-ply. Small ball 4-ply in Contrast colour (original used rem yarn from blanket). Pair No. 11 needles. Cotton material and Kapok for pillow.

Measurements: 11 × $6\frac{1}{2}$ in (plus edging).

Main Parts: Cast on 81 sts and work in moss st (every row * K1, P1; rep from * to last st, K1) until work measures $6\frac{1}{2}$ in from start. Cast off.
Work another piece the same.
Lace Border: With Contrast, cast on 6 sts. 1st row: (wrong side), * K1, P1; rep from * to end. 2nd row: P1, (K2tog, yf) twice, K1. 3rd to 6th row: Rep 1st and 2nd rows twice. 7th row: As 1st. 8th row: P1, K1, (yf, K2tog) twice. 9th to 12th row: Rep 7th and 8th rows twice. These 12 rows form patt. Rep last 12 rows 6 times more. Cast off. Work another piece the same.

TO MAKE UP

Observing general method on page 81, block and press. Take one piece of pillow slip for front and neatly oversew straight edge of border to each short end. With wrong side facing, stitch the two long edges of front of pillow slip to the corresponding long edges of back then turn right side out. Make pillow, place inside cover and stitch side edges of back to front.

Chapter 6

The Expert Touch

Knitting has changed very little over the years. The basic golden rules remain the same and should be followed very carefully to achieve finished work that has the professional touch. These rules apply to both the knitting and making up. This chapter deals with the work in progress – tension, the key to the correct size of a finished piece of work which involves not only the actual knitting but the use of correct materials, measuring the work, picking up dropped stitches, neat side edges, joining in new yarn and many other points. Making up and finishing touches follow in Chapter 8.

MATERIALS

The knitter should stick to the rule that the correct yarn as stated in the materials paragraph of a design should be used, as it will have been specially planned and checked for the specific yarn quoted. Changing the yarn may produce a result which is different in appearance and size; yarn quantities may be different too. Only very experienced knitters should attempt any variation and they should be completely familiar with the details given in the shopping guide in Chapter 2.

TENSION

Tension is the number of stitches and rows measured in inches. A knitting design is a mathematical calculation based on these measurements, thus working to a tension which differs from the stated pattern will produce a differently sized piece of fabric. Half a stitch out can build up to an increase or reduction of the all-round measurement by two or three inches, and the same applies to the length.

Tension should be checked before starting the actual garment as follows: take the correct needles and yarn and cast on the correct number of stitches for two or more inches. Now work correct number of rows to complete the square. Cast off. Lay it on a flat surface and measure with tape-measure and pins as in the diagram.

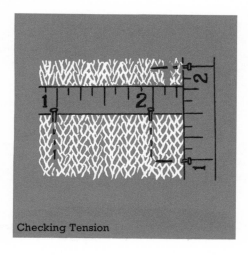

Checking Tension

If there are more or less stitches and rows to the inch than as given in the tension paragraph, then the work is too tight or too loose respectively. This can be corrected by using one size thicker or finer needles, and this is the accepted method for experienced knitters who also understand that the individual design must be taken into account. For example, a chunky design which already uses extra thick needles, might not stand up to an even thicker size, and there is a limit to the fineness of needles too. Nevertheless, this method of tension adjustment can be applied to most knitting worked in medium and double knitting yarns. Experienced knitters can use this method to vary sizes as well as to achieve the correct size. An approximate guide for tension is half a stitch and half a row to the inch for each needle change, so to adapt a tension requires a mathematical calculation to gauge the finished measurements required against the tension being achieved.

However, the beginner should start off in the right way by learning to knit to correct tension. A good lesson is to practise knitting several squares in stocking stitch using different yarns and needle sizes. Correct stocking stitch tension usually means the worker is an average knitter who could be expected to achieve a correct design tension. Hold the work lightly but firmly and work to an even rhythm.

STANDARD TENSIONS

Throughout this book only universally known classic yarns in various weights have been recommended. They can readily be matched by using the tension table below in conjunction with the table of knitting needle sizes in Chapter 3.

The following table indicates the recommended tensions for the principal classic yarns:

Needle Size	2-ply		3-ply		4-ply		Double Knitting		Double Double Knitting	
	Sts	Rows	Sts	Rows	Sts	Rows	Sts	Rows	Sts	Rows
12	9	11	$8\frac{1}{2}$	$10\frac{1}{2}$						
11	$8\frac{1}{2}$	$10\frac{1}{2}$	8	10	$7\frac{1}{2}$	$9\frac{1}{2}$				
10	8	10	$7\frac{1}{2}$	$9\frac{1}{2}$	7	9	6	8		
9	$7\frac{1}{2}$	$9\frac{1}{2}$	7	9	$6\frac{1}{2}$	$8\frac{1}{2}$	$5\frac{3}{4}$	$7\frac{3}{4}$		
8	7	9	$6\frac{1}{2}$	$8\frac{1}{2}$	6	8	$5\frac{1}{2}$	$7\frac{1}{2}$		
7			6	8	$5\frac{1}{2}$	$7\frac{1}{2}$	$5\frac{1}{4}$	7	$4\frac{3}{4}$	$6\frac{1}{4}$
6					5	7	5	$6\frac{1}{2}$	$4\frac{1}{2}$	$5\frac{3}{4}$
5							$4\frac{3}{4}$	6	$4\frac{1}{4}$	$5\frac{1}{4}$
4							$4\frac{1}{2}$	$5\frac{1}{2}$	4	$4\frac{3}{4}$

ADAPTING SIZES

The rules for adapting tension apply also to sizes as the instructions will have been prepared for the given size range. Simple adaptations to length can be made, but the beginner should not attempt to adapt sizes by changing stitches. This is where the experienced knitter can apply her knowledge of tension and stitch units, but she will consider many other factors. For example, adding extra stitches in width will lengthen decreasings for armholes and these must be adjusted accordingly.

Similarly, although changing needles to adjust a size is an accepted method, this requires experience, the accepted guide being approximately 2 inches difference either way to one size in needles. It must also be considered that any adaptations on these lines will involve using different yarn quantities.

MEASURING

For complete accuracy, lay the work on a flat surface. Measure carefully noting the difference in length between the straight fabric and sloping edges. For example, this should be checked when measuring a sleeve length and full length of garment from shoulder to lower edge.

It is correct to measure on the straight unless otherwise stated, that is, a sleeve measurement may refer specifically to the sleeve seam and this would be the sloping edge. Note if a measuring instruction includes the welt and cuff. Measurements should be checked frequently whilst the work is in progress.

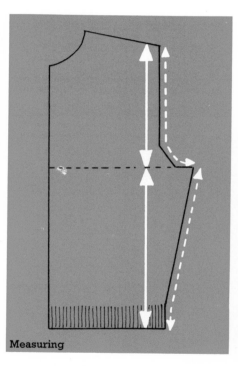

Measuring

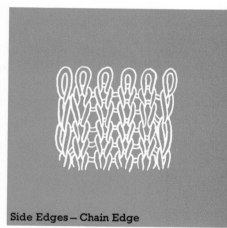

Side Edges — Chain Edge

SIDE EDGES

Good edges contribute to the finished appearance of a garment. Edges on flat pieces of fabric which are going to be seamed together must be firm and it is usual to work the first and last stitches in such a way that the edges do not curl and the rows can be matched exactly when sewing the pieces together. One method is to work a knit stitch at each end of every row. This forms a line of protruding loops down the edge which can be paired when making up.

The following two methods also give neat edges which will not curl: (1) Slip the first stitch purlways on every knit row, and slip the first stitch knitways on every purl row. (2) Slip the first stitch and knit the last stitch on every row (both knit and purl rows). For garter stitch, slip first stitch purlways on every row.

58

Open side edges must be firm and lie flat. The following method is recommended as it gives a decorative chain effect: slip first and last stitches knitways on knit rows and purl all stitches on purl rows. By slipping the stitch on knit rows only, one long stitch is stretched over 2 rows which tightens the edge.

It is important that in all methods the first and last few stitches should be worked firmly.

DROPPED STITCHES

These can usually be picked up without difficulty working the correct knit or purl action as required for the pattern. The first diagram shows a dropped knitted loop with the missed strand lying to the back. Insert right needle through this loop from front to back and pull the missed strand through to form a knitted stitch on right needle as in the second diagram. Finally, transfer stitch to left needle making sure the stitch lies the right way.

For a purl stitch the loose strand lies to the front. The right needle is inserted through the dropped loop from back to front and the loose strand is taken back through the loop to form a purl stitch then transferred to the left needle.

When a stitch has dropped down several rows, a good tip is to use a crochet hook for the picking up.

Picking up a Knit Stitch 1

Picking up a Knit Stitch 2

Picking up a Knit Stitch 3

Picking up a Purl Stitch 1

Picking up a Purl Stitch 2

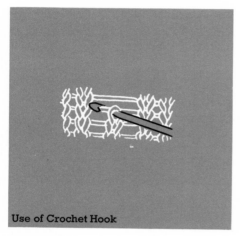

Use of Crochet Hook

SHAPINGS

Shaping in a garment is formed by increasing and decreasing the stitches as required. Some simple methods were given in Chapter 5. The principles of shaping are based on the fact that the angle formed by an increase or decrease shows on the fabric, so shapings must be planned to give the best appearance. For example, raglans involve a decrease at each end of a row, so a right decrease and a left decrease are used.

Single Right Decrease on a Knit Row. This produces a slope to the right and is usually worked at the beginning of a row as follows: K1, K2tog knitways, K1.

Single Left Decrease on a Knit Row. This produces a slope to the left and is worked at the end of a row as follows: K to last 3 sts, K2togtbl, K1. A left slope can also be made by working sl 1, K1, psso, K1.

In these examples the shapings are described as being worked one stitch in from the edge, but they are often worked inside two or more stitches.

A Double Knit Decrease to the Right is formed by working K3tog or sl 1 knitways, K2tog, psso.

Raglan decreasings are not usually worked on purl rows, but where these occur, work P2tog for a decrease to slope to the right on the right (knit) side of the work, and P2togtbl or sl 1 purlways, P1, psso for a left slope decrease.

Vertical Double Decrease. For a centred shaping, this gives a neat and even

60

effect with the decrease forming a slight decorative feature. Work as follows: sl 1, K2tog, psso, for a double decrease to the left, then for a double right decrease, sl 1, K1, psso, return st to left needle and pass next st over, then return the K st to right needle to complete the action. Thus four stitches have been decreased.

DARTS AND HORIZONTAL SHAPINGS

These are worked in steps on the principle of working forwards, turning and working back. Specific instructions will be given in the pattern and the following example will demonstrate the principle. With 48 stitches on the needle, K40, turn and P40. K32, turn and P32. K24, turn and P24. K12, turn and P12. K48 to complete shaping. Note: to avoid a hole at the turn, when this point is reached pick up loop lying before next stitch and knit through back of this loop together with the next stitch. To reverse the shaping, start with K12, turn and P12 and so on.

JOINING IN A NEW YARN

When knitting with two needles, always join in a new ball of yarn at the beginning of a row. As the end of the ball is reached gauge the yarn to ensure that this will not run out in the middle of a row (allow approximately 4 times the width of work), and join in the new ball at the beginning of the next row. A neat way of doing this is to trim existing yarn to length of 3 or 4 inches, knit first stitch with new ball leaving a 3- or 4-inch length, then continue with the new ball, taking the two short ends together and laying them over the new length before knitting 2nd stitch. This method can be used in the middle of a row by weaving the short ends over 2 or 3 stitches.

When working in rounds, the above method can be too bulky, and a neat join can be made by splicing the ends. Separate the strands of both yarns for 4 or 5 inches and cut away half the strands from each yarn. Lay the two trimmed ends over each other and twist them together to form one complete thickness again.

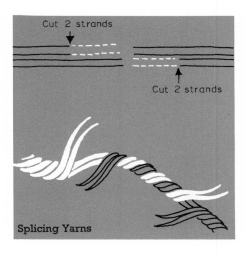

Splicing Yarns

BUTTONHOLES

These can be made in various ways such as the three examples which follow:

Round Buttonhole. This is made by the 'over' principle described in Chapter 5 and gives a small hole suitable for baby garments. The method on a knit row is: K to position of hole, yf, K2tog, K to end. On next row, purl through the 'yf' in the usual way. This gives a loose hole. The edge can be made firmer and neater by oversewing loosely round it.

Horizontal Buttonhole. The most widely used. K or work in pattern to position of hole. Cast off three or more stitches as required, K to end. Next row: work in pattern to cast-off stitches, cast on matching number, work to end of row. For a tighter edge, use thumb method for casting on. This is the basic method for this type of buttonhole. On next row, loose thread at base of buttonhole can be picked up purlways with right needle and worked together with next stitch. It is usual to work an edging of oversewing or buttonhole stitch round a horizontal buttonhole, but as this tightens the opening, test for size with button.

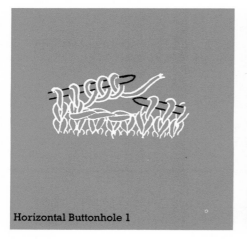

Horizontal Buttonhole 1

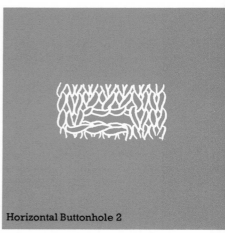

Horizontal Buttonhole 2

Vertical Buttonhole. This is made by dividing the work at the correct point, and working an equal number of rows on each half, using a 2nd ball of yarn for the left half. When buttonhole is correct depth, join top by working across all stitches. Short ends should be darned in neatly.

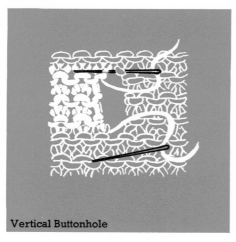

Vertical Buttonhole

HEMS

The two most widely used versions are the stitched hem in which the cast-on edge is folded up and slip-stitched to the wrong side of the work, and the knitted hem where the cast-on stitches are knitted together with the row of working stitches. These are worked as follows:

Stitched Hem in Stocking Stitch. Cast on an even number of stitches by the loose chain loop method described in Chapter 4. Do not knit into the backs of the stitches on the first row, and work straight in stocking stitch for required depth of hem, ending with wrong (purl) side of work facing. Knit next row into the backs of stitches to mark hemline, then carry on with main knitting as described in the pattern. When making up the garment, turn hem at hemline and slip-stitch loosely in position. *Note:* for a firm hem, the rows up to the hemline can be worked on a finer needle than the main part.

Stitched Hem in Stocking Stitch

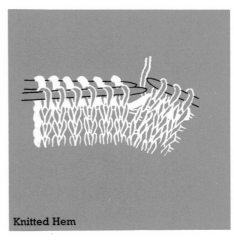

Knitted Hem

Picot Hem 1

Picot Hem 2

Knitted Hem. Work up to hemline as described above, then continue until hem is correct depth. Slip stitches from cast-on edge on to a 3rd needle and fold up behind working needle. Complete hem by knitting the stitches together in pairs, one from each needle, making sure the sides match exactly.

Picot Hem. Work as described for stitched hem to required hem depth, ending with right side of work facing. Next row: K1, * yf, K2tog; rep from * to end. When work is finished, fold hem at the row of holes and slip-stitch loosely in position.

Pretty Poncho provides
Perfect Practice

Shapings and making holes are illustrated in this popular design.
Trims – pompons, cords, and fringe – are dealt with in Chapter 8. Instructions
for Humpty are given in Chapter 17.

Materials: 6 (50g) balls Patons Double Knitting. Pair No 8 needles. Crochet hook.

Measurements: Length at side edge, 11½ in (excluding fringes).

Tension: 11 sts and 15 rows to 2 in over st st.

BACK AND FRONT (both alike)

Start at lower edge. With No 8 needles, cast on 163 sts.

1st row (on which holes for fringe are worked): K1, * yf, K2tog; rep from * to end. 2nd row: K.

Now work in patt with shaping, marking centre st with a length of coloured yarn, as follows:

1st row: K to within 2 sts of centre st, K2tog, K1 (centre st), K2togtbl, K to end. 2nd row: P. 3rd row: As 1st. 4th row: K. 5th row: K to within 4 sts of centre st, (K2tog) twice, K1, (K2togtbl) twice, K to end.

6th row: K. 7th row: K1, * yf, K2tog; rep from * to end. 8th row: P.

9th and 10th rows: As 5th and 6th. 11th row: As 1st. 12th row: K: 149 sts.

13th to 24th row: As 1st to 12th: 135 sts. Next row: K. Next row: P. Next row: K to within 4 sts of centre st, (K2tog) twice, yf, K1, yf, (K2togtbl), twice, K to end.

Next row: P.

Rep last 2 rows until 83 sts rem, ending with a P row.

Next row: K2, (K2tog, K5) 5 times, (K2tog) twice, yf, K1, yf, (K2togtbl) twice, (K5, K2togtbl) 5 times, K2: 71 sts.

Next row: K. Rep 3rd to 11th row of patt with shaping once: 59 sts. Cast off loosely.

TO MAKE UP

Observing general method on page 81, block and press. Join side edges. Press seams. See Chapter 8 for making pompons, cords, and a fringed edge. Make a four-inch fringe using groups of three lengths of yarn. For the cord, use three lengths of yarn each 150 inches long.

Crown of Glory

Swedish Motif

Norwegian Style

Danish Borders

Scandinavian Reindeer

Fair Isle Style

Oriental

Chapter 7
Special Effects and Techniques

FOLK KNITTING AND FASHION

Traditional Fair Isle designs look elaborate but are not difficult as they rarely use more than two colours on a row: multi-coloured effects are obtained by varying these pairs of colours. The Fair Isle look includes motifs such as the Armada Cross and Crown of Glory.

Shetland colour knitting is characterized by its use of soft colour effects – natural colours on browns and greys.

Scandinavian folk designs provide an interesting variety of different treatments: from Norway comes the look of bands of bold design, usually a deep colour on white against stripes of black. Danish designs are smaller, often in one colour on white, and Swedish designs are particularly effective with their use of white on a grey ground. The Reindeer and all-over spot effects called Seeding are features of Scandinavian design.

Further afield, peasant designs from mid-Europe are more complicated as their floral and wavy motifs can introduce three or more colours. Further east still, the designs are more exotic with bands of involved symmetrical patterning in rich colours.

Now that the changing face of fashion places such emphasis on new and sophisticated treatments of colour, designers have been quick to see the potentialities of these traditional patterns and have mixed and mingled them in the most unconventional ways to produce highly original effects. Similarly, elaborate patterned monochrome effects such as we associate with the Aran look, though still popular for knitted sportswear, have been taken up by fashion designers to give this tradition a completely different concept.

Simple Aran-type Stitches

Shetland lacy knitting is very beautiful with its delicate effects and perhaps nothing has surpassed the world-famous Shetland shawl. The true stitches are inspired by nature with intriguing names such as Old Shale, Fern, and Fir Cone. Shetland knitting is high in fashion today for evening shawls and accessories.

Shawl based on Traditional Shetland Stitches

FISHERMEN'S JERSEYS

Sometimes these jerseys were knitted by the fishermen themselves, but more often the womenfolk made them for their husbands, sons, and sweethearts according to a tradition which varied from region to region. 'Guernsey', from the Channel Island of that name, is a widely used generic term, often corrupted to 'gansey'. The original guernsey was knitted in stocking stitch with limited decoration which had no apparent regional significance. It was always in navy blue.

In Norfolk ports such as Sheringham and Caister ganseys were knitted to the recipient's choice from such dramatically named patterns as Lightning, Diamonds, Hailstones, and Flower Pot. They were knitted in the round using from four to eleven needles, sometimes in sizes as fine as 17s. They fitted so snugly that three or four fittings might be necessary and the wearer's ears might bleed as the gansey was pulled over his head for the first time.

The patterns used for fishermen's jerseys in Yorkshire ports had a specific regional association and a Filey man in his rope-and-ladder pattern could be readily distinguished from a Staithes man, who wore cable-and-moss stitch. There was also a tradition of port jerseys in Scotland at Peterhead. These patterned jerseys were worn as Sunday best to chapel or church. In Cornwall they were often known as bridal shirts and were knitted by sweethearts for their husbands-to-be.

CONTINENTAL KNITTING

Some experienced knitters consider this method to be quicker than the English method as the actual working movements are more compact. It is also suitable for both right- and left-handed knitters as both hands play an active part.

To hold the work. The diagram shows how the yarn in the left hand lies round the index finger and is held out and away from the needle. The yarn is arranged round the fingers of the left hand as follows (or in the most comfortable arrangement to suit the knitter): yarn comes from ball over little finger, under middle two fingers, then over and round index finger, thus the needle is held between the thumb and second finger leaving the index finger free to manipulate the yarn.

Holding the Work

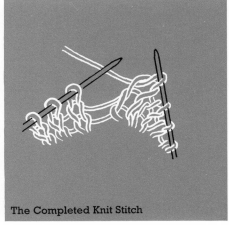

The Completed Knit Stitch

The Knit Stitch. Insert right needle through 1st stitch on left needle as in diagram above, pick up yarn and pull a loop through thus forming a stitch on the right needle at the same time slipping stitch off left needle.

The Purl Stitch. The needles are held in the same way but with the yarn at front. Insert right needle purlways through 1st stitch, behind yarn. Turn right needle over yarn to take a loop back through stitch (manipulate index finger of left hand to control yarn whilst doing this) at the same time slipping stitch off left needle, leaving loop on right needle to form the stitch.

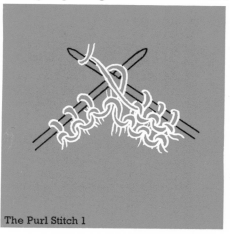 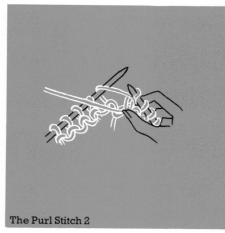

The Purl Stitch 1   The Purl Stitch 2

TUBULAR KNITTING ON TWO NEEDLES

Cast on an even number of stitches. Working row: * K1, bring wool to front, slip 1 purlways, take wool to back, rep from * all across row. This row is repeated throughout. When work is required length, cast off. For a firmer edge K2tog each time.

This gives a double fabric which is closed on all four edges, thus it is particularly suitable for articles where warmth is required such as rugs and covers. A narrow strip, worked on fine needles gives a reversible fabric for a tie.

Open-ended tubular knitting on two needles

The work can be finished off with an opening at the top edge to give a bag shape by dividing the casting-off stitches as follows (an extra needle is required): K1, slip next st on spare needle and leave at back of work, K1, cast off 1st st, slip next st on spare needle as before, K1, cast off 1. Cont thus along row until front sts are all cast off, then cast off the sts on spare needle.

SPIRAL KNITTING
This is a tube of ribbed fabric worked on a set of needles. The ribbing is worked in a continuous spiral. The tube has no knitted-in shapings as the character of the spiral allows the fabric to fit naturally into position where required.

An example of Spiral Knitting: cast on 36 sts, or a multiple of 6, on three needles, and mark start of round. Work 6 rounds K3, P3 rib. *Next 6 rounds:* P1, * K3, P3; rep from * ending P2. *Next 6 rounds:* P2, * K3, P3; rep from * ending P1. *Next 6 rounds:* P3, K3. *Next 6 rounds:* K1, * P3, K3; rep from * ending K2. Continue moving ribs 1 stitch on every 6 rounds.

A bedsock illustrates the principle as the spiral ribs are adjusted to appear straight on the leg and the heel fits comfortably into position.

LOOPED KNITTING
This gives very attractive effects particularly for borders. There are various ways of knitting loops including the following simple method. Cast on an odd number of stitches. 1st row: K. 2nd row: * K1, insert needle into next st, wrap yarn round needle point and index finger of right hand 3 times, then draw loops through the stitch, slip sts back on to left needle and knit all loops as 1 st; rep from * to last st, K1.

This is only one way of working a looped fabric. Attractive chunky and multi-coloured effects are made by using two or three colours together.

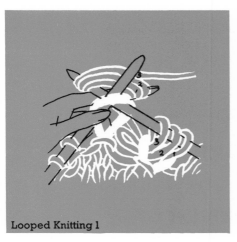

Looped Knitting 1

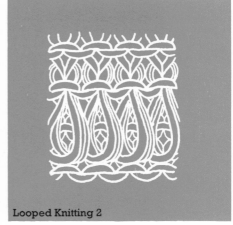

Looped Knitting 2

BEADED KNITTING
This form of decoration is made by working small beads into the fabric. Various sizes of beads can be used but the hole must take the yarn. A given number of beads is threaded on the yarn and these are slipped into place on the fabric as the knitting progresses. It is usual to thread the required number of beads on the yarn before starting the work where the number involved is not too many. For a large bead pattern, the beads can be threaded as required, breaking yarn and threading on more beads and joining in again at the beginning of the next row.

It is sometimes difficult to thread the beads on to the yarn, and a good tip for doing this is shown in the diagram.

Threading Beads

Thread a fine needle with double cotton then loop it through the folded end of the knitting yarn, pick up a bead with the needle point and it is then a simple matter to slip the bead along the cotton and on to the yarn. If the bead design forms a motif, perhaps in more than one colour, a working chart is usually given and this must be followed when threading the beads.

There are several ways of doing beaded knitting: the following two describe how to introduce the beads when, firstly, the knit side is the right side of the work which will carry the bead pattern, and secondly, the purl side is the right side. **Working Beads on a Knit Fabric.** With wrong side of work facing, knit to position of 1st bead, push up a bead close to the work at the back (right side of pattern) and K next st. Continue thus incorporating beads as required. **Working Beads on a Purl Fabric.** Purl to position of 1st bead. Keep yarn forward, pass a bead close to right needle and purl next stitch taking care bead does not slip through to other side of work.

PLEATED EFFECTS

Inverted pleats, overlapping pleats and box pleats can be knitted. They are all simple to do but add weight to a fabric so this must be considered when incorporating them into a garment. Mock pleating to give a ray effect is a satisfactory alternative suitable for most pleated fabrics. The effect is made by slipping a stitch at regular intervals on the right side of the work so that the slipped stitches form clearly defined edges. The pleats are worked over an odd number of stitches. Thus, for a sample of 9-stitch pleating, work as follows: cast on 44 sts. 1st row: (right side): * P2, K4, Sl 1P, K4; rep from * to end. 2nd row: * P9, K2; rep from * to end. These two rows form the pattern and are repeated throughout.

DIAGONAL KNITTING

Bias fabrics have the stitches running diagonally across the width and this is formed on the simple principle of working an increase at one end of the row and a decrease at the other so that the basic number of stitches does not change. The fabric can slope to the left or right. For a right bias fabric, work sample as follows: cast on required number of stitches. 1st row: K2tog, K to last st, M1 (use an invisible increase as described in Chapter 5), slip last st without knitting it. 2nd row: P. Repeat these two rows throughout. For a left bias, work the increase at beginning of row, and decrease at the end.

FISHERMAN'S RIB AND BRIOCHE STITCHES

These are similar in character both forming double fabrics which are rather slow to do and use more yarn, but they give excellent fabrics for heavy-knit sports garments and other items where extra warmth is required. There are several variations on these stitches, all based on the following simple version:

Fisherman's Rib. Cast on an even number of stitches. *Foundation row* (back of work but the fabric is reversible): K2, * P1, K1; rep from * to end. *Working row*: Sl 1 Knitways, * K1 below (see diagram), P1; rep from * to last st, K1. This row is repeated throughout.

Fisherman's Rib   Rib – K1 below

Five Designs to Mark Progress so Far

For children: boy's slipover with Fair Isle border, tot's classic jumper and girl's skirt. For the home: a folksy cushion. For evening: a beaded purse.

Boy's Slipover

Materials: 3/3/4 (50g) balls Natural and small ball each Green, Blue, Dark Red, and Yellow Patons Purple Heather 4-ply. Pair each Nos 10 and 12 needles.

Measurements: To fit 24/26/28 in chest. Length from top of shoulders, 13½/15/16½ in.

Tension: 14 sts and 18 rows to 2 in over st st on No 10 needles.

Additional Abbreviations (see page 29): N=Natural; G=Green; B=Blue; R=Dark Red; Y=Yellow.

BACK
** With No 12 needles and N cast on

86/**92**/100 sts and work K1, P1 rib for 2 in. Next row: Rib 8/**6**/10, (M1, rib 5/**5**/4) 14/**16**/20 times, M1, rib 8/**6**/10: 101/**109**/121 sts.

Change to No 10 needles and joining in colours as required, work rows 1 to 15 incl from chart A/**B**/B, rep the 12 patt sts 8/**9**/10 times across and last 5/**1**/1 sts on K rows, and first 5/**1**/1 sts on P rows as indicated, reading odd rows K from right to left and even rows P from left to right.

Break G, B, R, and Y.

Cont in N and st st thus: Next row: P. Next row: K 4/**8**/2, (K2tog, K 5/**4**/4) 13/**15**/19 times, K2tog, K 4/**9**/3: 87/**93**/101 sts. Cont straight in st st until Back measures 8/**9**/10 in, ending with a P row.**

Shape armholes by casting off 3 sts at beg of next 2 rows, then dec 1 st at each end of every row until 71/**77**/85 sts rem. Work 1 row straight.

Now dec 1 st at each end of next and every alt row until 61/**65**/69 sts rem. Work straight until Back measures 13½/**15**/16½ in, ending with a P row.

Shape shoulders by casting off 5/**5**/6 sts at beg of next 4 rows, then 5/**6**/5 sts at beg of foll 2 rows. Leave rem 31/**33**/35 sts on a length of yarn.

FRONT

Work as for Back from ** to **.

Shape armhole and divide for neck
Next row: Cast off 3 sts, K38/**41**/45 (incl st on needle), K2 tog, turn and leave rem sts on a spare needle: 39/**42**/46 sts. Cont on these sts for first side and P 1 row.

Dec 1 st at armhole edge on every row, at the same time dec 1 st at neck edge on every 3rd row from previous dec until 32/**35**/39 sts rem. Work 1 row straight.

Now dec 1 st at armhole edge on next and every alt row, at the same time cont dec 1 st at neck edge on every 3rd row as before until 24/**25**/26 sts rem.

Keeping armhole edge straight cont dec 1 st at neck edge on every 3rd row as before until 15/**16**/17 sts rem. Work straight until Front matches Back at armhole edge, ending with a P row.

Shape shoulder by casting off 5/5/6 sts at beg of next and foll alt row. Work 1 row straight. Cast off rem 5/**6**/5 sts.

With right side facing, leave centre st on a safety pin, rejoin yarn to rem sts, K2tog, K to end. Finish to correspond with first side, reversing shapings.

TO MAKE UP

Observing general method on page 81, block and press. Join right shoulder seam.

NECKBAND

With right side facing, No 12 needles and N, start at left shoulder on front and work thus: Knit up 40/**44**/48 sts down left side of neck, K 1 st from safety pin, (mark this st with coloured thread), knit up 40/**44**/48 sts up right side of neck, then K31/**33**/35 sts from Back inc 1 st at centre: 113/**123**/133 sts. (See Chapter 8 for hints on knitting up stitches for borders.)

Work 1 in K1, P1 rib, keeping marked st K on right side rows and dec 1 st at each side of marked st on every row. Cast off evenly in rib.

Join neckband and left shoulder seam.

ARMBANDS

With right side facing, No 12 needles, and N, knit up 82/**90**/98 sts all round each armhole. Work K1, P1 rib for ½ in. Cast off evenly in rib. Join side seams and armbands. Press seams.

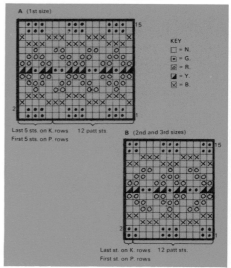

A (1st size)

KEY
□ = N.
⊡ = G.
◎ = R.
◪ = Y.
⊠ = B.

Last 5 sts. on K. rows   12 patt sts.
First 5 sts. on P. rows

B (2nd and 3rd sizes)

Last st. on K. rows   12 patt sts.
First st. on P. rows

Cushion

Materials: 7 (50g) balls Patons Double Knitting. Pair each Nos 8 and 10 needles. Cushion pad.

Measurements: 17 × 17 in (approx).

Tension: 11 sts and 15 rows to 2 in over st st on No 8 needles.

Additional Abbreviations (see page 29): Cr1BP=slip next st on cable needle to back of work, KB3, then P1 from cable needle. Cr3FP=slip next 3 sts on cable needle to front of work, P1, then KB3 from cable needle. K1BK=slip next st on cable needle to back of work, KB3, then K1 from cable needle.

K3FK=slip next 3 sts on cable needle to front of work, K1, then KB3 from cable needle. C4F=slip next 2 sts on cable needle to front of work, K2, then K2 from cable needle. C4B=slip next 2 sts on cable needle to back of work, K2, then K2 from cable needle.

MB5=Make bobble: K1, P1, K1, P1, K1 all in one st, turn, P5, turn, K5, turn, P5, turn, K5, pass 2nd, 3rd, 4th, and 5th sts over 1st 1st.

Aran Patt (referred to as Aran Patt 21) 1st row: K6, Cr1BP, K1, Cr3FP, K6. 2nd row: P6, PB3, K1, P1, K1, PB3, P6. 3rd row: K5, Cr1BP, K1, P1, K1, Cr3FP, K5.

4th row: P5, PB3, (K1, P1) twice, K1, PB3, P5. 5th row: K4, Cr1BP, (K1, P1) twice, K1, Cr3FP, K4. 6th row: P4, PB3, (K1, P1) 3 times, K1, PB3, P4.

7th row: K3, Cr1BP, (K1, P1) 3 times, K1, Cr3FP, K3. 8th row: P3, PB3, (K1, P1) 4 times, K1, PB3, P3. 9th row: K2, Cr1BP, (K1, P1) 4 times, K1, Cr3FP, K2.

10th row: P2, PB3, (K1, P1) 5 times, K1, PB3, P2. 11th row: K1, Cr1BP, (K1, P1) 5 times, K1, Cr3FP, K1. 12th row: P1, PB3, (K1, P1) 6 times, K1, PB3, P1.

13th row: K1, K3FK, (P1, K1) 5 times, P1, K1BK, K1. 14th row: As 10th. 15th row: K2, K3FK, (P1, K1) 4 times, P1, K1BK, K2. 16th row: As 8th.

17th row: K3, K3FK, (P1, K1) 3 times, P1, K1BK, K3. 18th row: As 6th. 19th row: K4, K3FK, (P1, K1) twice, P1, K1BK, K4.

20th row: As 4th. 21st row: K5, K3FK, P1, K1, P1, K1BK, K5. 22nd row: P6, PB3, K1, P1, K1, PB3, P6.

23rd row: K6, K3FK, P1, K1BK, K6. 24th row: P7, PB3, K1, PB3, P7. These 24 rows form patt.

Cable Patt (referred to as Cable 8) 1st row: K8. 2nd row: P8. 3rd row: C4B, C4F. 4th row: P8. 5th and 6th rows: As 1st and 2nd. These 6 rows form patt.

MAIN PARTS (both sides alike)

With No 8 needles, cast on 102 sts.
1st row: P2, Tw2F, P2, Cable 8 (1st row), P2, Tw2F, P2, Aran Patt 21 (1st row), P2, Tw2F, P2, Cable 8 (1st row), P2, Tw2B, P2, Aran Patt 21 (1st row), P2, Tw2B, P2, Cable 8 (1st row), P2, Tw2B, P2.

2nd row: K2, P2, K2, Cable 8 (2nd row), K2, P2, K2, Aran Patt 21 (2nd row), K2, P2, K2, Cable 8 (2nd row), K2, P2, K2, Aran Patt 21 (2nd row), K2, P2, K2, Cable 8 (2nd row), K2, P2, K2.

Keeping patts correct as placed (next row will be 3rd row of Aran and Cable patts) cont as on last 2 rows until 4 complete patts of Aran Patt 21 have been completed. Cast off.

BORDERS

With No 10 needles and right side facing, knit up 93 sts evenly along one side of one main part (see Chapter 8 for hints on knitting up stitches for borders). Work 4 rows moss st (every row * K1, P1; rep from * to last st, K1). Next row: Inc in first st, moss st to last 2 sts, inc in next st, moss st 1. Work 4 rows moss st.

Next row: Inc in first st, moss st 2 (MB5, moss st 7) 11 times, MB5, moss st 1, inc in next st, moss st 1.

Work 9 rows moss st, inc 1 st at each end as before on 5th row. Cast off. Complete other sides of main parts to match.

TO MAKE UP

Observing general method on page 81, block and press. Join corners and 3 sides. Insert cushion pad and join 4th side.

Raglan Jumper

Materials: 3/4 (50g) balls, Patons Double Knitting. Pair each Nos 11 and 9 needles, set of 4 No 11 needles with points at both ends. 2 stitch-holders.

Measurements: To fit 20/22 in chest. Length 10½/13 in; sleeve seam, 6½/9 in (adjustable).

Tension: 11½ sts and 15½ rows to 2 in over st st on No 9 needles.

BACK

With No 11 needles, cast on 60/66 sts. Work K1, P1 rib for 1½/2 in.

Change to No 9 needles and work in st st until Back measures 5½/7½ in from start, ending with a P row.

Shape raglan: 1st and 2nd rows: Cast off 2/2, work to end. 3rd row: K1, K2tog, K to last 3 sts, sl 1, K1, psso, K1. 4th row: K1, P to last st, K1. ** Rep 3rd and 4th rows until 18/20 sts rem. Work 1 row. Slip these sts on a stitch-holder.

FRONT
Work as Back to **. Rep 3rd and 4th rows until 30/34 sts rem, ending with a dec row.
Divide for neck: Next row: K1, P10/12, P next 8 sts on to a stitch-holder and leave, P to last st, K1. Work separately on each group of sts. Still dec at armhole edge as before, at the same time dec 1 st at neck edge on next and every alt row until 3 sts rem. Cont dec at armhole edge only until 1 st rem. Work 1 row. Fasten off.

SLEEVES
With No 11 needles, cast on 34/36 sts. Work K1, P1 rib for 1½/2 in. Next row: Rib 2/3, (inc in next st, rib 6) 4 times, inc in next st, rib to end: 39/41 sts.
Change to No 9 needles and work in st st, inc 1 st at each end of 3rd/5th row and every foll 7th/8th row until there are 49/53 sts. Cont on these sts until work measures 6½/9 in from start, ending with a P row (adjust length here).
Shape top by working 1st to 4th row of raglan shaping as on Back, then rep 3rd and 4th rows until 7 sts rem. Work 1 row. Cast off.

MAKE UP AND NECKBAND
Observing general method on page 81, block and press. Join side and sleeve seams, insert sleeves. With set of No 11 needles and right side of work facing, knit up 68/74 sts round neck incl sts from stitch-holders. Work 4/6 rnds K1, P1 rib. Cast off loosely. Press seams.

Pleated Skirt

Materials: 4 (50g) balls, Patons Purple Heather 4-ply. Pair No 12 needles. Belt.

Measurements: Length from belt, 11 in.

Tension: 16 sts and 20 rows to 2 in over st st.

BACK AND FRONT (both alike)
Cast on 208 sts and work in rib patt.
1st row (right side): * P2, K5, sl 1P, K5; rep from * to end. 2nd row: * P11, K2; rep from * to end. These 2 rows form rib patt.
Cont in rib patt until work measures 7 in, ending with right side facing.
Shape thus: Next row: * P2, K3, K2togtbl, sl 1P, K2tog, K3; rep from * to end: 176 sts. Work 9 rows straight.
Next row: * P2, K2, K2togtbl, sl 1P, K2tog, K2; rep from * to end: 144 sts. Work 9 rows straight.
Next row: * P2, K1, K2togtbl, sl 1P, K2tog, K1; rep from * to end: 112 sts.

Work straight until work measures 10 in ending with right side facing. Next row: * P2, K2togtbl, sl 1P, K2tog; rep from * to end: 80 sts. Work 7 rows, K1, P1 rib.
Make belt slots as follows breaking and rejoining yarn as required:
Rib 10, turn, work 6 rows rib on these 10 sts. Rib next 6 sts, turn, rib 6 rows on these 6 sts. Rib 12, turn, rib 6 rows on these 12 sts. Rib 6, turn, rib 6 rows on these 6 sts. Rib 12, turn, rib 6 rows on these 12 sts. Rib 6, turn, rib 6 rows on these 6 sts. Rib 12, turn, rib 6 rows on these 12 sts. Rib 6, turn, rib 6 rows on these 6 sts. Rib 10, turn, rib 6 rows on these 10 sts. Work 8 rows across all sts. Cast off in rib.

TO MAKE UP
Observing general method on page 81, join side seams. Tack down each pleat, then press edge of pleats. Remove tacks. Slot belt through waist. Press seams.

Beaded Purse

Materials: 1 (50g) ball Patons Purple Heather 4-ply. Pair No 10 needles. 476 small white beads (2 packets). $5\frac{1}{2} \times 7\frac{1}{2}$ in piece of lining material. 4 in zip.

Measurements: $4\frac{1}{2} \times 3\frac{1}{4}$ in.

Thread 238 beads on to ball of yarn. Push beads well down and draw up as required (see the foregoing chapter for beaded knitting).
Cast on 26 sts. 1st row: K. 2nd row: K1, * bring a bead up to needle, K2; rep from * to last st, bring a bead up to needle, K1. 3rd row: K. 4th row: K2, * bring a bead up to needle, K2; rep from * to end. These 4 rows form patt. Work these 4 rows 8 times more, then 1st, 2nd, and 3rd rows once. Cast off. Work another piece the same.

TO MAKE UP
Pin top edge of each piece to each side of zip and stitch in position. Open zip. With wrong side facing, stitch side and lower edges together. Turn right side out. Make lining to fit, slip inside purse, turn in hems at top edge and slip stitch to wrong side of zip.

Chapter 8

Making Up and Finishing Touches

No matter with what perfection of smoothness and regularity the fabric of a garment may have been knitted, its completely successful appearance when finished depends almost entirely on making up and those final professional touches. After all the work has scarcely begun at the comparable stage in dressmaking when the pieces of fabric have been cut out. The finishing of a handknit includes picking up stitches neatly for neckbands and borders, knitting buttonhole borders and pocket-tops, pressing and sewing the pieces together, sewing in zips, adding decorative trims and all those other details which can make or mar the finished result.

MAKING UP
Blocking and Pressing. Block and press knitted pieces as follows: lay out, wrong side up, on a flat padded surface suitable for ironing, such as a blanket and covering cloth on the table. Pat each piece of garment into shape and hold in positions with pins: this is called blocking the fabric. The secret is to use plenty of pins to make sure that all edges are flat as in diagram.

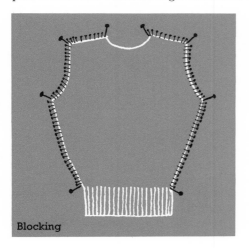

Blocking

The degree of pressing required will depend on the type of yarn used for the garment, so follow pressing instructions as given in the individual pattern. For example, some yarns made from synthetic fibres should be pressed with a cool iron over a dry cloth, and some should not be pressed at all as this could permanently damage the fabric. For wool, lay a lightly damped cloth over the blocked fabric and run the iron over the cloth so as to press the knitting underneath gently.

In all pressing, it is best to start off lightly and gradually increase the pressure as required so that stitch texture is not spoilt and the fabric is not pressed out of shape. It is usual to leave all ribbed edges unpressed to keep their elasticity.

Angora-type fabrics are not pressed: they are steamed by passing a hot iron over a wet cloth which is held about one inch away from the fabric so that the steam passes through. The cloth is weighted down at one side so that it can be held above the knitted fabric.

Seams. The garment pieces are sewn together after pressing as instructed. First of all, match pieces for size as follows: use the flat surface again and lay the matching pieces flat right side to right side, with wrong side uppermost and undermost. Now make up seams on wrong side using one of the two following accepted methods: *Back Stitch Seam* Match all joining edges exactly for size and hold in position by pinning at intervals. Take the two edges to be joined and use a tapestry needle and same yarn as for garment. Join with back stitching, working over one or two stitches. This gives a tailored seam and is used for most garments. *Flat Seam* Use this for finer garments such as baby clothes or any article where a flat joining is required. Ribbing on garments is usually made up with a flat seam. Place the two edges of fabric exactly together, right sides facing, matching ridge to ridge. Join by over-stitching through corresponding ridges on each edge thus giving a lacing effect; this is shown with the two edges laid flat to illustrate the stitch. All finished seams should be given a final light pressing as instructed.

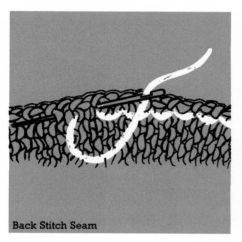

Back Stitch Seam

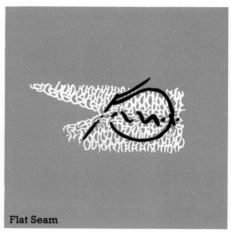

Flat Seam

KNITTING UP STITCHES FOR BORDERS

Many garments have neckbands, collars, and pocket-tops which are added when the main part is finished in the final stages of making up. This involves knitting up stitches and the technique for this causes dismay to many knitters. The aim is to avoid loose stitches, holes, and dragged effects, and the following diagrams and instructions will help in achieving a professional finish.

The three diagrams show three differently shaped edges with the stitches being knitted up through both loops of the stitch on both cast-off edge and row edge. This is important as separating the loops will loosen the stitches and cause ladder-like holes. A good tip is to use a finer needle than that to be used for the actual border.

In knitting up through a shaped (decreased) edge there are alternating long and short stitches. Wherever possible, knit up through the short stitches, omitting the long stitches, although this will depend on the number of stitches required.

V NECKBANDS

A neckband can be worked in rows or in rounds. For either method it is best to use a set of needles. For the row method, one shoulder seam is joined. With right side facing, stitches are picked up and knitted across back of neck, down one edge of neck slope and up the other using one needle for each of the three edges. The stitches must be knitted up equally up each side and a stitch knitted up at centre of V. A professional appearance is achieved by keeping this stitch as a knit stitch on the right side of the work all the way up, and decreases are worked on either

Knitting up through a Straight Edge

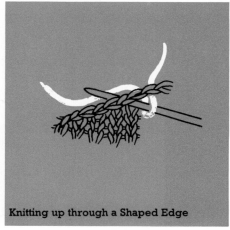

Knitting up through a Shaped Edge

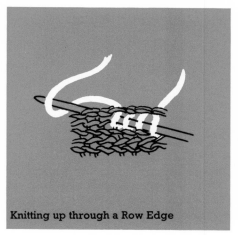

Knitting up through a Row Edge

side. Thus, when picking up stitches for a ribbed V neck, mark this centre stitch first, remember that it is to be a knit stitch, and calculate other stitches accordingly. A right decrease and a left decrease are worked on either side of centre stitch as required.

The principle is the same for a neckband worked on four needles, except that both shoulders are seamed and neck is worked in rounds. Stitches are picked up and knitted all round the neck edge, using one needle for each neck slope and third needle for back of neck. Keep centre front knit stitch as described above. The cast-off edge must not be tight, so when doing this the stitches must be tested for elasticity: if necessary use a larger needle.

POCKETS
There are many types of knitted pocket and the choice will depend on suitability for the garment being made. Two basic styles are as follows:

Patch Pocket. This is the simplest method of all. It means knitting a separate square or oblong of the main fabric and stitching it neatly on garment. The top edge can be a border of ribbing, or a hem. The knitted pocket should be pressed flat as instructed, then pinned carefully in correct position. With matching yarn, sew neatly in place round three sides using a flat oversewing stitch. Alternatively, use embroidered knitting stitch where suitable (see Chapter 9), following line of knitting stitches round the pocket edges and stitching through both fabrics.

Set-in Pocket. In this method the pocket is knitted in with the main work. Instructions will be given in the individual design, but the principle is to knit a pocket lining separately which is taken in with the main work at the correct point by knitting across the lining stitches in place of the corresponding pocket stitches on main work; the latter are either cast off or left on a spare needle to be picked up later for working border for top of pocket. The lining and border ends are slip-stitched neatly in position afterwards.

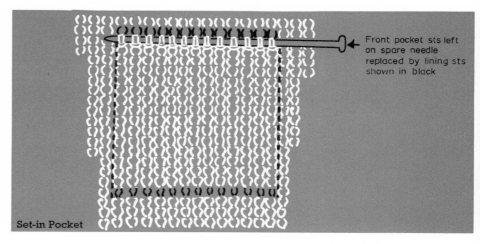

Front pocket sts left
on spare needle
replaced by lining sts
shown in black

Set-in Pocket

WAISTBANDS

The most popular finishing for a skirt waistband is a length of elastic placed round the inside top edge which stretches out to fit the waist. The elastic should be set within a casing and left unstitched so that it can move freely. This will be put in when the skirt has been pressed and made up as follows: allowing a slight stretch, cut elastic to required waist size plus one inch. Overlap ends for half an inch and over-sew neatly. Turn skirt to wrong side and lay elastic band in position round top. Using tapestry needle and appropriate yarn, work herringbone stitch in the row of stitches above and below elastic making sure that the stitching does not catch the elastic. An alternative method is to work a crochet chain casing. Both these methods are shown in the diagrams.

Herringbone Casing

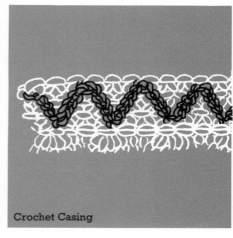

Crochet Casing

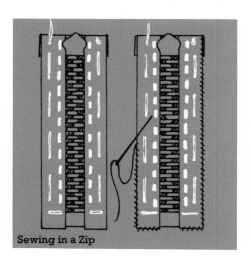

SEWING IN ZIPS

Depth of opening and length of zip should match exactly as if the opening is too short the zip will bulge, and if too long the opening will be dragged. This is seen in zip-fronted garments where the back hangs below the front.

Place zip carefully in position in garment and tack, then sew in position with small running stitches and oversewing stitch as in the diagrams. With modern zips, these can be put in almost invisibly.

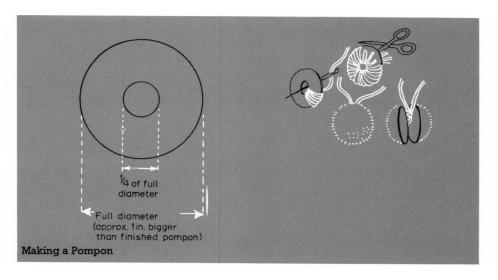

¼ of full diameter

Full diameter (approx. 1 in. bigger than finished pompon)

Making a Pompon

TRIMS

Pompons. These are made by winding yarn round twin cardboard rings. Size of pompon is governed by diameter of cardboard circle: this must be cut with a diameter one inch greater than required size of finished pompon. Hole should be one quarter of full diameter of circle.

Place the two rings together and wind yarn round and round until hole is filled (this gives a solid pompon: wind less yarn as required). Cut through the threads on the edge between the two cardboard rings but do not let the threads slip through the hole. Wind a double thread tightly between the cardboard circles and

85

fasten off, leaving long ends for joining to main cord as required. Remove circles and trim pompon ends. *Note:* Pompons must be added on cords after these have been threaded through.

Tassels. Cut a piece of cardboard to depth of finished tassel. Wind yarn round centre to required fullness. Break yarn leaving a long end. Thread under all strands, pull up tightly and tie. Remove cardboard and wrap yarn round loops about $\frac{1}{4}$ in down from knot. Fasten off. Cut through loops.

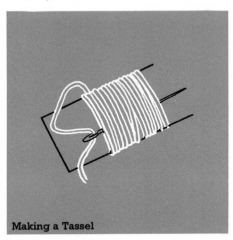

Making a Tassel

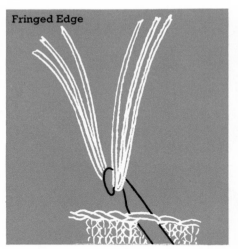

Fringed Edge

Fringed Edge. This is a quick and simple way of adding a trim to the edge of a fabric. A crochet hook is used to knot groups of threads through the edge as in the diagrams. The yarn is cut into short lengths depending on size of fringe required: allow twice the depth plus allowance for knot. Taking threads in groups, fold group in half, pull loop through edge of fabric, then pull cut ends through this loop.

Cords. This is a simple way of making a twisted cord. Allow approximately 25g double knitting yarn for a dress cord. Get a friend to help. Measure off six 5-yard lengths of yarn. Knot ends together, insert pencil at each end in front of knot between lengths of yarn (stage A in diagram). Facing each other and each holding yarn between thumb and finger in front of knot, turn pencils clockwise (stage B). Continue until strands are tightly twisted, then bring pencils together and allow cord to twist. Slip out pencils and knot ends (stage C).

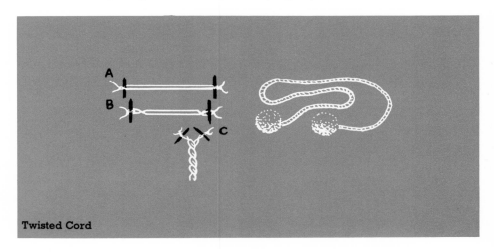

Twisted Cord

Chapter 9

Odds and Ends: After-care

DECORATIONS ON KNITTING

A hand-knitted fabric can be transformed by adding decorative touches using embroidery stitches, crochet trims, or the simple method of working a motif in knitting stitch (also known as Swiss darning): this is a quick way of achieving a Fair Isle effect or incorporating a motif such as those used to decorate children's garments: the design is usually worked from a chart with each square representing one embroidery stitch. Decoration by knitting in beads was described in Chapter 7.

Embroidered Knitting Stitch. This is worked on a stocking stitch fabric with each embroidery stitch exactly over a knitted stitch. Use a tapestry needle and appropriate yarn which ideally should be of the same thickness as the main yarn. Bring needle up through centre of stitch from back of work. Insert needle from right to left behind stitch immediately above (diagram shows needle in this position), then down through centre of original stitch. Now move one stitch to the left as indicated by arrow.

Embroidered Knitting Stitch

Other Embroidery Stitches. These can be used but care must be taken to avoid dragging the background fabric. Simple counted stitches are best, such as cross stitch, blanket stitch, and loop stitch.

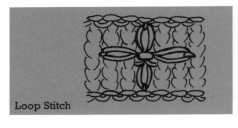

Loop Stitch

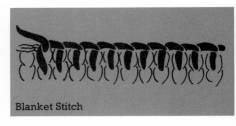

Blanket Stitch

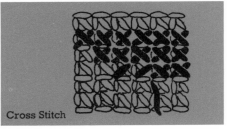

Cross Stitch

CHARTS

A collection of charts is a useful addition to a knitter's library. Following is a selection of motifs which are suitable for both knitting-in or embroidering in knitting stitch or cross stitch.

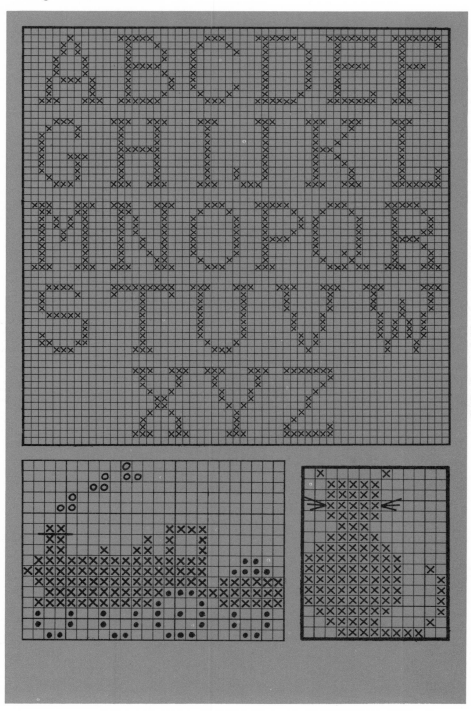

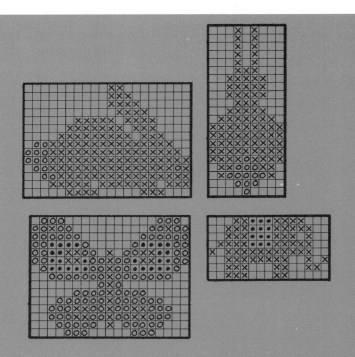

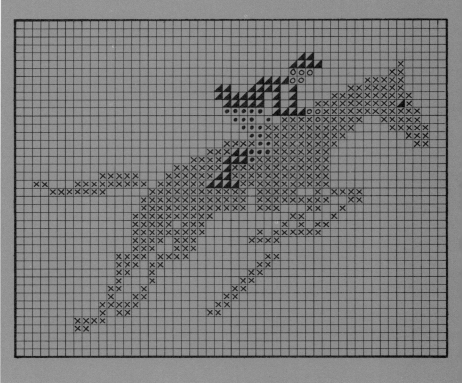

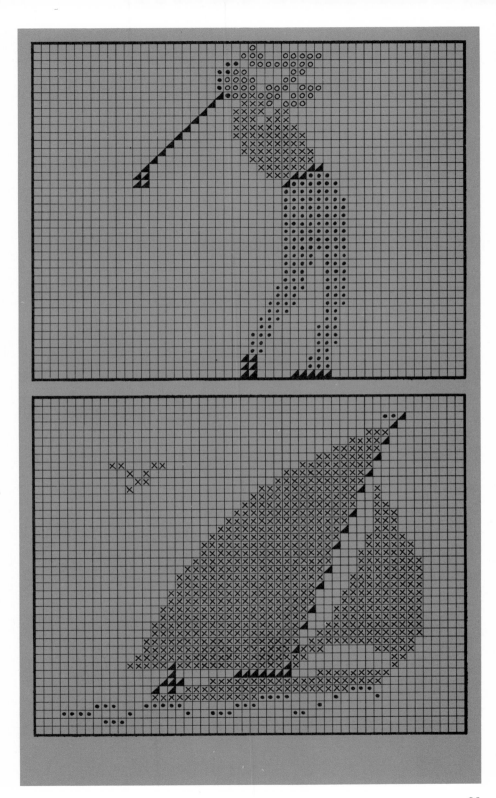

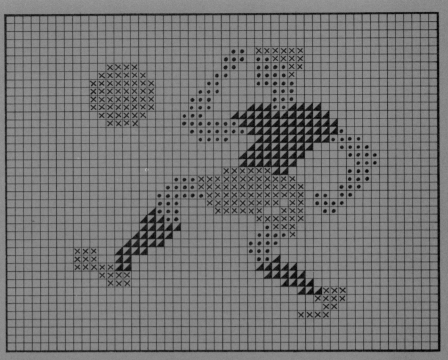

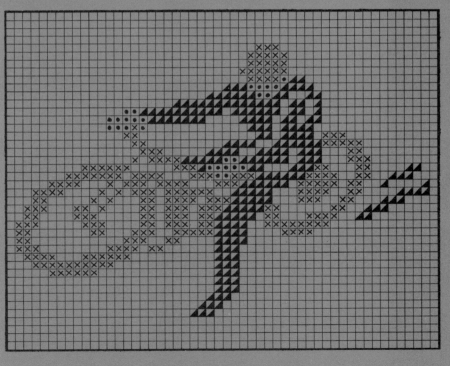

BOBBINS FOR COLOUR WORK – HOW TO MAKE THEM

These are useful for separate motifs using small amounts of colours. Use stiff cardboard and cut to shape shown in diagrams, making slit at top. Yarn is wound round centre of bobbin and working end passes through the slit. These bobbins are very useful for colour knitting as several can be kept in work on a design. They are easy to handle, and can hang at the back of the work keeping colours free from tangles.

Making a Colour Bobbin

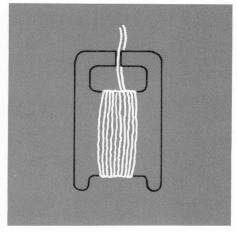

Diagrams illustrate a bobbin for medium-weight yarns: bobbins should be cut to sizes appropriate to the thickness of the yarn.

LEFT-HANDED KNITTING

Strictly speaking, this is a misnomer as both hands are used in knitting, the left hand holds and manipulates the stitches to be worked and the right hand works the yarn to make the knitting stitch, so both hands are equally important. However, some left-handed workers find it more natural to handle the yarn in the left hand, so in this sense, all the foregoing knitting diagrams must be seen in reverse. The simplest way of doing this is in a mirror as in the following diagram. The book is propped open at the appropriate page facing towards the mirror so that the worker can follow the reversed image.

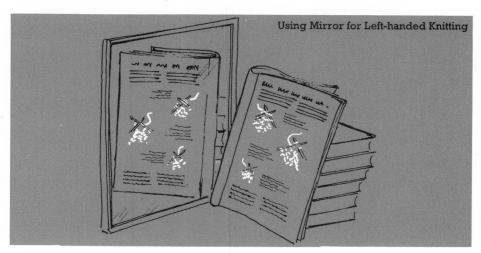

Using Mirror for Left-handed Knitting

Left-handed workers should also practise Continental knitting as the character of this method comes very naturally to them.

ADJUSTING LENGTH

The simplest way to lengthen a piece of knitting is to undo the cast-on edge and continue knitting as required. This involves snipping and pulling away the cast-on stitches then picking up the loops of the main fabric and knitting down. This means that in the extra rows, the stitches are upside down. If the above method is done as neatly as possible the pick-up row in simple fabrics can be almost invisible. This method is, obviously, not always practicable for finished garments.

For the majority of fabrics, the following method is the most successful for both shortening and lengthening the work as the joining row is invisible. The principle is to separate the fabric and adjust the length at this point either by adding rows or unpicking them. Mark the appropriate row, then insert needle point through side of one stitch close to edge of fabric. Gently pull up the thread forming this row of stitches, then break the yarn and the two sections will come apart leaving a clean row of loops on each edge. It is then a simple matter to pick up the bottom row of loops and knit on or unravel a few rows as required, before grafting the two edges together.

GRAFTING

This is the method for joining two sets of stitches together to form an invisible seam such as for adjusting length. The two sets of stitches are left on the needles and they must be equal and opposite each other. A blunt-ended needle is used and sufficient yarn to complete the row (at least four times the width of row on the needle). The diagrams show how grafting is actually a duplicate row of knitting. Various simple stitches can be grafted and these will be understood once the following two examples have been practised.

Grafting Knit Side of Work 1

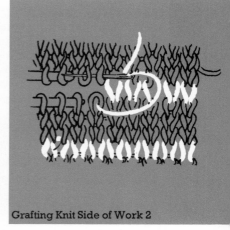
Grafting Knit Side of Work 2

Knit Side of Work. Lay the two pieces of fabric flat on a table so that the edges meet and withdraw needles as the join proceeds. Grafting thread is coloured in the diagrams, which show clearly how the stitching is following a line of knit stitches by threading the yarn through the side loops in pairs, thus linking open stitches alternately above and below, and moving on half a stitch each time, thus needle passes through each loop twice.

94

Purl Side of Work. The principle is the same for purl rows with the horizontal thread forming a line of purl ridges by threading the yarn over the loops, as in diagram.

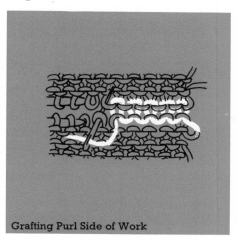

Grafting Purl Side of Work

KNITTING MACHINES

The growing popularity of home knitting machines has established them as part of today's knitting scene. All knitted fabrics whether produced on industrial machines or by knitting with needles at home are the same in character and the home knitting machine comes somewhere between the two combining the speed of the factory machine with the use of the hands. The home knitting machine is used where speed and quantity are the essential requirements. The fabric differs from hand knitting in that the mechanical working produces a much more regular and even appearance and the fabric is closer and tighter in contrast to the naturally soft character of hand knitting which is part of its appeal. Knitting machines have their limits, although with their continuing development their scope is increasing all the time. Already the modern home machine can produce fancy and decorative effects and many aspects of colour work including intricate patterns of the **Fair Isle** type, single colour motifs, and, of course, a limitless variety of simple stripes and borders. By using sophisticated speciality yarns and the new techniques available in the latest machines, couture fabrics and fashions can be achieved which are unique to this medium and could not be produced by hand knitting. In a family environment, however, the home knitting machine is useful where a regular supply of children's and classic garments is required. Knitters who use machines regularly will find that their speed and productivity consume substantial quantities of yarn very quickly.

Many women's magazines include instructions in their knitting sections and some of the machine makers have their own publications.

The expert worker can also translate hand-knitting instructions for the machine as stitch tensions can usually be matched. Row tensions are more difficult as these are sometimes tighter on the machine. Hand-knitting instructions where lengths are given in inches (cm) can often be adapted, therefore, with simple adjustments but where the row tension cannot be matched exactly expert knitting knowledge is required.

After-care

'Hand-made' deserves care. By their very nature, knitting and crochet call for a great deal of time and patience which most people like to use for lasting benefit, despite trends to lightning fashion changes and instant obsolescence. A widespread sentiment still persists that hand-made things should endure; hand-knits will last longer and stay softer if the simple, common-sense rules in this section are followed. *Wash them frequently.* Do not wait until hand-knits are visibly soiled. Wash them often to remove dirt and grit before these have had time to accumulate and spoil the handle and appearance of a garment by breaking its delicate fibres.

WASHING BY HAND IS ALWAYS SAFER – THE BASIC PROCEDURE

Although the use of washing machines is acceptable for some types of fibre and garment, as indicated below, every knitter should know the basic procedure for washing by hand as described in the following paragraphs. If ever in doubt, wash by hand. There are three stages: washing; rinsing; drying.

(i) *Washing.* Soap, soapflakes, soap powders, and detergents are all suitable; detergents are especially effective in hard water districts. Do pay attention to the instructions printed on the packet and use the quantities recommended by the maker. Dissolve the washing preparation completely in hot water and add cold water until the suds are just warm at a temperature of about 40 degrees centigrade. Make certain that no particles of undissolved detergent remain and that enough washing water has been prepared to cover the garment completely. Submerge the garment in the water and, using the hands, allow the suds to work through gently and quickly. *Never* add more powder after this stage because this could have disastrous results. *Never* boil hand-knits.

(ii) *Rinsing.* Rinse the garment thoroughly in cold water and keep changing the rinsing water until this becomes clear. Whenever the garment is lifted from the water, make sure it is supported with *both* hands. Wool, in particular, holds a lot of water and unsupported garments soon distort irreparably. Extra care is needed when washing heavy garments made from bulky yarns or those of lacy, open construction. Make sure the garment is constantly supported when wet and try not to lift it out of the water until rinsing is finished.

(iii) *Drying.* Get rid of as much water as possible as quickly as possible. Do not pull or twist the garment but simply squeeze between towels, or fold in a towel and pass through a light rubber wringer. Remove any buttons which may break and cause damage.

(a) *Spin Dryer – use with wool.* A spin dryer is excellent for removing excess water quickly from garments made from wool.

(b) *Spin Dryer – limited use with man-made fibres.* Special care is needed if a spin dryer is to be used in connection with hand-knits in man-made fibres such as Courtelle or Nylon. They quickly become distorted and creased if subjected to anything more than a short spin *when cold*; heat is harmful.

(c) *A Tumble Dryer should never be used with wool.* The tumbling action causes the wool to felt and shrink; this damage cannot afterwards be rectified.

(d) *A Tumble Dryer is excellent for drying hand-knits in man-made fibres.*

After excess moisture has been removed, the garment should be laid flat to dry and on no account should it ever be hung up. Use an airing cupboard if possible. Wool garments dried out of doors must be kept in the shade because wet wool scorches and turns brown in the sun; as already mentioned, this is particularly the case with optically-bleached white wool (Patons shade 504 Snow White) which turns to an unattractive yellowish tint if exposed to the sun when wet.

Pressing. Garments knitted from wool and wool mixtures look better if, after drying, they are lightly pressed under a damp cloth after being gently eased to the correct shape and size. Be careful to avoid ribbing when pressing. It is inadvisable to press knitwear containing certain man-made fibres because pressing them tends to flatten the yarn and spoil the appearance of the garment. A hand-knit should not be pressed after washing any more drastically than it was when first knitted.

THE USE OF SYMBOLS TO INDICATE AFTER-CARE

The basic hand wash procedure just described is easy enough to follow but, as the shopping guide section has shown, there are so many new and differing man-made fibres on the market today (with more to come) that it is sometimes difficult to decide which is the quickest and best after-care to give a hand-knitted garment, whether the use of a washing machine is permissible, and so on. In an endeavour to simplify the situation, the leading manufacturers have issued, under the auspices of the Home Laundering Consultative Council, a series of standardized symbols relating to after-care and these are now to be found on textiles of all kinds, detergent packs, washing machines, and other places where guidance may be helpful.

The symbols cover eight procedures: the Wash Tub symbol indicates that the article can be washed safely by machine or by hand. The Hand in Wash Tub symbol indicates that the article should be washed by hand only. Concise instructions accompany the symbols explaining the complete washing procedure required, the recommended water temperature, the intensity of machine-wash (minimum, medium, or maximum) and how the water should be extracted. The following symbols are of particular interest to hand-knitters:

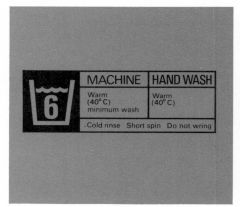

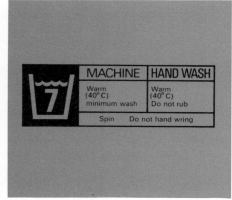

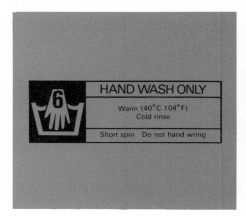

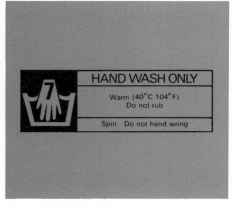

Continental Symbols. The Home Laundering Consultative Council are also publicizing a series of symbols used on the Continent which cover ironing and dry cleaning as well as washing. This type of symbol is often to be found on the ball bands of hand-knitting yarn imported from France and other European countries.

Treatment	Minimum Precaution Necessary	Some Caution Necessary	Special Care Necessary	Treatment Prohibited
Washing	95	60	30	✕
Bleaching (with chlorine)	Cl	–	–	✕
Ironing	•••	••	•	✕
Dry Cleaning	A	P	F	✕

Explanatory notes – Washing. The figure in the wash tub represents the Centigrade temperature recommended for the washing solution.

Bleaching. The symbol refers to *chlorine* bleach only and does not refer to the safe oxygen bleach (sodium perborate) incorporated in most heavy duty washing products.

Ironing. The dots in the iron symbol indicate the temperature recommended for the iron. One dot denotes a cool iron, two dots a warm iron and three dots a hot iron.

Dry Cleaning. The letter in the circle indicates the type of dry cleaning fluid which can be used on the fabric.

A – can be cleaned in any dry cleaning solvent.

P – clean in perchlorethylene or white spirit only.

F – clean in white spirit only.

Chapter 10

Crochet for Beginners

Crochet is easy and quick to do. It can be learnt very quickly and the beginner soon grasps the simplicity of the basic principle that the foundation is a simple chain stitch. The most difficult part for the beginner is learning how to hold the yarn and hook but this is quickly understood as soon as the first few chain stitches have been worked.

THE FIRST LOOP
This counts as the starting chain stitch. Take cut end (coloured in diagram) and make a loop, then take end up behind loop and pull a loop through with the crochet hook. Tighten loop on hook to form the first stitch.

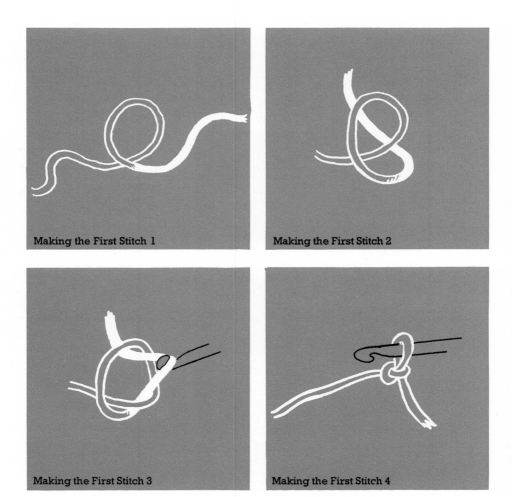

Making the First Stitch 1

Making the First Stitch 2

Making the First Stitch 3

Making the First Stitch 4

TAKING UP THE YARN

Each worker develops her own individual way of doing this. Here is a simple method for beginners:

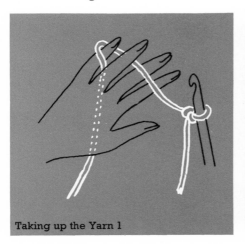

Taking up the Yarn 1

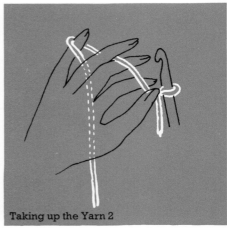

Taking up the Yarn 2

Yarn runs from ball across palm of left hand, round little finger, through to back of hand between 3rd and 2nd fingers, over 2nd and index fingers to be grasped firmly close to knot of 1st stitch on hook. Curve fingers slightly and curl little finger as required to hold yarn. This is seen in the following diagram which shows both hands in position for working. The yarn in work is controlled by the fingers which are opened out a little as required. From now on hands are omitted to make diagrams clearer.

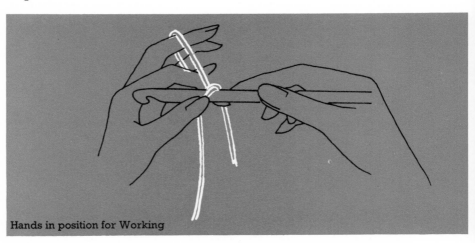

Hands in position for Working

CHAIN STITCH

All crochet fabrics start with a length of chain. The length of chain required will be given in the design instructions. Chain stitch is a length of loop stitches formed by catching the yarn with the hook and pulling it through loop already on hook so that first stitch drops down. Continue thus pulling a new loop through each time so that length of chain gets longer. **Note:** In crochet the work always hangs from one loop on the hook.

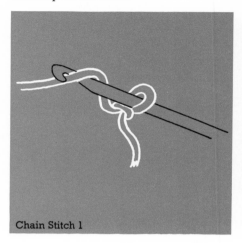

Chain Stitch 1

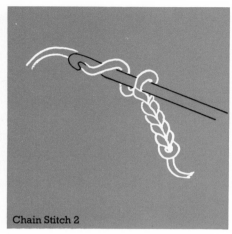

Chain Stitch 2

When the foundation chain is the required length, turn work round so that cut end of yarn lies to the left and work is in correct position to start foundation row of main fabric stitch. It is important to remember that the hook is always inserted under the two top threads of stitch as illustrated in the second diagram above.

The third diagram shows a length of foundation chain as seen from on top. In the next diagram, the work has been turned round to work the foundation row and shows chain stitch from the side with the hook inserted under the two top threads.

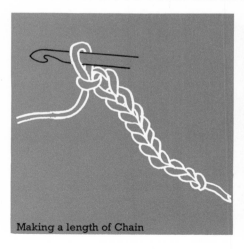

Making a length of Chain

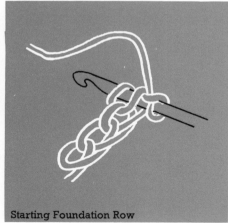

Starting Foundation Row

The following diagram illustrates this action in work.

Although reference is made to the two top threads in the following instructions, this rule is assumed in standard crochet wording unless there is a specific reference to working through only one thread to obtain a special effect as in ridged stitches.

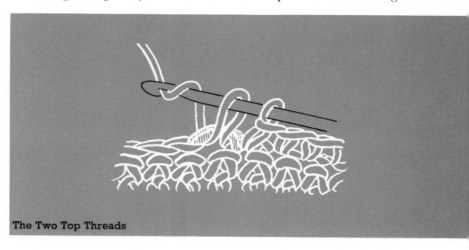

The Two Top Threads

The following two illustrations show both sides of a piece of double crochet fabric. The main fabric is reversible but the starting and working (top) edges are different.

The Top Edge of Work 1

The Top Edge of Work 2

THE BASIC WORKING STITCHES

These are double crochet and treble stitches and all other fabrics are variations on these and chain stitch. Slip stitch (or single crochet) is chain stitch in work on a fabric and is mainly used in edgings and joinings.

There are three stages in each basic stitch – length of chain, foundation row, and working row which is repeated to form the fabric.

Double Crochet. This is the main basic stitch. It produces a close firm fabric and many articles are made entirely in double crochet. Make a length of chain.

FOUNDATION ROW: Insert hook under 2 top threads of 2nd chain from hook (note – in counting stitches to start a row the number always excludes loop on hook).

Hook under yarn and draw a loop through to give 2 loops on hook. Hook under yarn and draw a loop through both loops on hook. Thus 1 loop remains on hook and 1 double crochet has been completed. The following diagrams illustrate these steps.

Working Double Crochet 1

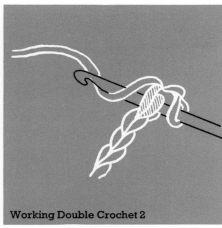

Working Double Crochet 2

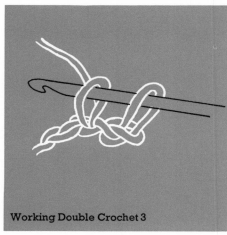

Working Double Crochet 3

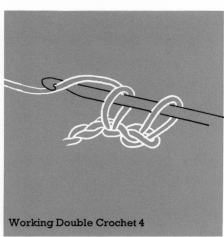

Working Double Crochet 4

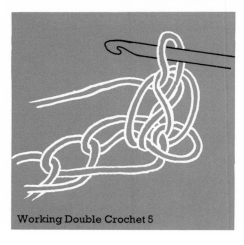

Working Double Crochet 5

Repeat this action into every chain to end. Make 1 turning chain which is the loop on the hook in the following diagram.

Turn work round so that worked strip lies to the left and hook with turning chain is in position to start the WORKING ROW: note that the top edge looks slightly different on the reverse side but the 2 top loops are still clearly seen.

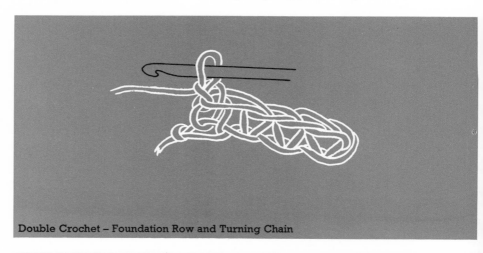

Double Crochet – Foundation Row and Turning Chain

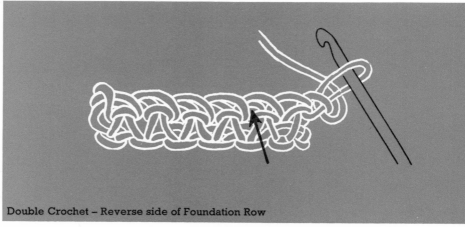

Double Crochet – Reverse side of Foundation Row

WORKING ROW: Miss the turning chain and 1st double crochet, insert hook under 2 top threads of 2nd double crochet and work 1 double crochet as described in the steps above, then work 1 double crochet into each double crochet to end (last double crochet will be worked into the missed stitches at beginning of previous row), make 1 chain for turning.

Treble Stitches

The next basic fabric stitch is the treble group of stitches. These are extensions of double crochet and those most widely used are half treble, treble, and double treble.

Half Treble. Make a length of foundation chain. FOUNDATION ROW: Yarn round hook, miss 2 chain, insert hook under 2 top threads of 3rd chain from hook (arrowed in 1st diagram), pull a loop through to give 3 loops on hook, yarn round hook (this is seen in the next diagram) and pull a loop through all 3 loops on hook

so that 1 loop remains on hook and 1 half treble has been completed.
Work 1 half treble into each chain to end, make 2 chain for turning. Turn work.

WORKING ROW: Miss 1st half treble (this will be the 2 turning chain), work 1 half treble into each half treble to end, make 2 chain for turning.

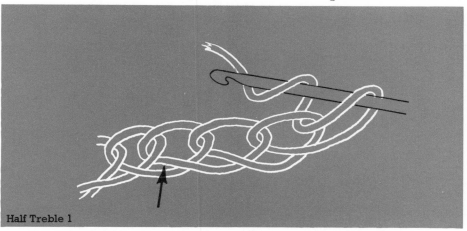

Half Treble 1

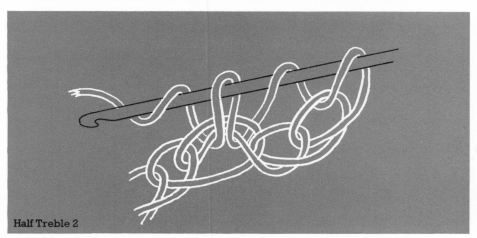

Half Treble 2

Half Treble 3

Treble. Make a length of foundation chain. FOUNDATION ROW: Yarn round hook, miss 2 chain, insert hook under 3rd chain from hook, pull a loop through (3 loops on hook), yarn round hook, pull a loop through 2 loops (2 loops on hook as shown in the 1st diagram), yarn round hook, pull loop through remaining 2 loops thus leaving 1 loop on hook and 1 treble has been worked as shown in the 2nd diagram. Work 1 treble into each chain to end, make 2 chain for turning. Turn work.

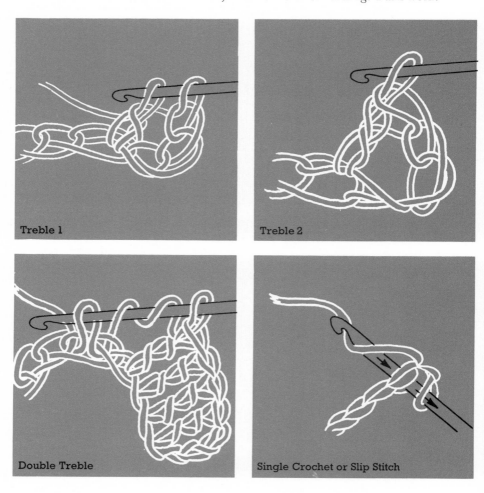

Treble 1

Treble 2

Double Treble

Single Crochet or Slip Stitch

WORKING ROW: Miss 1st treble (the 2 turning chain), work 1 treble into each treble to end (last stitch will be worked into the 2 turning chain of previous row), make 2 chain for turning.

Double Treble or Long Treble. This is worked as treble but with an extra step to give a higher stitch. Pass yarn twice round hook, insert hook under 4th chain of previous row and pull a loop through (4 loops on hook instead of 3 as in treble), yarn round hook, pull a loop through 2 loops (3 loops on hook), yarn round hook and pull a loop through 2 loops (2 loops on hook), yarn round hook and pull through remaining 2 loops. 1 double treble has been worked. Diagram shows the 6th double treble in work with the 3 chain stitches at beginning of row, forming the 1st double treble.

SINGLE CROCHET OR SLIP STITCH

This stitch is worked in one movement and is used where a firm edging is required. It is not normally used as a fabric stitch. Insert hook under next stitch, pass yarn round hook and pull a loop through stitch and loop on hook in one movement (diagram opposite), thus producing a chain stitch edge.

KEEPING SIDE EDGES STRAIGHT

A turning chain (or chains) is always worked at the end of a row and this chain (or chains) is always missed at the beginning of the next row, but at the other end, the chain stitch (or stitches) always counts as the first main stitch and must be worked into to keep a straight edge. Thus, at the beginning of rows where an instruction reads 'miss 1 double crochet' this is the turning chain. The principle is that a number of turning chains will be worked to match the height of the main stitch. For example, there could be 1 chain for double crochet, 2 chain for half treble, 2 or 3 chain for treble and so on.

PRACTICE SQUARES IN BASIC STITCHES

Use some Patons Double Knitting and a Milward Disc Hook No 5·00 mm. See Chapter 3 for crochet hook table and abbreviations. To help the beginner, the following exercises refer to the turning chain but in standard crochet wording this must be assumed.

Double Crochet. Make 13ch. FOUNDATION ROW: 1dc in 2nd ch from hook (1ch has been missed), 1dc into each remaining ch to end, 1ch, turn. WORKING ROW: Miss 1st dc (the turning ch), 1dc into each remaining ch to end (last st will be into the missed ch of foundation row), 1ch, turn. Rep Working Row as required. Fasten off.

Half Treble. Make 14ch. FOUNDATION ROW: 1htr in 3rd ch from hook (2ch have been missed), 1htr into each remaining ch to end, 2ch, turn. WORKING ROW: Miss 1st htr (the 2 turning ch), 1htr into each remaining htr to end (last st will be into the 2 missed ch of foundation row), 2ch, turn. Rep Working Row as required. Fasten off.

Double Crochet   Half Treble

INCREASING AND DECREASING

Increasing. If plain fabric is in work, an increase of 1 stitch can be made by working 2 stitches into 1 of previous row. For example, in the following diagram shading indicates the extra stitch.

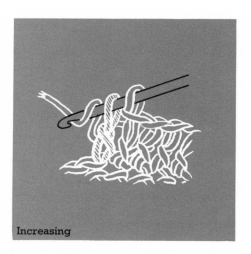

Increasing

Decreasing. If plain fabric is in work, a decrease of 1 stitch can be made by missing 1 stitch in previous row. For example, for fabric worked in trebles, a decrease of 1 stitch can be worked as follows: yarn over hook, draw a loop through next stitch, yarn over hook, draw a loop through next stitch, yarn over hook draw through 3 loops, yarn over hook, draw through 2 loops, 1 loop remaining on hook. In the diagram shading indicates the decreased stitch.

Note: Shapings in fancy patterns are usually given in detail in instructions.

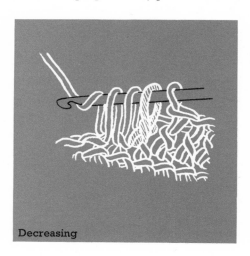

Decreasing

WORKING IN ROUNDS

Working in rounds in crochet is very simple and beginners will have no difficulty in doing this. The diagrams illustrate a practice example in double crochet: make 6ch and join with a sl st into 1st ch to form a circle. This is shown in the 1st two diagrams. **1st Round:** (Next diagram) Work 10dc into circle (working into centre hole and not into the ch sts) and join with sl st. Mark end of round with coloured thread. **2nd round:** Work in dc, working twice into every alternate st. **3rd and 4th Rounds:** As 2nd **5th Round:** Work 1dc in 1dc all round without increasing. This is a simple example of working in rounds. Specific instructions will be given in individual designs.

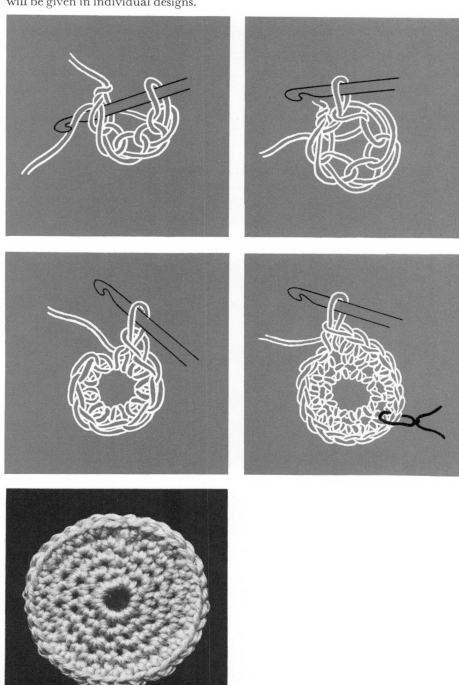

BLOCKS AND SPACES

These produce attractive effects in crochet and are widely used. A block is a group of stitches worked over a space, and a space is made by connecting two blocks with 2 or 3 chain. There are many variations of this type of open-work crochet and the following two examples will give simple practice for the beginner.

Example A

Make 22ch. 1st row: 1tr into 3rd ch from hook, 1tr into next ch, * 3ch, miss 3ch, 1tr into each of next 3ch; rep from * twice, 3ch, turn. 2nd row: Miss 1st tr, 1tr into each of next 2tr, * 3tr into 3ch sp, 3ch, miss 3tr; rep from * once, 3tr into 3ch sp, 2tr into last 2tr, 1tr into top of turning ch, 3ch, turn.

3rd row: Miss 1st tr, 1tr into each of next 2tr, * 3ch, miss 3tr, 3tr into 3ch sp; rep from * once, 3ch, miss 3tr, 2tr into last 2tr, 1tr into top of turning ch, 3ch, turn.

Rep 2nd and 3rd rows for pattern.

Example B

Make 21ch. 1st row: 1tr into 3rd ch from hook, 1tr into each rem ch, 3ch, turn: 20tr.

2nd row: Miss 1st tr, 1tr into each of next 2tr, (2ch, miss 2tr, 1tr into next tr) 4 times, 2ch, miss 2tr, 1tr into each of last 3tr, 3ch, turn.

3rd row: Miss 1st tr, 1tr into each of next 2tr, (2ch, miss 1 sp, 3tr into next sp) twice, 2ch, miss 1 sp, 1tr into each of last 3tr, 3ch, turn.

4th row: Miss 1st tr, 1tr into each of

Blocks and Spaces A

Blocks and Spaces B

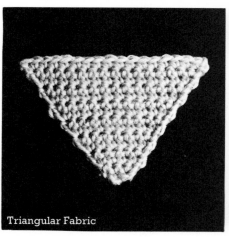

Triangular Fabric

Mesh Fabric

next 2tr, 2ch, miss 1 sp, 1tr into 1st tr of
block, 2ch, miss 2tr, 3tr into next sp,
2ch, miss 2tr, 1tr into 3rd tr of block,
2ch, miss 1 sp, 1tr into each of last 3tr.
5th row: As 3rd.
6th row: Miss 1st tr, 1tr into each of
next 2tr, (2ch, miss 1 sp, 1tr into 1st tr
of block, 2ch, 1tr into 3rd tr of block)
twice, 2ch, miss 1 sp, 1tr into each of
last 3tr.
7th row: Work 1tr into each tr and 2tr
into each sp all across. Fasten off.

TRIANGLES
Triangular pieces are very useful for
making up into simple articles in
crochet, and at the same time they give
practice in increasing and decreasing
side edges.

For a triangle with sides which shape
outwards, work as follows: Make 3ch.
Work 1dc into 2nd ch from hook, 1dc
into next ch, 1ch, turn.
Next row: Miss turning ch, 1dc into 1st
dc, 2dc into next dc (the missed turning
chain at start of previous row), 1ch,
turn. Next row: Miss turning ch, 1dc
into 1st dc, 1dc into next dc, 2dc into
last dc (turning ch of previous row), 1ch,
turn. Cont in dc, working 1dc into 1st
dc at beg of every row and working 2dc
into last dc of every row, thus shaping
sides outwards. Cont until triangle is
required size. Fasten off.

SIMPLE FANCY STITCHES
Mesh Fabric: Make foundation ch.

Multiple of 3+2.
1st row: (1tr, 3ch, 1tr) into 5th ch from
hook, * miss 2ch, (1tr, 3ch, 1tr) into
next ch; rep from * ending 1tr into last
ch, 3ch, turn.
2nd row: (1tr, 3ch, 1tr) into each 3ch
loop, ending 1tr into top of turning ch,
3ch, turn. Rep 2nd row for pattern.

Open Shell: Make foundation ch.
Multiple of 6+5.
1st row: (1tr, 3ch, 1tr) into 5th ch from
hook, * miss 2ch, (1tr, 3ch, 1tr) into
next ch; rep from * ending 1tr into last
ch, 3ch, turn.
2nd row: * 5tr into 1st ch sp, 1dc into
next ch sp; rep from * ending 1tr into
turning ch, 3ch, turn.
3rd row: * (1tr, 3ch, 1tr) into 1st dc,
(1 tr, 3ch, 1tr) into centre of 5tr; rep
from * ending 1tr into turning ch, 3ch,
turn.
4th row: * 1dc into 1st ch sp, 5tr into
next ch sp; rep from * ending 1dc into
turning ch, 3ch, turn.
5th row: * (1tr, 3ch, 1tr) into centre of
5tr, (1tr, 3ch, 1tr) into next dc; rep from
* ending 1 tr into turning ch, 3ch, turn.
Rep rows 2 to 5 for pattern.

Pyramid Shell: Make foundation ch.
Multiple of 6+2.
1st row: 1dc into 2nd ch from hook, 1dc
into next ch, * 3ch, miss 3ch, 1dc into
each of next 3ch; rep from * ending 3ch,
miss 3ch, 1dc into each of next 2ch, 1ch,
turn.
2nd row: 1dc into 1st st, * (1tr, 3dtr,

Open Shell

Pyramid Shell

III

1tr) into 3ch sp, miss 1dc, 1dc into next st; rep from * to end, turn.

3rd row: * 3ch, 1dc into each of 3dtr; rep from * ending 2ch, 1dc into last st, 4ch, turn.

4th row: (1dtr, 1tr) into 2ch sp, * 1dc into centre of 3dc, (1tr, 3dtr, 1tr) into 3 ch sp; rep from * ending 1dc into centre of 3dc, (1tr, 2dtr) into last sp, 1ch, turn.

5th row: 1dc into each dtr, * 3ch, 1dc into each dtr; rep from * ending 3ch, 1 dc into 2dtr, 1ch, turn. Rep rows 2 to 5 for pattern.

Crossed Half Trebles: Make foundation ch. Multiple of 2+1.

1st row: Miss 2ch, * hook under yarn, insert hook into next ch, hook under yarn, draw loop through, hook under yarn, insert hook into next ch, hook under yarn draw loop through, hook under yarn, draw loop through 5 loops on hook, 1ch; rep from * ending 1htr in last ch, 2 ch, turn.

2nd row: As 1st row, inserting hook under the ch sts at each side of 2 crossed half trebles on previous row. Rep 2nd row for pattern.

Three-colour Wave Stitch: Make foundation ch in 1st colour. Multiple of 4+1.

1st row: 1dc into 2nd ch from hook, 1dc into each rem ch.

Change to a larger hook. 2nd row: 3ch, 1tr into 1st st, * miss 3 sts, 3tr into next st; rep from * to last 4 sts, miss 3 sts, 2tr into last st.

Join in 2nd colour. 3rd row: 2ch, * 3tr

Crossed Half Treble

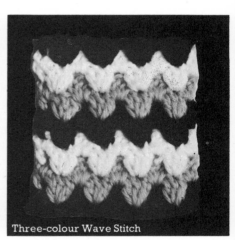

Three-colour Wave Stitch

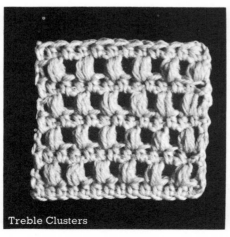

Treble Clusters

Arrow Pattern

into centre of 3 sts missed in previous row; rep from * ending 1htr into centre of 3ch.

Work in pattern as follows:

1st row: 3ch, 1tr into sp between htr and next group of tr, 3tr between each foll group of tr, ending 2tr into sp between last group and ch.

Change to 3rd colour. 2nd row: 2ch, 3tr into each centre tr of group 2 rows below, ending 1htr into centre of 3ch.

3rd row: As 1st.

Change to 1st colour. 4th row: As 2nd. 5th row: As 1st.

Change to 2nd colour. 6th row: As 2nd. Keeping colour sequence, work repeats of 6 pattern rows.

Treble Clusters: Make foundation ch.

1st row: 1htr into 2nd ch from hook, 1htr into each rem ch, 2ch, turn.

2nd row: (wrong side) * miss 1 st, 1 cluster into next st as follows: (hook under yarn, draw loop through) 3 times, hook under yarn, draw loop through all 7 loops, 2ch; rep from * ending 1tr into last st, 2ch, turn.

3rd row: 1htr into top of 1st cluster, * 1htr into ch sp, 1htr into top of next cluster; rep from * ending 1htr into top of 2 turning ch, 2ch, turn. Rep rows 2 and 3 for pattern.

Arrow Pattern: Make foundation ch. Multiple of 4+1.

1st row: 1dc into 2nd ch from hook, 1dc into each rem ch, 1ch, turn.

2nd row: Miss 1st dc, 1dc into each rem dc, 3ch, turn.

3rd row: Miss 1st dc, 1tr into next dc, * miss 3dc, 1dtr into next dc, 1tr into each of 3 missed dc working behind dtr; rep from * ending 1tr into each of last 2dc, 3ch, turn.

4th row: Miss 1st tr, 1tr into next tr, miss 3tr, 1dtr into dtr, 1tr into each of 3 missed tr working in front of dtr; rep from * ending as 3rd row, 1ch, turn.

5th row: Miss 1st tr, 1dc into each rem tr, 1ch, turn. Rep rows 2 to 5 for pattern.

SIMPLE EDGES AND BORDERS

Picot Edges. 1st Example: * 1ss into 1st st, 3ch, 1ss into same st, 1ss into each of next 2 sts; rep from * all along. Fasten off. **2nd Example:** 1ss into 1st st, * 5ch, ss into 3rd ch from hook, 2ch miss 2 sts, 1ss into next st; rep from * all along. Fasten off.

Shell Edges. 1st Example: 1ss into 1st st, * 3tr into next st, 1ss into each of next 2 sts; rep from * all along. Fasten off. **2nd Example:** 1ss into 1st st, * miss 2 sts, 5tr into next st, miss 2 sts, 1dc into next st; rep from * all along. Fasten off.

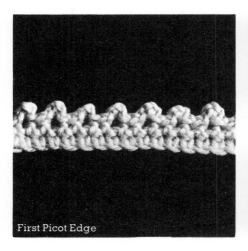
First Picot Edge

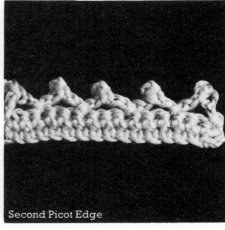
Second Picot Edge

3rd Example: 1st row: 1ss into 1st st, * 5ch, miss 1 st, 1ss into each of next 3 sts; rep from * all along, 1ch, turn.

2nd row: Work 5dc into each 5ch loop and 1ss into each centre ss all along. Fasten off.

Ribbon Insertion. 1st row: 5ch, miss 2 sts, 1tr into next st, * 1ch, miss 1 st, 1tr into next st; rep from * all along, turn. 2nd row: 1ch, * 1dc into sp, 1dc into next tr; rep from * ending 1dc into 3rd of 5ch, turn. 3rd row: * 3ch, miss 1 st, 1dc into next st; rep from * all along. Fasten off. Insert ribbon through holes in 1st row.

Corded Edge. 1st row: Work in dc all along, do not turn. 2nd row: Work in dc from left to right of work, removing hook after each st and reinserting for next st, i.e., remove hook from loop,

insert in next st, then reinsert in loop and complete dc. Fasten off.

MORE ELABORATE STITCHES

Ridge Stitch. A basic double crochet with ridges formed by working into the *back* loop only instead of through both loops.

Make foundation ch.

1st row: 1dc in 2nd ch from hook, 1dc in each rem ch, turn with 1ch.

2nd row: * 1dc in each st, inserting hook in back horizontal thread at top of st of previous row; rep from * to end, turn with 1ch.

2nd row forms pattern.

Waffle Stitch. A simple and reversible 1-row cluster pattern. These are formed by working half a treble through 1 st, half a treble through next st, then com-

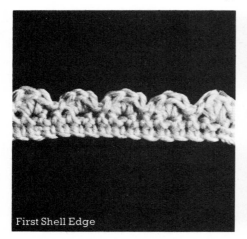

First Shell Edge

Second Shell Edge

Third Shell Edge

Ribbon Insertion

pleting the treble before continuing.
Foundation ch, even number.

1st row: Miss 1ch, * insert hook in next ch, yrh, draw a loop through, insert hook in next st, yrh, draw a loop through, yrh, draw a loop through 2 loops, yrh, draw a loop through last 2 loops, 1 ch; rep from * ending 1dc in last st.

2nd row: 1ch, * insert hook before vertical thread of previous row, yrh, draw a loop through, insert hook after vertical thread of previous row, yrh, draw a loop through, yrh, draw a loop through 2 loops, yrh, draw a loop through last 2 loops, 1 ch; rep from * ending 1dc in last st.

2nd row forms pattern.

Triangle Stitch. The triangles are formed by working 1tr, 1ch, 1tr into the ch sp of the triangle of the previous row. Multiple of 3+2.

1st row: 1tr in 5th ch from hook, * miss 2ch, (1tr, 1ch, 1tr) in next ch; rep from * to end, turn with 5ch.

2nd row: 1tr in first ch sp, * (1tr, 2ch, 1tr) in next ch sp; rep from * ending (1tr, 2ch, 1tr) into loop of 5ch, turn with 5ch.

2nd row forms pattern.

Loop Stitch. The main stitch is double crochet, with loops formed by placing the finger over the yarn and working the stitch over the top of it, thus forming a loop round the finger.

Make foundation ch.

1st row: 1dc in 2nd ch from hook and 1dc in each rem ch, turn with 1ch.

2nd row: (wrong side). Holding yarn over middle finger and under first finger

Corded Edge

Ridge Stitch

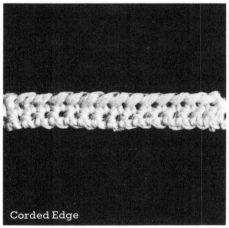

Waffle Stitch

Triangle Stitch

of left hand loosely, insert hook into next st, yoh and draw through st (thus forming a loop round first finger), yoh and draw through both loops on hook, work a very tight ch to lock (this is not counted as a st), slip loop from finger, work 1 loop st in each rem st, turn with 1 ch.

3rd row: 1dc in each loop st to end, turn with 1 ch.

2nd and 3rd rows form pattern.

Pineapple Stitch. The clusters are formed by following the basic treble stitch but working 4 times into the same stitch, thus forming 9 loops on the hook which are then secured by drawing the yarn through 8 loops, then through 2 loops and working 1 ch.

Multiple of 2+1.

Miss 2ch, yrh, insert hook in 3rd ch from hook, * (yrh, draw through long loop) 4 times in same ch, (9 loops on hook), yrh and draw through 8 loops, yrh, and draw through 2 loops, 1ch, miss 1ch, yrh, insert hook in next ch; rep from *, ending 1tr, 2ch, turn.

On following rows make the cluster in the ch sp between the clusters of previous row.

Two-colour Star Stitch. A 4-row pattern of alternating groups of 3dc and 3tr which in turn are again alternated when working in the contrasting colours.

Multiple of 6+4.

1st row: In Light, 1dc in 2nd ch from hook, 1dc in each rem ch.

2nd row: In Light, 3ch, miss 1st st, 1tr in each of next 2 sts, * 1dc in each of next 3 sts, 1tr in each of next 3 sts; rep from * to end.

3rd row: In Light, as 2nd.

4th row: In Dark, 1ch, 1dc in each of next 3 sts, * 1tr in each of next 3 sts, 1dc in each of next 3 sts; rep from * to end.

5th row: In Dark, as 4th.

Rows 2 to 5 form pattern.

Loop Stitch

Pineapple Stitch

Two-colour Star Stitch

SOME HINTS FOR
LEFT-HANDED WORKERS

The instructions are the same as for right-handed workers, except that the hook is held in the left hand, and the yarn in the right hand.

Follow the basic instructions starting on page 99, reading right for left, and vice versa. To see the diagrams in reverse, look at a reversed image as described for left-handed knitting in Chapter 9.

The two diagrams illustrate this easy way of reversing the diagrams for left-handed workers.

Left-Handed Crochet:
Reversed Image

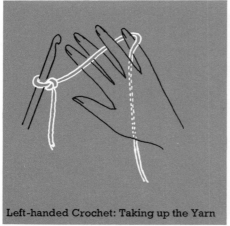

Left-handed Crochet: Taking up the Yarn

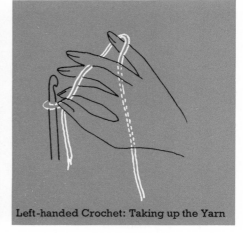

Left-handed Crochet: Taking up the Yarn

HINTS FOR COLOUR WORK –
using Treble as an example

Linking Up. Working in trebles and blocks of colour: hold second colour behind first colour, draw second colour through last two loops of last treble of first colour, then pass first colour upwards, over top of second colour and continue using second colour along row. Link colours at colour-change point on every row.

Two-colour Pattern. When working in trebles and two-colour pattern, colour to be used next is drawn through last two loops just worked, and colour in use is then worked over colour not in use.

JOINING IN YARN

When only a few inches are left, take end from new ball of yarn and complete last st with this. Lay short ends of old and new yarns along edge and work over them for a few sts continuing with new yarn.

Ready for Action

The five simple articles for which instructions are given below put into action the principles of crochet set out in this chapter. The cushion is worked in double crochet throughout and provides practice in increasing. It is followed by the treble stitch bag, which illustrates working in rounds, with corner increases to form a square. The pretty pinafore is worked in groups of trebles and chains; because it is a garment, it introduces simple shapings. Next comes a warm Afghan which is built up from a number of fancy motifs in double trebles and double crochet which are sewn together. Finally, lacy medallions are sewn together to create the diaphanous evening stole.

Cushion

Materials: 3 (50g) balls Main Shade, 2 (50g) balls Dark, 1 (50g) ball Light Patons Double Knitting. No 4·00 mm crochet hook. Cushion pad.

Measurements: 14 × 14 in square.

Additional Abbreviations (see page 29): M=Main Shade; D=Dark; L= Light.

Break and join colours as required.

With M, make 2 ch. 1st row: 3dc in 2nd ch from hook, 1ch, turn. 2nd row: Miss 1dc, 3dc, in next dc, 1dc, 1ch, turn. 3rd row: Miss 1dc, 1dc, 3dc in next dc, 2dc, 1ch, turn.

4th row: Miss 1dc, 6dc, 1ch, turn. 5th row: Miss 1dc, 2dc, 3dc in next dc, 3dc, 1ch, turn. 6th row: Miss 1dc, 3dc, 3dc in next dc, 4dc, 1ch, turn.

7th row: Miss 1dc, 4dc, 3dc in next dc, 5dc, 1ch, turn. 8th row: Miss 1dc, 12dc, 1ch, turn. 9th row: With D, miss 1dc, 5dc, 3dc in next dc, 6dc, 1ch, turn.

10th row: With D, miss 1dc, 6dc, 3dc in next dc, 7dc, 1ch, turn. 11th row: With L, miss 1dc, 7dc, 3dc in next dc, 8dc, 1ch, turn. 12th row: With L, miss 1dc, 18dc, 1ch, turn.

13th row: With D, miss 1dc, 8dc, 3dc in next dc, 9dc, 1ch, turn. 14th row: With D, miss 1dc, 9dc, 3dc in next dc, 10dc, 1ch, turn.

Working every 4th row without shaping as before, cont inc in this way in stripes of '8 rows M, 2D, 2L, and 2D', until 5th set of D and L stripes has been worked.

Work 8 rows M. Fasten off. Make another piece to match.

TO MAKE UP

Observing general method on page 81, block and press. Stitch pieces tog round 3 sides on wrong side. Turn right side out, insert pad and stitch up other side.

Toddler's Tunic

Materials: 1/2 (50g) balls Blue, 1/1 (50g) ball each in White and Yellow Patons Purple Heather 4-ply. No 3·50 mm crochet hook.

Measurements: To fit 22/24 in chest; length from top of shoulder, 16/18½ in.

Tension: 5 groups of trebles to 3 in; 6½ rows to 2 in.

Additional Abbreviations (see page 29): W=White; B=Blue; Y=Yellow.

Note: Carry yarns not in use loosely up side of work.

BACK AND FRONT (both alike)

With W, make 82/88ch. Foundation row: With W, 1tr in 4th ch from hook, * miss 2ch, 3tr in next ch; rep from * to last 3ch, miss 2ch, 2tr in last ch: 25/27 grs with ½ gr at each end (starting ch counts as 1st tr on every row).

Work in patt as follows: 1st row: With B, 3ch, 3tr in sp between ½ gr and 1st gr, 3tr in each foll sp between 2gr, ending 3tr in sp between last gr and ½ gr, 1tr in top of 3ch: 26/28 grs with 1tr at each end. 2nd row: With Y, 3ch, 1tr in sp between tr and first gr, 3tr in each foll sp, 2tr in sp between last gr and 3ch. 3rd row: With W, as 1st. 4th row: With B, as 2nd. 5th row: With Y, as 1st. 6th row: With W, as 2nd. These 6 rows form patt. Work rows 1 to 3 again.

1st shaping row: 3ch, 1tr in first sp, 5/6 grs, 2tr in next sp, 13 grs, 2tr in next sp, patt to end. 2nd shaping row: 3ch, 5/6 grs, 2tr in each of next 2 sps, 12 grs, 2 tr in each of next 2 sps, patt to end. 3rd shaping row: 3ch, 1tr in first sp, 5/6 grs, 1tr in next sp, 13 grs, 1tr in next sp, patt to end.

4th shaping row: 3ch, 5/6 grs, 1tr in each of next 2 sps, 12 grs, 1tr in each of next 2 sps, patt to end. 5th shaping row:

In patt, but missing each sp between the 2 single tr: 23/25 grs with $\frac{1}{2}$ gr at each end. Work 2/4 rows straight.

Next row: 3ch, 5/6 grs, 2tr in next sp, 12 grs, 2tr in next sp, patt to end. Next row: 3ch, 1tr in first sp, 4/5 grs, 2tr in each of next 2 sps, 11 grs, 2tr in each of next 2 sps, patt to end.

Next row: 3ch, 5/6 grs, 1tr in next sp, 12 grs, 1tr in next sp, patt to end. Next row: 3ch, 1tr in first sp, 4/5 grs, 1tr in each of next 2 sps, 11 grs, 1tr in each of next 2 sps, patt to end. Next row: As 5th shaping row: 22/24 grs.

Work 2/4 rows straight. Next row: 3ch, 1tr in first sp, 4/5 grs, 2tr in next sp, 11 grs, 2tr in next sp, patt to end. Next row: 3ch, 4/5 grs, 2tr in each of next 2 sps, 10 grs, 2tr in each of next 2 sps, patt to end. Next row: 3ch, 1tr in first sp, 4/5 grs, 1tr in next sp, 11 grs, 1tr in next sp, patt to end. Next row: 3ch, 4/5 grs, 1tr in each of next 2 sps, 10 grs, 1tr in each of next 2 sps, patt to end. Next row: as 5th shaping row: 19/21 grs, with $\frac{1}{2}$ gr at each end.

Work 2/4 rows straight. Next row: 3ch, 4/5 grs, 2tr in next sp, 10 grs, 2tr in next sp, patt to end. Next row: 3ch, 1tr in first sp, 3/4 grs, 2tr in each of next 2 sps, 9 grs, 2tr in each of next 2 sps, patt to end.

Next row: 3ch, 4/5 grs, 1tr in next sp, 10 grs, 1tr in next sp, patt to end. Next row: 3ch, 1tr in first sp, 3/4 grs, 1tr in each of next 2 sps, 9 grs, 1tr in each of next 2 sps, patt to end. Next row: as 5th shaping row: 18/20 grs. Break all yarns.

Shape armholes: Next row: rejoin appropriate colour to sp between 3rd and 4th gr, 3ch, 1tr in this sp, 11/13 grs, 2tr in next sp, turn. Work 7/9 rows straight. Shape neck and work straps: Next row: 3ch, 1tr in first sp, 2 grs, 2tr in next sp, turn. Work straight until work measures 5/5$\frac{1}{2}$ in from start of armhole shaping. Fasten off. Leaving 6/8 grs at centre unworked, rejoin appropriate colour to next sp, 3ch, 1tr in this sp, patt to end. Finish to correspond with first strap.

TO MAKE UP
Observing general method on page 81, block and press. Join side and shoulder seams. With B, work 1 row dc round neck and armholes.

Lower edge: 1st rnd: With right side facing, using Y, work 1 rnd dc all along lower edge by working 3dc in each ch sp. 2nd rnd: With B, * 1dc in each of next 3dc, 5ch, then work 1dc into 1st of these 5ch; rep from * to end of rnd. Fasten off.

Evening Stole

Materials: 7 (50g) balls Patons Purple Heather 4-ply. No 4·00 mm crochet hook.

Measurements: 22 × 66 in, excluding fringes.

Tension: Each large medallion measures approximately 3$\frac{3}{4}$ in across from loop to loop.

LARGE MEDALLION
Make 8ch and join in a ring with 1 ss.
1st rnd: 5ch, (1tr into ring, 2ch) 7 times, 1 ss into 3rd of the 5ch. ** 2nd rnd: 6ch, 1 ss into same st as ss of previous rnd, (2dc into ch sp, 1 ss into next tr, 6ch, 1 ss into same tr) 7 times, 2dc into ch sp. 3rd rnd: Ss to centre of first loop, 1dc into first loop, (8ch, 1dc into centre of next loop) 7 times, 8ch, 1 ss into first dc. 4th rnd: * Work (1dc 3ch) 3 times, 1dc into next ch sp, 1dc into next dc; rep from * 7 times more, ending last rep with 1 ss into first dc. Fasten off. Make 108 medallions in all.

SMALL MEDALLION

Work as Large Medallion to **.
Next rnd: (1dc 2tr 1dc into ch sp) 8
times, 1 ss into first dc of rnd. Fasten off.
Make 85 medallions in all.

TO MAKE UP

Join large and small medallions as illustrated; width 6 large medallions; length
18 large medallions. Make fringe at each
end of stole, as described in Chapter 9,
thus: With 4 strands of yarn 8 in long,
fold in half and knot into loops on outside edge of medallions, working 2
fringes into each loop. Press lightly.

Afghan (illustrated on page 124)

Materials: 6 (50g) balls Navy, 2 (50g)
balls each Emerald Green, Dark Green,
Dark Red, Scarlet, White, Dark Brown,
Yellow, Royal Blue, Sky Blue, and
Beige Patons Double Knitting. No
3·50 mm crochet hook.

Measurements: 38 × 38 in, excluding
fringe.

Tension: Across widest part of one
motif measures 3¼ in.

There are 121 small motifs in all, which
are sewn together to form the large
square.
With Scarlet, make 7ch and join in a
ring with ss, 4ch (this represents 1dtr),
23dtr into centre of ring. Join last dtr to
top of first 4ch with ss. Break yarn.
Join in White, 4ch, now work 5 more
dtr into same st, * miss 2dtr of previous
row, 1dc into 3rd st, miss 2dtr, make
12dtr into next st (this forms one half
circle) *; rep from * to * twice more,
miss 2dtr, 1dc into next st, miss last
2dtr, work 6dtr into same st as first 6dtr,

thus completing 4th half circle. Fasten
off by working ss into top of 4ch. Break
yarn.
Join in Navy and work a round of dc all
round outer edge, working 3dc into
centre st at top of each half circle to
keep fabric flat; fasten off with ss. This
completes one motif.
Make 120 more motifs in this way, varying colours as you wish but always using
Navy for the dc edging.

TO MAKE UP

Observing general method on page 81,
press.
With Navy, join motifs by sewing tog
round corners, leaving about 1¼ in free
in centre of each side. With Navy, work
a round of tr all round outer edges of
rug to form a border. Cut remaining
Navy into 5 in lengths and using 3
strands make fringe as described in
Chapter 9, knotting through every 2nd
stitch. Pin rug out carefully and give
a final press on wrong side.

Fringed Bag

Materials: 1 (50g) ball Black and oddments of White, Light Grey, Medium Grey, and Dark Grey, Patons Double Knitting. No 4·50 mm crochet hook. ⅜ yd of scarlet material for lining. Piece of thin plastic foam 12 × 24 in for interlining (optional).
Size: 12½ in square.

Start with Black then change colour for each round, shading out to White.

With Black, make 6 ch, join into ring with ss. 1st rnd: 3ch, 1tr, (1ch, 2tr) 3 times, 1ch, join with ss to top of 3ch. Break Black. Join in Dark Grey. 2nd rnd: 3ch, 3tr into 1ch sp, (1ch, 4tr) 3 times (making 4 groups of 4 trebles). Join with ss to top of 3ch. Break Dark Grey. Join in Medium Grey to centre of corner group. 3rd rnd: 3ch, 3tr into same sp; 2tr into each of next 3 sps, 4tr into corner.

Rep round rem 3 sides of square. Join to top of 3ch with ss. Rep 3rd rnd using Light Grey then White. Cont round the square, shading colours as from the start until 4 sets of colours have been worked.

To give a firm edge work one extra rnd in Black making 4tr into each corner as before but 3tr in each sp between corners. Work second square to match. Press on wrong side under a damp cloth. With Black, crochet the two sides tog along bottom edge in dc. Cut piece of lining same size and interlining $\frac{1}{2}$ in smaller. Tack spare lining over interlining and slip stitch to wrong side $\frac{1}{4}$ in inside the edge. Fold bag in half and with Black, join two sides tog with dc. Cut some of rem yarns into 6 in lengths and knot along bottom edge to form a fringe. Cut rest of yarn into 90 in lengths to form a thick plait of about 27 strands. Knot ends to form tassels and stitch firmly to sides of bag.

Chapter 11

Family Life
Baby Days

Having mastered the basic techniques of the crafts, the budding knitting or crochet expert naturally looks for some first-class designs on which to try her developing skill. Almost all the remaining pages of this book are devoted to a collection of different articles which brings the total in the book up to one hundred.

The instructions are not difficult and do not include any methods of working which have not already been discussed in the earlier part of the book. Each successive chapter is devoted to a group of designs associated with particular aspects of present-day life. Every effort has been made to ensure that their character does not date and that they remain of permanent interest. Because family life has a perpetual fascination, the first four chapters of the collection are devoted to the needs of a family at every stage of its development, starting with those enchanting first four or five years.

Dressed and Coated in Crochet

A clean, crisp, matching pair in the first size

Materials: Dress: 7 (25g) balls; **Coat:** 5 (25g) balls Patons Baby 4-ply, Courtelle. No 3·50 mm crochet hook. 4 buttons for Dress, 3 buttons for Coat. **Measurements:** To fit 18 in chest. **Dress:** Length from top of shoulder, 14 in; sleeve seam, 1 in. **Coat:** Length from top of shoulder, 10½ in; sleeve seam, 5 in. **Tension:** 10½ sts and 8 rows to 2 in over half trebles.

DRESS

FRONT

** Bodice: Make 50ch. Foundation row: (right side) 1htr in 3rd ch from hook, 1htr in each foll ch, turn with 2ch. 1st row: Miss first st, 1htr in each foll st, 1htr in top of turning ch, turn with 2ch: 49 sts. (Turning ch of previous row counts as first st). This row forms Bodice patt. Rep it once more, omitting turning ch at end.
Shape armholes: 1st row: Ss over 2 sts, 2ch, miss first st, work to last 2 sts, (incl turning ch), turn. 2nd row: Ss over 1 st, 2ch, miss first st, work to last st (turning ch), turn. Rep 2nd row 4 times more: 35 sts.** Work 5 rows straight.
Shape neck: 1st row: Miss first st, 1 htr in each of next 11 sts, turn. Dec 1 st at neck edge on next 3 rows: 9 sts.
Shape shoulder: Next row: Ss over 3 sts, work to end. Next row: Miss first st, 1htr in each of next 2 sts. Fasten off. Leaving centre 11 sts unworked, rejoin yarn to next st and make 2 ch, work to end. Finish to correspond with first side, reversing shapings.
Border: with wrong side facing, work 1 row dc along first shoulder, round neck and along second shoulder. Work buttonhole loops along shoulder and shells along neck edge thus:
Next row: (1dc in each of next 2 sts, 2ch, miss 2 sts) twice, 1dc in next st, cont along neck edge as follows: * Miss 2 sts, 1tr, (1ch, 1tr) 3 times all in next st, miss 2 sts, 1dc in next st; rep from * up to shoulder edge, 1dc in first st of shoulder, (2ch, miss 2 sts, 1dc in each of next 2 sts) twice. Fasten off.
Skirt: With right side facing, rejoin yarn to starting ch and work Foundation row: 3ch, 2tr in first ch loop, * miss 1 ch loop, 1tr 1ch 1tr all in next ch loop, miss 1ch loop, 2tr 1ch 2tr all in next ch loop; rep from * to last 4ch loops, miss 1ch loop, 1tr 1ch 1tr all in next ch loop, miss 1ch loop, 3tr in last ch loop, turn with 3ch.
Work in patt as follows: 1st row: 2tr in first st, * 1ch, 1tr in next ch sp, 1ch, 2tr 1ch 2tr all in next ch sp; rep from *, ending last rep 3tr in top of turning ch, turn with 3ch. 2nd row: 2tr in first st, * miss next 2 sts, 1tr 1ch 1tr all in next single tr, miss next ch sp, 2tr 1ch 2tr all in next ch sp; rep from *, ending last rep 3tr in top of turning ch, turn with 3ch. These 2 rows form skirt patt. Rep them until skirt measures approx 9½ in, ending with 1st patt row and turning with 4ch at end.
Work shells as follows: Next row: (1tr, 1ch) twice in first st, * 1dc in single tr, miss next ch sp, (1ch, 1tr) 4 times in next ch sp, 1ch; rep from *, ending last rep (1ch, 1tr) 3 times in top of turning ch. Fasten off.

BACK

Work as for front from ** to **. Work 9 rows straight.
Shape shoulders: Next row: Ss over 3 sts, 2ch, miss next st, 1htr in each of next 5 sts, turn with 2ch. Next row: Miss first st, 1htr in each of next 2 sts. Fasten off. Leaving centre 17 sts unworked, rejoin yarn to next st, work to last 3 sts, turn. Finish to correspond with first side, reversing shapings.
Border: With wrong side facing, work 1

row dc along shoulders and neck edges. Next row: Work 1 row dc along shoulder edges and work shells as for front along neck edge. Fasten off.

SKIRT
Work as for front.

SLEEVES
Make 34ch and work Foundation row and 2 rows bodice patt: 33 sts.
Shape top: Next row: Ss over 2 sts, work to last 2 sts, turn. Dec 1 st at each end of every row until 9 sts rem. Fasten off. With right side facing, work row of shells as for neck border along starting ch. Fasten off.

TO MAKE UP
Observing general method on page 81, block and press.
Join side and sleeve seams. Catch shoulder borders together, front overlapping back. Insert sleeves. Press seams. Sew on buttons.

COAT

Yoke: Starting at neck edge make 54ch and work Foundation row as for bodice of dress: 53 sts. Cont in bodice patt, shaping as follows: 1st row: Miss first st, 1htr in each of next 2 sts, * 2htr in next st, 1htr in each of next 4 sts; rep from * to end (noting that last st is worked in top of turning ch), turn with 2 ch: 63 sts. 2nd row: Miss first st, 1htr in each of next 3 sts, (2htr in next st, 1htr in each of next 5 sts) 9 times, 2htr in next st, 1htr in each of next 4 sts, turn with 2ch: 73 sts.
3rd row: Miss first st, 1htr in each of next 3 sts, (2htr in next st, 1htr in each of next 6 sts) 9 times, 2htr in next st, 1htr in each of next 5 sts, turn with 2ch: 83 sts. 4th row: Miss first st, 1htr in each of next 4 sts, (2htr in next st, 1htr in each of next 7 sts) 9 times, 2htr in next st, 1htr in each of next 5 sts, turn with 2ch: 93 sts.
5th row: Miss first st, 1htr in each of next 4 sts, (2htr in next st, 1htr in each of next 8 sts) 9 times, 2htr in next st, 1htr in each of next 6 sts, turn with 2ch: 103 sts. 6th row: Work straight.

7th row: Miss first st, 1htr in each of next 5 sts, (2htr in next st, 1htr in each of next 9 sts) 9 times, 2htr in next st, 1htr in each of next 6 sts, turn with 2ch: 113 sts. 8th row: Work straight. 9th row: Miss first st, 1htr in each of next 5 sts, (2htr in next st, 1htr in each of next 10 sts) 9 times, 2htr in next st, 1htr in each of next 7 sts, turn with 2ch: 123 sts. 10th row: Work straight. 11th row: Miss first st, 1htr in each of next 6 sts, (2htr in next st, 1htr in each of next 11 sts) 9 times, 2htr in next st, 1htr in each of next 7 sts, turn with 3ch: 133 sts.
Cont with left front as follows: Foundation row: 2tr in first st, (miss 1 st, 1tr 1ch 1tr all in next st, miss 1 st, 2tr 1ch 2tr all in next st) 4 times, miss 1 st, 1tr 1ch 1tr in next st, miss 1 st, 3tr in next st, turn with 3ch. Work 1st and 2nd rows of skirt patt as on dress. Place marker at end of last row.
Cont in skirt patt until front measures approx 6 in from marker, ending with a 1st patt row and turning with 4ch at end. Work shells as for lower edge of dress.
Cont with left sleeve as follows: Foundation row: Rejoin yarn to next st and make 3ch, 2tr in same st, (miss 1 st, 1tr 1ch 1tr in next st, miss 1 st, 2tr 1ch 2tr in next st) 5 times, miss 1 st, 1tr 1ch 1tr in next st, miss 1 st, 3tr in next st, turn with 3ch.
Work 1st and 2nd rows of skirt patt. Place markers at each end of last row. Cont in skirt patt until sleeve measures approx $4\frac{1}{2}$ in from marker, ending with a 1st row, omitting turning ch at end.
Work cuff: Next row: 1dc in each of next 3tr, * miss next 3 sts, (i.e. 1ch 1tr 1ch), 1dc in each of next 2tr, miss 1ch, 1dc in each of next 2tr; rep from *, ending 1dc in each of last 2tr, turn, leaving turning ch unworked: 25 sts. Work 1 row more dc, turning with 4ch at end of last row.
Work shells: Next row: 1tr 1ch 1tr in first st, * miss 1 st, 1dc in next st, miss 1 st, 1tr, (1ch, 1tr) 3 times in next st; rep from *, ending last rep 1tr, (1ch, 1tr) twice in last st. Fasten off.
Cont with Back: Foundation row: Re-

join yarn to next st and make 3ch, 2tr in same st, (miss 1 st, 1tr 1ch 1tr in next st, miss 1 st, 2tr 1ch 2tr in next st) 9 times, miss 1 st, 1tr 1ch 1tr in next st, miss 1 st, 3tr in next st, turn with 3ch. Complete as for left front, but placing markers at each end of row.

RIGHT SLEEVE
Work as for left sleeve.

RIGHT FRONT
Rejoin yarn to next st and make 3ch, 2tr in same st, work Foundation row as for left front from portion in brackets, then complete as for left front, but placing marker at beg of row.

TO MAKE UP
Observing general method on page 81, block and press.
Sew sleeves to fronts and back from yoke to markers, then join side and sleeve seams.
Borders: Work 2 rows dc along left front edge. Fasten off. Work 1 row dc up right front edge, then work another row, making 3 buttonloops, 1st immediately below neck edge, 3rd at end of yoke and rem one at centre.
To make a buttonloop: 2ch, miss 2 sts. Work shells as for neck edge of dress up right front edge, round neck and down left front edge, counting each buttonloop as 2 sts. Fasten off. Press seams. Sew on buttons.

Two for a Comfortable Start
Warm vests, for the first two years

RIBBED VEST

Materials: 2 (25g) balls Patons Baby 3-ply, Courtelle. Pair each Nos 10 and 11 needles. Stitch-holder.

Measurements: To fit 18 in chest; length, 10½ in; sleeve seam, 1 in.

Tension: 16 sts and 21 rows to 2 in over patt on No 10 needles.

BACK AND FRONT (both alike)
With No 11 needles, cast on 64 sts and work 10 rows K2, P2 rib as follows: 1st row: K1, * K2, P2; rep from * to last 3 sts, K3. 2nd row: K1, * P2, K2; rep from * to last 3 sts, P2, K1. Rep last 2 rows 4 times more.
Change to No 10 needles and rib patt as follows: 1st row: K3, * P2, K2; rep from * to last 5 sts, P2, K3. 2nd row: K1, P to last st, K1. These 2 rows form patt. Continue in patt until work measures 10 in, ending with right side facing, and placing a marker at each end when work measures 6½ in. Change to No 11 needles and work 10 rows K2, P2 rib as at start. Cast off evenly in rib.

SLEEVES
With No 11 needles, cast on 52 sts and work 4 rows K2, P2 rib as for start of back and front. Change to No 10 needles and rib patt and work 6 rows straight. Shape top by dec 1 st at each end of next and every alt row until 36 sts remain. Now dec 1 st at each end of next 3 rows. Cast off.

TO MAKE UP
Observing general method on page 81, block and press. Overlap ribbing at top of front and back and catch together at side edges. Join side seams to markers, then join sleeve seams. Insert sleeves.

GARTER STITCH YOKE

Materials: 2 (25g) balls Patons Baby 3-ply, Courtelle. Pair No. 11 needles. No 3·00 mm crochet hook. 1½ yds baby ribbon.

Measurements: To fit 18 in chest; length, 11 in; sleeve, 1½ in.

Tension: 16 sts to 2 in over garter stitch.

FRONT AND BACK (both alike)

Cast on 74 sts loosely. Work in fancy rib thus: 1st row: Sl 1P, * P1, KB1; rep from * to last st, P1. 2nd row: Sl 1P, * PB1, K1; rep from * to last st, P into back of st. Rep these 2 rows until work measures 8 in.

Change to garter st and inc 1st at each end of every alt row until there are 84 sts. Cast on 10 sts at beg of next 2 rows: 104 sts. Work straight for 34 rows.

Shape neck: K34 and leave on spare needle, cast off 36, and work 8 rows in garter st on last 34 sts. Leave on needle. Return to sts on spare needle and work to correspond.

TO MAKE UP

Observing general method on page 81, block and press. Join side seams and graft shoulders. Work a crochet edging round neck thus: 1st rnd: In dc. 2nd rnd: 3ch into first dc of previous rnd, * 2ch, miss 1dc, 1tr into foll dc; rep from * to end, fasten off. Thread ribbon through neck.

The Means and the Ends

Bonnet, mitts, and booties in knitting: set of mittens and booties in crochet

KNITTED SET

Materials: Bonnet: 1 (25g) ball; **Mitts:** 1 (25g) ball; **Booties:** 1 (25g) ball Patons Baby 3-ply, Courtelle. Pair each Nos 9 and 11 needles. No 3·00 mm crochet hook. 1¾ yds 1 in wide ribbon for Bonnet, narrow ribbon for Mitts and Booties. 2 25g balls are enough for the complete set.

Tension: 13 sts and 17 rows to 2 in over st st on No 9 needles.

BONNET

With No 11 needles, cast on 83 sts and work 4 rows st st, starting with a K row. Next row: K1, * yf, K2tog; rep from * to end. Starting with a P row, work 5 rows st st. Next row: Make picot hem by knitting tog 1 st from needle and 1 st from cast-on edge all across row.

Change to No 9 needles. Next row: P5, P2tog, * P6, P2tog; rep from * to last 4 sts, P4: 73 sts.

Work in lace patt as follows: 1st row: K1, * K1, K2tog, yf, K1, yf, sl 1, K1, psso, K2; rep from * to end. 2nd and alt rows: P. 3rd row: K1, * K2tog, yf, K3, yf, sl 1, K1, psso, K1; rep from * to end.

5th row: K2tog, * yf, K2, yf, K2tog, K1, yf, sl 1, K2tog, psso; rep from * to last 7 sts, yf, K2, yf, K2tog, K1, yf, sl 1, K1, psso. 7th row: K1, * yf, sl 1, K1, psso, K3, K2tog, yf, K1; rep from * to end.

9th row: K1, * K1, yf, sl 1, K1, psso, K1, K2tog, yf, K2; rep from * to end. 11th row: K1, K2, yf, sl 1, K2tog, psso, * yf, K2, yf, K2tog, K1, yf, sl 1, K2tog, psso; rep from * to last 3 sts, yf, K3. 12th row: P.

These 12 rows form lace patt. Cont until work measures approx 4 in, ending with a 6th patt row. Next row: P5, M1, * P8, M1; rep from * to last 4 sts, P4: 82 sts. Place marker at end of row.

Shape crown as follows: 1st row: K1, (K2tog, K7) 9 times. 2nd and every alt row: K1, P to last st, K1. 3rd row: K1, (K2tog, K6) 9 times. 5th row: K1, (K2tog, K5) 9 times.

Cont dec thus on every alt row until the row 'K1, (K2tog, K1) 9 times' has been worked. Next row: K1, P to last st, K1. Next row: K1, (K2tog) 9 times: 10 sts. Break yarn and thread through rem sts, draw up and fasten off securely.

TO MAKE UP

Observing general method on page 81, block and press. Join seam from centre of crown to marker.

With right side facing, work 2 rows dc along neck edge. Press seam. Make rosettes with ribbon leaving ends to tie, stitch to sides of bonnet.

MITTS

With No 11 needles, cast on 33 sts and work 4 rows in st st, starting with a K row.

** Next row: K1, * yf, K2tog; rep from * to end. Starting with a P row work 5 rows in st st. Next row: Make picot hem by knitting tog 1 st from needle and 1 st from cast-on edge all across row.

Change to No 9 needles and st st, starting with a P row, until work measures 1½ in, ending with right side facing for next row.

Work holes for ribbon: Next row: K1, * yf, K2tog; rep from * to end.** Next row: K, dec 1 st in centre: 32 sts.

Cont in st st, starting with a K row until work measures 3½ in, ending with right side facing.

Shape top as follows: 1st row: (K1, K2togtbl, K10, K2tog, K1) twice. 2nd and alt rows: P. 3rd row: (K1, K2tog tbl, K8, K2tog, K1) twice. 5th row: (K1, K2togtbl, K6, K2tog, K1) twice. 7th row: (K1, K2togtbl, K4, K2tog, K1) twice. Cast off.

TO MAKE UP

Observing general method on page 81, block and press. Join seam and press. Thread ribbon through holes at wrist and tie in a bow.

BOOTIES

With No 11 needles, cast on 33 sts and work 4 rows in st st, starting with a K row. Now work as for mitts from ** to **. Next row: K, dec 2 sts evenly: 31 sts. Divide for foot as follows: 1st row: K21, turn. 2nd row: K1, P9, K1, turn. 3rd row: K11, turn. Rep 2nd and 3rd rows 8 times more, then 2nd row again. Break yarn.

Rejoin yarn to inside edge where sts were left, and pick up and K11 along side of foot, K across sts on needle, pick up and K11 along other side of foot, K to end: 53 sts. K11 rows.

Shape foot as follows: 1st row: (K1, K2tog, K21, K2tog) twice, K1. 2nd and alt rows: K. 3rd row: (K1, K2tog, K19, K2tog) twice, K1. 5th row: (K1, K2tog, K17, K2tog) twice, K1. Cast off.

TO MAKE UP

Observing general method on page 81, block and press. Join seams. Press seams. Thread ribbon through row of holes and tie in bow.

CROCHET SET

Materials: 2 (25g) balls Patons Baby 3-ply, Courtelle. No 3·00 mm crochet hook. 1½ yds baby ribbon.

MITTS

** Make 41ch. 1st row: 1htr in 2nd ch from hook, 1htr in next 39ch, 5ch, turn. 2nd row: (on which holes for ribbon are worked) * Miss 2 sts, 1tr in next 2 sts, 2ch; rep from * to end of row.**

3rd row: Miss first tr, 1htr in next tr, * 2htr in 2ch sp, 1htr in each of next 2tr; rep from * to end of row, ending with 2htr in 2ch sp, 1ch, turn. 4th row: Miss first st, 1htr in next 39 sts, 1ch, turn. Rep 4th row until work measures 2½ in from start.

Shape top: Next row: Miss first 2 sts, 1htr in next 16 sts, miss 1 st, 1htr in next 2 sts, miss 1 st, 1htr in next 16 sts, miss 1 st, 1htr in last st, 1ch, turn: 36 sts. Next row: Miss 2 sts, 1htr in next 14 sts, miss 1 st, 1htr in next 2 sts, miss 1 st, 1htr in next 14 sts, miss 1 st, 1htr in last st, 1ch, turn: 32 sts.

Next row: Miss 2 sts, 1htr in next 12 sts, miss 1 st, 1htr in next 2 sts, miss 1 st, 1htr in next 12 sts, miss 1 st, 1htr in last st, 1ch, turn: 28 sts. Next row: Miss 2 sts, 1htr in next 10 sts, miss 1 st, 1htr in next 2 sts, miss 1 st, 1htr in next 10 sts, miss 1 st, 1htr in last st, 1ch, turn: 24 sts. Fasten off.

CUFF

With right side of work facing, join in yarn to first st on starting edge and make 3ch. 1st row: * Miss 2 sts, 2tr 1ch 2tr all in next st; rep from * to last 3 sts, miss 2 sts, 1tr in last st, 3ch, turn. 2nd row: Work 2tr 1ch 2tr all in 1ch sp of each cluster on previous row, 1tr into last tr, 3ch, turn. 3rd row: As 2nd but omitting '3ch' at end of row. Fasten off.

BOOTIES

Work as mitts from ** to **. Fasten off. With right side facing, join in yarn to 14th st from right-hand side and work in htr across centre 14 sts (13 sts unworked at each side of centre sts). Work 2¼ in of htr on centre 14 sts for foot. Fasten off.

With right side of work facing, rejoin yarn to first st of 13 sts left unworked at right side of foot and work in htr across these sts; work 13 htr along side of foot; 14htr across end of 13 sts left unworked at other side of foot, 1ch, turn: 66 sts.

Shape foot: 1st row: Miss 2 sts, 1htr in next 29 sts, miss 1 st, 1htr in next 2 sts, miss 1 st, 1htr in next 29 sts, miss 1 st, 1htr in last st, 1ch, turn: 62 sts. 2nd row: Miss 2 sts, 1htr in next 27 sts, miss 1 st, 1htr in next 2 sts, miss 1 st, 1htr in next 27 sts, miss 1 st, 1htr in last st, 1ch, turn: 58 sts.

3rd row: Miss 2 sts, 1htr in next 25 sts, miss 1 st, 1htr in next 2 sts, miss 1 st, 1htr in next 25 sts, miss 1 st, 1htr in last st, 1ch, turn: 54 sts. 4th row: Miss 2 sts, 1htr in next 23 sts, miss 1 st, 1htr in next 2 sts, miss 1 st, 1htr in next 23 sts, miss 1 st, 1htr in last st: 50 sts. Fasten off.

Work cuff as for mitts but noting that 2nd row is worked twice, thus giving 4 rows for bootie instead of 3.

TO MAKE UP

Observing general method on page 81, press. Join side seams of all pieces on wrong side. Cut ribbon into 4 equal lengths and thread through holes at wrists and ankles.

Promising Jumper

Matching pants complete a smart twosome

Materials: 3 (25g) balls each for **Jumper and Briefs,** Patons Baby 4-ply, Courtelle. Pair each Nos 11, 10 and 9 needles. 1 stitch-holder. 3 buttons. Length of elastic for waist of Briefs.

Measurements: Jumper: To fit 18–20 in chest; length from top of shoulders, $9\frac{1}{2}$ in; sleeve seam, $5\frac{1}{2}$ in. **Briefs:** Length at centre front, $8\frac{1}{2}$ in.

Tension: 14 sts and 18 rows to 2 in over st st on No 10 needles.

JUMPER

FRONT

With No 11 needles, cast on 61 sts and work K1, P1 rib for 1 in, rows on right side having a K1 at each end, and ending with right side facing.

Change to No 9 needles and patt as follows: 1st row: K1, * (K1, P1) twice, K2; rep from * to end. 2nd row: * P3, K1, P2; rep from * to last st, P1. These 2 rows form patt.

Cont straight in patt until front measures $5\frac{1}{4}$ in, ending with right side facing. Keeping continuity of patt, shape raglans by casting off 3 sts at beg of next 2 rows. 1st row: K1, K2togtbl, patt to last 3 sts, K2tog, K1. 2nd row: K1, P1, patt to last 2 sts, P1, K1. 3rd row: K2, patt to last 2 sts, K2. 4th row: K1, P1, patt to last 2 sts, P1, K1. Rep last 4 rows 3 times more, then 1st and 2nd rows only until 33 sts rem, ending with right side facing.

Shape neck: Next row: K1, K2togtbl, patt 10, turn and leave rem sts on stitch-holder. Cont on these sts for first side as follows: Next row: Patt to last 2 sts, P1, K1. Next row: K1, K2togtbl, patt to last 2 sts, K2tog. Rep last 2 rows until 4 sts rem, ending with right side facing. Next row: K1, K2togtbl, patt 1. Next row: Patt 1, P1, K1. Next row: K1, K2togtbl. Next row: P1, K1. K2tog and fasten off.

With right side facing, slip centre 7 sts on a length of yarn, rejoin yarn to rem sts and finish to correspond with first side, reversing shapings and working tog in place of togtbl at raglan edge.

BACK

Work as for front until 45 sts rem in raglan shaping, ending with right side facing.

Divide for back opening: Next row: K1, K2togtbl, patt 18, K3, turn and leave rem sts on stitch-holder. 1st row: K3, patt to last 2 sts, P1, K1. 2nd row: K1, K2togtbl, patt to last 3 sts, K3. Rep last 2 rows until 19 sts rem, ending with right side facing.

Make a buttonhole in next row thus: K1, K2togtbl, patt to last 3 sts, yf, K2tog, K1. Rep 1st and 2nd rows 4 times, then 1st row again.

Make a buttonhole in next row as before. Rep 1st and 2nd rows twice more, then 1st row again: 11 sts. Leave sts on a safety-pin.

With right ride facing, rejoin yarn to rem sts, cast on 3 for underflap, K these 3 sts, patt to last 3 sts, K2tog, K1. Finish to correspond with first side, reversing shapings, working tog in place of togtbl and omitting buttonholes.

SLEEVES

With No 11 needles, cast on 34 sts and work K1, P1 rib for 1 in, inc 3 sts evenly across on last row: 37 sts.

Change to No 9 needles and patt as follows: 1st row: K1, * P1, K3, P1, K1; rep from * to end. 2nd row: K1, * P5, K1; rep from * to end. These 2 rows form patt. Cont in patt, shaping sides by inc 1 st at each end of 9th and every foll 12th row, until there are 43 sts, taking inc sts into patt. Work a few rows straight until sleeve seam measures $5\frac{1}{2}$ in, ending with right side facing.

Shape raglans by casting off 3 sts at beg of next 2 rows. 1st row: K1, K2togtbl, patt to last 3 sts, K2tog, K1. 2nd row: K1, P1, patt to last 2 sts, P1, K1. 3rd row: K2, patt to last 2 sts, K2. 4th row: K1, P1, patt to last 2 sts, P1, K1.

Rep last 4 rows 5 times more, then 1st and 2nd rows only until 5 sts rem, ending with right side facing. Leave sts on a safety-pin.

TO MAKE UP

Observing general method on page 81, block and press. Join side, sleeve seams and raglans. With right side facing and

No 11 needles, start at top of back opening and work thus: K11 from safety-pin, K5 from sleeve, knit up 17 down left side of neck, K7 sts from centre inc 2 sts, knit up 17 up right side, K5 sleeve sts, then K11 from safety-pin: 75 sts. Work in rib. 1st row: K3, P1, * K1, P1; rep from * to last 3 sts, K3. 2nd row: K4, * P1, K1; rep from * to last 3 sts, K3. Rep last 2 rows once more then 1st row again.

Work a buttonhole in next row, then work 1st row again. Cast off. Catch down cast-on st for underflap at base of opening.

Press seams. Sew on buttons.

BRIEFS

FRONT

With No 11 needles, cast on 72 sts and work K1, P1 rib for 1 in.

Change to No 10 needles and st st, starting with a K row, and work straight until front measures 6¾ in, ending with right side facing.

Shape crutch by casting off 4 sts at beg of next 10 rows, then dec 1 st at each end of every row until 20 sts rem. Work 5 rows straight. Cast off.

BACK

With No 11 needles, cast on 72 sts and work K1, P1 rib for 1 in.

Change to No 10 needles and work 2 rows st st, starting with a K row.

Shape Back: 1st row: K66, turn. 2nd row: Sl 1, P59, turn. 3rd row: Sl 1, K53, turn. Cont in this way, working 6 sts less on every row until the row 'Sl1, P23, turn' has been worked. Next row: Sl 1, K to end. Cont in st st across all sts until back matches front at side edge, ending with right side facing. Shape crutch by dec 1 st at each end of every row until 20 sts rem. Work 5 rows straight. Cast off.

TO MAKE UP

Observing general method on page 81, block and press. Join side seams.

Leg Bands: With right side facing and No 11 needles, knit up 68 sts all round each leg. Work K1, P1 rib for 1½ in. Cast off in rib.

Join crutch and leg bands. Fold waist and leg ribbing in half to wrong side and slip-hem loosely in position, leaving an opening at waist for elastic; insert elastic, join ends, sew up opening. Press seams.

Peta Piper Picked a Poncho

In crochet, with hood, mitts, and pompons

Materials: Poncho: 6 (25g) balls; **Hat and Mitts:** 1 (25g) ball each, Patons Baby 4-ply, Courtelle. Nos 3·50 mm and 3·00 mm crochet hooks. 1 button.

Measurements: Poncho: To fit 18–20 in chest; length at centre front, 10 in.

Tension: 10 sts and 5 rows to 2 in on No 3·50 hook, over patt.

PONCHO

BACK AND FRONT (both alike)

With No 3·50 hook, start at neck edge by making 54 ch.

1st row: (wrong side): 1dc in 2nd ch from hook, 1dc in each ch to end, turn: 53 sts. 2nd row: 2ch, miss first st, * 1ch, miss next st, 1htr in next st; rep from * to end. 3rd row: 1dc in first st, * 1dc in ch sp, 1dc in next st; rep from *, ending 1dc in turning ch.

4th row: 2ch, miss 2 sts, * 4tr in next st, miss 1 st, 1tr in next st, miss 1 st; rep from * to last 3 sts, 4tr in next st, miss 1 st, 1tr in last st, turn with 2ch.

5th row: * 4tr into centre sp of 4tr of previous row, miss 2 sts, 1tr in next st; rep from * 5 times more, 8tr into centre sp of 4tr of previous row, ** miss 2 sts, 1tr in next st, 4tr into centre sp of 4tr of previous row; rep from ** to last 3 sts, miss 2 sts, 1tr in last st, turn with 2ch.

6th row: * 4tr into centre sp of 4tr of

previous row, miss 2 sts, 1tr in next st; rep from * 5 times more, 4tr into sp between 2nd and 3rd tr of previous row, 1tr into sp between 4th and 5th tr of previous row, 4tr into sp between 6th and 7th tr of previous row, ** miss 2 sts, 1tr in next st, 4tr into centre sp between 4tr of previous row; rep from ** to last 3 sts, miss 2 sts, 1tr in last st, turn with 2ch.

7th row: * 4tr into centre sp of 4tr of previous row, miss 2 sts, 1tr in next st; rep from * 5 times more, 4tr into centre sp of 4tr of previous row, miss 2 sts, 6tr in next st, ** 4tr into centre sp of 4tr of previous row, miss 2 sts, 1tr in next st; rep from ** to end, turn with 2ch.

8th row: * 4tr into centre sp of 4tr of previous row, miss 2 sts, 1tr in next st; rep from * 6 times more, 4tr into centre sp of 6tr of previous row, ** miss 2 sts, 1tr in next st, 4tr into centre sp of 4tr of previous row; rep from ** to last 3 sts, miss 2 sts, 1tr in last st, turn with 2ch.

9th, 10th and 11th rows: As 5th, 6th and 7th, but working patt rep 6 times more in place of 5.

12th, 13th, 14th and 15th rows: As 8th, 5th, 6th and 7th, but working patt rep 7 times more.

16th, 17th, 18th and 19th rows: As 8th, 5th, 6th and 7th, but working patt rep 8 times more.

20th, 21st, 22nd and 23rd rows: As 8th, 5th, 6th and 7th, but working patt rep 9 times more.

24th row: As 8th, but working patt rep 10 times more and omitting turning ch. Fasten off.

TO MAKE UP

Observing general method on page 81, block and press.

Join side seams. Make a twisted cord, thread through holes at neck and tie at centre front. Make 2 pompons and sew to ends of cord. Cut rem yarn into 6 in lengths and taking 3 strands tog, knot all round lower edge to form fringe as described in Chapter 8. Press seams.

HAT

With No 3·50 hook, make 82ch.

1st row: (right side), 1dc in 2nd ch from hook, 1dc in each ch to end, turn with 1ch: 81 sts.

2nd row: Miss first dc, * 1dc in next dc; rep from * to end, turn with 1ch. 3rd row: Miss first dc, * 1dc in next dc; rep from * to last 4 sts, 2ch, miss 1dc, 1dc in each of next 3dc, turn with 1ch. 4th row: As 2nd, working 1dc in 2ch sp. 5th row: As 2nd, omitting turning ch.

6th row: Ss over 10 sts, 2ch, miss first dc, * miss 1dc, 4tr in next dc, miss 1dc, 1tr in next st; rep from * 14 times more, turn with 2ch.

7th row: * 4tr into centre sp of 4tr of previous row, miss 2 sts, 1tr in next st; rep from * to end, turn with 2ch.

Rep last row until work measures 5½ in from start, ending with right side facing, omitting turning ch on last row.

Next row: Ss over 10 sts, 2ch, (4tr into centre sp of 4tr of previous row, miss 2 sts, 1tr in next st) 11 times, turn.

Next row: Ss over 10 sts, 2ch, (4tr into centre sp of 4tr of previous row, miss 2 sts, 1tr in next st) 7 times, turn.

Next row: Ss over 10 sts, 2ch, (4tr into centre sp of 4tr of previous row, miss 2 sts, 1tr in next st) 3 times. Fasten off.

TO MAKE UP

Observing general method on page 81, press.

Join back seam. With No 3·00 hook, work 2 rows dc all round neck edge. Sew on button to correspond with buttonhole. Press seam.

MITTS

With No 3·50 hook, make 19ch, turn.

1st row: (right side), 1dc in 2nd ch from hook, * 1dc in next ch; rep from * to end, turn with 1ch: 18 sts.

2nd row: 2dc in first dc, 1dc in each of next 7dc, (2dc in next dc) twice, 1dc in each of next 7dc, 2dc in last dc, turn with 1ch: 22 sts.

3rd row: 1dc in each dc to end, turn with 1ch. 4th row: 2dc in first dc, 1dc in each of next 9dc, (2dc in next dc) twice, 1dc in each of next 9dc, 2dc in last dc, turn with 1ch: 26 sts. 5th row: As 3rd.

6th row: 2dc in first dc, 1dc in each of next 11dc, (2dc in next dc) twice, 1dc in each of next 11dc, 2dc in last dc, turn with 1ch: 30 sts. 7th row: As 3rd. Rep last row until work measures 2½ in from start, ending with right side facing.

Next row: 1dc in each of next 14dc, miss 1dc, * 1dc in next st; rep from * to end, turn with 3ch: 29 sts.

Next row: * Miss first 2dc, 1htr in next dc, * 1ch, miss 1dc, 1htr in next dc; rep from * to end, turn with 1ch.

Next row: 1dc in each st to end, turn with 2ch. Next row: Miss first dc, * miss next dc, 4tr in next dc, miss 1dc, 1tr in next st; rep from * to end, turn with 2ch. Next row: * 4tr into centre sp of 4tr of previous row, miss 2 sts, 1tr in next st; rep from * to end, turn with 2ch. Rep last row once more, omitting turning ch. Fasten off.

TO MAKE UP

Observing general method on page 81, press.

Join seam. Make a twisted cord and thread through holes at wrist and tie at front. Make 2 small pompons and sew to ends of cord.

For to Take the Air

Raglan coat and leggings for the first two years
(Instructions for Faithful Teddy are in Chapter 17)

Materials: Coat: 3 (50g) balls; **Leggings:** 3 (50g) balls Patons Purple Heather 4-ply. Pair each Nos 12 and 10 needles. 1 stitch-holder. 5 buttons. Length of elastic for waist.

Measurements: Coat: To fit 20–22in chest; length from top of shoulders, 14 in; sleeve seam, 6 in. **Leggings:** centre front seam, 9 in; leg seam, 7 in.

Tension: 14 sts and 18 rows to 2 in over st st on No 10 needles.

COAT (Boy's Version)
BACK
With No 10 needles, cast on 117 sts and work 7 rows in garter st (every row K).

Cont in patt as follows: 1st row: K.

2nd row: P. 3rd row: * K2, yf, K2tog; rep from * to last st, K1. 4th row: P. These 4 rows form patt. Rep them 17 times more. Next row: (K1, K2tog) 17 times, (K2tog) 6 times, (K2tog, K1) 18 times: 76 sts. Next row: P.

Change to No 12 needles and work 6 rows K1, P1 rib.

Change to No 10 needles and st st, starting with a K row, and shape raglans by casting off 2 sts at beg of next 2 rows. Next row: K1, K2togtbl, K to last 3 sts, K2tog, K1. Work 3 rows straight.

Cont dec as before but on next and every alt row until 24 sts rem, ending with right side facing. Cast off.

LEFT FRONT

With No 10 needles, cast on 63 sts and work 7 rows in garter st.

Cont in patt as follows: 1st row: K. 2nd row: K6, P57. 3rd row: * K2, yf, K2tog; rep from * to last 7 sts, K7. 4th row: K6, P57. Rep these 4 rows 17 times more. Next row: (K1, K2tog) 7 times, (K2tog) 6 times, (K2tog, K1) 8 times, K6: 42 sts. Next row: K6, P to end.

Change to No 12 needles. 1st row: * K1, P1; rep from * to last 6 sts, K6. 2nd row: K6, * K1, P1; rep from * to end. 3rd and 4th rows: As 1st and 2nd. Next row (Buttonhole row): * K1, P1; rep from * to last 6 sts, K1, K2tog, yf, K3. 6th row: As 2nd.

Change to No 10 needles and st st, starting with a K row, shape raglan by casting off 2 sts at beg of next row. Work 1 row straight. Next row: K1, K2togtbl, K to end. Next row: K6, P to end. Work 2 rows straight. Next row: K1, K2togtbl, K to end. Next row: K6, P to end. Rep last 2 rows once more.

Work a buttonhole: Next row: K1, K2togtbl, K to last 5 sts, K2tog, yf, K3. Next row: K6, P to end.

Cont shaping raglan as before and work 8 rows. Rep last 10 rows twice more. Next row: K1, K2togtbl, K to last 5 sts, K2tog, yf, K3. Next row: K6, P to end. Next row: K1, K2togtbl, K to end. Next row: K6, P to end. Next row: K1, K2togtbl, K to end: 19 sts.

Shape neck by casting off 9 sts at beg of next row. Dec 1 st at raglan edge as before on next and every alt row, and at the same time dec 1 st at neck edge on every row until 2 sts rem. Next row: P2, turn, K2tog and fasten off.

RIGHT FRONT

Work to correspond with Left Front omitting buttonholes and reversing shapings, working K2tog in place of K2togtbl.

SLEEVES

With No 10 needles, cast on 34 sts and work 15 rows K1, P1 rib. Next row: Inc in first 2 sts, (inc in next st, P1) 15 times, inc in last 2 sts: 53 sts. Cont in patt as for back until sleeve seam measures 6 in, ending with wrong side facing. Inc 1 st at each end of next row: 55 sts.

Shape raglan top by casting off 2 sts at beg of next 2 rows. Next row: K1, K2togtbl, K to last 3 sts, K2tog, K1. Work 3 rows straight. Cont dec as before, but on next and every alt row until 5 sts rem, ending with right side facing. Next row: K1, sl 1, K2tog, psso, K1. Next row: P. Cast off.

COLLAR

With No 10 needles, cast on 73 sts. 1st row: K2, * P1, K1; rep from * to last st, K1. 2nd row: * K1, P1; rep from * to last st, K1. 3rd row: K1, M1P, rib to last st, M1P, K1. 4th to 6th row: K1, rib to last st, K1. 7th row: K1, M1K, rib to last st, M1K, K1. 8th to 10th row: K1, rib to last st, K1. Cont inc 1 st at each end of next and every foll 4th row as before, until collar measures 2 in at centre. Cast off.

COAT (Girl's Version)

As for Boy's Version, but working buttonholes on Right Front.

TO MAKE UP

Observing general method on page 81, block and press. Join raglan, side and sleeve seams. Sew collar in position from centre of right front band to centre of left front band. Press seams. Sew on buttons.

LEGGINGS
RIGHT LEG
**With No 10 needles, cast on 72 sts.
1st row: K2, * P1, K1; rep from * to end. 2nd to 4th row: As 1st. 5th row: K2, * yf, K2tog, P1, K1; rep from * to last 2 sts, yf, K2tog. Rep 1st row 7 times more.
Slipping first st on every row throughout, cont as follows: 1st row: K5, turn. 2nd and every alt row: K to end. 3rd row: K10, turn. 5th row: K15, turn. Cont thus until the row 'K50, turn' has been worked. Next row: K to end. Cont in garter st inc 1 st at each end of 7th and every foll 8th row until there are 92 sts. Cont straight until work measures 9 in along short side. Place a marker at each end. Dec 1 st at each end of next and every foll 3rd row until 56 sts rem, then every foll 6th row until 46 sts rem. Work straight until leg measures 7 in down centre from marker, ending with right side facing.**
Shape foot: 1st row: K41, turn. 2nd row: K16, turn: 16 sts. Work 38 rows in garter st on these 16 sts. Next row: K2togtbl, K12, K2tog. Next row: K2togtbl, K10, K2tog. Break yarn and leave rem sts on stitch-holder.
Rejoin yarn to inside edge of 25 sts which were left and work as follows: Knit up 17 sts along side of foot, K12 sts from stitch-holder, knit up 17 sts along other side of foot, K5 sts on needle: 76 sts.
Work 9 rows in garter st. Next row: K7, K2tog, K2, K2tog, K32, K2tog, K2, K2tog, K25. Next row: K. Next row: K6, K2tog, K2, K2tog, K30, K2tog, K2, K2tog, K24. Next 2 rows: K. Cast off rem sts.

LEFT LEG
Work as for right leg from ** to **.
Next row: K. Finish to correspond with left foot, reversing shapings.

TO MAKE UP
Observing general method on page 81, block and press. Join front, back and inside leg and foot seams. Cut elastic to fit waist, thread through holes at waist ribbing and join ends. Press seams.

With Cables and Raglans

Chunky cardigan in two sizes up to three years
(Instructions for the woolly ball are given in Chapter 17)

Materials: 4/5 (25g) balls Patons Baby 4-ply, Courtelle. Pair each Nos 9 and 11 needles. 5 buttons. Cable needle.

Measurements: To fit 18–20/21–23 in chest; length from top of shoulders, 9½/10½ in; sleeve seam, 5½/6½ in.

Tension: 16 sts and 17 rows to 2 in over st st on No 9 needles.

Additional Abbreviations (see page 29): C4=slip next 2 sts on cable needle to front of work, K2, then K2 from cable needle.

BACK
With No 11 needles, cast on 64/70 sts and work K1, P1 rib for 1 in.
Next row: Rib 2/5, M1, * rib 4, M1; rep from * to last 2/5 sts, rib 2/5: 80/86 sts.
Change to No 9 needles and patt as follows: 1st row: P2, * K2, yf, K2tog, P2; rep from * to end. 2nd row: K2, * P2, yrn, P2tog, K2; rep from * to end. 3rd to 6th row: Rep 1st and 2nd rows twice. 7th row: P2, * C4, P2; rep from * to end. 8th row: As 2nd.
These 8 rows form patt. Cont straight in patt until Back measures 5/5½ in, ending with right side facing.
Shape raglans by casting off 3 sts at beg of next 2 rows. Next row: K1, K2tog, patt to last 3 sts, K2togtbl, K1. Next row: K1, P1, patt to last 2 sts, P1, K1. Rep last 2 rows until 42/44 sts rem. Next row: K1, P2togtbl, patt to last 3

sts, P2tog, K1. Next row: K1, K2tog, patt to last 3 sts, K2togtbl, K1. Rep last 2 rows until 24/26 sts rem. Cast off.

LEFT FRONT

With No 11 needles, cast on 30/34 sts and work K1, P1 rib for 1 in. Next row: Rib 5/3, M1, * rib 3, M1; rep from * to last 4 sts, rib 4: 38/44 sts. Change to No 9 needles and patt as for back until front matches back at side edge, ending with right side facing.

Shape raglan and neck: Cast off 3 sts at beg of next row. 1st row: Patt to last 2 sts, P1, K1. 2nd row: K1, K2tog, patt to last 2 sts, K2tog. Cont dec 1 st at raglan edge on every alt row, and at the same time dec 1 st at neck edge on every foll 4th/3rd row until 12 sts rem, ending with right side facing. Next row: K1, K2tog, patt to end. Next row: patt to last 3 sts, P2tog, K1. Rep last 2 rows until 2 sts rem, K2tog and fasten off.

RIGHT FRONT

Work to correspond with left front, reversing shapings and working togtbl in place of tog.

SLEEVES

With No 11 needles, cast on 32/34 sts and work K1, P1 rib for 1 in. Next row: Rib 5/2, M1, * rib 2, M1; rep from * to last 5/2 sts, rib 5/2: 44/50 sts.

Change to No 9 needles and patt as for back, shaping sides by inc 1 st at each end of 5th/3rd and every foll 5th/7th row, until there are 56/62 sts, taking inc

sts into patt. Work a few rows straight until sleeve seam measures $5\frac{1}{2}$/$6\frac{1}{2}$ in, ending with right side facing.

Shape raglans by casting off 3 sts at beg of next 2 rows. Next row: K1, K2tog, patt to last 3 sts, K2togtbl, K1. Next row: K1, P1, patt to last 2 sts, P1, K1. Rep last 2 rows until 14/18 sts rem.

Next row: K1, P2togtbl, patt to last 3 sts, P2tog, K1. Next row: K1, K2tog, patt to last 3 sts, K2togtbl, K1. Rep last 2 rows until 4 sts rem. Cast off.

TO MAKE UP

Observing general method on page 81, block and press. Join raglan, side and sleeve seams.

FRONT BANDS

Left: With No 11 needles, cast on 7 sts and work in rib.

1st row: K2, P1, K1, P1, K2. 2nd row: * K1, P1; rep from * to last st, K1. Rep these 2 rows until strip fits up front edge to centre back, when slightly stretched. Sew in position as you go along. Cast off.

Right: Work as for left band with the addition of 5 buttonholes, first to come $\frac{1}{4}$ in up from lower edge, fifth $\frac{1}{4}$ in down from start of neck shaping and rem 3 spaced evenly.

First mark position of buttons on left front with pins to ensure even spacing, then work buttonholes to correspond thus: Rib 3, yf, work 2tog, rib 2. Join bands at centre back. Press seams. Sew on buttons.

Here we come a-tasselling

In this cosy cap and scarf

Materials: 5 (25g) balls Patons Baby 4-ply, Courtelle. Pair each Nos 10 and 8 needles. No 3·00 mm crochet hook.

Measurements: Hat: To fit 3–7 years

Scarf: 5 × 48 in (approx).

Tension: 13 sts and 17 rows to 2 in over st st on No 8 needles.

Additional Abbreviations (see page 29): P1B=purl into next st but through loop of row below, at the same time slipping st above off needle.

HAT

With No 10 needles, cast on 96 sts and

work K1, P1 rib for 2 in, inc 1 st in centre of last row: 97 sts.

Change to No 8 needles and work in patt, noting that 1st row of patt is wrong side of work. 1st to 8th row: K. 9th row: K1, * P1B, K1; rep from * to end. 10th row: K2, * P1B, K1; rep from * to last st, K1. 11th to 16th row: As 9th and 10th, 3 times. These 16 rows form patt. Rep them twice more, dec 1 st at end of last row: 96 sts.

Shape top: 1st row: (K10, K2tog) 8 times. 2nd and every alt row: K. 3rd row: (K9, K2tog) 8 times. 5th row: (K8, K2tog) 8 times. Cont dec in this way until the row '(K1, K2tog) 8 times' has been worked: 16 sts. Next row: (K2tog) 8 times. Break yarn and thread through rem sts, draw up tightly and fasten off.

SCARF

With No 10 needles, cast on 3 sts and K 1 row. Next row: K1, K three times in next st by working into front, back and front of it, K1.

Continue shaping point: 1st and every alt row: K. 2nd row: K1, K twice in next st, K to last 2 sts, K twice in next st, K1. Rep last 2 rows until there are 31 sts, ending with 1st row.

Change to No 8 needles and starting with 9th patt row, rep the 16 patt rows as for hat until scarf measures approx 46 in from point, ending with 16th patt row.

Change to No 10 needles and shape point: 1st row: K. 2nd row: K1, K2tog, K to last 3 sts, K2tog, K1. Rep these 2 rows until 5 sts rem. Work 1 row straight. Next row: K2tog, K1, K2tog. Cast off.

TO MAKE UP

Observing general method on page 81, press.

Hat: With crochet hook, using yarn double, make a 1 in long ch and sew one end to top of hat. With 7 in lengths of yarn, make a tassel and sew to other end.

Scarf: With 8 in lengths of yarn, make 2 tassels, and sew one to each end of scarf.

Lining up the Favourite

Classic raglan cardigan with contrast edgings in four sizes up to nine years

Materials: 3/4/4/5 (50g) balls in Main Shade and 1/1/1/1 (50g) ball Light, Patons Purple Heather 4-ply. Pair each Nos 10 and 12 needles. 5/5/6/6 buttons. 3 stitch-holders.

Measurements: To fit 22/24/26/28 in chest; length from top of shoulders, 12½/14/15½/17 in; sleeve seam, 7/8½/10/11½ in.

Tension: 14 sts and 18 rows to 2 in over st st on No 10 needles.

Additional Abbreviations (see page 29): M=Main Shade; L=Light.

BACK

** With No 12 needles and M, cast on 82/88/96/102 sts and work K1, P1 rib in stripes of 2 rows M, 2 rows L for 10 rows. Break L.**

Change to No 10 needles and M, starting with a K row work straight in st st until back measures 7½/8½/9½/10½ in at centre, ending with a P row.

Shape raglans by casting off 3 sts at beg of next 2 rows. Next row: K2, K2togtbl, K to last 4 sts, K2tog, K2. Next row: P. Rep last 2 rows until 34/36/38/40 sts rem, ending with right side facing.

Next row: K2, K2togtbl, K to last 4 sts, K2tog, K2. Next row: P2, P2tog, P to last 4 sts, P2togtbl, P2. Rep last 2 rows once more: 26/28/30/32 sts.

Change to No 12 needles, join in L and work 10 rows striped rib as for lower edge. With M, cast off in rib.

LOWER POCKET LININGS (2)

With No 10 needles and M, cast on 23/**24**/28/**29** sts and starting with a P row, work 1**7**/**17**/21/**21** rows st st. Leave sts on a spare needle.

BREAST POCKET LINING

With No 10 needles and M, cast on 14/16/16/**18** sts and work 16/**16**/18/**18** rows st st. Leave sts on a spare needle.

LEFT FRONT

With No 12 needles and M, cast on 40/**44**/48/**50** sts and work as for back from ** to **.

Change to No 10 needles. Next row: K,

inc 1 st at centre on 1st and 4th sizes only: 41/**44**/48/**51** sts. Work a further 17/**17**/21/**21** rows st st.

Place Pocket: Next row: K9/**10**/10/**11**, slip next 23/**24**/28/**29** sts on a stitch-holder and in place of these K across sts of one pocket lining, K9/**10**/10/**11**. Work straight until front matches back at side edge, ending with right side facing.

Shape raglan and front edge as follows: 1st row: Cast off 3, K to last 2 sts, K2tog. 2nd row: P. 3rd row: K2, K2togtbl, K to end. 4th row: P. 5th row: K2, K2togtbl, K to last 2 sts, K2tog. Rep rows 2 to 5 incl 1/**1**/2/**2** times more, then 2nd row again: 31/**34**/35/**38** sts.

Place breast pocket: Next row: K2, K2togtbl, K2, slip next 14/**16**/16/**18** sts on a stitch-holder and in place of these, K across sts of breast pocket lining, K to end. Cont dec 1 st at raglan edge as before on every alt row, and at the same time dec 1 st at neck edge on foll alt row, then on every 4th row until 4/**4**/5/**5** sts rem.

3rd and 4th sizes only: Work 1 more dec at raglan edge, ending with wrong side facing.

All sizes: Keeping front edge straight, dec 1 st at raglan edge on every row until all sts are worked off.

RIGHT FRONT

Work to correspond with left front, reversing shapings and omitting breast pocket. When shaping raglan work 'K2tog, K2'.

SLEEVES

With No 12 needles and M, cast on 42/**44**/46/**48** sts and work as for back from ** to **. Change to No 10 needles and M, starting with a K row, work in st st, shaping sides by inc 1 st at each end of 3rd and every foll 6th/**6th**/7th/**7th** row until there are 58/**62**/66/**70** sts. Work straight until sleeve seam measures 7/

8½/**10**/**11½** in, ending with right side facing.

Shape raglans by casting off 3 sts at beg of next 2 rows. Work 0/**0**/2/**2** rows straight. Next row: K2, K2togtbl, K to last 4 sts, K2tog, K2. Next row: P. Rep last 2 rows until 6 sts rem, ending with a P row. Leave sts on a safety-pin.

TO MAKE UP

Observing general method on page 81, block and press. Join front raglan seams. Left Border: With right side facing, No 12 needles and M, start at top of left sleeve and K 6 sts from safety-pin, knit up 40/**44**/48/**52** sts down left front slope, then 60/**68**/76/**84** sts down to lower edge: 106/**118**/130/**142** sts.

Work 1 row K1, P1 rib in M, then join in L and rib 2 rows.

Work next 2 rows in M, making button-holes thus: rib 49/**53**/55/**62**, (cast off 3, rib 10/**12**/11/**12**) 4/**4**/5/**5** times, cast off 3, rib to end and back, casting on 3 over those cast off. Cont in rib and work 2 rows L, 2 rows M. Cast off in rib in M. Right Border: Starting at lower edge, work to correspond with left border, omitting buttonholes.

Pocket Tops: With right side facing, No 12 needles and M, work across 23/**24**/28/**29** sts on lower pockets thus: K2/**1**/3/**2**, inc in next st, (K8/**6**/6/**11**, inc in next st) 2/**3**/3/**2** times, K2/**1**/3/**2**: 26/**28**/32/**32** sts. Cont in K1, P1 rib in stripes, 1 row M, 2 rows L, 2 rows M, 2 rows L, 1 row M. Cast off in rib in M.

With right side facing, No 12 needles and M, work across 14/**16**/16/**18** breast pocket sts thus: K3/**3**/3/**4**, inc in next st, K6/**8**/8/**8**, inc in next st, K3/**3**/3/**4**: 16/**18**/18/**20** sts. Finish as for lower pocket tops.

Catch down Pocket Linings lightly on wrong side and sides of Pocket Tops neatly on right side. Join back raglan seams, then join ribbed borders. Join side and sleeve seams. Press seams. Sew on buttons.

Chapter 12
Family Life
Growing Up

From starting school up to the early teens the classic line in handknits is the most rewarding, particularly in double or double double knitting yarns which are robust, warm, and knit up quickly. As well as variations on the classic sweater and cardigan, this group includes sports and outdoor wear, not forgetting cold weather specialities such as the perennially popular bobble cap and balaclava.

Gradus ad Parnassum

The classic raglan sweater in double knitting with V or round neck in a range of sizes up to big school age

V NECK VERSION

Materials: 5/5/6/**7** (50g) balls Patons Double Knitting. Pair each Nos 10 and 8 needles. Set of 4 No 10 needles with points at both ends.

Measurements: To fit 24/26/28/**30** in chest; length from top of shoulders, 14¾/16½/17¾/**19** in; sleeve seam, 10½/12½/14/**15½** in.

Tension: 11 sts and 15 rows to 2 in over st st on No 8 needles.

FRONT

With No 10 needles, cast on 68/74/80/**86** sts. Work K1, P1 rib for 2¼/2¼/2½/**2½** in.
Change to No 8 needles and st st until work measures 8¾/10/10¾/**11½** in from start, ending with a P row.
Shape raglans by casting off 2/3/3/**4** sts at beg of next 2 rows.**

Cont to shape raglan and divide for V neck as follows: Next row: K2tog, K30/**32**/35/**37,** turn. Next row: P.
Work on this group of sts, dec 1 st at raglan edge on next and every alt row, at the same time dec 1 st at neck edge on next and every foll 4th row until 5/**4**/4/**6** sts rem.
Cont without further dec at neck edge but still dec at raglan edge as before until 1 st rem. Work 1 row. Fasten off.
Rejoin yarn to rem sts and complete to match first half, reversing all shapings.

BACK

Work as front to **. Dec 1 st at each end of next and every alt row until 20/**22**/24/**24** sts rem. Work 1 row. Cast off.

SLEEVES

With No 10 needles, cast on 34/36/38/**40** sts. Work K1, P1 rib for 2¼/2¼/2½/2½ in. Next row: Rib 3/**4**/5/**6**, (inc in next st, rib 3) 7 times, inc in next st, rib to end: 42/**44**/46/**48** sts.

Change to No 8 needles and st st, inc 1 st at each end of 5th/**3rd**/5th/**5th** and every foll 9th/**10th**/9th/**9th** row until there are 54/**58**/64/**70** sts. Cont on these sts until work measures 10½/**12½**/14/**15½** in from start, ending with a P row.
Shape top by casting off 2/3/3/**4** sts at beg of next 2 rows. Dec 1 st at each end of next and every alt row until 6/6/8/**8** sts rem. Work 1 row. Cast off.

MAKE UP AND NECKBAND

Observing general method on page 81, block and press. Join side and sleeve seams. Insert sleeves.
With set of No 10 needles and right side facing, knit up 126/**134**/142/**150** sts round neck, incl 1 st from centre V by picking up loop at centre V and knitting into back of it. Work 6/**7**/7/**8** rounds in K1, P1 rib, dec 1 st at each side of st knitted up at centre V on every rnd. Cast off loosely in rib. Press seams.

ROUND NECK VERSION

Materials: 4/5/6/**7** (50g) balls Patons Double Knitting. Pair each Nos 10 and 8 needles. Set of 4 No 10 needles with points at both ends. 2 stitch-holders.

Measurements: To fit 24/26/28/**30** in chest; length at centre back 14½/**16**/18/**19½** in; sleeve seam 9/**10**/12/**13½** in.

Tension: 11 sts and 15 rows to 2 in over st st on No 8 needles.

BACK

With No 10 needles, cast on 72/**78**/82/**88** sts. Work K1, P1 rib for 2/2¼/2¼/2½ in. Change to No 8 needles and st st until work measures 8½/**9½**/11/**12** in from start, ending with a P row.
Shape raglans: 1st and 2nd rows: Cast off 1, work to end. 3rd row: K2, K2togtbl, K to last 4 sts, K2tog, K2.
4th row: K2, P to last 2 sts, K2. Rep

3rd and 4th rows until 24/**26**/28/**30** sts rem, ending with a 4th row. Slip sts on to a stitch-holder.

FRONT

Work as back until 40/**44**/46/**50** sts rem at raglan shaping, ending with a 4th row.

Shape neck: Next row: K2, K2togtbl, K22/**24**/26/**28**, slip the last 12/**12**/14/**14** of these sts on to a stitch-holder and leave, K to last 4 sts, K2tog, K2.

Work on each group of sts thus: Dec 1 st at neck edge on next and every alt row until 5/**6**/6/**7** dec have been worked at neck edge, at the same time cont dec at raglan edge on every alt row as before until 1 st rem, noting that when 3 sts rem raglan dec will be worked at raglan edge. Work 1 row. Fasten off.

SLEEVES

With No 10 needles, cast on 34/**36**/38/**40** sts. Work K1, P1 rib for 2/**2¼**/2¼/**2½** in. Next row: Rib 1/**2**/3/**2**, (inc in next st, rib 5/**5**/5/**6**) 5 times, inc in next st, rib to end: 40/**42**/44/**46** sts.

Change to No 8 needles and st st, inc 1 st at each end of 3rd/**3rd**/5th/**5th** row and every foll 7th/**7th**/8th/**8th** row until there are 54/**58**/60/**64** sts. Cont on these sts until work measures 9/**10**/12/**13½** in from start, ending with a P row.

Shape top by working 1st to 4th row of raglan shaping as on back, then rep 3rd and 4th rows until 6 sts rem, ending with a 4th row. Cast off.

MAKE UP AND NECKBAND

Observing general method on page 81, block and press. Join side and sleeve seams. Insert sleeves.

With right side facing, using set of No 10 needles, knit up 86/**92**/96/**102** sts round neck, incl sts from stitch-holder. Work in rnds of K1, P1 rib for 1½/**2**/2/**2½** in. Cast off in rib.

Fold neckband at centre to wrong side and flat-stitch cast-off edge to knitted-up edge to form a double band. Press seams.

Never too Many

The basic raglan cardigan in 4-ply weight, so suitable for school – with V or button-up neck in a range of sizes

Materials: Button-through Version: 4/**4**/5/**5** (50g) balls; **V Neck Version:** 4/**4**/5/**5** (50g) balls Patons Purple Heather 4-ply. Pair each Nos 12 and 10 needles. 8/**9**/9/**10** buttons for Button-through Version; 5/**6**/6/**6** buttons for V Neck Version.

Measurements: To fit chest 24/**26**/28/**30** in; length from top of shoulders, 14/**15**/16½/**18** in; sleeve seam, 11/**12½**/13¾/**15½** in (adjustable).

Tension: 14 sts and 18 rows to 2 in over st st on No 10 needles.

BUTTON-THROUGH VERSION

RIGHT FRONT

With No 12 needles, cast on 38/**40**/44/ 48 sts. Work 23/**25**/27/**29** rows K1, P1 rib. Next row: Rib 3/**3**/3/**3**, (inc next st, rib 9/**7**/8/**9**) 3/**4**/4/**4** times, inc in next st, rib to end: 42/**45**/49/**53** sts.

Change to No 10 needles and st st until work measures 8/**8½**/9½/**10½** in from start, ending at side edge.

Shape raglan: 1st row: Cast off 3/**3**/4/**5**, P to end. 2nd row: K to last 3 sts, K2tog, K1. 3rd row: K1, P to end. Rep 2nd and 3rd rows 21/**23**/25/**27** times more: 17/**18**/19/**20** sts.

Shape neck: Next row: Cast off 7/**8**/9/ **10**, K to last 3 sts, K2tog, K1. Dec 1 st at neck edge on next 4 rows, at the same time cont dec at armhole edge on every alt row as before until 1 st rem. Work 0/**0**/0/**1** row.
Fasten off.

LEFT FRONT

Work to match right front reversing all shapings, noting that togtbl in place of tog will be worked at raglan edge.

BACK

With No 12 needles, cast on 78/**84**/92/**100** sts. Work 23/**25**/27/**29** rows, K1, P1 rib. Next row: Rib 5/**5**/6/**7**, (inc in next st, rib 10/**11**/12/**13**) 6 times, inc in next st, rib to end: 85/**91**/99/**107** sts. Change to No 10 needles and st st until work measures same as right front to raglan shaping, ending with a P row.

Shape raglans: 1st and 2nd rows: Cast off 3/**3**/4/**5**, work to end. 3rd row: K1, K2togtbl, K to last 3 sts, K2tog, K1. 4th row: K1, P to last st, K1. Rep 3rd and 4th rows 25/**27**/29/**31** times more, then 3rd row once: 25/**27**/29/**31** sts. Work 0/**0**/0/**1** row. Cast off.

SLEEVES

With No 12 needles, cast on 44/**46**/48/**50** sts. Work 23/**25**/27/**29** rows K1, P1 rib. Next row: Rib 1/**2**/3/**4**, (inc in next st, rib 9) 4 times, inc in next st, rib to end: 49/**51**/53/**55** sts.

Change to No 10 needles and st st, inc 1 st at each end of 9th/**9th**/3rd/**1st** row and every foll 7th/**8th**/8th/**8th** row until there are 67/**71**/77/**83** sts. Cont on these sts until work measures 11/**12½**/13¾/**15½** in from start, ending with a P row (adjust length here).

Shape top by working 1st to 4th row of raglan shaping as on back. Rep 3rd and 4th rows 25/**27**/29/**31** times more, then 3rd row once: 7 sts. Work 0/**0**/0/**1** row. Cast off.

RIGHT FRONT BAND

With No 12 needles, cast on 9 sts. 1st row: K2, (P1, K1) 3 times, K1. 2nd row: (K1, P1) 4 times, K1.

1st, 2nd and 3rd sizes only: Rep 1st and 2nd rows once more.

All sizes: Next row: Rib 3, cast off 3, rib to end. Next row: Rib 3, cast on 3, rib to end.

Cont in rib, working a buttonhole as on last 2 rows on every 17th and 18th/**17th and 18th**/19th and 20th/**19th and 20th** rows from previous buttonhole,

until 7/**8**/8/**9** buttonholes in all have been worked. Work 13/**13**/15/**15** rows. Slip these sts on to a safety-pin.

LEFT FRONT BAND

Omitting buttonholes, work to match right front band, working 1 row less.

MAKE UP AND NECKBAND

Observing general method on page 81, block and press. Join side and sleeve seams and insert sleeves.

Slip 9 sts from right front band on to No 12 needle, using the same needle with right side facing, knit up 75/**79**/83/**89** sts round neck, rib across sts on left front band: 93/**97**/101/**107** sts. 1st row: * K1, P1; rep from * to last st, K1. 2nd row: K2, * P1, K1; rep from * to last st, K1. Work 5 more rows in rib, working a buttonhole as before on 2nd and 3rd rows. Cast off in rib. Stitch on front bands. Press seams. Sew on buttons.

V NECK VERSION
RIGHT FRONT

Work as right front of button-through version to raglan shaping, ending with a P row.

Shape front slope and raglan: 1st row: K2tog, K to end. 2nd row: Cast off 3/**3**/4/**5**, P to end. 3rd row: K to last 3 sts, K2tog, K1. 4th row: K1, P to end.

Cont dec 1 st at raglan edge on next and every alt row as before, at the same time dec 1 st at front edge on next and every foll 4th row until 23/**26**/29/**32** sts rem, every 5th row until 6/**5**/5/**4** sts rem. Cont dec at raglan edge only until 1 st rem. Work 0/**0**/0/**1** row. Fasten off.

LEFT FRONT

Work to match right front, reversing all shapings, noting that togtbl in place of tog will be worked at raglan edge.

BACK AND SLEEVES

Work as button-through version.

FRONT BAND

With No 12 needles, cast on 9 sts. 1st row: K2, (P1, K1) 3 times, K1. 2nd row: (K1, P1) 4 times, K1. Rep 1st and

152

2nd rows twice more. Next row: Rib 3, cast off 3, rib to end. Next row: Rib 3, cast on 3, rib to end. Cont in rib, working a buttonhole as on last 2 rows on every 17th and 18th/**15th and 16th**/ 17th and 18th/**19th and 20th** rows from previous buttonhole until 5/6/6/6 buttonholes in all have been worked. Cont in rib without further buttonholes until

work measures $31\frac{1}{2}$/**34**/$37\frac{1}{2}$/**40$\frac{1}{2}$** in from start. Cast off in rib.

TO MAKE UP
Observing general method on page 81, block and press.
Join side and sleeve seams and insert sleeves. Stitch on front band.
Press seams. Sew on buttons.

The Same but More So

Another basic raglan cardigan but this time in double knitting

Materials: V Neck Version: 5/5/7/7 (50g) balls; **Button-through Version:** 5/6/7/8 (50g) balls Patons Double Knitting. Pair each Nos 10 and 8 needles. 5 buttons for V Neck Version and 6 buttons for Button-through Version.

Measurements: To fit 24/26/28/**30** in chest; length at centre back, 15/**16½**/18/**19½** in; sleeve seam, 9/**10½**/12/**13** in.

Tension: 11 sts and 15 rows to 2 in over st st on No 8 needles.

V NECK VERSION

BACK
With No 10 needles, cast on 72/**78**/82/**88** sts and work K1, P1 rib for 1½/**1½**/1½/**2** in. Change to No 8 needles and work in st st, starting with a K row until back measures 9/**10**/11/**12** in, ending with right side facing.

Shape raglans by casting off 4 sts at beg of next 2 rows. Next row: K1, K2tog, K to last 3 sts, K2togtbl, K1. Work 3 rows straight. Rep the last 4 rows until 54/**60**/64/**70** sts rem, ending with a dec row. Work 1 row. Next row: K1, K2tog, K to last 3 sts, K2togtbl, K1. Next row: P. Rep last 2 rows until 24/**26**/26/**28** sts rem, ending with right side facing. Cast off.

POCKET LININGS (2)
With No 8 needles, cast on 17/**17**/22/**22** sts and work 3/3/4/4 in st st, ending with right side facing. Leave sts on a length of yarn.

LEFT FRONT
** With No 10 needles, cast on 36/**38**/40/**44** sts and work K1, P1 rib for 1½/**1½**/1½/**2** in, inc 0/**1**/1/**0** st at end of last row: 36/**39**/41/**44** sts.

Change to No 8 needles and work straight in st st, starting with a K row until front measures 4½/4½/5½/6 in, ending with right side facing.

Place Pocket: Next row: K11/**12**/11/**12**, slip next 17/**17**/22/**22** sts on to a length of yarn and leave, with right side facing, slip sts of pocket lining on to left-hand needle, K across these sts, K to end.

Cont straight in st st until front matches

back at side edge, ending with right side facing.**

Shape raglan and neck: Next row: Cast off 4, K to last 2 sts, K2tog. Next row: P. Next row: K1, K2tog, K to end. Work 3 rows straight. Next row: K1, K2tog, K to last 2 sts, K2tog.

Cont dec 1 st at neck edge on every foll 6th row, at the same time, cont dec 1 st at raglan edge as before on every foll 4th row until 23/**26**/28/**31** sts rem. Work 1 row.

Now dec 1 st at raglan edge as before on next and every alt row, at the same time, dec 1 st at neck edge on every 4th row from previous dec until 5/5/7/7 sts rem. Keeping neck edge straight, cont dec 1 st at raglan edge on every alt row as before, until 2 sts rem. Next row: P. K2tog and fasten off.

RIGHT FRONT
Work to correspond with left front reversing all shapings and working togtbl in place of tog at raglan edge and placing pocket as follows: Next row: K8/**10**/8/**10**, slip next 17/**17**/22/**22** sts on to a length of yarn and leave, with right side facing slip sts of pocket lining on to left-hand needle, K across these sts, K to end.

POCKET TOPS
With right side facing and No 10 needles, K across sts of pocket tops as follows: Next row: K3/3/3/3, M1, * K4, M1; rep from * to last 2/**2**/3/**3** sts, K2/**2**/3/3: 21/**21**/27/**27** sts.

Work ¾ in rib as for Front Borders, starting with a 2nd row. Cast off in rib.

Sew pocket linings in position on wrong side, pocket tops on right side.

SLEEVES
With No 10 needles, cast on 36/**38**/40/**42** sts and work K1, P1 rib for 1/1½/2/2 in.

Change to No 8 needles and work in st st, starting with a K row, inc 1 st at each end of 5th/**3rd**/9th/**9th** row and every foll 5th/**6th**/6th/**7th** row until there are 56/**58**/60/**62** sts.

Work straight until sleeve seam measures 9/**10½**/12/**13** in, ending with right side facing (adjust length here).

Shape raglan top by casting off 4 sts at beg of next 2 rows. Next row: K1, K2tog, K to last 3 sts, K2togtbl, K1. Work 3 rows straight. Rep the last 4 rows until 40 sts remain, ending with a dec row. Work 1 row. Next row: K1, K2tog, K to last 3 sts, K2togtbl, K1. Next row: P.

Rep last 2 rows until 6 sts rem, ending with right side facing. Cast off.

TO MAKE UP

Observing general method on page 81, block and press.

Join raglan, side, and sleeve seams.

FRONT BORDER

With No 10 needles, cast on 9 sts and work in rib as follows: 1st row: K2, * P1, K1; rep from * to last st, K1. 2nd row: * K1, P1; rep from * to last st, K1. Rep these 2 rows once more.

Make a buttonhole in next 2 rows as follows:

Rib 3, cast off 3, rib to end and back, casting on 3 over those cast off. Work a strip in rib to fit up right front to start of neck shaping when slightly stretched and working 4 more buttonholes—4th to come at start of neck shaping and rem 3 spaced evenly between. First mark position of buttons on left front to ensure even spacing, then work buttonholes to correspond.

Continue until strip fits all round neck and down left front when slightly stretched. Sew in position as you go along. Cast off. Press seams. Sew on buttons.

BUTTON-THROUGH VERSION

BACK AND POCKET LININGS

Work as V neck version.

LEFT FRONT

Work as v neck version from ** to **. Shape raglan by casting off 4 sts at beg of next row. Next row: P. Next row: K1, K2tog, K to end. Work 2 rows straight. Rep last 4 rows until 27/30/32/35 sts rem, ending with a dec row. Work 1 row. Next row: K1, K2tog, K

to end. Next row: P. Rep the last 2 rows until 20/21/22/23 sts rem, ending with right side facing.

Shape neck: Next row: K1, K2tog, K12/12/14/14, turn and leave rem sts on a safety-pin. Next row: P. Next row: K1, K2tog, K to last 2 sts, K2tog. Rep last 2 rows until 4 sts rem. Keeping neck edge straight, cont dec 1 st at raglan edge on every alt row as before until 2 sts rem. Next row: P. K2tog and fasten off.

RIGHT FRONT

Work to correspond with left front reversing all shapings, working togtbl in place of tog at raglan shaping and placing pocket as follows: Next row: K8/10/8/10, slip next 17/17/22/22 sts on to a length of yarn and leave, with right side facing slip sts of pocket lining on to left-hand needle, K across these sts, K to end.

POCKET TOPS AND SLEEVES

Work as for V neck version.

TO MAKE UP

As V neck version.

LEFT FRONT BORDER

With No 10 needles, cast on 9 sts. 1st row: K2, * P1, K1; rep from * to last st, K1. 2nd row: * K1, P1; rep from * to last st, K1. Rep these 2 rows until border fits up left front to start of neck shaping, ending with a 2nd row. Slip sts on to a safety-pin. Sew border in position.

RIGHT FRONT BORDER

Work as for Left Border, working 1 row more and leaving sts on needle, with the addition of 5 buttonholes, the first to come ½ in up from lower edge and last to come 2/2½/2½/3 in down from start of neck shaping and rem 3 spaced evenly between. First mark position of buttons on left front with pins to ensure even spacing, then work buttonholes to correspond. To work a buttonhole: 1st row: Rib 3, cast off 3, rib to end. 2nd row: Rib 3, cast on 3, rib to end.

NECKBAND

With same needle as for Right Front Border, with right side facing, K5/6/5/6 sts from safety-pin, knit up 13/13/15/15 up right side of neck, K 6 sleeve sts, knit up 23/25/25/27 across back, K 6 sleeve sts, knit up 13/13/15/15 down left side of neck, K5/6/5/6 from safety-pin, rib 9 border sts: 89/93/95/99 sts. Work 9 rows in rib, working a buttonhole as before in 4th and 5th rows.
Cast off in rib. Press seams. Sew on buttons.

Double it Again
A husky sports sweater in double double knitting

Materials: 4/5/5/6 (50g) balls each Dark and Medium; 1/1/1/1 (50g) ball each Contrast and Light Patons Doublet. Pair each Nos 8 and 5 needles.

Measurements: To fit 26/28/30/32 in chest; length from top of shoulders, 17/18½/20/21½ in; sleeve seam, 11/12½/14/15½ in.

Tension: 8½ sts and 10½ rows to 2 in over st st on No 5 needles.

Additional Abbreviations (see page 29): A=Dark; B=Light; C=Medium; D=Contrast.

BACK

** With No 8 needles and A, cast on 54/58/62/66 sts and work K1, P1 rib for 2 in, inc 4 sts evenly across on last row: 58/62/66/70 sts.
Change to No 5 needles and work straight in st st, starting with a K row, until back measures 7/8/9/10 in, ending with right side facing. Break A.
Cont in st st, working 22 rows in stripes as follows:
*** Join in B and work 6 rows. Break B. Join in C and work 6 rows. Leave C hanging. Join in D and work 6 rows. Break D. Work 4 rows in C. ***
Cont in C, shaping armholes by casting off 3 sts at beg of next 2 rows. Now dec 1 st at each end of every row until 48/52/52/56 sts rem, then on next and every alt row until 42/44/46/48 sts rem.**
Work straight until back measures 17/18½/20/21½ in, ending with right side facing.
Shape shoulders by casting off 3/4/4/5 sts at beg of next 2 rows, then 4 sts at beg of next 4 rows. Leave rem 20/20/22/22 sts on a spare needle.

FRONT

Work as for back from ** to **. Work straight until front measures 15/16½/18/19½ in, ending with right side facing.
Shape neck: Next row: K15/16/16/17, turn and leave rem sts on a spare needle. Cont on these sts for first side, dec 1 st at neck edge on next and every alt row, until 11/12/12/13 sts rem. Work a few rows straight until front matches back at armhole shaping, ending with right side facing.
Shape shoulder by casting off 3/4/4/5 sts at beg of next row, then 4 sts at beg of foll 2 alt rows.
With right side facing, slip centre 12/12/14/14 sts on a spare needle, rejoin yarn to rem sts and finish to correspond with first side, reversing shapings.

SLEEVES

With No 8 needles, and A, cast on 28/30/32/34 sts and work K1, P1 rib for 2 in, inc 2 sts evenly on last row: 30/32/34/36 sts.
Change to No 5 needles and st st, starting with a K row, shaping sides by inc 1 st at each end of 3rd/7th/5th/7th and every foll 9th/10th/10th/9th row, until there are 36/38/42/46 sts. Work 3/5/3/3 rows straight. Break A.

Cont in st st, working 22 rows in stripes as for back from *** to ***, and at the same time cont inc 1 st at each end of every foll 9th/**10th**/10th/**9th** row as before, until there are 40/**42**/46/**50** sts. Cont straight until the 22 rows of stripes have been completed.

Cont in C, shaping sleeve top by casting off 3 sts at beg of next 2 rows, then dec 1 st at each end of next and every alt row, until 16/**16**/20/**24** sts rem. Now dec 1 st at each end of foll 1/**1**/1/**3** rows: 14/**14**/18/**18** sts.
Cast off.

MAKE UP AND POLO NECK

Observing general method on page 81, block and press. Join right shoulder, side, and sleeve seams. With right side facing, No 8 needles and C, start at top of left shoulder on front and work thus: knit up 13 sts down left side of neck, K12/**12**/14/**14** from spare needle inc 1 st in centre, knit up 13 sts up right side, K20/**20**/22/**22** from spare needle inc 1 st in centre: 60/**60**/64/**64** sts. Work K1, P1 rib for 4½/**5**/5/**5½** in. Cast off evenly in rib. Join rem shoulder seam, then join polo. Insert sleeves. Press seams.

Knee-high to Smartness

These socks, knitted on four needles, are popular and practical

Materials: 2/2/3 (50g) balls Patons Purple Heather 4-ply. Set of 4 No 13 needles with points at both ends.

Measurements: Length of foot, 7½/8/8½ in; length from top to base of heel, 11/13/14½ in.

Tension: 17 sts and 21 rows to 2 in over st st on No 13 needles.

Cast on 66/72/78 sts, 21/24/27 sts on 1st needle; 24/24/24 sts on 2nd needle; and 21/24/27 sts on 3rd needle. Work in rnds of K1, P1 rib for 1 in.
Work in patt: 1st rnd: * K1, yf, K2tog; rep from * to end of rnd. 2nd rnd: * Sl 1 knitways, K1, psso, yf, K1; rep from * to end of rnd. These 2 rnds form patt. Cont in patt until work measures 3½/4½/5 in from start.
Shape leg: ** Next rnd: K1, K2tog, patt to last 3 sts, K1, K2tog. Keeping patt correct, work 12/13/14 rnds without shaping.** Work from ** to ** twice more: 60/66/72 sts. Cont without further shaping until work measures 8¼/10/11 in from start.
Divide for heel: K15/18/18 sts, slip last 15/18/18 sts of rnd on to the other end of same needle (these 30/36/36 sts are for heel). Divide rem sts on to 2 needles and leave for instep.
Start heel: 1st row: Sl 1 purlways, P to end. 2nd row: Sl 1 knitways, K to end.

Rep these 2 rows 10/11/15 times more, then 1st row once.
Turn heel: 1st row: K21/24/24 sts, sl 1, K1, psso, turn. 2nd row: P13, P2tog, turn. 3rd row: K13, sl 1, K1, psso, turn. Rep 2nd and 3rd rows 6/9/9 times more, then 2nd row once. Next row: K7 thus completing heel (7 sts rem unworked on left-hand needle). Slip all instep sts on to one needle.
Using spare needle K7 heel sts, knit up 12/13/17 sts along side of heel, using 2nd needle patt across instep sts, using 3rd needle knit up 12/13/17 sts along other side of heel, K7 heel sts: 68/70/84 sts.
Shape instep: 1st rnd: 1st needle: K; 2nd needle: patt all across; 3rd needle: K. 2nd rnd: 1st needle: K to last 3 sts, K2tog, K1; 2nd needle: patt all across; 3rd needle: K1, sl 1, K1, psso, K to end. Rep these 2 rnds until 58/58/70 sts rem. Cont on these sts until work measures 4¼/4½/4¾ in from where sts were knitted up at heel. Next rnd: 1st needle: K; 2nd needle: K1, sl 1, K1, psso, patt to last 3 sts, K2tog, K1; 3rd needle: K.
Shape toe: 1st rnd: 1st needle: K to last 3 sts, K2tog, K1; 2nd needle: K1, sl 1, K1, psso, K to last 3 sts, K2tog, K1; 3rd needle: K1, sl 1, K1, psso, K to end. 2nd rnd: K. Rep these 2 rnds until 24/24/28 sts rem, K sts from 1st needle on to end of 3rd needle. Graft sts or cast off sts from needles tog. Press.

Cricket Champion

Traditional cables for this double knitting sweater

Materials: 6/7/7 (50g) balls Patons Double Knitting. Pair each Nos 10 and 8 needles. Set of 4 No 10 needles with points at both end. Cable needle.

Measurements: To fit 26/28/30 in chest; length from top of shoulders, 16½/18/19 in; sleeve seam, 12½/13½/15 in.

Tension: 11 sts and 15 rows to 2 in over st st on No 8 needles.

Additional Abbreviations (see page 29): C4=cable 4 by working across next 8 sts thus: slip next 4 sts on to cable needle and leave at front of work, knit next 4 sts, then knit 4 sts from cable needle.

FRONT
With No 10 needles, cast on 66/70/76 sts. Work K1, P1 rib for 2½ in. Next

row: Rib 3/**5**/8, (inc in next st, rib 11) 5 times, inc in next st, rib to end: 72/**76**/82 sts.

Change to No 8 needles and work in cable panels as follows:
1st row: K9/**10**/11, * P2, K8, P2, K9 **10**/12 *; rep from * to * once, P2, K8, P2, K9/**10**/11. 2nd row: P9/**10**/11, * K2, P8, K2, P9/**10**/12 *; rep from * to * once, K2, P8, K2, P9/**10**/11. 3rd and 4th rows: As 1st and 2nd.
5th row: K9/**10**/11, * P2, C4, P2, K9/ **10**/12 *; rep from * to * once, P2, C4, P2, K9/**10**/11. 6th row: As 2nd. 7th to 12th row: Rep 1st and 2nd rows 3 times. These 12 rows form patt.

Cont in patt until work measures 11/ **12**/12½ in from start, ending with right side facing. Keeping patt correct, shape armholes by casting off 3/**4**/5 sts at beg of next 2 rows.**

Cont to shape armholes and divide for neck: Next row: K2tog, patt 31/**32**/34, turn. Cont in patt on this group of 32/ **33**/35 sts, dec 1 st at armhole edge on every row until 4 more dec (5 in all) have been worked at armhole edge, at the same time dec 1 st at neck edge on next and foll 3rd row: 26/**27**/29 sts.

Cont without further dec at armhole edge, but still dec at neck edge on every 3rd row from previous dec until 22/**23**/25 sts rem, then every foll 3rd/**4th**/4th row until 18/**19**/20 sts rem.

Cont on these sts until work measures 5½/ **6**/6½ in from start of armhole shaping, ending at armhole edge.

Shape shoulder: 1st row: Cast off 6/**6**/7 sts, patt to end. 2nd row: Patt all across. Rep these 2 rows once. Cast off. Rejoin yarn to sts on needle and complete to match first half.

BACK
Work as front until ** is reached.
Cont to shape armholes by dec 1 st at each end of every row until 56/**58**/62 sts rem. Cont on these sts until work measures same as front up to shoulder shaping. Shape shoulders by casting off

6/**6**/7 sts at beg of next 4 rows: 6/**7**/6 sts at beg. of foll 2 rows.
Cast off.

SLEEVES
With No 10 needles, cast on 34/**38**/42 sts. Work K1, P1 rib for 2½ in, inc 1 st at end of last row on 1st size only: 35/**38**/42 sts.
Next row: Rib 2/**4**/6 (inc in next st, rib 5) 5 times, inc in next st, rib to end: 41/ **44**/48 sts.

Change to No 8 needles and work in cable panels as follows:
1st row: K4/**5**/6, P2, K8, P2, K9/**10**/12, P2, K8, P2, K4/**5**/6. 2nd row: P4/**5**/6, K2, P8, K2, P9/**10**/12, K2, P8, K2, P4/ **5**/6. 3rd and 4th rows: As 1st and 2nd.
5th row: K4/**5**/6, P2, C4, P2, K9/**10**/12, P2, C4, P2, K4/**5**/6. 6th row: As 2nd. 7th to 12th row: Rep 1st and 2nd rows 3 times. These 12 rows form patt. Cont in patt inc 1 st at each end of next and every foll 9th/**9th**/10th row until there are 53/**58**/62 sts, working extra sts in st st. Cont on these sts until work measures 12½/**13½**/15 in from start.

Shape top by casting off 3 sts at beg of next 2 rows. Dec 1 st at each end of next and every alt row until 19/**22**/24 sts rem. Cast off 3/**4**/4 sts at beg. of next 4 rows.
Cast off.

MAKE UP AND NECKBAND
Observing general method on page 81, block and press.

Join shoulders of back and front. With set of No 10 needles and right side of work facing, starting at top of left shoulder knit up 42/**44**/46 sts along side of neck, knit up 1 st from centre V by picking up loop that lies at centre V and knitting into back of it, knit up 42/**44**/46 sts along other side of neck, finally knit up 21/**21**/23 sts across back of neck: 106/ **110**/116 sts. Dec 1 st at each side of centre st on every rnd, work 6 rnds in K1, P1 rib. Cast off loosely in rib. Join side and sleeve seams, insert sleeves. Press seams.

Ballet Class

Authentic hug-me-tight design, knitted in 4-ply

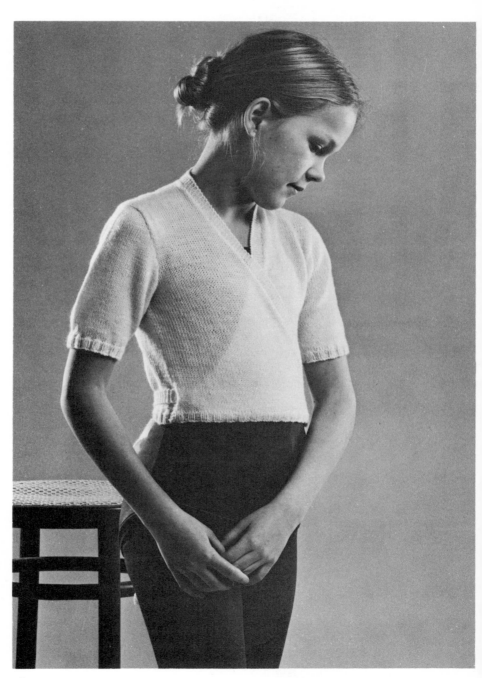

Materials: 3/4 (50g) balls Patons Purple Heather 4-ply. Pair each Nos 12 and 10 needles.

Measurements: To fit 26–28/30–32 in chest/bust; length from top of shoulders, 13½/17 in; sleeve seam, 4/5 in.

Tension: 14 sts and 18 rows to 2 in over st st on No 10 needles.

BACK

With No 12 needles, cast on 92/96 sts and work K2, P2 rib for ½/1 in.

1st size: Change to No 10 needles and work straight in st st until work measures 7 in.

2nd size: Change to No 10 needles and st st, inc 1 st at each end of 7th and every foll 6th row until there are 118 sts, then cont straight until work measures 10 in.

Both sizes: Shape armholes by casting off 4/5 sts at beg of next 2 rows, then K2tog at each end of next and every alt row until 72/90 sts rem. Work straight in st st until back measures 13/17 in.

Shape shoulders by casting off 9/10 sts at beg of next 6 rows.

Cast off.

FRONTS

1st size only

Left: With No 12 needles cast on 64 sts and work K2, P2 rib for ½ in.

Change to No 10 needles and st st, dec 1 st at front edge on 5th and every foll 4th row until side edge measures 7 in. Still dec at front edge on every 4th row, shape armhole by casting off 4 sts at beg of next row (side edge), then K2tog on every alt row at this edge 6 times in all. Now keep this edge straight and cont dec on every 4th row at front edge until 27 sts rem. Work straight until front matches back to shoulder shaping, ending at armhole edge. Shape shoulder by casting off 9 sts at beg of next 3 alt rows.

Right: Work to correspond with left front, reversing shapings.

2nd size only

Left: With No 12 needles cast on 72 sts and work P2, K2 rib for 1 in.

Change to No 10 needles and st st, inc 1 st at side edge on 7th and every foll 6th row 11 times in all, at the same time, dec 1 st at front edge on next and every foll 4th row 22 times.

Cont dec at front edge on every 3rd row, and when work measures 10 in, shape armhole by casting off 5 sts at beg of next row (side edge), then K2tog at same edge on every alt row 9 times. Keeping armhole edge straight, cont dec at front edge on every 3rd row until 30 sts rem. Work straight until front matches back, ending at armhole edge. Shape shoulder by casting off 10 sts at beg of next and foll 2 alt rows.

Right: Work to correspond with left front, reversing shapings.

SLEEVES

With No 12 needles, cast on 68/78 sts and work K2, P2 rib for ½/1 in.

Change to No 10 needles and st st, inc 1 st at each end of 7th/next and every foll 4th/4th row until there are 74/96 sts. Work straight until sleeve seam measures 4/5 in.

Shape top: Cast off 4/4 sts at beg of next 2/2 rows, then K2tog at each end of next and every alt row until 50/56 sts rem, then at each end of every row until 24/20 sts rem.

Cast off.

BAND

With No 12 needles, cast on 6/8 sts and work a strip in garter st long enough to go up left front, round back of neck and down right front when slightly stretched. Sew strip in position as you work, to ensure a good fit.

TIES (make 2)

With No 12 needles, cast on 8/8 sts and work in garter st for 26/28 in.

Cast off.

TO MAKE UP

Observing general method on page 81, block and press. Join side seams, leaving a small opening about 1 in from bottom on right side: join shoulder and sleeve seam; insert sleeves. Sew ties to front edge at waist.

Cold Comfort

Warm gloves and extra-warm mitts knitted on two needles

GLOVES

Materials: 2(50g) balls Patons Double Knitting. Pair each Nos 10 and 8 needles.

N.B.: To make the large size use No 9 needles in place of No 10 and No 7 in place of No 8.

Measurements: Width all round above thumb, 7/7½ in; length from lower edge to top of middle finger, 8/8½ in.

Tension: 11 sts and 15 rows to 2 in over st st on No 8 needles.

RIGHT GLOVE

With No 10 needles, cast on 36 sts. 1st row: K2, * P1, K1; rep from * to end. Cont in rib as on 1st row until work measures 1¾ in from start.

Change to No 8 needles and work thumb gusset: 1st row: K1, P2, (KB1, P3) 4 times, inc twice by knitting into front, back and front of next st, P1, K15. 2nd row: K1, P14, K1, P3, K3, (PB1, K3) 4 times. 3rd row: K1, P2, (KB1, P3) 4 times, K twice into each of next 2 sts, K1, P1, K15.

4th row: K1, P14, K1, P5, K3, (PB1, K3) 4 times. 5th row: K1, P2, (KB1, P3) 4 times, K twice into next st, K2, K twice into next st, K1, P1, K15. 6th row: K1, P14, K1, P7, K3, (PB1, K3) 4 times. 7th row: K1, P2, (KB1, P3) 4 times, inc in next st, K4, inc in next st, K1, P1, K15.

8th row: K1, P14, K1, P9, K3, (PB1, K3) 4 times. 9th row: K1, P2, (KB1, P3) 4 times, inc in next st, K6, inc in next st, K1, P1, K15. 10th row: K1, P14, K1, P11, K3, (PB1, K3) 4 times: 46 sts. Keeping patt and st st correct, work 4 rows without shaping.

Work Thumb: 1st row: patt 18, P1, K11, turn. 2nd row: K1, P10, cast on 2 sts, turn. 3rd row: K13. Work 13 rows in st st.

Shape top: 1st row: (K2tog) 6 times, K1. 2nd row: (P2tog) 3 times, P1. Break off yarn, thread through rem sts, draw up and fasten off securely.

With right side of work work facing, re-join yarn and knit up 3 sts from cast-on

sts at base of thumb, K across rem 16 sts on left-hand needle. Keeping patt and st st correct, work 11 rows.

First Finger: 1st row: K26, turn. 2nd row: K1, P10, cast on 1. Work 16 rows on these 12 sts. Shape top: 1st row: (K2tog) 6 times. 2nd row: (P2tog) 3 times. Fasten off as thumb.

Second Finger: Knit up 2 sts from base of first finger, K across 4 sts from left-hand needle, turn. Next row: K1, P11, cast on 1. Work 18 rows. Next row: (K2tog) 6 times, K1. Next row: (P2tog) 3 times, P1. Fasten off as thumb.

Third Finger: Knit up 2 sts from base of 2nd finger, K across 4 sts from left-hand needle, turn. Next row: K1, P10, cast on 1. Work 16 rows. Complete as first finger.

Fourth Finger: Knit up 1 st from base of 3rd finger, K rem 4 sts on left-hand needle. Next row: K1, P7, K1. Work 14 rows. Next row: (K2tog) 4 times, K1. Next row: (P2tog) twice, P1. Fasten off as thumb.

LEFT GLOVE

Work ribbing as for right glove. Change to No 8 needles: 1st row: K15, P1, inc twice in next st, (P3, KB1) 4 times, P2, K1. 2nd row: (K3, PB1) 4 times, K3, P3, K1, P14, K1. Complete to match right glove noting that the extra sts are cast on for thumb and fingers at end of first row in place of 2nd row.

TO MAKE UP

Observing general method on page 81, block and press. Join thumb, finger, and side seams. Press seams.

MITTS

Materials: 2 (50g) balls Patons Doublet. Pair each Nos 5 and 8 needles.

Measurements: Width all round above thumb, 6½ in; length, 8 in.

Tension: 8½ sts and 10½ rows to 2 in over st st on No 5 needles.

RIGHT MITT

With No 8 needles, cast on 26 sts and work K1, P1 rib for 2 in.

Change to No 5 needles and work diamond patt and shapings as follows: 1st row: K13, P1, K1, P1, K10. 2nd row: P10, K1, P1, K1, P13. 3rd row: (K6, P1) twice, inc twice in next st (by knitting into front, back and front of it), P1, K10: 28 sts. 4th row: P10, K1, P3, K1, P5, K1, P1, K1, P5. 5th row: K4, P1, K3, P1, K4, P1, inc in next st, K1, inc in next st, P1, K10: 30 sts.

6th row: P10, K1, P5, K1, P3, K1, P5, K1, P3. 7th row: K4, P1, K3, P1, K4, P1, inc in next st, K3, inc in next st, P1, K10: 32 sts. 8th row: P10, K1, P7, K1, P5, K1, P1, K1, P5. 9th row: K6, P1, K6, P1, inc in next st, K5, inc in next st, P1, K10: 34 sts. 10th row: P10, K1, P9, K1, P5, K1, P1, K1, P5. 11th row: K4, P1, K3, P1, K4, P1, K9, P1, K10. 12th row: P10, K1, P9, K1, P3, K1, P5, K1, P3.

Divide for thumb: 1st row: K4, P1, K3, P1, K4, P1, K9, turn. 2nd row: P9, cast on 2. Work 8 rows st st on these 11 sts. Shape top: Next row: K2tog, (K1, K2tog) 3 times: 7 sts. Next row: P1, (P2tog, P1) twice: 5 sts. Break yarn, thread through rem sts, draw up tightly and fasten off.

With right side facing knit up 3 sts from base of thumb, K across rem 11 sts. Next row: P20, K1, P1, K1, P5.

Cont straight on these 28 sts, keeping diamond patt correct until 3 diamonds in all have been worked, then cont in st st until work measures $7\frac{1}{2}$ in from start, ending with right side facing.

Shape top: 1st row: K1, K2togtbl, K8, K2tog, K2, K2togtbl, K8, K2tog, K1. 2nd row: P1, P2tog, P6, P2togtbl, P2, P2tog, P6, P2togtbl, P1. 3rd row: K1, K2togtbl, K4, K2tog, K2, K2togtbl, K4, K2tog, K1. Cast off.

LEFT MITT

Work rib as for right mitt. Change to No 5 needles: 1st row: K10, P1, K1, P1, K13. 2nd row: P13, K1, P1, K1, P10. 3rd row: K10, P1, inc twice in next st, (P1, K6) twice. 4th row: P5, K1, P1, K1, P5, K1, P3, K1, P10.

Complete to match Right Mitt reversing shaping and noting that 2 sts at base of thumb are cast on at end of first division row in place of second.

TO MAKE UP

Observing general method on page 81, press. Join thumb, side and top. Press seams.

Cosy in Crochet

This beanie and scarf are warm with a dash of fashion, too

Materials: Hat: 1 (50g) ball; **Scarf:** 4 (50g) balls Patons Double Knitting. No 4·00 mm crochet hook.

Measurements: Hat: To fit child 8 to 10 yrs. **Scarf:** Width 6 in; length approx 56 in.

Tension: 11 sts to 2 in over patt.

HAT

Make 4ch and join into ring with ss. 1st rnd: 1ch, 12dc into ring, join with ss to first dc. 2nd rnd: 3ch, 1tr in 1st st, 2tr in each foll st, join with ss to top of ch: 24 sts (starting ch counts as 1st st). 3rd rnd: 3ch, 1tr in each of next 2 sts, * 2tr in next st, 1tr in next st; rep from * to end, join with ss to top of ch: 36 sts. 4th rnd: 3ch, 1tr in each of next 3 sts, * 2tr in next st, 1tr in each of next 2 sts; rep from * to end, join with ss to top of ch: 48 sts. 5th rnd: 3ch, 1tr in each of next 4 sts, * 2tr in next st, 1tr in each of next 3 sts; rep from * to end, join with ss to top of ch: 60 sts. 6th rnd: 3ch, 1tr in each of next 5 sts, * 2tr in next st, 1tr in each of next 4 sts; rep from * to end, join with ss to top of ch: 72 sts.

Work in patt as follows: 7th rnd: 1dc in 1st st, * 3ch, miss 2 sts, 1dc in next st; rep from * to last 2 sts; 3ch, miss 2 sts, join with ss to 1st dc: 96 sts. 8th rnd: Ss into 1st ch sp, 3ch, 2tr in this ch sp, * 1ch, 3tr in next ch sp; rep from * to end, 1ch, join with ss to top of ch. 9th rnd: Work 1dc back into last ch sp of previous rnd, * 3ch, 1dc in next ch sp; rep from *, ending 3ch, ss in 1st dc. Rep 8th and 9th rnds 5 times more, then 8th rnd again.

Next rnd: Work 1dc back into last ch sp of previous rnd, * 2ch, 3tr in next ch sp, 2ch, 1dc in next ch sp, 2ch, 1dc in next ch sp; rep from *, but ending last rep ss in 1st dc. Fasten off.

SCARF

Start at centre by making 26ch. Next row: 1dc in 2nd ch from hook, 1dc in each foll ch, turn with 1ch: 25 sts.

Work in patt. Foundation row: 1dc in 1st st, * 3ch, miss 2 sts, 1dc in next st; rep from * to end, turn with 3ch: 33 sts. 1st row: Right side facing, 3tr in 1st ch sp, * 1ch, 3tr in next ch sp; rep from * to end, 1tr in last dc, turn with 1ch. 2nd row: 1dc in sp between 1st and 2nd tr, * 3ch, 1dc in next ch sp; rep from *, ending last rep 1dc in sp between last tr and turning ch, turn with 3ch. Rep 1st and 2nd rows until work measures approx 28 in, ending with a 1st patt row. Fasten off.

With wrong side facing, work foundation row along starting ch (using free ch loops to work into), then finish to correspond with 1st side.

Observing general method on page 81, press.

Fringes: Cut yarn into 10 in lengths and using 6 strands tog each time, knot a fringe into each ch sp at short edges as described in Chapter 8.

Wild Weather Chums

Winter sport and play demand a bobble cap and a balaclava

BOBBLE CAP

Materials: 2 (50g) balls Patons Double Knitting. Pair No 8 needles.

Measurements: Width all round lower edge (not stretched), 15 in.

Tension: 11 sts and 15 rows to 2 in over st st on No 8 needles.

Cast on 110 sts and work K1, P1 rib for 7 in, ending with wrong side facing for next row, dec 1 st at beg of last row: 109 sts.

Shape Crown: 1st row: P2tog, * (K1, P1) 4 times, K1, sl 2, K1, P2sso; rep from * to last 11 sts, (K1, P1) 4 times, K1, P2tog. 2nd row: (K1, P1) 5 times, * P2, (K1, P1) 4 times; rep from * to last st, K1. 3rd row: (P1, K1) 5 times, * K2, (K1, P1) 4 times; rep from * to last st, P1.

4th row: As 2nd. 5th row: K2tog, * (P1, K1) 3 times, P1, sl 2, K1, P2sso; rep from * to last 9 sts, (P1, K1) 3 times, P1, K2tog. 6th row: * P1, K1; rep from * to last st, P1. 7th row: * K1, P1; rep from * to last st, K1. 8th row: As 6th.

9th row: P2tog, * (K1, P1) twice, K1, sl 2, K1, P2sso; rep from * to last 7 sts, (K1, P1) twice, K1, P2tog. 10th row: (K1, P1) 3 times, * P2, (K1, P1) twice; rep from * to last st, K1. 11th row: (P1, K1) 3 times, * K2, (P1, K1) twice; rep from * to last st, P1. 12th row: As 10th. 13th row: K2tog, * P1, K1, P1, sl 2, K1, P2sso; rep from * to last 5 sts, P1, K1, P1, K2tog. 14th row: As 6th. 15th row: P2tog, * K1, sl 2, K1, P2sso; rep from * to last 3 sts, K1, P2tog. 16th row: P1, * P2tog; rep from * to end. Thread yarn through rem sts and fasten off securely.

TO MAKE UP

Observing general method on page 81, press. Join seam, taking care to reverse seam for turn up at lower edge. Press seam. Make a pompon and attach to centre of crown.

BALACLAVA

Materials: 2/2 (50g) balls Patons Double Knitting. Pair No 8 needles.

Measurements: To fit 8 to 10 years/ 12 years upwards.

Tension: 11 sts and 15 rows to 2 in over st st on No 8 needles.

Starting at neckband, cast on 68/70 sts loosely.
Work in rib: 1st row: K2, * P1, K1; rep from * to end. Rep 1st row 19/21 times. Next row: Rib to last 11/12 sts, slip these 11/12 sts on to a safety-pin. Next row: Rib to last 11/12 sts, slip these 11/12 sts on to a safety-pin: 46 sts.
Small size: Next row: K6, (inc in next st, K2) 11 times, inc in next st, K to

end: 58 sts. Large size: Next row: K2 (inc in next st, K2) 13 times, inc in next st, K to end: 60 sts.
Both sizes: Starting with a P row, work in st st until work measures 9½/10 in, from start, ending with a P row.
Shape top: 1st row: K36/38, sl 1, K1, psso, turn. 2nd row: P15/17, P2tog, turn. 3rd row: K15/17, sl 1, K1, psso, turn. Work 2nd and 3rd rows 19 times more, then 2nd row once: 16/18 sts. Break yarn.
With right side of work facing, slip 11/12 sts left on 2nd safety-pin on to a needle, rejoin yarn and using same needle, knit up 34/38 sts along side of balaclava, knit across 16/18 sts on needle, knit up 34/38 sts along other side, rib across 11/12 sts from first safety-pin: 106/118 sts. Next row: K2, * P1, K1; rep from * to end. Rep this row 5 times. Cast off in rib.

TO MAKE UP

Observing general method on page 81, press. Join ribbing tog to form neck-band. Press seam.

Chapter 13

Family Life
The Breadwinners

In the modern family, teamwork is everything; husbands and wives both go out to work and share the home jobs, too, whether it be cooking boeuf stroganoff or papering the spare room. It is hardly surprising, then, that they should wish to dress as a team. Knitting or crochet makes it particularly easy for them to do this because sizes and colours are so much easier to mix and match. All the designs in this group except two are equally suitable for him or her and the styling is intended to be basic rather than in passing fashion.

Casually Classic

Decoratively ribbed, this round-necked raglan sweater is in double knitting

Materials: 11/**11**/12/**12**/13/**13** (50g) balls Patons Double Knitting. Pair each Nos 10 and 8 needles. Set of 4 No 12 needles with points at both ends. 1 stitch-holder.

Measurements: To fit 34/**36**/38/**40**/42/**44** in bust; length from top of shoulders, 22/**22½**/23½/**24**/25/**25½** in; sleeve seam, 16½/**16½**/16½/**17**/17/**17** in.

Tension: 11 sts and 15 rows to 2 in over st st on No 8 needles.

BACK

With No 10 needles, cast on 98/**104**/110/**116**/122/**128** sts and work in K1, P1 rib for 2 in. Next row: Rib 9/7/11/**12**/11/**16**, M1, (rib 20/**18**/22/**23**/25/**32**, M1) 4/**5**/4/**4**/4/**3** times, rib 9/7/11/**12**/11/**16**: 103/**110**/115/**121**/127/**132** sts.

Change to No 8 needles and work in lace rib patt as follows:
1st, 3rd and 5th sizes only: 1st row: P/o/1/2, * K3, P2, yon, K2togtbl, K1, P2; rep from * to last 3/4/5 sts, K3, P/o/1/2. 2nd row: K/o/1/2, * P3, K2; rep from * to last 3/4/5 sts, P3, K/o/1/2. 3rd row: P/o/1/2, * K3, P2, K1, K2tog, yrn, P2; rep from * to last 3/4/5/ sts, K3, P/o/1/2. 4th row: As 2nd. These 4 rows form patt.
2nd, 4th and 6th sizes only: 1st row: * K2, P2, yon, K2togtbl, K1, P2, K2; rep from * to end. 2nd row: * P2, K2, P3, K2, P2; rep from * to end. 3rd row: * K2, P2, K1, K2tog, yrn, P2, K2; rep from * to end. 4th row: As 2nd. These 4 rows form patt.

All sizes: Cont in patt until back measures 13/**13**/13½/**13½**/14/**14** in, ending with wrong side facing.

Shape raglans: ** Next row: Cast off 3/**4**/3/**3**/3/**3** sts. P4 incl st on needle, patt to last 7/**8**/7/**7**/7/**7** sts, P4 cast off rem sts. Break yarn.
Rejoin yarn and cont shaping raglans:

1st row: K4, patt to last 4 sts, K4. 2nd row: P4, patt to last 4 sts, P4. 3rd row: K1, K3tog, patt to last 4 sts, sl 1, K2tog, psso, K1. 4th row: P4, patt to last 4 sts, P4.**
Rep 1st to 4th row until 33/**34**/37/**39**/41/**42** sts rem, ending with a 3rd shaping row. Work 7 rows on these sts. Leave these sts on a spare needle.

FRONT

Work as for back until 45/**46**/49/**51**/53/**54** sts rem in raglan shaping, ending with a 3rd shaping row.
Divide for neck: Next row: P4, patt 12, turn and leave rem sts on a spare needle.
Cont on sts for first half as follows: Still dec at raglan edge as before, at the same time cast off at neck edge on next and foll alt rows, 3 sts twice, 2 sts once, 1 st once: 3 sts. Next row: P. Next row: K. Next row: P. Next row: K3tog. Fasten off.
With wrong side facing, slip centre 13/**14**/17/**19**/21/**22** sts on stitch-holder, rejoin yarn to rem sts, work to end. Complete to match first half, reversing shapings.

SLEEVES

With No 10 needles, cast on 54/**56**/58/**60**/62/**64** sts and work K1, P1 rib for 2 in. Next row: Rib 3/**5**/5/**3**/3/**5**, M1, (rib 6/**5**/6/**6**/7/**6**, M1) 8/**9**/8/**9**/8/**9** times, rib 3/**6**/5/**3**/3/**5**: 63/**66**/67/**70**/71/**74** sts.
Change to No 8 needles and work in patt as follows:
1st, 3rd and 5th sizes only: 1st row: o/P2/K2, P2, * K3, P2, yon, K2togtbl, K1, P2; rep from * to last 3/5/7 sts, K3/K3, P2/K3, P2, K2. 2nd row: o/K2/P2, K2, * P3, K2; rep from * to last 3/5/7 sts, P3/P3, K2/P3, K2, P2. 3rd row: o/P2/K2, P2, * K3, P2, K1, K2tog, yrn, P2; rep from * to last 3/5/7 sts, K3/K3, P2/K3, P2, K2. 4th row: As 2nd.

171

2nd, 4th and 6th sizes only: 1st row: 0/K2/P2, K2, * K2, P2, yon, K2togtbl, K1, P2, K2; rep from * to last 0/2/4 sts, 0/K2/K2, P2. 2nd row: 0/P2/K2, P2, * P2, K2, P3, K2, P2; rep from * to last 0/2/4 sts, 0/P2/P2, K2. 3rd row: 0/K2/P2, K2, * K2, P2, K1, K2tog, yrn, P2, K2; rep from * to last 0/2/4 sts, 0/K2/K2, P2. 4th row: As 2nd.

All sizes: Cont in lace rib patt, shaping sides by inc 1 st at each end of 5th/**3rd**/5th/**5th**/next/**next** and every foll 9th/**8th**/7th/**7th**/7th/**7th** row until there are 85/**90**/93/**96**/101/**104** sts, taking inc sts into lace rib patt.
Cont straight until sleeve seam measures 16½/**16½**/16½/**17**/17/**17** in, ending with wrong side facing. Work as back from ** to **, then rep 1st to 4th row until 15/**14**/15/**14**/15/**14** sts rem, ending with a 3rd shaping row.
1st Sleeve: Next row: Cast off 8/**7**/8/**7**

8/**7** sts, patt to end. Slip rem 7 sts on a safety-pin.
2nd Sleeve: Next row: Patt 7, slip these 7 sts on a safety-pin, cast off rem sts.

TO MAKE UP
Observing general method on page 81, block and press.
Join raglans, matching shapings and stitching 7 rows at top of back to cast-off sts at top of sleeve, join side and sleeve seams. Press seams.
Collar: With right side facing, and set of No 12 needles, starting at left sleeve, K7 sts from sleeve, knit up 16 sts down left side of neck, K13/**14**/17/**19**/21/**22** from front dec 1 st in centre on 4th size only, knit up 16 up right side of neck, K7 from right sleeve, 33/**34**/37/**39**/41/**42** from back inc 2/**4**/2/**3**/2/**4** sts evenly: 94/**98**/102/**106**/110/**114** sts.
Work in rnds of K1, P1 rib for 2½ in. Cast off evenly in rib.

Essence of Cardigan

Here is fundamental simplicity which can be knitted with a V or button-up neck in six sizes

Materials: V Neck Version: 9/**10**/11/11/**12**/12 (50g) balls; **Button-through Version:** 10/**11**/11/**12**/12/**13** (50g) balls, Patons Double Knitting. Pair each Nos 10 and 8 needles. 5 buttons for V Neck Version; 8 buttons and 1 press-stud for Button-through Version.

Measurements: To fit 32/**34**/36/**38**/40/**42** in bust/chest; length from top of shoulders, 23½/**24**/24½/**25**/25½/**26** in; sleeve seam, 16/**16**/16½/**16½**/17/**17½** in.

Tension: 11 sts and 15 rows to 2 in over st st on No 8 needles.

V NECK VERSION
BACK
With No 10 needles, cast on 90/**96**/102/**108**/114/**120** sts. Work K1, P1 rib for 1½ in. Change to No 8 needles and st st until work measures 14¼ in from start, ending with a K row.

Shape raglans: ** Next row: Cast off 3/**3**/4/**4**/4/**5**, P to last 3/**3**/4/**4**/4/**5** sts, cast off these sts. Break off yarn. Rejoin yarn. 1st row: K. 2nd row: P. 3rd row: K2, sl 1, K2tog, psso, K to last 5 sts, K3tog, K2. 4th row: P. ** Rep 1st to 4th row until 28/**30**/30/**32**/34/**34** sts rem, ending with a 3rd row. Work 10 rows. Cast off.

RIGHT FRONT
With No 10 needles, cast on 44/**48**/50/**54**/56/**60** sts. Work K1, P1 rib for 1½ in, inc 1 st at beg of last row on 1st, 3rd and 5th sizes only: 45/**48**/51/**54**/57/**60** sts. Change to No 8 needles and st st until work measures 14¼ in from start, ending with a K row.
Shape raglan and front slope: Next row: Cast off 3/**3**/4/**4**/4/**5**, P to end. 1st row: K2tog, K to end. 2nd row: P. 3rd row: K to last 5 sts, K3tog, K2. 4th row: P.

Dec 2 sts at raglan edge on every foll 4th row from previous dec as before, at the same time dec 1 st at front edge on every 4th/**4th**/5th/**5th**/5th/**5th** row from previous dec until 17/**20**/24/**27**/30/**32** sts rem, every 4th row until 5/**5**/3/**3**/3/**5** sts rem.

Cont dec at raglan edge only as before until 1 st rem.

Fasten off.

LEFT FRONT

Work as right front to raglan shaping. Shape raglan and front slope: Next row: P to last 3/**3**/4/**4**/4/**5** sts, cast off 3/**3**/4/**4**/4/**5**. Break off yarn. Rejoin yarn and complete to match right Front reversing all shapings noting that sl 1, K2tog, psso in place of K3tog will be worked at raglan shaping.

SLEEVES

With No 10 needles, cast on 42/**44**/46/**48**/50/**52** sts. Work K1, P1 rib for 2½ in. Next row: Rib 4/**1**/2/**3**/0/**1**, (inc in next st, rib 3/**4**/3/**3**/3/**3**) 8/**8**/10/**10**/12/**12** times, inc in next st, rib to end: 51/**53**/57/**58**/63/**65** sts.

Change to No 8 needles and st st, inc 1 st at each end of 3rd/**7th**/5th/**3rd**/3rd/**7th** row foll and every foll 7th/**6th**/6th/**6th**/6th/**5th** row until there are 79/**83**/89/**93**/97/**103** sts. Cont on these sts until work measures 16/**16**/16½/**16½**/17/**17½** in from start, ending with a K row.

Shape top by working as back from ** to **, then rep 1st to 4th row until 17 sts rem, ending with a 3rd row. Cast off.

FRONT BAND

With No 10 needles, cast on 13 sts. 1st row: K2, (P1, K1) 5 times, K1. 2nd row: (K1, P1) 6 times, K1. Rep these 2 rows twice more. Next row: Rib 5, cast off 3, rib to end. Next row: Rib 5, cast on 3, rib to end. Cont in rib working a buttonhole as on last 2 rows on every foll 27th and 28th rows from previous buttonhole until 5 button-holes in all have been worked. Cont in rib, without further buttonholes until band measures 54/**55¼**/56½/**57¾**/58/**58¼** in from start. Cast off in rib.

TO MAKE UP

Observing general method on page 81, block and press.

Join side and sleeve seams. Insert sleeves, stitching 10 rows at back of neck to 8 of the cast-off sts at top of sleeve. Stitch front band in position, placing buttonholes on right side for Woman, left side for Man. Press seams. Sew on buttons.

BUTTON-THROUGH VERSION

Work back and sleeves as V neck version.

RIGHT FRONT

Work as right front of V neck version to raglan shaping.

Shape raglan: Next row: Cast off 3/**3**/4/**4**/4/**5**, P to end. 1st row: K. 2nd row: P. 3rd row: K to last 5 sts, K3tog, K2. 4th row: P. Dec 2 sts at raglan edge on every foll 4th row from previous dec as before until 18/**19**/21/**22**/23/**23** sts rem, ending with a 4th/**4th**/2nd/**2nd**/4th/**4th** row.

Shape neck: 1st, 2nd, 5th and 6th sizes only: Next row: Cast off 8/9/10/10, K to end. 3rd and 4th sizes only: Next row: Cast off 9, K to last 5 sts, K3tog, K2. All sizes: Dec 2 sts at raglan edge as before, at the same time, dec 1 st at neck edge on every row until 5/5/5/6/6/6 dec have been worked at neck edge. Work 0/0/2/1/3/3 rows. Next row: K3tog. Fasten off.

LEFT FRONT

Work as right front to raglan shaping. Shape raglan: Next row: P to last 3/**3**/4/**4**/4/**5** sts, cast off 3/3/4/4/4/5. Break off yarn. Rejoin yarn. 1st row: K. 2nd row: P. 3rd row: K2, sl 1, K2tog, psso, K to end. 4th row: P. Complete to match right front, reversing all shapings.

FIRST FRONT BAND

With No 10 needles, cast on 13 sts. 1st row: K2, (P1, K1) 5 times, K1. 2nd row: (K1, P1) 6 times, K1. Rep these 2 rows 0/**1**/2/**2**/0/**0** times more. Next row: Rib 5, cast off 3, rib to end. Next row: Rib 5, cast on 3, rib to end. Cont in rib working a buttonhole as on last 2 rows on every foll 25th and 26th/**25th and 26th**/25th and 26th/**25th and 26th**/27th and 28th/**27th and 28th** rows from previous buttonhole until 7 buttonholes in all have been worked. Work 21/**21**/23/**23**/21/**23** rows for Woman, 20/**20**/22/**22**/20/**22** rows for Man. Slip these sts on a length of yarn.

SECOND FRONT BAND
Omitting buttonholes, work as first front band, working one row less for Woman, one row more for Man.

MAKE UP AND NECKBAND
Observing general method on page 81, block and press.

Join side and sleeve seams. Insert sleeves, stitching 10 rows at back of neck to 8 of the cast-off sts at top of sleeve.

With No 10 needles and right side facing, slip 13 sts from top of first front band for woman or second front band for man, on to right-hand needle; with same needle and right side facing, knit up 77/**81**/85/**89**/93/**97** sts round neck, rib across 13 sts from rem front band: 103/**107**/111/**115**/119/**123** sts. Work 6/**6**/6/**6**/8/**8** rows in rib, working a buttonhole as before on 4th and 5th/**4th and 5th**/2nd and 3rd/**2nd and 3rd**/6th and 7th/**4th and 5th** rows. Cast off in rib. Stitch front bands in position. Press seams. Sew on buttons and press stud at top of neck.

Sporting Double
This round-necked raglan sweater is very quick to knit in double double knitting

Materials: 15/**16**/17/**18**/19/**21** (50g) balls Patons Doublet. Pair each Nos 5 and 8 needles and set of 4 No 8 needles with points at both ends.

Measurements: To fit 36/**38**/40/**42**/44/**46** in bust/chest; length at centre back, 25/**25½**/25½/**26**/26/**26½** in; sleeve seam, 17½/**18**/18/**18**/18½/**18½** in.

Tension: 8½ sts and 10½ rows to 2 in over st st on No 5 needles.

BACK
With No 8 needles, cast on 76/**80**/84/**88**/92/**96** sts and work K1, P1 rib for 2½ in. Next row: Rib 7/**9**/9/**11**/10/**12**, (inc in next st, rib 11/**11**/12/**12**/13/**13**) 5 times, inc in next st, rib to end: 82/**86**/90/**94**/98/**102** sts.
Change to No 5 needles and work in st st until back measures 16/**16**/15½/**15½**/15/**15** in, ending with a P row. Shape raglan: 1st and 2nd rows: Cast off 4,

work to end. 3rd row: K2, K2togtbl, K to last 4 sts, K2tog, K2. 4th row: P.** Rep 3rd and 4th rows until 26/**26**/28/**28**/30/**30** sts rem, ending with a 4th row. Leave sts on a length of yarn.

FRONT
Work as back to **. Rep 3rd and 4th rows until 40/**40**/42/**44**/46/**46** sts rem at raglan shaping, ending with a 4th row. Shape neck: Next row: K2, K2togtbl, K11/**10**/11/**12**/13/**12**, turn and leave rem sts on a spare needle. Dec 1 st at neck edge on every row, at the same time cont dec at raglan edge on every alt row as before until 5/**6**/5/**6**/6/**6** sts rem. Cont dec at raglan edge only until 3 sts rem. Next row: P. Next row: K1, K2togtbl. Next row: P. K2tog and fasten off.
With right side facing leave centre 10/**12**/12/**12**/12/**14** sts on spare needle, rejoin yarn to rem sts and complete to match first side reversing shapings.

SLEEVES

With No 8 needles, cast on 34/**36**/38/**40**/42/**44** sts and work K1, P1 rib for $2\frac{1}{2}$ in. Next row: Rib 4/**4**/5/**4**/5/**5**, (inc in next st, rib 7/**8**/8/**9**/9/**10**) 3 times, inc in next st, rib to end: 38/**40**/42/**44**/46/**48** sts.

Change to No 5 needles and work in st st inc 1 st at each end of 3rd/**5th**/5th/**3rd**/3rd/**next** and every foll 7th/**6th**/6th/**6th**/6th/**6th** row until there are 60/**64**/66/**70**/72/**76** sts. Cont on these sts until sleeve seam measures $17\frac{1}{2}$/**18**/18/**18**/$18\frac{1}{2}$/**$18\frac{1}{2}$** in, ending with a P row. Shape top by working rows 1 to 4 of raglan shaping as on back, then rep 3rd and 4th rows until 8 sts rem, ending with a 4th row. Next row: K2, K2togtbl, K2tog, K2. Next row: P. Next row: K1, K2togtbl, K2tog, K1. Next row: P. Leave sts on a safety-pin.

TO MAKE UP

Observing general method on page 81, block and press. Join raglan, side and sleeve seams.

NECKBAND

With right side facing and set of No 8 needles, K4 sleeve sts, knit up 16/**16**/16/**18**/18/**18** down left side of neck, K across sts at centre front inc 2/**2**/2/**0**/0/**0** sts evenly, knit up 16/**16**/16/**18**/18/**18** sts up right side of neck, K4 sleeve sts, K across sts on back: 78/**80**/82/**84**/86/**88** sts. Work in rounds of K1, P1 rib for $2\frac{1}{2}$ in.

Cast off loosely in rib. Fold Neckband at centre to wrong side and slip-stitch loosely in position. Press seams.

POLO NECK

With right side facing and set of No 8 needles, K4 sleeve sts, knit up 16/**16**/16/**18**/18/**18** sts down left side of neck, K across sts at centre front inc 2/**4**/2/**2**/4/**2** sts evenly, knit up 16/**16**/16/**18**/18/**18** sts up right side of neck, K4 sleeve sts, K across sts on back inc 6/**4**/6/**6**/4/**6** sts evenly: 84/**86**/88/**92**/94/**96** sts. Work in rounds of K1, P1 rib for 6 in. Cast off loosely in rib. Press seams.

Zipper Jackets for Two

Double moss stitch and cable-style panels prove that a jacket in double double knitting can be ornamental as well as useful

Materials: 14/16 (50g) balls Patons Doublet. Pair each Nos 7 and 4 needles. Cable needle. 22/24 in open-ended zip.

Measurements: To fit 34/40 in bust/chest. Length at centre back, 25/27 in; sleeve seam, $17\frac{1}{2}$/$18\frac{1}{2}$ in.

Tension: 8 sts and 10 rows to 2 in over st st on No 4 needles.

Additional Abbreviations (see page 29): C4F=Cable 4 Front by working across next 4 sts as follows: Slip next 2 sts on to cable needle and leave at front of work, knit next 2 sts, then knit 2 sts from cable needle.

C4B=Cable 4 Back as C4F, but leave sts at back of work in place of front.

Tw2F=Twist 2 Front by knitting into front of 2nd st, then front of first st on left-hand needle and slipping 2 sts off needle tog.

Tw2B=Twist 2 Back by knitting into back of 2nd st, then back of first st on left-hand needle and slipping 2 sts off needle tog.

BACK

With No 4 needles, cast on 73/81 sts. 1st row: * P1, KB1; rep from * to last st, P1. 2nd row: * K1, PB1, rep from * to last st, K1. 3rd row: P2, * KB1, P1; rep from * to last st, P1. 4th row: K2, * PB1, K1; rep from * to last st, K1. Work in all-over patt with centre cable panel as follows:

1st row: (P1, KB1) 13/15 times, P1, Tw2F, P3, K9, P3, Tw2B, P1, (KB1, P1) 13/15 times. 2nd row: (K1, PB1) 13/15 times, K1, P2, K3, P9, K3, P2, K1, (PB1, K1) 13/15 times. 3rd row: P2, (KB1, P1) 11/13 times, KB2, P1,

Tw2F, P3, C4F, K1, C4B, P3, Tw2B, P1, KB2, (P1, KB1) 11/13 times, P2. 4th row: K2, (PB1, K1) 11/13 times, PB2, K1, P2, K3, P9, K3, P2, K1, PB2, (K1, PB1) 11/13 times, K2. These 4 rows form patt.

Cont in patt until work measures 15¾/16½ in from start, ending with wrong side facing. Next row: Cast off 5/4, patt to last 5/4 sts, cast off these sts. Break off yarn.

Rejoin yarn and shape raglan: 1st row: P2tog, patt to last 2 sts, P2tog. 2nd row: K1, patt to last st, K1. Rep these 2 rows until 19/23 sts rem, ending with a dec row. Work 2 rows on these sts. Cast off.

RIGHT FRONT
With No 4 needles, cast on 41/45 sts. 1st row: P2, * KB1, P1; rep from * to last st, P1. 2nd row: K2, * PB1, K1; rep from * to last st, K1. 3rd row: * P1, KB1; rep from * to last st, P1. 4th row: * K1, PB1; rep from * to last st, K1.

Work as follows: 1st row: K1, P1, Tw2F, P3, K9, P3, Tw2B, P1, (KB1, P1) 9/11 times, P1. 2nd row: K1, (K1, PB1) 9/11 times, K1, P2, K3, P9, P3, P2, K2. 3rd row: K1, P1, Tw2F, P3, C4F, K1, C4B, P3, Tw2B, P1, KB2, (P1, KB1) 8/10 times, P1. 4th row: (K1, PB1) 8/10 times, K1, PB2, K1, P2, K3, P9, K3, P2, K2. These 4 rows form patt.

Cont in patt until work measures same as back to raglan shaping, ending with wrong side facing. Next row: Cast off 7/6, patt to end.

Shape raglan: 1st row: Patt to last 2 sts, P2tog. 2nd row: K1, patt to end. Rep these 2 rows until 19/21 sts rem, ending at front edge.

Shape neck: Next row: Cast off 3/5, patt to last 2 sts, P2tog. Next row: K1, patt to last 2 sts, work 2tog. Still dec at raglan edge on next and every alt row as before, at the same time dec 1 st at neck edge on every row until 8 dec in all have been worked at neck edge. Cont dec at armhole edge on every alt row as before until all sts are worked off.

LEFT FRONT
With No 4 needles, cast on 41/45 sts. Work 4 rows of rib as on Right Front. 1st row: P2, (KB1, P1) 9/11 times, Tw2F, P3, K9, P3, Tw2B, P1, K1. 2nd row: K2, P2, K3, P9, K3, P2, K1, (PB1, K1) 9/11 times, K1. 3rd row: (P1, KB1) 8/10 times, P1, KB2, P1, Tw2F, P3, C4F, K1, C4B, P3, Tw2B, P1, K1. 4th row: K2, P2, K3, P9, K3, P2, K1, PB2, (K1, PB1) 8/10 times, K1. These 4 rows form patt. Cont in patt until work matches back to raglan shaping, ending with wrong side facing. Next row: Patt to last 7/6 sts, cast off these sts. Break off yarn.

Rejoin yarn and shape raglan: 1st row: P2tog, patt to end. 2nd row: Patt to last st, K1. Rep these 2 rows until 19/21 sts rem, ending at neck edge.

Shape neck: Next row: Cast off 3/5, patt to last st, K1. Next row: P2tog, patt to last 2 sts, work 2 tog. Still dec at raglan edge on every alt row as before, at the same time dec 1 st at neck edge on every row until 8 dec in all have been worked at front edge. Cont dec at raglan edge only on every alt row as before until all sts are worked off.

SLEEVES
With No 7 needles, cast on 40/42 sts. Work K1, P1 rib for 3 in. Next row: Rib 4/3, (inc in next st, rib 7/5) 4/6 times, inc in next st, rib to end: 45/49 sts.

Change to No 4 needles and work as follows: 1st row: (P1, KB1) 6/7 times, P1, Tw2F, P3, K9, P3, Tw2B, P1, (KB1, P1) 6/7 times. 2nd row: (K1, PB1) 6/7 times, K1, P2, K3, P9, K3, P2, K1, (PB1, K1) 6/7 times. 3rd row: P2, (KB1, P1) 4/5 times, KB2, P1, Tw2F, P3, C4F, K1, C4B, P3, Tw2B, P1, KB2, (P1, KB1) 4/5 times, P2. 4th row: K2, (PB1, K1) 4/5 times, PB2, K1, P2, K3, P9, K3, P2, K1, PB2, (K1, PB1) 4/5 times, K2.

Working extra sts into all-over patt, inc 1 st at each end of 5th row and every foll 12th row until there are 55/59 sts. Cont on these sts until work measures 16½/17½ in from start, ending with

179

wrong side facing (adjust length here). Inc 1 st at each end of next and every alt row until there are 61/65 sts. Work 1 row thus ending with wrong side facing.

Shape raglan top: Next row: 1st sleeve —Cast off 5/4 sts, patt to last 7/6 sts, cast off these sts. Next row: 2nd sleeve— Cast off 7/6 sts, patt to last 5/4 sts, cast off these sts.

Cont for both sleeves: 1st row: P2tog, patt to last 2 sts, P2tog. 2nd row: K1, patt to last st, K1. Rep these 2 rows until 5 sts rem, ending with a dec row. Cast off.

COLLAR

With No 4 needles, cast on 79/87 sts. 1st row: (wrong side), K2, P2, * K1, P1; rep from * to last 5 sts, K1, P2, K2. 2nd row: K1, P1, Tw2F, * P1, K1; rep from * to last 5 sts, P1, Tw2B, P1, K1. Rep these 2 rows until work measures $2\frac{1}{4}/2\frac{1}{2}$ in from start.

Change to No 7 needles and cont until work measures $3\frac{1}{2}/3\frac{3}{4}$ in from start, ending with a 1st row. Cast off in rib.

TO MAKE UP

Observing general method on page 81, block and press.

Join side and sleeve seams and insert sleeves, matching shapings, stitching 2 rows at top of back to 2 of the cast-off sts at top of sleeve.

Stitch collar with cast-off edge to neck from edge of right front to edge of left front. Stitch zip in position. Press seams.

T-Shirt, Crochet Style

A modern classic in an up-to-date craft

Materials: 9/**10**/11/**12**/13/**14** (50g) balls Patons Double Knitting. Nos 5·00 mm and 4·00 mm crochet hooks. 5 buttons.

Measurements: To fit bust/chest 34/**36**/38/**40**/42/**44** in; length from top of shoulders, $22\frac{1}{2}$/**$22\frac{1}{2}$**/$22\frac{1}{2}$/**$25\frac{1}{2}$**/$26\frac{1}{2}$/**$26\frac{1}{2}$** in; sleeve seam, $5\frac{1}{2}$/**$5\frac{1}{2}$**/$5\frac{1}{2}$/**$6\frac{1}{2}$**/$6\frac{1}{2}$/**$6\frac{1}{2}$** in.

Tension: 8 sts and 6 rows to 2 in over patt using No 5·00 hook.

FRONT

** With No 5·00 hook, make 71/**75**/79/**85**/89/**93** ch. 1st row: 1htr in 3rd ch from hook, 1htr in each foll ch, turn with 2ch. 2nd row: Miss first st, (turning ch counts as first st), 1htr in each foll st, 1htr in top of turning ch, turn with 2ch: (70/**74**/78/**84**/88/**92** sts incl turning ch of previous row).

2nd row forms patt. Rep it until front measures $12\frac{1}{2}$ / **$12\frac{1}{2}$** / $12\frac{1}{2}$ / **$14\frac{1}{2}$** / $14\frac{1}{2}$ / **$14\frac{1}{2}$** in.**

Divide for front opening: Next row: Work 33/**35**/37/**40**/42/**44** sts (incl turn-ing ch), turn with 2ch. Cont on these sts for first side as follows: Work 2 rows straight.

Shape armhole: 1st row: Patt to last 2/**3**/4/**4**/4/**4** sts (incl turning ch), turn. 2nd row: Ss over 1 st, make 2ch, patt to end, turn with 2ch. 3rd row: Patt to last st (turning ch), turn. Rep 2nd and 3rd rows 2/**2**/2/**3**/3/**3** times more.

1st, 2nd and 3rd sizes only: Work 2nd row again.

All sizes: Work 8/**8**/8/**7**/11/**11** rows straight on rem 24/**25**/26/**28**/30/**32** sts.

Shape neck: Next row: Ss over 5/**6**/6/**6**/7/**8** sts, patt to end, turn with 2ch. 1st row: Patt to last st, turn. 2nd row: Ss over 1 st, make 2ch, patt to end, turn. Rep last 2 rows once more, then 1st row again on 4th, 5th and 6th sizes only: 15/**15**/16/**17**/18/**19** sts. Work 3/**3**/3/**4**/4/**4** rows straight.

Shape shoulders: Next row: Work 10/**10**/11/**11**/12/**13** sts, turn. Next row: Ss over 5/**5**/5/**6**/6/**6** sts, patt to end. Fasten off. Leaving 4 sts at centre unworked,

rejoin yarn to next st and make 2ch, patt to end. Work 2 rows straight.

Shape armhole: Next row: Ss over 2/3/ 4/4/4/4 sts, patt to end. Dec 1 st at armhole edge on every row until 24/25/26/ **28**/30/**32** sts rem. Work straight until work matches first side to start of neck shaping.

Shape neck: Next row: Patt to last 5/6/ 6/6/7/**8** sts, turn. Complete to match first side, reversing shapings.

BACK

Work as for front from ** to **. Work 3 rows straight, omitting turning ch at end of last row.

Shape armholes: Next row: Ss over 2/ **3**/4/4/4/4 sts, patt to last 2/3/4/4/4/4 sts, turn. Dec 1 st at each end of every row until 52/**54**/56/**60**/64/**68** sts rem. Work straight until back matches front at armhole edge.

Shape shoulders: Next row: Ss over 5/ 5/5/**6**/6/6 sts, patt to last 5/5/5/**6**/6/6 sts, turn. Rep last row once more. Fasten off.

SLEEVES

With No 5·00 hook, make 43/**45**/47/**53**/ 57/**61** ch. Work 1st and 2nd rows as on front: 42/**44**/46/**52**/56/**60** sts. Next row: 1htr in 1st st, 1htr in each st to last 2 sts, 2htr in next st, 1htr in top of turning ch, turn with 2ch: 44/**46**/48/**54**/58/**62**

sts. Inc 1 st at each end as before on every foll 4th/**4th**/4th/**5th**/5th/**5th** row until there are 48/**50**/52/**58**/62/**66** sts. Work straight until sleeve seam measures 4½/4½/4½/5½/5½/5½ in. omitting turning ch at end of last row.

Shape top: Next row: Ss over 2/3/4/**4**/ 4/4 sts, work to last 2/3/4/**4**/4/4 sts, turn. Dec 1 st at each end of every row until 14/**14**/14/**16**/16/**20** sts rem. Fasten off.

TO MAKE UP

Observing general method on page 81, block and press. Join shoulder seams.

Neck Border: With right side facing for first row and No 4·00 hook, work 6 rows dc along neck edge, dec 4 sts evenly on 3rd and 5th rows. Fasten off.

Front Borders: With right side facing for first row and No 4·00 hook, work 6 rows dc along front edges, making 5 buttonholes in 4th row on right side for Lady's Version and on left side for Man's Version, the first, 1 in from division, the last just below neck edge, rem evenly spaced. To make a buttonhole: 2ch, miss 2 sts.

With right side facing for first row and No 4·00 hook, work 6 rows dc along lower and cuff edges. Join side and sleeve seams. Insert sleeves. Catch down short edges of front borders at base. Press seams and borders. Sew on buttons.

Great Outdoors

A knitted hat for all sporting occasions – or whenever it is cold

Materials: 2/3 (50g) balls Patons Double Knitting. Pair No 8 needles.

Measurements: His/Hers average head size.

Tension: 11 sts and 15 rows to 2 in over st st on No 8 needles.

Additional Abbreviations (see page 29): Tie 3 = Insert point of right needle between 3rd and 4th sts on left needle and pull loop through, place loop on

point of left needle, then knit it tog with next st, K2.

Cast on 132/138 sts and work in patt as follows: 1st to 4th row: * Tie 3, P3; rep from * to end. 5th to 8th row: * K3, P3; rep from * to end. These 8 rows form patt. Cont in patt until 2 patts and 4 rows have been worked.

Change to st st and shape top as follows: Next row: K4/2, * K2tog, K9/10; rep

from * to last 7/4 sts, K2tog, K5/2: 120/
126 sts. Work 21/25 rows straight.
Cont in st st shaping top: Next row:
* K6/7, K2tog; rep from * to end; 105/
112 sts. Work 5/5 rows straight. Next
row: * K5/6, K2tog; rep from * to end:
90/98 sts. Work 3/5 rows straight.
Next row: * K4/5, K2tog; rep from * to
end: 75/84 sts. Work 3/3 rows straight.
Next row: * K3/4, K2tog; rep from * to
end: 60/70 sts. Next row: P. Next row:
* K2/3, K2tog; rep from * to end: 45/
56 sts. Next row: P. Next row: * K1/2,
K2tog; rep from * to end: 30/42 sts.
Next row: P.

1st size: Next row: (K2tog) 15 times.
Next row: (P2tog) 7 times, P1. Break

yarn, thread through rem sts, draw up
and fasten off.

2nd size: Next row: * K1, K2tog; rep
from * to end: 28 sts. Next row: P.
Next row: (K2tog) 14 times. Next row:
(P2tog) 7 times. Break yarn, thread
through rem sts, draw up and fasten off.

TO MAKE UP

Observing general method on page 81,
block and press.

Join centre back seam neatly. Press
seams. Cut 2 cardboard circles 4½ in
across then cut away centres of circles,
so that 2 rings 1¼ in wide rem. From
rem yarn make a pompon as described
in Chapter 9 and sew to top of cap.

Hers and Hers

Crochet beanie or knitted beret with scarf to match

KNITTED BERET AND SCARF

Materials: Scarf: 2 (50g) balls Medium Shade, 5 (50g) balls Contrast; **Beret:** 1 (50g) ball Medium Shade, 1 (50g) ball Contrast, Patons Double Knitting. Pair each No 8 needles for Scarf; Nos 10 and 9 needles for Beret.

Measurements: Scarf: Length (excluding fringes), 66 in. **Beret:** To fit average head.

Tension: 11 sts and 15 rows to 2 in over st st on No 8 needles.

Additional Abbreviations (see page 29): MS = Medium Shade; C = Contrast.

SCARF

With No 8 needles and MS, cast on 80 sts and work in rib patt as follows: 1st row: K1, * K2, P2; rep from * to last 3 sts, K3. 2nd row: K1, * P2, K2; rep from * to last 3 sts, P2, K1. These 2 rows form rib patt.
Cont in rib patt working stripes thus: Work 6 rows more in MS, then (2 rows C, 2 rows MS) 20 times. Break MS.
Work straight in C until scarf measures 54 in, ending with a 2nd row. Join in MS and work (2 rows MS, 2 rows C) 20 times. Break C.
Work 8 rows MS. Cast off evenly in rib. Cut rem MS into 8 in lengths and knot through ends of scarf to form tassels.

BERET

With No 10 needles and MS, cast on 114 sts. Work 8 rows K1, P1 rib. Next row: P, thus forming ridge. Starting with a P row, work 9 rows st st. Next row: K4, * M1, K3; rep from * to last 5 sts, M1, K5: 150 sts. Next row: P.
Change to No 9 needles, join in C and cont in st st, working stripe patt thus: 2 rows C, 2 rows MS. These 4 rows form patt. Cont in patt until work measures 5 in from ridge, ending with right side facing.
Keeping stripe patt correct, shape crown as follows: 1st row: (K13, K2tog) 10 times. 2nd and alt rows: P. 3rd row: (K12, K2tog) 10 times. 5th row: (K11, K2tog) 10 times. Cont in this way until the row '(K1, K2tog) 10 times' has been

worked. Next row: P. Next row: K2tog all across. Break off yarn, thread through rem sts and fasten off securely.

TO MAKE UP

Observing general method on page 81, block and press. Join seam. Fold ribbing at ridge to wrong side and flat stitch in position to form double band. Press seam.

CROCHET BEANIE AND SCARF

Materials: 3 (50g) balls Dark and 3 (50g) balls Light Patons Double Knitting. Nos 4·00 mm and 3·50 mm crochet hooks.

Measurements: Hat: To fit average head. **Scarf:** Width, 6 in; length, 80 in (excluding fringes).

Tension: 4 rows and 1 patt rep = 2 in.

Additional Abbreviations (see page 29): L = Light; D = Dark.

HAT

With No 4·00 hook and L, make 4ch, join with ss to form ring.
1st rnd: In L, 2ch, 11htr into ring, join with ss in top of 2ch: 12 sts.
Join in D. 2nd rnd: In D, 3ch, 1tr in first st, * 2tr in next st; rep from * ending ss in top of 3ch: 24 sts. 3rd rnd: In L, 3ch, 1tr in first st, * 1tr in next st, 2tr in next st; rep from * to last st, 1tr in last st, join with ss in top of 3ch: 36 sts.
4th rnd: In D, 3ch, 1tr in first st, * miss 1 st, (1tr, 2ch, 1tr) in next st, miss 1 st, (2tr, 1ch, 2tr) in next st; rep from * ending last rep 2tr in first st, 1 ch, ss in top of 3ch. 5th rnd: In D, 6 ch, 1tr in base of 6ch, * (2tr, 1ch, 2tr) in next ch sp, (1tr, 3ch, 1tr) in next ch sp; rep from * ending last rep (2tr, 1ch, 2tr) in last ch sp, ss in 3rd of 6ch.
6th rnd: In L, ss in first ch sp, 3ch, 2tr in 1st ch sp, * (1tr, 3ch, 1tr) in next ch sp, (3tr, 1ch, 3tr) in next ch sp; rep from * ending 3tr in 1st ch sp, 1ch, ss in top of 3ch. 7th rnd: In L, 6ch, 1tr in base of 6ch, * (3tr, 1ch, 3tr) in next ch sp, (1tr, 3ch, 1tr) in next ch sp; rep from * ending last rep (3tr, 1ch, 3tr) in last ch sp, ss in 3rd of 6ch. 8th rnd: In D, as

6th. 9th rnd: In D, as 7th. Rep last 4 rnds until hat measures approx 7 in, ending with 7th rnd in L, turn.
Change to No 3·50 hook and with wrong side facing, work as follows: Next rnd: In D, 3dc in first ch sp, * miss 1tr, 1dc in each of next 3tr, 1dc in next ch sp, 1dc in each of next 3tr, miss 1tr, 3dc in next ch sp; rep from *, join with ss in first dc. Next rnd: In D, 1ch, 1dc in first st, 1dc in each st to end, join with ss in 1ch. Rep last rnd 3 times more. Fasten off.

SCARF

With No 4·00 hook and D, make 34ch, turn.
1st row: In D, 2tr in 4th ch from hook, * miss 4ch, (1tr, 3ch, 1tr) in next ch, miss 4ch, (3tr, 1ch, 3tr) in next ch; rep from * to last 10ch, miss 4ch, (1tr, 3ch, 1tr) in next ch, miss 4ch, 3tr in last ch.

** Join in L. 2nd row: In L, 4ch, 1tr in first tr, * (3tr, 1ch, 3tr) in next ch sp, (1tr, 3ch, 1tr) in next ch sp; rep from * ending last rep (1tr, 1ch, 1tr) in last st. 3rd row: In L, 3ch, 2tr in first ch sp, * (1tr, 3ch, 1tr) in next ch sp, (3tr, 1ch, 3tr) in next ch sp; rep from * ending last rep 3tr in 3rd of 4ch. 4th row: In D, as 2nd. 5th row: In D, as 3rd. Rep last 4 rows until scarf measures approx 40 in, ending with 5th patt row. Fasten off.**
With right side facing, rejoin D to original ch and work thus: 3tr in first ch, * miss 4ch, (1tr, 3ch, 1tr) in next ch, miss 4ch, (3tr, 1ch, 3tr) in next ch; rep from * ending 3tr in last ch. Work as for first half from ** to **.
Cut rem D yarn into 10 in lengths and using 4 strands tog, knot along short ends to form fringe as described in Chapter 9. Do not press.

Choice of Gloves

Hers are knitted sideways, his are straight up: both pairs on two needles

HERS

Materials: 1 (50g) ball Patons Purple Heather 4-ply. Pair No 11 needles.

Tension: 15 sts to 2 in over garter st on No 11 needles.

Cast on 55 sts. 1st row: K. 2nd row: Inc in first st, K to end. 3rd row: K to last 2 sts, inc in next st, K1. 4th row: K to last 14 sts, turn. 5th row: K all across, picking up loop where work was turned, and working it tog with next st to avoid a hole. 6th row: K all across.
7th row: K to last 2 sts, K2tog. 8th row: K2tog, K to end. 9th row: K.
10th row: Cast off 15 sts, cast on 19, K the cast-on sts, K to end. 11th to 19th row: Rep 1st to 9th row incl once. 20th row: Cast off 19 sts, cast on 21, K the cast-on sts, K to end. 21st to 29th row: Rep 1st to 9th row incl once. 30th row: Cast off 21 sts, cast on 19, K the cast-on

sts, K to end. 31st to 39th row: Rep 1st to 9th row incl once.
40th row: Cast off 28 sts, cast on 17, K the cast-on sts, K2, turn. 41st row: K19. 42nd row: inc in first st, K20, turn. 43rd row: K20, inc in next st, K1. 44th row: K25, turn. 45th row: K25. 46th row: K27, turn. 47th row: K25, K2tog. 48th row: K2tog, K26, turn. 49th row: K27. Cast off. Make 3 more pieces the same.

TO MAKE UP

Observing general method on page 81, block and press. Sew up neatly on wrong side.

HIS

Materials: 2 (50g) balls Patons Double Knitting. Pair No 11 needles. Cable needle.

Tension: 13½ sts and 18 rows to 2 in over st st on No 11 needles.

PANEL PATT (16 sts)

1st row: (right side), P2, K1, P2, K6, P2, K1, P2. 2nd row: K2, P1, K2, P6, K2, P1, K2. 3rd row: P2, K1, P2, sl next 2 sts on cable needle to back of work, K1, then K2 from cable needle, sl next st on cable needle to front of work, K2, then K1 from cable needle, P2, K1, P2. 4th row: As 2nd. These 4 rows form patt.

RIGHT GLOVE

Note: Figures in brackets refer to left glove only.

Cast on 56 sts and work in rib. 1st row: (right side), P1, * K2, P2; rep from * to last 3 sts, K2, P1. 2nd row: K1, * P2, K2; rep from * to last 3 sts, P2, K1. Rep these 2 rows 8 times more.

Change to st st and patt as follows: 1st row: K6 (34), work 1st row of panel patt over next 16 sts, K to end. 2nd row: P34 (6), patt 16 as on 2nd row of panel patt, P to end. 3rd row: K6 (34), patt 16 as on 3rd row of panel patt, K to end. 4th row: P34 (6), patt 16 as on 4th row, P to end.

Keeping 16 panel patt sts correct, shape thumb: 1st row: Work 29 (25), inc 1, K2, inc 1, work to end. Work 3 rows straight. 5th row: Work 29 (25), inc 1, K4, inc 1, work to end. Work 3 rows straight. 9th row: Work 29 (25), inc 1, K6, inc 1, work to end. Cont thus, inc 2 sts on every 4th row until there are 70 sts.

Your last inc row will read: Work 29 (25), inc 1, K14, inc 1, work to end. Work 1 row straight. Next row: Work 45 (41), turn and cast on 2 sts. Next row: P18, turn and cast on 2 sts. Work 24 rows straight in st st on these 20 thumb sts. ** Next row: * K2tog; rep from * to end. Next row: * P2tog; rep from * to end. Break yarn, thread through rem sts, draw up and fasten off. Join seam.**

Next row: (right side), knit up 4 sts from base of thumb, then K across 25 (29) sts left unworked. Work 15 rows straight over all sts.

With right side facing, cont in st st for fingers: 1st finger: K37, turn and cast on 2 sts. Next row: P18, turn. Work 28 rows straight on these 18 sts. ***Next row: * K2tog; rep from * to end. Next row: P1, * P2tog; rep from * to end. Break yarn and finish as for thumb.***

2nd finger: With right side facing, knit up 2 sts at base of 1st finger, K7, turn and cast on 2. Next row: P18, turn. Work 32 rows straight on these 18 sts, then finish as for 1st finger from *** to ***.

3rd finger: Work as for 2nd finger, but working only 28 rows straight.

4th finger: With right side facing, knit up 2 sts from base of 3rd finger, K rem 7 sts. Next row: P16. Work 20 rows straight, then finish as for thumb from ** to **.

LEFT GLOVE

Work as for right glove, reading figures in brackets where 2 sets of figures are given, thus reversing shaping.

TO MAKE UP

Observing general method on page 81, press. Join side seams. Press seams.

The Four-needle Technique

Is used for these socks for men in 4-ply

Materials: 3 (50g) balls Patons Purple Heather 4-ply. Set of 4 No 12 needles with points at both ends.

Measurements: Length of foot, 10½ in; length from top to lower edge, 13½ in.

Tension: 16 sts and 20 rows to 2 in over st st on No 12 needles.

Cast on 72 sts, 24 on each of 3 needles. Work in rnds of K1, P1, rib for 3½ in. Work in st st (every rnd K) for 2½ in.

189

Shape leg: 1st rnd: K2tog, K to last 3 sts, K2togtbl, K1. Work 5 rnds without shaping. Rep these 6 rnds until 60 sts rem. Cont without further shaping until work measures 10½ in from start.

Divide sts for heel: K14, slip last 15 sts of rnd on to other end of same needle (these 29 sts are for heel). Divide rem sts on to 2 needles and leave for instep. Start heel: 1st row: Sl 1P, P to end. 2nd row: Sl 1K, * K1, keeping yarn at back of needle sl 1P; rep from * to last 2 sts, K2. Work the last 2 rows 16 times more, then 1st row once.

Turn heel: 1st row: K17, sl 1, K1, psso, turn. 2nd row: P6, P2tog, turn. 3rd row: K7, sl 1, K1, psso, turn. 4th row: P8, P2tog, turn. Cont in this manner until all sts are worked on to one needle again. Next row: K9, thus completing heel (8 sts rem unworked on left-hand needle). Slip all instep sts on to one needle.

With spare needle, K8 heel sts, knit up 18 sts along side of heel; with 2nd needle K across instep sts; with 3rd needle knit up 18 sts along other side of heel, K9 heel sts: 84 sts.

Shape instep: 1st rnd: K. 2nd rnd: 1st needle: K to last 3 sts, K2tog, K1; 2nd needle: K; 3rd needle: K1, K2togtbl, K to end. Rep these 2 rnds until 58 sts rem in round. Cont on these sts until foot measures 7¼ in from where sts were knitted up at heel. Slip first st of 2nd needle on to end of first needle and last st of second needle onto third needle.

Shape toe: 1st rnd: 1st needle: K to last 3 sts, K2tog, K1; 2nd needle: K1, K2togtbl, K to last 3 sts, K2tog, K1; 3rd needle: K1, K2togtbl, K to end. 2nd rnd: K. Rep these 2 rnds until 26 sts rem. K sts from first needle on to end of third needle. Graft sts or cast off sts from 2 needles tog. Press.

Chapter 14

Family Life
Special Privileges

One of the pleasantest aspects of knitting and crochet is their adaptability in providing for the 'special cases' in the family — those with extra-inch problems, the chilly mortals, the aged, and the infirm. The designs in this group are intended to help those who are not stock size or require that little extra warmth, or added comfort which hand knitted or crocheted things can so easily supply.

A Kindly Sweater

With its patterned panels and long or short sleeves, this sweater caters for the larger-than-stock sizes

Materials: Long Sleeve Version: 8/**9**/9 (50g) balls; **Short Sleeve Version:** 7/**8**/8 (50g) balls Patons Purple Heather 4-ply. Pair each Nos 12 and 10 needles, and set of 4 No 12 needles with points at both ends.

Measurements: To fit 40–41/**42–43**/44–45 in bust; length from top of shoulders, 23/**23½**/23½ in; sleeve seam: Long, 15/**15½**/15½ in (adjustable); Short, 5/**5**/5 in.

Tension: 14 sts and 18 rows to 2 in over st st on No 10 needles.

PATT PANEL 29

1st row: Tw2, P2, K1, * K1, K2tog, yf K1, yf, K2tog; rep from * twice more, K2, P2, Tw2. 2nd row: P2, K2, P1, P2tog, yrn, * P3, yrn, sl 1, P2tog, psso, yrn; rep from * once more, P3, yrn, P2tog, P1, K2, P2.

3rd row: Tw2, P2, K1, * K1, yf, K2tog, K1, K2tog, yf; rep from * twice more, K2, P2, Tw2. 4th row: P2, K2, P1, * P2 yrn, sl 1, P2tog, psso, yrn, P1; rep from * twice more, P2, K2, P2. These 4 rows form patt.

BACK

** With No 12 needles, cast on 150/**156**/164 sts, and work K1, P1 rib for 2 in, inc 1 st at end of last row: 151/**157**/165 sts.

Change to No 10 needles and work in reverse st st, placing patt panels as follows: 1st row: P22/**23**/24, patt panel 29 1st row, (P10/**12**/15, patt panel 29 1st row) twice, P22/**23**/24. 2nd row: K22/**23**/24, patt panel 29 2nd row, (K10/**12**/15, patt panel 29 2nd row) twice, K22/**23**/24.

Work straight in patt until back measures 14/**14**/13½ in, ending with right side facing. *Note:* The largest size is shorter at this point, the extra length being adjusted in the armhole shaping. Shape armhole by casting off 4 sts at

beg of next 2 rows, then dec 1 st at each end of every row until 123/**129**/137 sts rem. Now dec 1 st at each end of next and every alt row until 111/**115**/121 sts rem, ending with right side facing.**

Work straight in patt until back measures 23/**23½**/23½ in, ending with right side facing.

Shape shoulders by casting off 11/**12**/12 sts at beg of next 2 rows, then 12/**12**/13 sts at beg of next 4 rows. Leave rem sts on a length of yarn.

FRONT

Work as back from ** to **.

Work straight until front measures 19/**19½**/19½ in, ending with right side facing.

Shape neck: Next row: Patt 46/**48**/50, turn and leave rem sts on a length of yarn. Next row: In patt. Dec 1 st at neck edge on every row until 42/**44**/46 sts rem. Now dec 1 st at neck edge on next and every alt row until 35/**36**/38 sts rem. Cont straight until Front matches back at armhole edge, ending with right side facing.

Shape shoulder by casting off 11/**12**/12 sts at beg of next row, 12/**12**/13 sts at beg of foll 2 alt rows. With right side facing, leave centre 19/**19**/21 sts on length of yarn, rejoin yarn to rem sts and work to end. Complete to match first side reversing all shapings.

LONG SLEEVES

With No 12 needles, cast on 60/**62**/64 sts and work K1, P1 rib for 2 in. Next row: Rib 2/**3**/4, M1, * rib 5/5/5, M1; rep from * to last 3/4/5 sts, rib 3/**4**/5: 72/**74**/76 sts.

Change to No 10 needles and work in reverse st st, starting with a P row, inc 1 st at each end of 7th/**3rd**/3rd and every foll 7th row until there are 100/**106**/112 sts. Work straight until sleeve seam measures 15/**15½**/15½ in, ending with right side facing (adjust length here).

Shape top by casting off 4 sts at beg of next 2 rows, then dec 1 st at each end of next and every alt row until 48/**52**/56 sts rem. Now dec 1 st at each end of every row until 14 sts rem. Cast off.

SHORT SLEEVES

With No 12 needles, cast on 86/**92**/98 sts and work K1, P1 rib for 1 in. Next row: Rib 13/**13**/14, M1, (rib 12/**13**/14, M1) 5/5/5 times, rib 13/**14**/14: 92/**98**/104 sts.

Change to No 10 needles and work in reverse st st, starting with a P row, inc 1 st at each end of 3rd and every foll 8th row until there are 100/**106**/112 sts. Work straight until sleeve seam measures 5 in, ending with right side facing. Shape top as for long sleeves.

MAKE UP AND NECKBAND

Observing general method on page 81, block and press. Join shoulder, side and sleeve seams and insert sleeves.

With right side facing and set of No 12 needles, start at top of left shoulder and knit up 40 sts down left side of neck, K19/**19**/21 sts across front, knit up 40 sts up right side of neck, K41/**43**/45 across back: 140/**142**/146 sts.

Work K1, P1 rib for 1 in. Cast off evenly in rib. Press seams.

Edge-to-edge Casual

A classic sleeveless style in a range of sizes which can be slipped on as a chill-chaser

Materials: 8/**9**/9/**10** (50g) balls Patons Double Knitting. Pair each Nos 8 and 10 needles. 2 stitch-holders.

Measurements: To fit 38/**40**/42/**44** in bust/chest; length from top of shoulders, 24½/**25**/25½/**26** in.

Tension: 11 sts and 15 rows to 2 in over st st on No 8 needles.

BACK

With No 10 needles, using the chain method, cast on 103/**109**/115/**121** sts and work in st st for 1½ in, ending with a K row. Next row: K thus forming ridge for hemline. Starting with a K row, work st st for a further 1½ in, ending with wrong side facing. Next row: P5/**4**/7/7, inc in next st, (P12/**13**/13/**14**, inc in next st) 7 times, P to end: 111/**117**/123/**129** sts.

Change to No 8 needles and cont in st st until back measures 15½/**15½**/16/**16** in from ridge, ending with right side facing. Shape armholes by casting off 5/5/6/6 sts at beg of next 4 rows, then dec 1 st at each end of next and every alt row until 83/**87**/89/**93** sts rem. Work straight until back measures 24½/**25**/25½/**26** in from ridge, ending with right side facing.

Shape shoulders by casting off 8/8/9/9 sts at beg of next 4 rows, then 8/**9**/8/**9** sts at beg of next 2 rows. Cast off rem sts.

POCKET LININGS (2)

With No 8 needles, cast on 28 sts and work in st st for 4 in, ending with a P row. Leave these sts on a spare needle.

LEFT FRONT

With No 10 needles, using the chain method, cast on 49/**52**/55/**58** sts and work in st st for 1½ in, ending with a K row. Next row: K, thus forming ridge for hemline. Starting with a K row, work in st st for a further 1½ in, ending with wrong side facing. Next row: P inc 4 sts evenly: 53/**56**/59/**62** sts.

Change to No 8 needles and cont in st st until front measures 5½ in from ridge, ending with right side facing. Place pocket. Next row: K15/**16**/17/**18**, slip next 28 sts on to a stitch-holder and

in place of these, K across sts from 1st pocket lining, K10/**12**/14/**16**. Cont in st st until front measures 14½/**14½**/15/**15** in from ridge, ending with right side facing.

Shape front edge by dec 1 st at end of next and every foll 4th row, at the same time when side edge measures the same as back, and with right side facing, shape armhole by casting off 5/**5**/6/**6** sts at beg of next and foll alt row, then dec 1 st at same edge on next and foll 3/**4**/4/**5** alt rows.

Now keeping armhole edge straight cont dec at front edge on every 4th row from previous dec as before until 24/**25**/26/**27** sts rem. Work straight until front measures same as back at arm hole edge, ending with right side facing.

Shape shoulder by casting off 8/**8**/9/**9** sts at beg of next and foll alt row. Work 1 row. Cast off rem sts.

RIGHT FRONT
Work to correspond with left front reversing all shapings. Row placing pocket reads: K10/**12**/14/**16**, slip next 28 sts on to a stitch-holder and in place of these K across sts from 2nd pocket lining, K15/**16**/17/**18**.

ARMHOLE BORDERS
Join shoulder seams. With right side facing and No 10 needles, knit up 100/**106**/106/**112** sts round armhole. Work K1, P1 rib for 1 in. Cast off evenly in rib.

POCKET TOPS
With right side facing and No 10 needles, K across sts from stitch-holder. Work 3 rows st st. Next row: P. Work 4 rows more in st st, starting with a P row. Cast off.

TO MAKE UP
Observing general method on page 81, block and press. Join side seams. Fold hems at ridge to wrong side and slip-hem in position. Stitch pocket linings in position on wrong side. Fold pocket tops at ridge to wrong side and slip-hem lightly in position. Neatly stitch side of pocket tops on right side.

FRONT BORDER
With No 10 needles, cast on 9 sts and work K1, P1 rib, rows on right side having a K1 at each end, until strip fits up one front edge, round neck and down other front edge, when slightly stretched. Cast off in rib. Sew Border neatly in position. Press seams.

Accommodating Cardigan
In three sizes up to a 44-inch bust

Materials: 10/**11**/11 (50g) balls Patons Purple Heather 4-ply. Pair each Nos 13 and 11 needles. 2 stitch-holders. Cable needle. 7 buttons.

Measurements: To fit 40/**42**/44 in bust; Length from shoulder to lower edge, 24¼/**24½**/24¾ in; sleeve seam, 18 in.

Tension: 15 sts and 19 rows to 2 in over st st on No 11 needles.

BACK
With No 11 needles, cast on 160/**168**/176 sts. Work K1, P1 rib for 1½ in. Work in st st until back measures 16½ in from start.

Shape armholes by casting off 8/**9**/10 sts at beg of next 2 rows, then dec 1 st at each end of next and every alt row until 122/**128**/134 sts rem. Cont on these sts until work measures 7¾/**8**/8¼ in from start of armhole shaping.

Change to No 13 needles and shape shoulders by casting off 14/**15**/16 sts at beg of next 4 rows, 15/**16**/17 sts at beg of next 2 rows. Cast off.

POCKET

With No 13 needles, cast on 38 sts. Work in st st for 4¼ in, ending with a K row. Slip sts on to a stitch-holder.

RIGHT FRONT

With No 11 needles, cast on 80/**84**/88 sts. Work ribbing to match back.

Work in st st with chequer cable panel as follows:

1st row: K26/**28**/30, (P4, KB4) 3 times, P4, K26/**28**/30. 2nd row: P26/**28**/30, (K4, PB4) 3 times, K4, P26/**28**/30. 3rd row: As 1st. 4th row: P26/**28**/30, (K4, cable 2 back by slipping next 2 sts on to cable needle and leaving at back, PB2, then PB2 across sts on cable needle) 3 times, K4, P26/**28**/30.

5th, 6th and 7th rows: Rep 1st, 2nd and 1st. 8th row: P26/**28**/30, (PB4, K4) 3 times, PB4, P26/**28**/30. 9th row: K26/**28**/30, (KB4, P4) 3 times, KB4, K26/**28**/30. 10th row: As 8th.

11th row: K26/**28**/30, (cable 2 front by slipping next 2 sts on to cable needle and leaving at front, KB2, then KB2 across sts on cable needle, P4) 3 times, cable 2 front, K26/**28**/30. 12th, 13th and 14th rows: As 8th, 9th and 8th. These 14 rows form patt. Rep 1st to 14th row incl twice more.

Place Pocket: Next row: K21/**23**/25, K next 38 sts on to a stitch-holder and leave, K21/**23**/25. Next row: P21/**23**/25, slip sts from pocket on to left-hand needle, P5, patt 28 (2nd row), P5 across these sts, P21/**23**/25.

Noting that next row will be 3rd row, cont in patt until work measures 15 in from start, ending at front edge.

Shape front slope by dec 1 st at front edge on next and every foll 5th row until work measures same as back to armhole shaping, ending at side edge.

Still dec on every 5th row from previous dec at front edge, shape armhole by casting off 8/**9**/10 sts at beg of next row, then dec 1 st at armhole edge on next and every alt row until 11 dec in all have been worked at armhole edge.

Cont dec at front edge only on every 5th row as before until 43/**46**/49 sts rem. Cont on these sts until work measures same as back to shoulder shaping, ending at armhole edge.

Change to No 13 needles and shape shoulder: 1st and 3rd rows: Cast off 14/**15**/16, work to end. 2nd and 4th rows: Work all across. Cast off rem 15/**16**/17 sts.

POCKET TOP

Slip 38 sts from stitch-holder on a No 13 needle: right side facing for 1st row. 1st row: K2 (P1, K1) 8 times, P1, M1K, (P1, K1) 8 times, P1, K2. 2nd row: * K1, P1; rep from * to last st, K1. 3rd row: K2, * P1, K1; rep from * to last st, K1. Rep 2nd and 3rd rows until Pocket Top measures ¾ in from start. Cast off in rib.

POCKET, LEFT FRONT, AND POCKET TOP

Work to match right front, reversing all shapings.

SLEEVES

With No 13 needles, cast on 70/**74**/78 sts. Work K1, P1 rib for 3 in. Next row: Rib 5/**2**/4, (inc in next st, rib 5/**6**/6) 10 times, inc in next st, rib to end: 81/**85**/89 sts.

Change to No 11 needles and work in st st, inc 1 st at each end of 7th and every foll 9th row until there are 109/**113**/117 sts. Cont on these sts until work measures 18 in from start.

Shape top by casting off 8/**9**/10 sts at beg of next 2 rows, then dec 1 st at each end of next and every alt row until 71/**73**/75 sts rem. Cast off 3 sts at beg of next 14 rows. Cast off.

FRONT BAND

With No 13 needles, cast on 13 sts. 1st row: K2, (P1, K1) 5 times, K1. 2nd row: (K1, P1) 6 times, K1.

3rd to 6th row: Rep 1st and 2nd rows twice. 7th row: Rib 5, cast off 3, rib to end. 8th row: Rib 5, cast on 3, rib to end. Cont in this manner working a buttonhole as on 7th and 8th rows on every 23rd and 24th rows from previous buttonhole until 7 buttonholes in all have been completed. Cont in rib until work measures 52½/**53**/53½ in from start. Cast off.

TO MAKE UP

Observing general method on page 81, block and press. Stitch pockets in position on wrong side and pocket tops on right side. Join shoulder, side and sleeve seams and insert sleeves. Stitch on front band. Press seams. Sew on buttons.

A Spencer is Snug

This traditional 'in-between' bodice takes its title from a jacket named after the nineteenth-century Earl Spencer

Materials: 3 (50g) balls Patons Baby 3-ply Courtelle. Pair each Nos 10 and 6 needles. A spare No. 6 needle.

Measurements: To fit 34–36 in bust; length from top of shoulders, 18 in (after pressing); sleeve seam, 18 in (after pressing).

Note: By using No 9 needles in place of No 10 and No 5 in place of No 6, a garment can be knitted to fit 37–39 in bust.

The Spencer is worked in one piece up to division for armholes. The first st should be slipped purlways on every row thus forming a chain edge.

With No 6 needles, cast on 110 sts very loosely, and K 28 rows. Make holes at waist: Next row: K1, * K2tog, yf; rep from * to last 3 sts, K2tog, K1: 109 sts. K 1 row.

Commence dart shaping as follows: 1st row: K21, yf, K23, yf, K21, yf, K23, yf, K21. 2nd and alt rows: K. 3rd row: K22, (yf, K23) 3 times, yf, K22. 5th row: (K23, yf) twice, K25, (yf, K23) twice. 7th row: K24, yf, K23, yf, K27, yf, K23, yf, K24. Cont in this manner, inc on front and back panels on every alt row until the row 'K41, yf, K23, yf, K61, yf, K23, yf, K41' has been worked: 193 sts. K 5 rows.

Work first half of Front: 1st row: K44, turn. K 23 rows on these 44 sts.

Shape neck: 1st row: K1, K2tog, yf, K2tog, K to end. 2nd row: K. Rep these 2 rows 12 times, then 1st row once: 30 sts. Next row: (K2tog, K2) 7 times, K2. Cast off.

Slip first 20 sts on needle on to a length of yarn and leave for sleeve. Rejoin yarn and work Back as follows: 1st row: K65, turn. K 23 rows on these 65 sts.

Shape shoulders: 1st row: K2, K2tog, K to last 4 sts, K2tog, K2. 2nd row: K. Rep these 2 rows 17 times, then 1st row once. Next row: * K2tog, yf; rep from * to last st, K1. K 2 rows. Cast off. Slip first 20 sts on needle on to a length of yarn and leave. Rejoin yarn to rem 44 sts and work second half of Front: K 24 rows.

Shape neck: 1st row: K to last 5 sts, K2tog, yf, K2tog, K1. 2nd row: K. Rep these 2 rows 12 times, then 1st row once: 30 sts. Next row: K2, (K2, K2tog) 7 times. Cast off.

Sleeves: Using a flat seam join cast-off shoulders on front to shaped portion on back. Divide 20 sts left for sleeve on to 2 No 6 needles.

With No 6 needles incl spare needle, with right side of work facing, starting at centre of these 20 sts, K10, knit up 44 sts round armhole, K rem 10 sts: 64 sts. K 3 rows. Next row: K2, K2tog, K to last 4 sts, K2tog, K2. Cont dec as on last row on every foll 8th row until 40 sts rem. Change to No 10 needles and work 24 rows K1, P1 rib. Cast off loosely in rib. Work second sleeve in same manner.

TO MAKE UP

Observing general method on page 81, press, stretching to size. Looping tog sl st edges, join centre front and sleeve seams. Press seams. Make a cord and thread through holes at waist.

This Bedjacket Flatters

The pleats hang from a well-fitting yoke to give a smartly comfortable fit

Materials: 13 (25g) balls Patons Baby 4-ply Courtelle. Pair No 10 needles. Cable needle. 4 buttons.

Measurements: To fit 34–37 in bust; length from top of shoulders, 19½ in;

sleeve seam, 17 in.

Tension: 14½ sts and 18½ rows to 2 in over st st on No 10 needles.

Additional Abbreviations (see page 29): C4F=Slip next 2 sts on to cable

needle and leave at front of work, K next 2 sts, then K 2 sts from cable needle.

Note: All sl sts are slipped knitways throughout.

LEFT FRONT

Cast on 93 sts. K 8 rows. Work in lace rib with garter st border as follows:
1st row: * K7, yf, sl 1, K2tog, psso, yf; rep from * to last 13 sts, K13. 2nd row: Sl 1, K5, P to last st, K1. 3rd row: * K7, P3; rep from * to last 13 sts, K13. 4th row: Sl 1, K5, P to last st, K1. These 4 rows form patt.

Cont in patt until work measures 11½ in from start, ending with a 4th patt row. Shape armholes: Next row: Cast off 7, patt to end. Next row: Patt to last st, K1. Next row: K1, K2togtbl, patt to end. Cont thus, dec 1 st at armhole edge on every alt row until 69 sts rem. Next row: Sl 1, K5, * (P2tog, P3) twice, P2tog, P3tog, P2tog, P3; rep from * to last 3 sts, P3tog: 49 sts. Sl sts on a length of yarn.

SLEEVES

Cast on 38 sts. K 21 rows. Next row: K2, inc once in each of next 15 sts, K4, inc once in each of next 14 sts, K3: 67 sts. Work in lace rib patt as follows:
1st row: * K7, yf, sl 1, K2tog, psso, yf; rep from * to last 7 sts, K7. 2nd row: K1, P to last st, K1. 3rd row: * K7, P3; rep from * to last 7 sts, K7. 4th row: K1, P to last st, K1. Cont in patt as on these 4 rows, inc 1 st at each end of next and every foll 8th row until there are 97 sts, working extra sts into patt. Cont on these sts until work measures 17 in from start, ending with a 4th row of patt. Shape top by casting off 7 sts at beg of next 2 rows. Next row: K1, K2togtbl, patt to last 3 sts, K2 tog, K1. Next row: K1, patt to last st, K1. Cont thus, dec 1 st at each end of 3rd and every foll 4th row until 65 sts rem. Work 1 row. Sl sts on a length of yarn.

BACK

Cast on 157 sts. K 8 rows. Work in lace rib patt as 1st to 4th row of sleeves until work matches left front to arm-

hole shaping. Shape armholes by casting off 7 sts at beg of next 2 rows. Next row: K1, K2togtbl, patt to last 3 sts, K2tog, K1. Next row: K1, patt to last st, K1. Cont thus, dec 1 st at each end of next and every alt row until 109 sts rem. Next row: K1, P2, * (P3, P2tog) 3 times, P3tog, P2tog; rep from * to last 6 sts, P5, K1: 79 sts. Sl sts on a length of yarn.

RIGHT FRONT

Cast on 93 sts. K 8 rows. Work in lace rib patt with garter st border as follows:
1st row: Sl 1, K12, * yf, sl 1, K2tog, psso, yf, K7; rep from * to end. 2nd row: K1, P to last 6 sts, K6. 3rd row: Sl 1, K12, * P3, K7; rep from * to end. 4th row: K1, P to last 6 sts, K6. Cont in patt as on these 4 rows until work measures 11½ in from start, ending with a 1st row of patt.

Keeping patt correct, shape armhole: Next row: Cast off 7, patt to end. Next row: Patt to last 3 sts, K2tog, K1. Next row: K1, patt to end. Cont thus, dec 1 st at armhole edge on next and every alt row until 69 sts rem. Next row: K1, P2tog, * P3, P2tog, P3tog, P2tog, (P3, P2tog) twice; rep from * to last 6 sts, K6: 50 sts.

Start yoke: (right side facing), Next row: Sl 1, K5, P to end, then sl sts left on lengths of yarn on to left-hand needle in the foll order: first left Front, then one sleeve, back and finally second sleeve. With right side facing, P across these sts to last 6 sts, K6: 308 sts.

Work yoke as follows: 1st row (button-hole started): Sl 1, K5, * C4F; rep from * to last 6 sts, K2, cast off 2, (1 st on needle after cast-off), K1. 2nd row: Sl 1, K1, cast on 2, K2, P to last 6 sts, K6. 3rd row: Sl 1, K5, P5, (P2tog, P2) 72 times, P3, K6: 236 sts. 4th row: Sl 1, K to end. 5th row: Sl 1, K5, P to last 6 sts, K6. 6th to 9th row: Rep 4th and 5th rows twice. 10th row: Sl 1, K5, P to last 6 sts, K6.

11th and 12th rows: As 1st and 2nd. 13th row: Sl 1, K5, P1, (P2tog, P2) 55 times, P2tog, P1, K6: 180 sts. 14th to 22nd row: As 4th to 12th. 23rd row:

Sl 1, K5, P1, (P2tog, P2) 41 times, P2tog, P1, K6: 138 sts. 24th to 27th row: Rep 4th and 5th rows twice. 28th row: As 4th. 29th row: Sl 1, K5, P5, (P2tog, P2) 30 times, P1, K6: 108 sts. 30th row: As 10th. 31st and 32nd rows: As 1st and 2nd. 33rd row: Sl 1, P6, (P2tog, P2) 23 times, P2tog, P6, K1: 84 sts.

Work picot edge: 1st row: Sl 1, K to end. 2nd row: Sl 1, P to last st, K1. 3rd row: Sl 1, * yf, K2tog; rep from * to last st, K1. 4th row: As 2nd. 5th row: Sl 1, K to end. Cast off loosely purlways.

TO MAKE UP

Observing general method on page 81, block and press, taking care not to stretch yoke.

Join side and sleeve seams and sleeve shaping up to start of yoke. Fold over picot edge at row of holes and stitch to wrong side of work. Press seams. Sew on buttons.

Bedsocks in Crochet: Kneecaps in Knitting

They raise a smile sometimes but their extra warmth brings extra comfort to elderly or aching bones

BEDSOCKS

Materials: 2 (50g) balls Patons Purple Heather 4-ply. No. 3·50 mm crochet hook. 1½ yds ribbon.

Note: Eyelet is worked as follows: 1tr, 1ch, 1tr all into one st.

Using yarn double, make 50ch. Break off 1 strand of yarn. Foundation row: 1htr in 2nd ch from hook, 1htr in next 48ch, 1ch, turn. Work in patt as follows: 1st row: 3ch, 1tr in base of 3ch, * miss 2 sts, 1 Eyelet in next st; rep from * to end of row, 1ch, turn. 2nd row: Miss first st, 1htr in next 48 sts, turn. These 2 rows form patt. Cont in patt until work measures 6½ in from start, ending with a 2nd row of patt.

Make holes for ribbon: Next row: 1ch, 1htr in first st, * 3ch, miss 2 sts, 1htr in next 3 sts; rep from * to last 3 sts, 3ch, miss 2 sts, 1htr in last st, 1ch, turn. Next row: Miss first st, * 2htr in 3ch sp, 1htr in next 3 sts; rep from *, ending 2htr in last 3ch sp, 1htr in each of last 2 sts: 50 sts. Fasten off.

Turn work to right side and rejoin yarn to 18th st from right-hand side of work and start to work top of foot: 1st row: 3ch, 1tr into same st, (miss 2 sts, 1 Eyelet in next st) 5 times, 1ch, turn. 2nd row: Miss first st, 1htr in next 15 sts, 1ch, turn. Rep last 2 rows 8 times more. Shape toe: Next row: Miss 2 sts, 1htr in each st to last 2 sts, miss next st, 1htr in last st, 1ch, turn. Rep last row 3 times more: 8 sts.

Work foot: Next row: Work across 8 sts, work 31htr down side of instep, miss first st of next 17 sts, then work 1htr into next 16 sts, 1ch, turn. Next row: Miss first st, work 1htr in next and every st to end, work 31htr down other side of instep, miss first st of rem 17 sts, then work 1htr into next 16 sts, 1ch, turn: 102 sts.

Shape toe: 1st row: Miss first st, 1htr in next 46 sts, miss 1 st, 1htr in next 6 sts, miss 1 st, 1htr in next 47 sts, 1ch, turn. 2nd row: Miss first st, 1htr to end, 1ch, turn. 3rd row: Miss first st, 1htr in next 46 sts, miss 1 st, 1htr in next 4 sts, miss 1 st, 1htr to end, 1ch, turn. 4th row: As 2nd. 5th row: Miss first st, 1htr in next 46 sts, miss 1 st, 1htr in next 2 sts, miss 1 st, 1htr to end, 1ch, turn. 6th row: As 2nd. 7th row: Miss first st, 1htr in next 45 sts, miss 1 st, 1htr in next 2 sts, miss 1 st, 1htr to end, 1ch, turn.

Shape heel and cont toe shaping as follows: 8th row: Miss 2 sts, 1htr in next and every st to last 2 sts, miss 1 st, 1htr in last st, 1ch, turn. 9th row: Miss 2 sts, 1htr in next 42 sts, miss 1 st, 1htr in next 2 sts, miss 1 st, 1htr in next 42 sts, miss 1 st, 1htr in last st, 1ch, turn. 10th row: Miss 2 sts, 1htr in next 40 sts, miss 1 st, 1htr in next 2 sts, miss 1 st, 1htr in next 40 sts, miss 1 st, 1htr in last st, 1ch, turn. 11th row: Miss 2 sts, 1htr in next 38 sts, miss 1 st, 1htr in next 2 sts, miss 1 st, 1htr in next 38 sts, miss 1 st, 1htr in last st, 1ch, turn. 12th row: Miss 2 sts, 1htr in next 36 sts, miss 1 st, 1htr in next 2 sts, miss 1 st, 1htr in next 36 sts, miss 1 st, 1htr in last st, 1ch, turn. Fasten off.

TO MAKE UP

Observing general method on page 81, press. Join side edges tog. Press seams. Thread ribbon through holes at ankle.

KNEECAPS

Materials: 3 (25g) balls Patons Baby 4-ply Courtelle. Pair No 11 needles.

Tension: 15 sts and 19 rows to 2 in over st st on No 11 needles.

Cast on 92 sts loosely and work K2, P2 rib for 2¾ in.

Shape Cap: 1st row: Rib 53, turn. 2nd row: K14, turn. 3rd row: K15, turn. 4th row: K16, turn. 5th row: K17, turn.

Cont thus taking 1 more st into garter st on every row until 22 ribbed sts are left unworked at each side, turn.

Cont working on centre 48 sts. Next row: K45, K2tog, K1, turn. Next row: K to last 3 sts of cap, K2tog, K1, turn. Rep last row until 14 sts rem in centre. Now pick up and K17 sts along side of cap, then work next 22 sts in rib. Next row: Rib 53, pick up and P17 sts along other side of cap, rib rem 22 sts. Work K2, P2 rib for 2¾ in. Cast off loosely in rib.

Join back seam.

Comfort above the Waist...

This cape and draught-excluding shawl are both in knitting

CAPE

Materials: 7 (50g) balls Patons Double Knitting. Pair each Nos 8 and 3 needles. 1½ yds of 1 in ribbon.

Measurement: Length at side seams, 16 in.

Tension: 9 sts and 9 rows to 2 in over patt on No 3 needles.

BACK

With No 3 needles, cast on 188 sts and K 2 rows.
Change to patt as follows: 1st row (wrong side facing): K2, * yrn, P4tog; rep from * to last 2 sts, yon, K2. 2nd row: K2, * (K1, P1, K1) in next st, K1; rep from * to last st, K1. 3rd row: K2, * P4tog, yrn; rep from * to last 5 sts, P4tog, K1. 4th row: K2, * (K1, P1, K1) in next st, K1; rep from * to last 2 sts, K2. These 4 rows form patt.
Keeping continuity of patt, shape back as follows: 1st row: K2, * (yrn, P4tog) 22 times, * yrn, (P4tog) twice, sl 2nd st on right needle over 1st st; rep from * to *, yon, K2. 2nd row: As 2nd patt row. 3rd row: K2, (P4tog, yrn) 22 times, (P4tog) twice, sl 2nd st on right needle over 1st st, (yrn, P4tog) 22 times, K1. 4th row: As 4th patt row.
5th row: K2, * (yrn, P4tog) 21 times*, yrn, (P4tog) twice, sl 2nd st on right needle over 1st st; rep from * to *, yon, K2. 6th row: As 2nd patt row. 7th row: K2, (P4tog, yrn) 21 times, (P4tog) twice, sl 2nd st on right needle over 1st st, (yrn, P4tog) 21 times, K1. 8th row:

As 4th patt row. Cont dec thus over centre 8 sts until 52 sts rem.
Note: Your last 4 dec rows will read: 1st row: K2, * (yrn, P4tog) 5 times*, yrn, (P4tog) twice, sl 2nd st on right needle over 1st st; rep from * to *, yon, K2. 2nd row: As 2nd patt row. 3rd row: K2, (P4tog, yrn) 5 times, (P4tog) twice, sl 2nd st on right needle over 1st st, (yrn, P4tog) 5 times, K1. 4th row: As 4th patt row. K 2 rows.
Cast off.

FRONTS

Right: With No 3 needles, cast on 92 sts and K 2 rows, then work 4 patt rows as for Back.

Shape front as follows: 1st dec row: K2, (yrn, P4tog) 20 times, * yrn, (P4tog) twice, sl 2nd st on right needle over 1st st, yon, K2 *. 2nd row: As 2nd patt row. 3rd row: As 3rd patt row. 4th row: As 4th patt row. 5th row: K2, (yrn, P4tog) 19 times, work as for 1st dec row from * to *. 6th to 8th row: As 2nd to 4th. Cont dec thus until 24 sts rem, ending with 4th patt row. K 2 rows. Cast off.

Left: Work as for right front reversing shapings. Your first dec row will read: 1st row: K2, yrn, (P4tog) twice, sl 2nd st on right needle over 1st st, (yrn, P4tog) 20 times, yon, K2.

TO MAKE UP

Observing general method on page 81, block and press. Join side seams.

Border: With No 8 needles, cast on 4 sts: 1st and 2nd rows: K. 3rd row: Sl 1, K2, pass 2nd and 3rd sts over 1st st, K1. 4th row: K. 5th row: Cast on 2 sts, K4.

Rep rows 2 to 5 incl until strip fits up right front, round neck and down left front when slightly stretched. Sew in position as you go along. Cast off. Press seams.
Cut ribbon in half and sew a piece to each front at neck edge.

Fringe: Cut rem yarn into 9 in lengths and taking 8 strands tog each time, knot a fringe all round lower edge of cape as described in Chapter 8.

TWO-COLOUR SHAWL

Materials: 4 (50g) balls Light and 6 (50g) balls Dark Patons Double Knitting. Pair each Nos 7 and 9 (14 inch needles) and 2 spare No 7 needles.

Measurements: Length at centre back, excluding fringe, approx 38 in.

Tension: $10\frac{1}{2}$ sts and 14 rows to 2 in over st st on No 7 needles.

Additional Abbreviations (see page 29): L=Light; D=Dark.

Note: Carry yarns not in use loosely up side of work.

With the 4 No 7 needles and L, cast on 437 sts and to facilitate working, divide sts evenly on 3 needles and patt as follows:

1st row: (wrong side), With L, K2, * yf, K1; rep from * to last 2 sts, K2. 2nd row: With L, K, dropping all yfs of previous row. 3rd row: With L, K2, K3tog, * yf, yrn, K1, yf, yrn, sl 2, K3tog, P2sso; rep from * to last 6 sts, yf, yrn, K1, yf, yrn, K3tog, K2.

Join in D. 4th row: With D, K2, * K1, K into front of yrn and back of yf of previous row; rep from * to last 3 sts, K3.

5th row: With D, as 1st. 6th row: With D, as 2nd.

7th row: With D, K2, * K1, yf, yrn, sl 2, K3tog, P2sso, yf, yrn; rep from * to last 3 sts, K3. 8th row: With L, as 4th. These 8 rows form patt. Rep 1st and 2nd rows once more.

1st dec row: With L, K1, sl 3, K4tog, P3sso, K3tog, * yf, yrn, K1, yf, yrn, sl 2, K3tog, P2sso; rep from * 33 times more, yf, yrn, sl 3, K4tog, P3sso, ** yf, yrn, sl 2, K3tog, P2sso, yf, yrn, K1; rep from ** to last 11 sts, yf, yrn, K3tog, sl 3, K4tog, P3sso, K1: 419 sts.

Rep 4th, 5th and 6th rows once more.

2nd dec row: With D, patt 206, yf, yrn, sl 3, K4tog, P3sso, * yf, yrn, sl 2, K3tog, P2sso, yf, yrn, K1; rep from * to last 2 sts, K2: 413 sts.

Rep 8th, 1st and 2nd rows once more.

3rd dec row: With L, patt 203, yf, yrn, sl 3, K4tog, P3sso, * yf, yrn, sl 2, K3tog, P2sso, yf, yrn, K1; rep from * to last 5

sts, yf, yrn, K3tog, K2: 407 sts. Rep 4th, 5th and 6th rows once more.

4th dec row: With D, patt 200, yf, yrn, sl 3, K4tog, P3sso, * yf, yrn, sl 2, K3tog, P2sso, yf, yrn, K1; rep from * to last 2 sts, K2: 401 sts.

Rep 8th, 1st and 2nd rows once more.

5th dec row: With L, K1, sl 3, K4tog, P3sso, K3tog, * yf, yrn, K1, yf, yrn, sl 2, K3tog, P2sso; rep from * 30 times more, yf, yrn, sl 3, K4tog, P3sso, ** yf, yrn, sl 2, K3tog, P2sso, yf, yrn, K1; rep from ** to last 11 sts, yf, yrn, K3tog, sl 3, K4tog, P3sso, K1: 383 sts.

Rep 4th, 5th and 6th rows once more.

Keeping continuity of patt, cont dec 6 sts thus at centre, on next and every foll 4th row, and 6 sts at each end of every 16th row from previous dec until 23 sts rem, ending with 3rd patt row.

Next row: With L, K1, (sl 3, K4tog, P3sso) 3 times, K1: 5 sts. Next row: With L, sl 2, K3tog, P2sso. Fasten off.

TO MAKE UP

With right side facing, No 9 needles and D, knit up 280 sts along the top edge of shawl and work 4 rows garter st. Cast off.

Cut rem D yarn into 10 in lengths and taking 4 strands tog each time, knot along cast-on edge to form fringe as described in Chapter 8. Trim ends. Do not press.

... and Below

The frail and immobile will find that this knee-rug keeps the legs and feet warm

KNEE-RUG

Materials: 9(50g) balls Patons Double Knitting. Pair No 8 needles.

Measurements: 40 × 40 in (approx).

Tension: 11 sts and 15 rows to 2 in over st st on No 8 needles.

Cast on 202 sts. Work 8 rows in garter st (every row sl 1, K to end). Work drop st row as follows:

Next row: Sl 1, K5, * yf, K2tog, K7; rep from * to last 7 sts, yf, K2tog, K5.

Cont in garter st until work measures 39½ in from beg.

Next row: Sl 1, K5, * drop one st to 9th row from beg, yf, K8; rep from * to last 7 sts, drop one st to 9th row from beg, yf, K6.

Work 7 rows in garter st. Cast off.

Observing general method on page 81, block and press very lightly.

Chapter 15

Follow the Trend with Knitting and Crochet

The woman who knits and crochets finds it easy to keep in step with fashion – her scope is not confined to run-of-the-mill sweaters and twin sets. She can experiment to her heart's content; as soon as a new trend is launched, she can respond. Whether skirt lengths go up or down, whether sleeves lengthen, shorten, or disappear, there is no problem in conforming. New stitches and new fabrics can be produced at a moment's notice, and the very texture of knitting and crochet has repeatedly inspired such great designers as Dior and Cardin. The whole wide world of colour is open to her in all its infinite variety and freedom of choice. The designs in this group are not intended to represent trendy extremes but, in a simple way, to provide themes on which the individual can improvise. They are all uncomplicated to make and are supremely wearable.

The Long Line and Chunky Look

Give this sleeveless cardigan an unmistakably modern air

Materials: 10/**11**/11/**12** (50g) balls Patons Doublet. Pair each Nos 4, 5 and 8 needles. 2 stitch-holders. 8 buttons.

Measurements: To fit bust 34/**36**/38/**40** in; length, 29/**30**/31/**32** in.

Tension: 8½ sts and 17 rows to 2 in over patt on No 5 needles.

BACK

With No 8 needles, cast on 83/**87**/91/**95** sts and work K1, P1 rib for 1 in, rows on right side having K1 at each end.

Change to No 4 needles and patt as follows: 1st row: (right side), K. 2nd row: P. 3rd row: K3, * sl 1, K3; rep from * to end. 4th row: K3, * yft, sl 1, yb, K3; rep from * to end. 5th and 6th rows: As 3rd and 4th. 7th row: K. 8th row: P. 9th row: K1, * sl 1, K3; rep from * to last 2 sts, sl 1, K1. 10th row: K1, * yft, sl 1, yb, K3; rep from * to last 2 sts, yft, sl 1, yb, K1. 11th and 12th rows: As 9th and 10th. These 12 rows form patt.

Cont straight in patt until back measures 5/**5½**/6/**6½** in, ending with right side facing. Keeping continuity of patt, shape sides by dec 1 st at each end of next and every foll 16th row until 75/**79**/83/**87** sts rem.

Change to No 5 needles and cont in patt until back measures 20½/**21**/21½/**22** in, ending with right side facing.

Shape armholes by casting off 3 sts at beg of next 2 rows, then dec 1 st at each end of every row until 59/**63**/67/**71** sts rem. Work 1 row. Now dec 1 st at each end of next and every alt row until 49/**53**/57/**61** sts rem. Work straight until back measures 29/**30**/31/**32** in, ending with right side facing.

Shape shoulders by casting off 4/**4**/5/**5** sts at beg of next 4 rows, then 4/**5**/4/**5** sts at beg of foll 2 rows. Leave rem 25/**27**/29/**31** sts on a length of yarn.

POCKET LININGS (2)

With No 5 needles, cast on 23 sts and work in st st for 4 in, ending with a P row. Leave sts on a length of yarn.

LEFT FRONT

With No 8 needles, cast on 41/**43**/45/**47** sts and work K1, P1 rib for 1 in as for back.

Change to No 4 needles and patt as follows: 1st and 3rd sizes: 1st row: (right side), K. 2nd row: P. 3rd row * K3, sl 1; rep from * to last st, K1.

4th row: K1, * yft, sl 1, yb, K3; rep from * to end. 5th and 6th rows: As 3rd and 4th. 7th row: K. 8th row: P. 9th row: K1, * sl 1, K3; rep from * to end. 10th row: * K3, yft, sl 1, yb; rep from * to last st, K1. 11th and 12th rows: As 9th and 10th. These 12 rows form patt. 2nd and 4th sizes: Work in patt as for back.

All sizes: Cont straight in patt until front measures 5/**5½**/6/**6½** in, ending with right side facing. Keeping continuity of patt, shape side by dec 1 st at beg of next and foll 16th row: 39/**41**/43/**45** sts. Work 1 row.

Place pocket: Next row: Patt 8/**9**/10/**11**, slip next 23 sts on to a stitch-holder and in place of these, patt across 23 sts from first pocket lining, patt 8/**9**/10/**11**. Work 13 rows straight in patt. Now dec 1st at beg of next and foll 16th row: 37/**39**/41/**43** sts.

Change to No 5 needles and cont in patt until front measures 20½/**21**/21½/**22** in, ending with right side facing.

Shape armhole and front neck as follows:

Next row: Cast off 3 sts, patt to last 5/**6**/7/**8** sts, turn and leave these 5/**6**/7/**8** sts on a safety-pin. Dec 1 st at neck edge on every row, at the same time dec 1 st at armhole edge on foll alt row, then every row until 18/**19**/20/**21** sts rem. Next row: Work 2tog, patt to end.

Keeping neck edge straight dec 1 st at armhole edge on next and every alt row until 12/**13**/14/**15** sts rem. Work straight in patt until front matches back at armhole edge, ending with right side facing.

Shape shoulder by casting off 4/**4**/5/**5** sts at beg of next and foll alt row. Work 1 row. Cast off rem 4/5/4/**5** sts.

RIGHT FRONT

With No 8 needles, cast on 41/**43**/45/**47** sts and work K1, P1 rib for 1 in as for Back.

Change to No 4 needles and patt as follows: 1st and 3rd sizes: 1st row: (right side), K. 2nd row: P. 3rd row: K1, * sl 1, K3; rep from * to end. 4th row: * K3, yft, sl 1, yb; rep from * to last st, K1. 5th and 6th rows: As 3rd and 4th. 7th row: K. 8th row: P. 9th row: * K3, sl 1; rep from * to last st, K1. 10th row: K1, * yft, sl 1, yb, K3; rep from * to end. 11th and 12th rows: As 9th and 10th. These 12 rows form patt. 2nd and 4th sizes: Work in patt as for back.

All sizes: Complete to correspond with left front, reversing shapings.

TO MAKE UP

Observing general method on page 81, block and press. Join shoulder seams. Neckband: With right side facing and No 8 needles, start at neck edge on right front and work as follows: K5/**6**/7/**8** sts from safety-pin, knit up 40/**42**/46/**48** sts up right side of neck, K25/**27**/29/**31** sts from back, knit up 40/42/46/**48** sts down left side, then K5/6/7/**8** sts from safety-pin: 115/**123**/135/**143** sts. Work K1, P1 rib for 1 in as for back. Cast off evenly in rib.

ARMBANDS

With right side facing and No 8 needles, knit up 78/**82**/86/**90** sts all round each armhole. Work K1, P1 rib for 1 in. Cast off evenly in rib. Join side seams and armbands.

POCKET TOPS

With right side facing and No 8 needles, K across 23 pocket sts, inc 2 sts evenly: 25 sts. Work K1, P1 rib for ½ in as for back. Cast off evenly in rib. Catch down sides of pocket tops neatly to right side of garment and pocket linings to wrong side.

LEFT FRONT BORDER

With No 8 needles, cast on 7 sts. 1st row: (right side), K2, (P1, K1) twice, K1. 2nd row: (K1, P1) 3 times, K1. Rep last 2 rows until border fits up left front to top of neckband, when slightly stretched. Cast off evenly in rib. Sew borders neatly in position.

RIGHT FRONT BORDER

Work as for left border with the addition of 8 buttonholes, first to come ½ in above lower edge, 8th ½ in below top of neck-band, and rem spaced evenly. First mark position of buttons on left border with pins to ensure even spacing, then work buttonholes to correspond as follows: (right side), rib 3, cast off 2, rib to end and back casting on 2 sts over those cast off. Sew border neatly in position. Press seams. Sew on buttons.

Tunic in Crochet

More sleeveless fashion-thinking for teaming up with trousers

Materials: 9/**9**/10 (50g) balls Patons Double Knitting. No 3·50 mm crochet hook.

Measurements: To fit 34/**36**/38 in bust; length from top of shoulders, 23½/**24**/24½ in.

Tension: 37 sts (6 patts)=6½ in; 6 rows=2 in.

BACK AND FRONT (**both alike**)

Make 100/**106**/112 ch loosely.

Next row: Miss 3ch, 2dtr in next ch, * miss 2ch, 1dc in next ch, miss 2ch, 5dtr in next ch; rep from * to last 6ch, miss 2ch, 1dc in next ch, miss 2ch, 3dtr in last ch: 97/**103**/109 sts.

Work in patt as follows: 1st row: (wrong side), 1ch, * 2ch, 1dtr in dc of previous row, 2ch, 1dc in 3rd of 5dtr of previous row; rep from * to last 6 sts, 2ch, 1dtr in dc of previous row, 2ch, 1dc in first (top) of 3ch of previous row. 2nd row: 3ch, 2dtr in dc of previous row, * 1dc in dtr of previous row, 5dtr in dc of previous row; rep from * to last 6 sts, 1dc in dtr of previous row, 3dtr in last (edge) ch of previous row. These 2 rows form patt. Rep them until work measures 17/**17**/17½ in, ending with a 1st patt row.

Shape armholes: Next row: Ss over 3, 1dc in dtr of previous row, patt to last 3 sts (thus ending dc), turn. Next row: Ss over 3, 1dc in 3rd of 5dtr of previous row, patt to last 3 sts (thus ending dc), turn. Rep these 2 rows once more; this completes armhole shaping: 73/**79**/85 sts rem. Cont straight in patt until armhole measures 4½/5/5 in, measured at centre and ending with 1st patt row.

Shape neck: 1st row: Patt across 28 sts (thus ending dc), turn. 2nd row: Ss over 3, patt to end. 3rd row: Patt across 22 sts, turn. 4th row: As 2nd. Now work 2 more rows in patt. Armhole should now measure 6½/**7**/7 in.

Shape shoulder: Next row: Ss over 3, patt to end. Next row: Patt 7 sts (thus ending dc). Fasten off.

Leaving 16/**22**/28 sts at centre unworked, with right side facing, rejoin yarn to next st and draw a loop through, 1dc in next st, patt to end. Next row: Patt 25, turn. Next row: Ss over 3, patt to end. Next row: Patt 19, turn. Work 2 more rows straight.

Shape shoulder: Next row: Patt to last 3 sts, turn. Next row: Ss over 9, patt across rem 7 sts. Fasten off.

MAKE UP AND BORDERS

Observing general method on page 81, block and press.

Join shoulder and side seams. Starting at left shoulder work 96/**108**/120 dc all round neck.

** Next rnd: * 1dc in next st, miss 2 sts, 5tr in next st, miss 2 sts; rep from * all round, ending with ss in 1st dc. Fasten off.**

Armholes: Starting at side seam, work 66/**72**/72 dc all round armhole edge, then work as for neck from ** to **. Press seams.

Ribby Raglan with Matching Hat

The long line again – it's just as wearable without the belt

COAT

Materials: 14/**15**/16/**17** (50g) balls Patons Double Knitting. Pair each Nos 8 and 10 needles. 2 stitch-holders. 7 buttons.

Measurements: To fit bust 34/**36**/38/**40** in; length from top of shoulders, 29/**29½**/30/**30½** in; sleeve seam, 16½/**16½**/17/**17** in.

Tension: 11 sts and 15 rows to 2 in over st st on No 8 needles.

BACK

With No 10 needles, cast on 107/**113**/117/**123** sts. ** Work 7 rows st st, starting with a K row. Next row: K, thus forming ridge for hemline.**

Change to No 8 needles and work in patt as follows: 1st row: * K1, P1; rep from * to last st, K1. 2nd row: P. These 2 rows form patt.

Cont in patt until back measures 12½ in from ridge at hemline, ending with right side facing.

Keeping continuity of patt, shape sides

by dec 1 st at each end of next and every foll 12th row until 101/**107**/111/**117** sts rem. Cont straight on these sts until back measures 20 in from ridge at hemline, ending with right side facing.

Keeping continuity of patt, shape raglans by casting off 4 sts at beg of next 2 rows. 1st row: K2, K2togtbl, patt to last 4 sts, K2tog, K2. 2nd row: P. 3rd row: K3, patt to last 3 sts, K3. 4th row: P. Rep last 4 rows 4/4/5/5 times more: 83/**89**/91/**97** sts. Now rep 1st and 2nd rows only until 33/**35**/37/**39** sts rem, ending with right side facing. Cast off.

POCKET LININGS (2)

With No 8 needles, cast on 27 sts and work in st st for 4 in, ending with a P row. Leave sts on a spare needle.

LEFT FRONT

With No 10 needles, cast on 53/55/59/**61** sts and work as back from ** to **. Change to No 8 needles and work in patt as for back until front measures 12 in from ridge at hemline, ending with right side facing.

Place Pocket Lining as follows: Next row: Patt 12/**12**/14/**16**, slip next 27 sts on to a stitch-holder and in place of these, patt across sts from 1st pocket lining, patt to end. Work a few rows straight until front measures 12½ in from ridge at hemline, ending with right side facing.

Keeping continuity of patt, shape side by dec 1 st at beg of next and every foll 12th row until 50/**52**/56/**58** sts rem. Cont on these sts until front measures same as back at side edge, ending with right side facing.

Shape raglan and neck edge: 1st row: Cast off 4, patt to end. 2nd row: P. 3rd row: K2, K2togtbl, patt to last 2 sts, work 2 tog. 4th row: P. 5th row: K3, patt to end. 6th row: P. Rep 3rd to 6th row 4/**4**/5/**5** times more: 36/**37**/40/**42** sts.

Now dec at raglan edge as before on next and every foll alt row, at the same time dec 1 st at neck edge on next and every foll 4th row until 10/**12**/8/**10** sts rem. Keeping neck edge straight, cont

dec at raglan edge as before until 2 sts rem, ending with right side facing. K2tog and fasten off.

RIGHT FRONT

Work to correspond with left front reversing all shapings, and noting that K2tog will be worked in place of K2togtbl at raglan shaping. The row placing pocket lining will read thus: Patt 14/**16**/18/**18**, slip next 27 sts on to a stitch-holder, in place of these sts, patt across sts from 2nd pocket lining, patt to end.

SLEEVES

With No 10 needles, cast on 45/**47**/51/**53** sts and work as back from ** to **.

Change to No 8 needles and work in patt as on back, shaping sides by inc 1 st at each end of 3rd/**3rd**/7th/**7th** row and every foll 8th row until there are 73/**75**/79/**81** sts. Cont on these sts until sleeve seam measures 16½/**16½**/17/**17** in from ridge at hemline, ending with right side facing.

Shape raglan by casting off 4 sts at beg of next 2 rows. Now work rows 1 to 4 of raglan shaping as on Back 6/**7**/7/**8** times: 53/**53**/57/**57** sts. Rep 1st and 2nd rows only until 7 sts rem, ending with right side facing. Cast off.

TO MAKE UP

Observing general method on page 81, block and press.

Join raglan, side and sleeve seams. Fold hems at ridge to wrong side and neatly slip-stitch in position.

LEFT FRONT BORDER

With No 10 needles, cast on 11 sts and work in rib: 1st row: K2, * P1, K1; rep from * to last st, K1. 2nd row: * K1, P1; rep from * to last st, K1. Rep these 2 rows until strip fits up left front and up left side of neck to centre back, when slightly stretched. Cast off in rib. Sew in position as you go along.

RIGHT FRONT BORDER

Work as left border to fit up right front to centre back with the addition of 7 buttonholes, 1st to come 4½ in up from lower edge, 7th to come $\frac{1}{2}$ in down from neck shaping and rem spaced evenly between. First mark position of buttons on left front with pins to ensure even spacing then work buttonholes to correspond.

To make a buttonhole: (right side), rib 4, cast off 3, rib to end and back casting on 3 over those cast off. Join border neatly at centre back.

POCKET TOPS

With right side facing and No 10 needles, K across pocket sts. Work P1, K1 rib for 1 in, rows on right side having a K1 at each end. Cast off in rib. Catch down sides of pocket tops neatly on right side and linings on wrong side. Press seams. Sew on buttons.

BELT

With No 10 needles, cast on 15 sts and work in rib as for left front border until belt measures 50/**52**/**54**/**56** in. Cast off in rib.

HAT TO MATCH

Materials: 2(50g) balls Patons Double Knitting. Pair each Nos 8 and 10 needles.

Measurements: To fit average head.

Tension: 11 sts and 15 rows to 2 in over st st on No 8 needles.

With No 10 needles, cast on 117 sts and work in patt as for back of coat until hat measures $2\frac{1}{2}$ in, ending with right side facing. Next row: P (thus reversing patt). Cont in patt starting with a 1st row until hat measures $3\frac{1}{2}$ in from start. Change to No 8 needles and cont in patt until hat measures 8 in from start, ending with right side facing.

Now work in st st shaping crown thus: Next row: * K2tog, K7; rep from * to end: 104 sts. Next row: P. Next row: * K2tog, K6; rep from * to end: 91 sts. Next row: P. Next row: * K2tog, K5; rep from * to end: 78 sts. Cont dec thus until the row '* K2tog; rep from * to end' has been worked: 13 sts. Next row: P.

Break yarn, thread through rem sts, draw up tightly and fasten off.

TO MAKE UP

Observing general method on page 81, press. Join seam. Fold $2\frac{1}{2}$ in of patt to right side to form brim. Press seam.

The Line of the Thirties

But purl fabric and lacy rib create that inside-out look of the present day

Materials: 9/**11**/12 (25g) balls Patons Baby Quickerknit Courtelle. Pair each Nos 10 and 11 needles. No 2·50 mm crochet hook. 6 small buttons.

Measurements: To fit 33–34/**35–36**/37–38 in bust; length from top of shoulders, $19\frac{1}{2}$/**20**/21 in; sleeve seam, 5/5/$5\frac{1}{2}$ in.

Tension: 14 sts and 18 rows to 2 in over st st on No 10 needles.

BACK

With No 11 needles, cast on 114/**120**/126 sts and work 11 rows KB1, P1 rib,

inc 1 st at end of last row: 115/**121**/127 sts.

Change to No 10 needles and patt as follows: 1st row: (right side), P. 2nd row: K1/**4**/7, yf, sl 1, K2tog, psso, yf, * K7, yf, sl 1, K2tog, psso, yf; rep from * to last 1/**4**/7 sts, K1/**4**/7. The last 2 rows form patt. Cont straight in patt until back measures $12\frac{1}{2}$/**$12\frac{1}{2}$**/13 in, ending with right side facing.

Shape raglans by casting off 7 sts at beg of next 2 rows, then dec 1 st at each end of next and every alt row until 75/**75**/75 sts rem, ending with right side facing.

Divide for back opening: Next row:

P2tog, P34, P2tog, turn and leave rem 37 sts on a spare needle. Cont on these sts for first side, dec 1 st at raglan edge on every alt row as before until 17 sts rem, ending with right side facing. Leave sts on a spare needle.

With right side facing, rejoin yarn to last 37 sts, P to last 2 sts, P2tog. Finish to correspond with first side.

FRONT

Work as for back until 51 sts rem in raglan shaping, ending with right side facing.

Shape neck: Next row: P2tog, P13, turn and leave rem sts on a spare needle. Cont on these sts for first side, dec 1 st at neck edge on every row, and at the same time dec 1 st at raglan edge on alt rows as before, until 7 sts rem. Now keep neck edge straight and cont dec at raglan edge on alt rows until 2 sts rem, ending with right side facing. K2tog and fasten off.

With right side facing, slip centre 21 sts on a spare needle, rejoin yarn to rem 15 sts, P to last 2 sts, P2tog. Finish to correspond with first side.

SLEEVES

With No 11 needles, cast on 72/76/80 sts and work 11 rows twisted rib as for welt, inc 5 sts evenly across on last row: 77/81/85 sts. Change to No 10 needles and work the 2 patt rows. Cont as follows:

1st size: 1st row: P. 2nd row: K7, * yf, sl 1, K2tog, psso, yf, K7; rep from * to end.

2nd size: 1st row: P. 2nd row: K2tog, yf, K7, * yf, sl 1, K2tog, psso, yf, K7; rep from * to last 2 sts, yf, K2tog.

3rd size: 1st row: P. 2nd row: K1, * yf, sl 1, K2tog, psso, yf, K7; rep from * to last 4 sts, yf, sl 1, K2tog, psso, yf, K1.

All sizes: Work a further 2 rows in patt, then shape sides by inc 1 st at each end of next and every foll 6th/5th/5th row until there are 85/91/97 sts, taking inc sts into patt. Cont straight until sleeve seam measures 5/5/5½ in, ending with right side facing.

Shape top by casting off 7 sts at beg of next 2 rows, then dec 1 st at each end of next and every alt row until 5 sts rem, ending with right side facing. Slip these sts on a safety-pin.

MAKE UP AND NECKBAND

Observing general method on page 81, block and press.

Join raglan seams, matching lace ribs. With right side facing and No 11 needles, K17 sts from left back, then K5 sleeve sts, knit up 15 down left side of neck, K21 from spare needle inc 4 sts evenly, knit up 15 up right side, K5 sleeve sts, then K17 from back: 99 sts. Next row: P1, * KB1, P1; rep from * to end. Work a further 18 rows in twisted rib. Cast off loosely in rib.

Join side and sleeve seams. Fold neckband in half to wrong side and slip-hem loosely in position. With right side facing and crochet hook, work a row of double crochet up left side of back opening. Fasten off. Work a row on right side making 6 buttonloops evenly spaced. To make a buttonloop: 3ch, miss 2 sts. Press seams. Sew on buttons.

The Rightness of Simplicity

Stamps this openwork crochet cardigan with approval

Materials: 7/7/8 (50g) balls Patons Double Knitting. Nos 4·00 mm and 3·50 mm crochet hooks.

Measurements: To fit 34/36/38 in bust; length from top of shoulders, 21½ in (all sizes).

Tension: 4 triangles to 2¼ in; 5 rows to 2 in on No 4·00 mm hook.

Additional Abbreviations (see page 29): Tri=Triangle, made by working 1tr, 1ch, 1tr all in same ch or sp.

BACK

With No 4·00 hook, make 100/106/112ch. 1st row: 1Tri in 5th ch from hook, * miss 2ch, 1Tri in next ch; rep from * to last 2ch, miss 1ch, 1tr in last ch, turn with 3ch: 32/34/36Tri. 2nd row: * 1Tri into next 1ch sp of previous Tri; rep from * to end, 1tr in top of turning ch, turn with 3ch. 2nd row forms patt. Rep this row until back measures 12½ in, omitting turning ch at end of last row.

Shape armholes: 1st row: Ss over 7 sts (first tr and 2Tri), 3ch, work 28/30/32 Tri, 1tr in first tr of next Tri, turn. 2nd row: Ss over 4 sts, 3ch, patt to last Tri, 1tr in first tr of this Tri, turn. Rep 2nd row 3 times more: 20/22/24 Tri. Work straight until back measures 21½ in up centre.

Shape shoulders: Next row: Ss over 7/10/13 sts, patt to last 2/3/4 Tri, 1tr in first tr of last Tri. Fasten off.

LEFT FRONT

With No 4·00 hook, make 52/55/58 ch (16/**17**/18 Tri) and work straight until front matches back to start of armhole shaping.

Shape armhole and neck: 1st row: Ss over 7 sts, 3ch, patt to end omitting last tr, turn with 3ch. 2nd row: 1tr in ch sp of first Tri, patt to last Tri, 1tr in first tr of this Tri, turn. 3rd row: Ss over 4 sts, 3ch, 1Tri in each Tri, 1tr in last tr, turn with 3ch. 4th row: 1Tri in each Tri up to last Tri, 1tr in first tr of this Tri, turn. 5th row: Ss over 4 sts, 3ch, patt to end omitting last tr, turn with 3ch.

Keeping armhole edge straight, cont shaping neck: 1st row: 1tr in ch sp of first Tri, patt to end. 2nd row: 1Tri in each Tri, 1tr in last tr, turn with 3ch. 3rd row: Work straight in patt. 4th row: Patt to end omitting last tr, turn with 3ch. Rep last 4 rows twice more, then rows 1 to 3 again: 5/**6**/7 Tri.

Work a few rows straight until front matches back at armhole edge, ending at neck edge. Shape shoulder: Next row: Patt across 3Tri. Fasten off.

RIGHT FRONT

As patt is reversible, work right front as for left front.

MAKE UP AND BORDERS

Observing general method on page 81, block and press. Join side and shoulder seams. With No 3·50 hook, start at left side seam. Work 2 rnds dc along lower, front and neck edges, joining with ss at end of each rnd. Work 1 more rnd dc, but working from left to right, thus making a raised edge, join with ss. Fasten off. Work armhole borders in the same way. Press seams and edges.

Tunic in Knitting

Bold and bluff in double double knitting yarn which grows quick-as-a-wink

Materials: 13/**14**/15/16 (50g) balls Patons Doublet. Pair each Nos 5 and 8 needles. Cable needle.

Measurements: To fit 32/**34**/36/**38** in bust; length from top of shoulders, 28/**29**/30/**31** in.

Tension: 8½ sts and 10½ rows to 2 in over st st on No 5 needles.

Additional Abbreviations (see page 29): C3B=slip next stitch on cable needle to back of work, K2, then P1 from cable needle; C3F=slip next 2 sts on cable needle to front of work, P1, then K2 from cable needle; C4F=slip next 2 sts on cable needle to front of work, K2, then K2 from cable needle.

PANEL PATT 10

1st row: (right side), P3, K4, P3. 2nd row: K3, P4, K3. 3rd row: P2, C3B, C3F, P2. 4th row: (K2, P2) twice, K2. 5th row: P1, C3B, P2, C3F, P1. 6th row: K1, P2, K4, P2, K1. 7th row: C3B, P4, C3F. 8th row: P2, K6, P2. 9th row: C3F, P4, C3B. 10th row: As 6th. 11th row: P1, C3F, P2, C3B, P1. 12th row: As 4th. 13th row: P2, C3F, C3B, P2. 14th row: As 2nd. 15th row: P3, C4F, P3. 16th row: As 2nd. 17th row: P2, C3B, C3F, P2. 18th row: As 4th. 19th row: P2, C3F, C3B, P2. 20th row: As 2nd. 21st row: As 15th. Rows 2 to 21 incl form the Panel Patt.

BACK

** With No 8 needles, cast on 84/**88**/92/**96** sts and work K2, P2 rib for 1 in.

1st and 2nd sizes: Next row: Rib 10, M1, rib 4/**2**, M1, rib 18/**20**, M1, rib 20/**24**, M1, rib 18/**20**, M1, rib 4/**2**, M1, rib to end: 90/**94** sts.

3rd and 4th sizes: Next row: Rib 12/**10**, M1, (rib 2/**4**, M1, rib 20, M1) 3 times, rib 2/**4**, M1, rib to end: 100/**104** sts.

All sizes: Change to No 5 needles: 1st row: (right side), K4/2/5/3, * P3/4/4/5, panel patt 10 (1st row), P3/4/4/5, K6; rep from *, ending last rep K4/2/5/3. 2nd row: P4/2/5/3, * K3/4/4/5, panel patt 10 (2nd row), K3/4/4/5, P6; rep from *, ending last rep P4/2/5/3.

Keeping panel patts correct, rep these 2 rows until work measures 11/11/12/12 in, ending with wrong side facing. Next row: P4/2/5/3, * K2tog, patt 12/13/14/16, K2togtbl, P6; rep from *, ending last rep P4/2/5/3: 82/86/92/96 sts. Keeping continuity of patt throughout, work straight until back measures 19½/20/21/21½ in, ending with right side facing.

Shape armholes by casting off 4 sts at beg of next 2 rows, then dec 1 st at each end of every row until 50/54/56/60 sts rem.** Work straight in patt until back measures 28/29/30/31 in, ending with right side facing.

Shape shoulders by casting off 6/6/7/7 sts at beg of next 2 rows, then 6/7/7/8 sts at beg of foll 2 rows. Leave rem 26/28/28/30 sts on a spare needle.

FRONT

Work as for back from ** to **. Work straight in patt until front measures 24½/25½/26½/27½ in, ending with right side facing.

Divide for neck: Next row: Patt 20/21/22/23, turn and leave rem sts on a spare

needle. Cont on these sts for first side, dec 1 st at neck edge on every row until 12/13/14/15 sts rem. Work straight until front matches back at armhole edge, ending with right side facing. Shape shoulder by casting off 6/6/7/7 sts at beg of next row. Work 1 row straight. Cast off.

With right side facing, leave centre 10/12/12/14 sts on a spare needle, rejoin yarn to rem sts and finish to correspond with 1st side, reversing shapings.

TO MAKE UP

Observing general method on page 81, block and press.
Join right shoulder seam.

NECKBAND

With right side facing and No 8 needles, starting at left shoulder on front, knit up 16 sts down left side of neck, K10/12/12/14 sts from spare needle, knit up 16 sts up right side, K26/28/30/30 sts from spare needle dec 2 sts evenly: 66/70/70/74 sts. Work 6 rows, K1, P1 rib. Cast off evenly in rib. Join left shoulder seam and neckband.

ARMHOLE BORDERS

With right side facing and No 8 needles, knit up 80/86/86/90 sts all round armhole. Work 6 rows K1, P1 rib. Cast off evenly in rib. Join side seams. Press seams.

Blouse in Crochet

It's feminine because it's in 4-ply

Materials: 7/8 (50g) balls Patons Purple Heather 4-ply. No 2·50 mm crochet hook.

Measurements: To fit 36/38 in bust; length from shoulder to lower edge, 21/22½ in; sleeve seam, 4 in.

Tension: 3 patts = 3½ in across; 7 rows = 2 in deep.

BACK

Make 96/102ch (approx 19/20 in). Foundation row: 1tr into 3rd ch from hook, 3tr into same ch, * miss 2ch, (1tr, 2ch, 1tr) into next ch, miss 2ch, 5tr into next ch; rep from * to last 3ch, miss 2ch, (1tr, 2ch, 1tr) into last ch, turn: 16/17 patts.

1st row: (right side), 1ch, * (1tr, 3ch, 1tr) into 2ch sp, 4tr into 5tr of previous row; rep from * to end, turn. 2nd row: 1ch, * (1tr, 2ch, 1tr) between 2nd and 3rd trs of 4tr block of previous row, 5tr into 3ch sp; rep from * to end, turn. 3rd row: 1ch, * 4tr into 5tr of previous row, (1tr, 3ch, 1tr) into 2ch sp; rep from * to end, turn.

4th row: 1ch, * 5tr into 3ch sp, (1tr, 2ch, 1tr) between 2nd and 3rd tr of 4tr block of previous row; rep from * to end, turn. 1st to 4th row form patt. Cont in patt until work measures 13½/14½ in from start.

Shape armholes: Next row: Ss across 1½/2 patts, work to within 1½/2 patts of end of row, turn. Keeping patt correct cont until work measures 7/7½ in from armhole shaping.

Shape shoulders: Next row: Ss across 1 patt, work to beg of last patt, turn. Rep last row 3 times more. Fasten off: 5/5 patts left for neck.

FRONT

Work as for back until front measures 5/5½ in from armhole shaping: 13/13 patts.

Shape neck: Next row: Work across 6/6 patts, turn. Next row: Ss across 2 sts, work to end. Next row: Work to last 2 sts, turn. Rep last 2 rows until 4 patts rem, ending at neck edge.

Shape shoulder: 1st row: Work to beg of last patt, turn. 2nd row: Ss across first patt, work to end. 3rd and 4th rows: As 1st and 2nd. Omitting 1/1 patt at centre front, rejoin yarn and work second half to match first half.

SLEEVES

Make 60/66ch (approx 10/11 in). Work foundation row: 10/11 patts. Work as on back, inc 1 st at each end of every row until there are 12/13 patts in row. Cont in patt until work measures 4 in from start.

Shape top: Ss across ½ patt at beg of next 18 rows. Fasten off.

MAKE UP AND BORDERS

Observing general method on page 81, block and press. Join shoulder, side and sleeve seams and insert sleeves. Work a shell border of 6tr, 1ss round neck, lower edge and edge of sleeves. Press seams.

After his Fashion

Knitted fabric is so appropriate to modern styling for men

Materials: 9/**10**/11 (50g) balls Patons Double Knitting. Pair each Nos 10 and 8 needles. Cable needle. 2 stitch-holders. 5 buttons.

Measurements: To fit 40/**42**/44 in chest; length at centre back, 26/**26¼**/26½ in; sleeve seam, 18 in (adjustable).

Tension: 11 sts and 15 rows to 2 in over st st on No 8 needles.

Additional Abbreviations (see page 29): Cr1F = Cross 1 Front by slipping next st on cable needle, leave at front, P1, K st from cable needle; Cr1B = Cross 1 Back by slipping next st on cable needle, leave at back, K1, P st from cable needle.

BACK

With No 8 needles, cast on 146/**154**/162 sts. Work 10 rows K1, P1 rib.

Work in cross stitch rib patt as follows: 1st row: * K2, P2; rep from * to last 2 sts, K2. 2nd row: * P2, K2; rep from * to last 2 sts, P2. 3rd and 4th rows: As 1st and 2nd. 5th row: P1, * Cr1F, Cr1B, rep from * to last st, P1. 6th row: * K2, P2; rep from * to last 2 sts, K2. 7th row: * P2, K2; rep from * to last 2 sts, P2. 8th row: * K2, P2; rep from * to last 2 sts, K2. 9th and 10th rows: As 7th and 8th. 11th row: K1, * Cr1B, Cr1F; rep from * to last st, K1. 12th row: * P2, K2; rep from * to last 2 sts, P2. These 12 rows form patt.

Cont in patt until work measures 16 in from start for all sizes, ending with wrong side facing.

Start raglan shaping: Next row: Cast off 8/10/12, patt to last 8/10/12 sts, cast off 8/10/12. Break yarn. Rejoin and shape raglans by working 2tog at each end of next 11 rows, then every alt row until 40/42/44 sts rem. Work 3 rows on these sts. Cast off.

POCKET

With No 8 needles, cast on 36 sts. Work K1, P1 rib for 4½ in. Slip sts on to a stitch-holder.

RIGHT FRONT

With No 8 needles, cast on 70/74/78 sts. Work 10 rows K1, P1 rib. Work in patt as on back until work measures 4½ in from top of ribbing, ending with right side facing.

Place Pocket: Next row: Patt 53/55/57, slip the last 36 of these sts on to a stitch-holder and leave, patt 17/19/21. Next row: Patt 17/19/21, slip sts from top of pocket on to left-hand needle, patt to end. Cont in patt until work measures 14½ in from start, ending at front edge.

Shape front slope: Dec 1 st at front edge on next and every foll 5th row until work matches back to cast-off row at raglan shaping, ending with wrong side facing. Still dec at front edge on every 5th row from previous dec, at the same time shape raglan by casting off 8/10/12 sts at beg of next row, then dec 1 st at raglan edge on next 11 rows, then on every alt row at raglan edge until 16/17/18 front dec in all have been worked. Cont dec at raglan edge only on every alt row as before until all sts are worked off.

POCKET TOP

Slip 36 sts from top of pocket on to No 10 needle, right side facing for 1st row. 1st row: K2, P1, K1, M1P, (K1, P1) 7 times, M1K, (P1, K1) 7 times, M1P, K1, P1, K2: 39 sts. 2nd row: * K1, P1; rep from * to last st, K1. 3rd row: K2, * P1, K1; rep from * to last st, K1. 4th and 5th rows: As 2nd and 3rd. Cast off in rib.

POCKET, LEFT FRONT AND POCKET TOP

Reversing front shapings, work as right front until cast-off row at raglan shaping is reached, ending with wrong side facing. Next row: Work to last 8/10/12 sts, cast off these sts. Break yarn. Rejoin yarn and complete to match right front, reversing all shapings.

SLEEVES

With No 10 needles, cast on 58/62/66 sts. Work 23 rows K1, P1 rib. Next row: Rib 6/8/2, (inc in next st, rib 2/2/3) 15 times, inc in next st, rib to end: 74/78/82 sts.

Change to No 8 needles and work in patt as on back, inc 1 st at each end of 5th/3rd/7th row and every foll 6th/6th/5th row until there are 112/118/124 sts. Cont on these sts until work measures 18 in from start, ending with wrong side facing (adjust length here).

Next row: Cast off 8/10/12, patt to last 8/10/12 sts, cast off 8/10/12. Break yarn. Rejoin yarn and dec 1 st at each end of next 11 rows, then every alt row until 6 sts rem, ending with a dec row. Cast off.

FRONT BAND

With No 10 needles, cast on 11 sts. 1st row: K2, (P1, K1) 4 times, K1. 2nd row: (K1, P1) 5 times, K1. 3rd to 6th row: Rep 1st and 2nd rows twice. 7th row: Rib 4, cast off 3, rib to end. 8th row: Rib 4, cast on 3 rib to end. Cont in rib working a buttonhole as on last 2 rows on every 31st and 32nd rows from previous buttonhole until 5 buttonholes in all have been worked. Cont in rib until band measures 58/59/60 in from start (slightly stretched). Cast off.

TO MAKE UP

Observing general method on page 81, block and press.

Stitch pockets in position on wrong side and pocket tops on right side. Join side and sleeve seams and insert sleeves, stitching 3 rows at top of back to 3 of the cast-off sts at top of sleeve. Stitch front band in position. Sew on buttons. Press seams.

A Coat for the Car

Or anywhere else which calls for the style and the warmth of double double knitting

Materials: 17/**18**/19/**19**/20/**20** (50g) balls Patons Doublet. Pair each Nos 4 and 6 needles. **7** buttons. 1 press stud.

Measurements: To fit 32/**34**/36/**38**/ 40/**42** in bust; length from top of shoulders, 25/**25½**/26/**26½**/27/**27½** in; sleeve seam, 16/**16**/16/**16½**/16½/**16½** in.

Tension: 8 sts and 9½ rows to 2 in over st st on No 4 needles.

BACK

With No 6 needles, cast on 66/**74**/78/ **82**/90/**94** sts and work 7 rows garter st (every row K), inc 6 sts evenly across on last row: 72/**80**/84/**88**/96/**100** sts.

Change to No 4 needles and patt as follows:

1st row: (right side), K. 2nd row: K1, * P2, yon, K2, pass the yon over the K2; rep from * to last 3 sts, P2, K1. 3rd row: K. 4th row: P1, * yon, K2, pass the yon over the K2, P2; rep from * to last 3 sts, yon, K2, pass the yon over the K2, P1. These 4 rows form patt. Cont in patt until back measures 16½ in, ending with right side facing.

Shape raglans by casting off 4 sts at beg of next 2 rows, then dec 1 st at each end of next 4/8/8/10/12/14 rows: 56/56/60/60/64/64 sts. Now dec 1 st at each end of next and every alt row until 18/20/22/22/24/24 sts rem, ending with right side facing. Cast off.

LEFT FRONT

With No 6 needles, cast on 33/33/36/39/39/43 sts and work 7 rows garter st, inc 3/3/4/5/5/5 sts evenly across on last row: 36/36/40/44/44/48 sts.

Change to No 4 needles and patt as for back until front matches back at side edge, ending with right side facing.

Shape raglan: Next row: Cast off 4, K to end. Next row: In patt. Dec 1 st at raglan edge on next 4/4/8/14/10/16 rows. Now dec 1 st at raglan edge on next and every alt row until 16/14/16/16/16/16 sts rem, ending with right side facing. Cont shaping raglan and shape neck by dec 1 st at each end of next and every alt row until 2 sts rem. P2, then K2tog and fasten off.

RIGHT FRONT

Work as left front, reversing shapings.

SLEEVES

With No 6 needles, cast on 26/28/28/30/30/32 sts and work 7 rows garter st, inc 2/4/4/6/6/8 sts evenly across on last row: 28/32/32/36/36/40 sts.

Change to No 4 needles and patt as for back, shaping sides by inc 1 st at each end of 7th and every foll 6th row until there are 46/50/50/54/54/58 sts, taking inc sts into patt. Work straight until sleeve seam measures 16/16/16/16½/16½/16½ in, ending with right side facing.

Shape top by casting off 4 sts at beg of next 2 rows. Next row: K2tog, K to last 2 sts, K2tog. Work 3 rows straight in patt. Rep the last 4 rows 2/1/2/1/3/2 times more: 32/38/36/42/38/44 sts. Next row: K2tog, K to last 2 sts, K2tog. Next row: In patt. Rep the last 2 rows until 2 sts rem, ending with right side facing. Cast off.

COLLAR

With No 6 needles, cast on 68/68/72/72/76/76 sts and work 7 rows garter st. Next row: K4, sl these 4 sts on a safety-pin, change to No 4 needles and K to last 4 sts, turn and sl last 4 sts on a safety-pin. Cont in patt on centre 60/60/64/64/68/68 sts, starting with 2nd patt row and work 3 rows straight. Cont in patt dec 1 st at each end of next and every foll 3rd row until collar measures 4 in at centre. Cast off. With No 6 needles, cont in garter st on each set of 4 border sts until borders fit up short sides of collar to cast-off edge, when slightly stretched. Cast off.

MAKE UP AND BORDERS

Observing general method on page 81, block and press. Join raglan, side and sleeve seams. Join garter st borders to collar.

Left Front Border: With No 6 needles, cast on 8 sts and work a strip in garter st to fit, when slightly stretched, up Left Front to start of neck shaping. Sew in position as you go along. Cast off.

Right Front Border: Work to correspond with Left Border with the addition of 7 buttonholes, first to come 4 in up from lower edge, 7th 1 in below neck edge and rem 5 spaced evenly between. First mark position of buttons on Left Border with pins to ensure even spacing, then work buttonholes to correspond. To make a buttonhole: K3, cast off 2, K to end and back casting on 2 over those cast off. Sew in position as you go along. Cast off.

Sew collar in position round neck, starting and ending in centre of front borders. Press seams. Sew on buttons and a press stud at neck edge.

Chapter 16
Leisure International

In these days of package tours and charter flights it is appropriate that the group of holiday and outdoor handknits in this chapter should embody national styles from all over the world. Many holiday-makers have had the opportunity of seeing these very distinctive patterns and stitches being worn by the men and women who live in the countries where they were created. Just as folk songs and traditional ballads have become increasingly popular year by year in the musical field, so has folk knitting increased its appeal as a craft because it, too, represents living history and legend. Some of the designs have histories going back hundreds of years in the more remote communities where life was hard and people were dependent on everyday objects and crafts for some small degree of glamour. These communities include a number of island groups such as the Aran Isles, Fair Isle and, of course, the Channel Islands.

Aran-Style Jacket
for Him and Her

The embossed effects and contrasting fabrics are characteristic of the wind-swept group of islands in Galway Bay

Materials: 14/**15**/16/**17** (50g) balls Patons Double Knitting. Pair each Nos 9 and 7 needles. Cable needle. 2 stitch-holders. 8 buttons. 2 press studs.

Measurements: To fit 34/**36**/38/**40** in bust/chest; length from top of shoulders to lower edge, 25/**25¼**/25½/**25¾** in; sleeve seam, 18 in (adjustable).

Tension: 10½ sts and 14 rows to 2 in over st st on No 7 needles.

Additional Abbreviations (see page 29): C2F = Cable 2 front by working across next 4 sts thus: Slip next 2 sts on to cable needle and leave at front of work, knit next 2 sts, then knit 2 sts from cable needle; C2B = Cable 2 back as C2F but leave sts at back of work in place of front.

Tw2F = Twist 2 front by knitting into front of 2nd st, then front of first st on left-hand needle and slipping 2 sts off needle tog; Tw2B = Twist 2 back by knitting into back of 2nd st, then back of first st on left-hand needle and slipping 2 sts off needle tog.

Tw3 = Twist 3, insert point of right-hand needle knitways into front of 3rd st: keeping point of this needle at front of work, knit the st in the ordinary way, work the 2nd st in the same manner, now knit into front of the first st, then slip all 3 sts off left-hand needle tog.

Cr2B = by slipping next 2 sts on cable needle, leave at back, K4, P1, KB1 across sts on cable needle; Cr4F = by slipping next 4 sts on cable needle, leave at front, KB1, P1, K across 4 sts on cable needle.

Tw4/2F = by slipping next 4 sts on cable needle, leave at front, P2, K4 sts from cable needle; Tw2/4B = by slipping next 2 sts on cable needle, leave at back, K4, P2 sts from cable needle.

TRAVELLING ARAN PATT
(**referred to as Patt 31 throughout**)
1st row: KB3, P7, K4, P1, KB1, P1, K4, P7, KB3. 2nd row: PB3, K7, P4, K1, PB1, K1, P4, K7, PB3. 3rd row: Tw3, P7, C2B, KB1, P1, KB1, C2F, P7, Tw3.

4th row: PB3, K7, P4, PB1, K1, PB1, P4, K7, PB3. 5th row: KB3, P5, Cr2B, P1, KB1, P1, Cr4F, P5, KB3. 6th row: PB3, K5, P4, (K1, PB1) 3 times, K1, P4, K5, PB3. 7th row: Tw3, P5, C2B, (KB1, P1) 3 times, KB1, C2F, P5, Tw3. 8th row: PB3, K5, P4, (PB1, K1) 3 times, PB1, P4, K5, PB3. 9th row: KB3, P3, Cr2B, (P1, KB1) 3 times, P1, Cr4F, P3, KB3. 10th row: PB3, K3, P4, (K1, PB1) 5 times, K1, P4, K3, PB3. 11th row: Tw3, P3, C2B, (KB1, P1) 5 times, KB1, C2F, P3, Tw3.

12th row: PB3, K3, P4, (PB1, K1) 5 times, PB1, P4, K3, PB3. 13th row: KB3, P1, Cr2B, (P1, KB1) 5 times, P1, Cr4F, P1, KB3. 14th row: PB3, K1, P4, (K1, PB1) 7 times, K1, P4, K1, PB3. 15th row: Tw3, P1, C2B, (KB1, P1) 7 times, KB1, C2F, P1, Tw3.

16th row: PB3, K1, P4, (PB1, K1) 7 times, PB1, P4, K1, PB3. 17th row: KB3, P1, Tw4/2F, (P1, KB1) 5 times, P1, Tw2/4B, P1, KB3. 18th row: PB3, K3, P4, (K1, PB1) 5 times, K1, P4, K3, PB3. 19th row: Tw3, P3, C2B, (KB1, P1) 5 times, KB1, C2F, P3, Tw3.

20th row: As 12th. 21st row: KB3, P3, Tw4/2F, (P1, KB1) 3 times, P1, Tw2/4B, P3, KB3. 22nd row: PB3, K5, P4, (K1, PB1) 3 times, K1, P4, K5, PB3.

23rd row: Tw3, P5, C2B, (KB1, P1) 3 times, KB1, C2F, P5, Tw3. 24th row: As 8th. 25th row: KB3, P5, Tw4/2F, P1, KB1, P1, Tw2/4B, P5, KB3. 26th row: K7, P4, K1, PB1, K1, P4, K7, PB3.

27th row: Tw3, P7, C2B, KB1, P1, KB1, C2F, P7, Tw3. 28th row: PB3, K7, P4, PB1, K1, PB1, P4, K7, PB3. 5th to 28th rows form patt.

POCKET

With No 7 needles, cast on 35 sts. Foundation row: (wrong side), K2, PB3, K7, P4, K3, P4, K7, PB3, K2.

1st row: P2, patt 31 (1st row), P2. 2nd row: K2, patt 31 (2nd row), K2. 3rd to 28th row: Keeping patt 31 correct throughout (next row 3rd row), work as 1st and 2nd rows 13 times more. Do not break off yarn. Slip sts on to a stitch-holder and leave.

RIGHT FRONT

With No 9 needles, cast on 50/54/56/60 sts. Work K1, P1 rib for $1\frac{1}{4}$ in, inc 1 st at beg of last row on 34 and 38 in sizes only: 51/54/57/60 sts.

Change to No 7 needles and work in Aran Patt (referred to as patt 31 throughout front):

1st row: KB8/9/11/12, P2, patt 31 (1st row), P2, KB8/10/11/13. 2nd row: P8/10/11/13, K2, patt 31 (2nd row), K2, P8/9/11/12. 3rd to 28th row: Keeping patt 31 correct (next row 3rd row), work as 1st and 2nd rows 13 times more.

Next row: (5th row of Patt 31), KB8/9/11/12, with No 9 needle P across next 35 sts, slip these 35 sts on to a stitch-holder, break off yarn and leave; with right side facing slip 35 sts from top of pocket on to left-hand needle, P2, patt 31 (5th row), P2 across these sts, KB8/10/11/13.

Next row: (6th row of patt 31), P8/10/11/13, K2, patt 31, K2, P8/9/11/12.

Keeping Patt 31 correct (next row 7th row) cont until 28th row of patt has been completed.

Now cont until work measures $17\frac{1}{2}$ in from start, noting that for rem of front, patt 31 is a rep of 5th to 28th row throughout; end with wrong side facing.

Keeping patt correct shape armholes by casting off 3/4/5/6 sts at beg of next row, then dec 1 st at armhole edge on next and every alt row until 43/45/47/49 sts rem. Cont on these sts until work mea-

sures $4\frac{1}{2}$/$4\frac{3}{4}$/5/$5\frac{1}{4}$ in from start of arm-hole shaping, ending at front edge.

Shape neck by casting off 6/7/8/9 sts at beg of next row, then dec 1 st at neck edge on next and every alt row until 31/32/33/34 sts rem. Cont on these sts until work measures $7\frac{1}{4}$/$7\frac{1}{2}$/$7\frac{3}{4}$/8 in from start of armhole shaping, ending at armhole edge.

Shape shoulder: 1st row: Cast off 15/16/16/17 sts, work to end. 2nd row: Work all across. 3rd row: Cast off 16/16/17/17.

POCKET TOP

Slip sts from stitch-holder on a No 9 needle, with wrong side facing, rejoin yarn and P one row. 1st row: K2, * P1, K1; rep from * to last st, K1. 2nd row: * K1, P1; rep from * to last st, K1. Rep last 2 rows once more. Cast off.

POCKET, LEFT FRONT AND POCKET TOP

Work pocket as on right front.

With No 9 needles, cast on 50/54/56/60 sts. Work ribbing as on right front: 51/54/57/60 sts.

Change to No 7 needles and cont as follows: 1st row: KB8/10/11/13, P2, Patt 31 (1st row), P2, KB8/9/11/12. 2nd row: P8/9/11/12, K2, patt 31 (2nd row), K2, P8/10/11/13. 3rd to 28th row: Keeping patt 31 correct (next row 3rd row), work as 1st and 2nd rows 13 times more.

Next row: (5th row of patt), KB8/10/11/13, with No 9 needles P35, slip these 35 sts on to a stitch-holder and leave, place pocket as on right front, P2, Patt 31, P2 across pocket sts, KB8/9/11/12. Next row: (6th row of patt) P8/9/11/12, K2, patt 31, K2, P8/10/11/13.

Complete to match right front, reversing all shapings.

BACK

With No 9 needles, cast on 98/104/110/116 sts. Work K1, P1 rib to match right front, inc 1 st at beg of last row: 99/105/111/117 sts.

Change to No 7 needles. 1st row: KB8/10/11/13, P2, Patt 31 (1st row), P2,

KB13/**15**/19/**21**, P2, Patt 31 (1st row), P2, KB8/**10**/11/**13**. 2nd row: P8/**10**/11/**13**, K2, patt 31 (2nd row), K2, P13/**15**/19/**21**, K2, patt 31 (2nd row), K2, P8/**10**/11/**13**.

Keeping patt 31 correct, working 3rd to 28th row once, then rep of 5th to 28th row throughout, cont as on these 2 rows until work matches front to armhole shaping.

Shape armholes by casting off 3/**4**/5/**6** sts at beg of next 2 rows, then dec 1 st at each end of next and every alt row until 83/**87**/91/**95** sts rem. Cont on these sts until work matches Front to shoulder shaping.

Shape shoulders. 1st and 2nd rows: Cast off 15/**16**/16/**17**, work to end. 3rd and 4th rows: Cast off 16/**16**/17/**17**, work to end. 5th row: Cast off 21/**23**/25/**27**.

SLEEVES

With No 9 needles, cast on 52/**54**/56/**58** sts. Work K1, P1 rib for 2½ in. Next row: Rib 5/**2**/3/**4**, (inc in next st, rib 4/**5**/5/**5**) 8 times, inc in next st, rib to end: 61/**63**/65/**67** sts.

Change to No 7 needles. 1st row: KB13/**14**/15/**16**, P2, patt 31 (1st row), P2, KB13/**14**/15/**16**. 2nd row: P13/**14**/15/**16**, K2, patt 31 (2nd row), K2, P13/**14**/15/**16**.

Keeping patt correct working 3rd to 28th row once, then rep of 5th to 28th row throughout, cont as on these 2 rows, inc 1 st at each end of 5th row and every foll 9th row, working extra sts into twisted st st throughout until there are 81/**83**/85/**87** sts. Cont on these sts until work measures 18 in from start (adjust length here).

Shape top by casting off 3/**4**/5/**6** sts at beg of next 2 rows, then dec 1 st at each end of next and every alt row until 65 sts rem. Cast off 3 sts at beg of next 4/**6**/8/**10** rows. Cast off.

BUTTONHOLE BAND

With No 9 needles, cast on 11 sts. Foundation row: (wrong side), K1, P2, (K1, P1) twice, K1, P2, K1.

1st row: K1, Tw2B, (P1, K1) twice, P1, Tw2F, K1. 2nd row: K1, P2, (K1, P1) twice, K1, P2, K1. Rep these 2 rows 1/**2**/3/**4** times more. Next row: K1, Tw2B, P1, cast off 3, Tw2F, K1. Next row: K1, P2, K1, cast on 3, K1, P2, K1.

Cont thus working a buttonhole as on last 2 rows on every 21st and 22nd rows from previous buttonhole until 8 buttonholes in all have been worked. Work 4 rows after last buttonhole. Cast off.

BUTTON BAND

Omitting buttonholes, work to match buttonhole band.

COLLAR

With No 7 needles, cast on 105/**109**/113/**117** sts. Foundation row: (wrong side), K2, P2, * K1, P1; rep from * to last 5 sts, K1, P2, K2.

1st row: K2, Tw2B, * P1, K1; rep from * to last 5 sts, P1, Tw2F, K2. 2nd row: K2, P2, * K1, P1; rep from * to last 5 sts, K1, P2, K2. Rep these 2 rows until work measures 2 in from start.

Change to No 9 needles and cont until work measures 3½ in from start. Cast off.

TO MAKE UP

Observing general method on page 81, block and press. Fold pocket tops at ridge to wrong side and flat-stitch to form hems. Stitch pockets in position on wrong side. Stitch front bands in position, buttonhole band on right side for woman and left side for man. Join shoulder, side and sleeve seams, and insert sleeves matching shapings. Stitch cast-off edge of collar from centre of right front band to centre of left front band. Press seams. Stitch press studs at top of front bands. Sew on buttons.

For Junior's Sweater, Too

Stitches like these were knitted by the women of Aran for their men

Materials: 5/5/6/6/7/7 (50g) balls Patons Double Knitting. Pair each Nos 10 and 8 needles. Cable needle. 2 stitch-holders.

Measurements: To fit 20/**22**/24/**26**/28/**30** in chest. Length from top of shoulders, 12½/**14**/15½/**17**/18½/**20** in; sleeve seam, 9/**10**/11/**12**/13/**14** in.

Tension: 11 sts and 15 rows to 2 in over st st on No 8 needles.

Additional Abbreviations (see page 29): Cr3F=slip next 2 sts on cable needle to front of work, P1, then KB2 from cable needle; Cr3B=slip next st on cable needle to back of work, KB2, then P1 from cable needle; C8=slip next 4 sts on cable needle to back of work, K4, then K4 from cable needle; C4=slip next 2 sts on cable needle to front of work, KB2, then KB2 from cable needle.

BACK

With No 10 needles, cast on 60/**66**/70/**76**/80/**86** sts and work K1, P1 rib for 2 in. Next row: Rib 6/**6**/5/**8**/7/**7**, M1, * rib 8/**9**/10/**10**/11/**12**, M1; rep from * to last 6/**6**/5/**8**/7/**7** sts, rib 6/**6**/5/**8**/7/**7**: 67/**73**/77/**83**/87/**93** sts.

Change to No 8 needles and work in patt as follows: 1st row: K5/**8**/10/**13**/15/**18**, P2, K8, (P2, KB2) twice, P2, Tw2, P1, (K5, P1) twice, Tw2, (P2, KB2) twice, P2, K8, P2, K5/**8**/10/**13**/15/**18**. 2nd row: P5/**8**/10/**13**/15/**18**, K2, P8, (K2, PB2) 3 times, (K1, P5) twice, K1, (PB2, K2) 3 times, P8, K2, P5/**8**/10/**13**/15/**18**.

3rd row: K5/**8**/10/**13**/15/**18**, P2, K8, (P2, KB2) twice, P2, Tw2, P1, K4, P1, K1, P1, K4, P1, Tw2, (P2, KB2) twice, P2, K8, P2, K5/**8**/10/**13**/15/**18**. 4th row: P5/**8**/10/**13**/15/**18**, K2, P8, (K2, PB2) 3 times, K1, P4, K1, P1, K1, P4, K1, (PB2, K2) 3 times, P8, K2, P5/**8**/10/**13**/15/**18**. 5th row: K5/**8**/10/**13**/15/**18**, P2, K8, (P2, KB2) twice, P2, Tw2, P1, K3, (P1, K1) twice, P1, K3, P1, Tw2, (P2, KB2) twice, P2, K8, P2, K5/**8**/10/**13**/15/**18**.

6th row: P5/**8**/10/**13**/15/**18**, K2, P8, (K2, PB2) 3 times, K1, P3, (K1, P1) twice, K1, P3, K1, (PB2, K2) 3 times, P8, K2, P5/**8**/10/**13**/15/**18**. 7th row: K5/**8**/10/**13**/15/**18**, P2, K8, (P2, KB2) twice, P2, Tw2, P1, K2, (P1, K1) 3 times, P1, K2, P1, Tw2, (P2, KB2) twice, P2, K8, P2, K5/**8**/10/**13**/15/**18**. 8th row: P5/**8**/10/**13**/15/**18**, K2, P8, (K2, PB2) 3 times, K1, P2, (K1, P1) 3 times, K1, P2, K1, (PB2, K2) 3 times, P8, K2, P5/**8**/10/**13**/15/**18**.

9th row: K5/**8**/10/**13**/15/**18**, P2, K8, P2, Cr3F, Cr3B, P2, Tw2, P1, (K1, P1) 6 times, Tw2, P2, Cr3F, Cr3B, P2, K8, P2, K5/**8**/10/**13**/15/**18**. 10th row: P5/**8**/10/**13**/15/**18**, K2, P8, K3, PB4, K3, PB2, (K1, P1) 6 times, K1, PB2, K3, PB4, K3, P8, K2, P5/**8**/10/**13**/15/**18**. 11th row: K5/**8**/10/**13**/15/**18**, P2, C8, P3, C4, P3, Tw2, P2, (K1, P1) 5 times, P1, Tw2, P3, C4, P3, C8, P2, K5/**8**/10/**13**/15/**18**.

12th row: P5/**8**/10/**13**/15/**18**, K2, P8, K3, PB4, K3, PB2, K2, (P1, K1) 5 times, K1, PB2, K3, PB4, K3, P8, K2, P5/**8**/10/**13**/15/**18**. 13th row: K5/**8**/10/**13**/15/**18**, P2, K8, P2, Cr3B, Cr3F, P2, Tw2, (P1, K1) 6 times, P1, Tw2, P2, Cr3B, Cr3F, P2, K8, P2, K5/**8**/10/**13**/15/**18**. 14th row: P5/**8**/10/**13**/15/**18**, K2, P8, (K2, PB2) 3 times, (K1, P1) 6 times, K1, (PB2, K2) 3 times, P8, K2, P5/**8**/10/**13**/15/**18**. 15th row: As 7th. 16th row: As 8th.

17th row: K5/**8**/10/**13**/15/**18**, P2, K8, (P2, KB2) twice, P2, Tw2, P1, K3, (P1, K1) twice, P1, K3, P1, Tw2, P2, (KB2, P2) twice, K8, P2, K5/**8**/10/**13**/15/**18**. 18th row: P5/**8**/10/**13**/15/**18**, K2, P8, (K2, PB2) 3 times, K1, P3, (K1, P1) twice, K1, P3, K1, (PB2, K2) 3 times, P8, K2, P5/**8**/10/**13**/15/**18**. 19th row: K5/**8**/10/**13**/15/**18**, P2, K8, P2, Cr3F, Cr3B, P2, Tw2, P1, K4, P1, K1, P1, K4, P1, Tw2, P2, Cr3F, Cr3B, P2, K8, P2, K5/**8**/10/**13**/15/**18**.

20th row: P5/**8**/10/**13**/15/**18**, K2, P8, K3, PB4, K3, PB2, K1, P4, K1, P1, K1, P4, K1, PB2, K3, PB4, K3, P8, K2, P5/**8**/10/**13**/15/**18**. 21st row: K5/**8**/10/**13**/15/**18**, P2, C8, P3, C4, P3, Tw2, P1, (K5, P1) twice, Tw2, P3, C4, P3, C8, P2, K5/**8**/10/**13**/15/**18**. 22nd row: P5/**8**/10/**13**/15/**18**, K2, P8, K3, PB4, K3, PB2, K1, (P5, K1) twice, PB2, K3, PB4, K3, P8, K2, P5/**8**/10/**13**/15/**18**.

23rd row: K5/8/10/**13**/15/**18**, P2, K8, P2, Cr3B, Cr3F, P2, Tw2, P1, K4, P1, K1, P1, K4, P1, Tw2, P2, Cr3B, Cr3F, P2, K8, P2, K5/8/10/**13**/15/**18**.

Rows 4 to 23 incl form patt. Cont in patt until work measures 8/**9**/10/**11**/12/**13** in from start, ending with right side facing.

Shape armholes by casting off 2/2/3/3/**4**/**4** sts at beg of next 2 rows, then dec 1 st at each end of every row until 57/**63**/65/**71**/73/**79** sts rem. Now dec 1 st at each end of next and every alt row until 51/**55**/57/**61**/63/**67** sts rem.**

Cont on these sts until work measures 12½/**14**/15½/**17**/18½/**20** in from start, ending with right side facing.

Shape shoulders by casting off 5/6/6/**7**/7/**6** sts at beg of next 2 rows, then 6/**6**/6/6/6/**7** sts at beg of next 4 rows. Slip rem 17/**19**/21/**23**/25/**27** sts on a stitch-holder.

FRONT

Work as for back from ** to **: 51/**55**/57/**61**/63/**67** sts. Cont on these sts until work measures 10½/**12**/13½/**15**/16/**17**½in, ending with right side facing.

Divide for neck: Next row: Patt 21/**22**/22/**23**/24/**25**, turn. Next row: Patt to end. Cont on these sts, dec 1 st at neck edge on next and every alt row until 17/**18**/18/**19**/19/**20** sts rem. Cont until work measures same as back at armhole edge, ending at this edge.

Shape shoulder by casting off 5/6/6/**7**/7/**6** sts at beg of next row, then 6/6/6/6/6/**7** sts at beg of foll 2 alt rows. With right side facing, slip centre 9/**11**/13/**15**/15/**17** sts on a stitch-holder, rejoin yarn to rem 21/**22**/22/**23**/24/**25** sts and work to correspond with first side, reversing shapings.

SLEEVE PATTERN

1st row: K7/**8**/9/**10**/11/**12**, P2, Tw2, P1, (K5, P1) twice, Tw2, P2, K7/**8**/9/**10**/11/**12**. 2nd row: P7/**8**/9/**10**/11/**12**, K2, PB2, K1, (P5, K1) twice, PB2, K2, P7/**8**/9/**10**/11/**12**. 3rd row: K7/**8**/9/**10**/11/**12**, P2, Tw2, P1, K4, P1, K1, P1, K4, P1, Tw2, P2, K7/**8**/9/**10**/11/**12**. 4th row: P7/**8**/9/**10**/11/**12**, K2, PB2, K1,

P4, K1, P1, K1, P4, K1, PB2, K2, P7/**8**/9/**10**/11/**12**.

5th row: K7/**8**/9/**10**/11/**12**, P2, Tw2, P1, K3, (P1, K1) twice, P1, K3, P1, Tw2, P2, K7/**8**/9/**10**/11/**12**. 6th row: P7/**8**/9/**10**/11/**12**, K2, PB2, K1, P3, (K1, P1) twice, K1, P3, K1, PB2, K2, P7/**8**/9/**10**/11/**12**.

7th row: K7/**8**/9/**10**/11/**12**, P2, Tw2, P1, K2, (P1, K1) 3 times, P1, K2, P1, Tw2, P2, K7/**8**/9/**10**/11/**12**. 8th row: P7 8/**9**/10/**11**/12, K2, PB2, K1, P2, (K1, P1) 3 times, K1, P2, K1, PB2, K2, P7/**8**/9/**10**/11/**12**. 9th row: K7/**8**/9/**10**/11/**12**, P2, Tw2, (P1, K1) 6 times, P1, Tw2, P2, K7/**8**/9/**10**/11/**12**. 10th row: P7/**8**/9/**10**/11/**12**, K2, PB2, (K1, P1) 6 times, K1, PB2, K2, P7/**8**/9/**10**/11/**12**.

11th row: K7/**8**/9/**10**/11/**12**, P2, Tw2, P1, (P1, K1) 5 times, P2, Tw2, P2, K7/**8**/9/**10**/11/**12**. 12th row: P7/**8**/9/**10**/11/**12**, K2, PB2, K1, (K1, P1) 5 times, K2, PB2, K2, P7/**8**/9/**10**/11/**12**. 13th row: As 9th. 14th row: As 10th. 15th row: As 7th. 16th row: As 8th. 17th row: As 5th. 18th row: As 6th. 19th row: As 3rd. 20th row: As 4th. These 20 rows form patt.

SLEEVES

With No 10 needles, cast on 32/**34**/36/**38**/40/**42** sts and work K1, P1 rib for 2 in. Next row: Rib 1/**2**/3/**4**/5/**6**, (inc in next st, rib 13) twice, inc in next st, rib to end: 35/**37**/39/**41**/43/**45** sts.

Change to No 8 needles and sleeve patt, inc 1 st at each end of 7th and every foll 11th/**10th**/9th/**8th**/8th/**9th** row until there are 43/**47**/51/**55**/59/**61** sts, taking inc sts into st st. Cont on these sts until sleeve seam measures 9/**10**/11/**12**/13/**14** in, ending with right side facing.

Shape top by casting off 2/2/3/3/4/**4** sts at beg of next 2 rows. Now dec 1 st at each end of next and every foll alt row until 23/**27**/27/**31**/31/**31** sts rem, then at each end of every row until 9 sts rem. Cast off.

TO MAKE UP

Observing general method on page 81, block and press. Join shoulder, side, and sleeve seams, insert sleeves.

NECKBAND

With right side facing and set of No 10 needles, starting at top of left shoulder, knit up 19/**19**/19/**19**/21/**21** sts down left side of neck, K9/**11**/13/**15**/15/**17** from centre front, knit up 19/**19**/19/**19**/21/**21** up right side, K17/**19**/21/**23**/25/**27** from back inc 4 sts evenly: 68/**72**/76/**80**/86/**90** sts. Work in rounds of K1, P1 rib for 2 in. Cast off in rib. Fold neckband in half to wrong side and slip-hem loosely in position. Press seams.

Canadian Character

Canadians from the Rockies are fond of husky woolly jackets decorated with big, colourful designs

Materials: 14/15 (50g) balls Ground Shade, 3/3 (50g) balls Medium, 4/4 (50g) balls Contrast Patons Doublet. Pair each Nos 6 and 4 needles. 7 buttons. 2 press-studs.

Measurements: To fit 36–38/40–42 in bust/chest. Length from shoulder to lower edge, 24/25 in; sleeve seam, 17½ in.

Tension: 7½ sts and 9½ rows to 2 in over st st on No 4 needles.

Additional Abbreviations (see page 29): GS=Ground Shade; M=Medium; C=Contrast.

FRONTS AND BACK (worked in one piece up to armhole shaping)

With No 4 needles and GS, cast on 153/161 sts. 1st row: K2, * P1, K1; rep from * to last st, K1. 2nd row: * K1, P1; rep from * to last st, K1. 3rd row: As 1st. 4th row: With M, as 2nd. 5th and 6th rows: With GS, as 1st and 2nd. 7th and 8th rows: With C, as 1st and 2nd. 9th and 10th rows: With GS, as 1st and 2nd. 11th row: With M, as 1st. 12th to 14th row: With GS, as 2nd, 1st and 2nd.

Work as follows: With GS, work 4 rows in st st. Work rows 1 to 9 incl from Chart A. With GS, work 4 rows in st st. With M, work rows 1 to 15 incl from Chart B, placing position of motifs as follows: Next row: (1st row of Chart), P12/14GS, (1M, 8GS) twice, 1M, 20/22GS, (1M, 8GS) twice, 1M, 13GS, (1M, 8GS) twice, 1M, 20/22GS, (1M, 8GS) twice, 1M, 12/14GS. Cont working rows 2 to 15 incl of Chart, the motif position having been placed on last row.

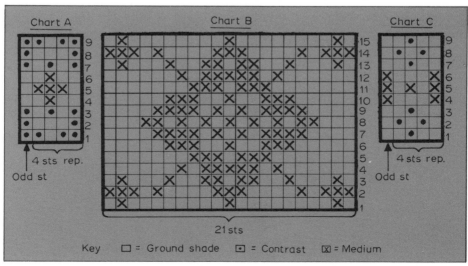

Key   □ = Ground shade   ⊡ = Contrast   ☒ = Medium

237

With GS, work 4 rows in st st. Work rows 1 to 9 incl of Chart C. With GS, work 4 rows in st st.

Next row: (1st row of Chart B), P12/14GS, (1M, 8GS) twice, 1M, 20/22GS, (1M, 8GS) twice, 1M, 13GS, (1M, 8GS) twice, 1M, 20/22GS, (1M, 8GS) twice, 1M, 12/14GS. Working motifs as placed on last row, work rows 2 to 7 from Chart B.

Divide for Fronts and Back: Next row: (8th row of Chart), work across 37/39 sts, cast off 6/7 sts, work across 66/68 sts (67/69 sts on needle after cast-off), cast off 6/7 sts, work to end.

Work on first group of 37/39 sts for first front: keeping motif correct until 15th row of motif has been completed (rem rows to be worked in GS), dec 1 st at armhole edge on every alt row until 32/34 sts rem.

With GS for rem of front cont in st st on these sts until work measures 6½/6½in from start of armhole shaping, ending at front edge.

Shape neck by casting off 7/8 sts at beg of next row. Dec 1 st at neck edge on every row until 19/19 sts rem. Cont on these sts until work measures 8¾/9 in from start of armhole shaping, ending at armhole or neck edge.

Shape shoulder by casting off 9/9 sts at beg or end of next row at armhole edge. Work 1 row. Cast off.

Rejoin yarn to next group of 67/69 sts and working patt from Chart as on first Front, shape armholes by dec 1 st at each end of every alt row until 57/59 sts rem. Cont on these sts until work matches front to shoulder shaping.

Shape shoulders by casting off 9/9 sts at beg of next 2 rows, 10/10 sts at beg of foll 2 rows. Cast off. Rejoin yarn to rem group of sts and complete to match first front, reversing shapings.

SLEEVES

With No 6 needles and GS, cast on 45/47 sts. Work rows 1 to 14 of ribbing as on Fronts and Back. Change to No 4 needles and with GS, work 3 rows in st st, inc 1 st at each end of 3rd row: 47/49 sts.

Work from Chart B as follows: Next row: (1st row of Chart), P14/15GS, (1M, 8GS) twice, 1M, 14/15GS. Work rows 2 to 8 from Chart. Next row: (9th row of Chart), inc in first st, work to last st, inc in last st: 49/51 sts. Work rows 10 to 15 incl from Chart.

With GS, work 3 rows in st st. Next row: Work across 9/12 sts, (inc in next st, work 9/24 sts) 3/1 times, inc in next st, work to end: 53/53 sts. Work rows 1 to 9 from Chart A. With GS, P1 row. Next row: Inc in first st, K to last st, inc in last st: 55/55 sts. Work 2 more rows in st st.

Next row: (1st row of Chart B), P18/18GS, (1M, 8GS) twice, 1M, 18/18GS. Work rows 2 to 15 incl from Chart B, inc 1 st at each end of 10th row: 57/57 sts. With GS, work 4 rows in st st. Work rows 1 to 9 incl from Chart C. With GS, work 2 rows in st st, inc 1 st at each end of first row: 59/59 sts.

Start top shaping as follows: (wrong side facing): 1st and 2nd rows: With GS, cast off 3 sts, work to end. 3rd row: Placing motif from Chart B, work thus: Using GS, cast off 3, P13/13 sts, (14/14 sts on needle after cast-off), (1M, 8GS) twice, 1M, P17/17GS. 4th row: With GS, cast off 3, work to end.

Keeping patt correct, cast off 2 sts at beg of next 4 rows. Dec 1 st at each end of every row until 31/33 sts, every alt row until 23/25 sts, every foll 3rd row until 19/21 sts rem, noting that when 15th row of Chart B has been worked rem of sleeve is worked in GS throughout. Cast off 3/3 sts at beg of next 4 rows. Cast off.

FIRST FRONT BAND (worked in C)

With No 6 needles, cast on 7 sts. 1st row: K2, P1, K1, P1, K2. 2nd row: (K1, P1) 3 times, K1. Rep 1st and 2nd rows once.

Make buttonhole: Next row: K2, P1, yrn, P2tog, K2. Next row: (K1, P1) 3 times, K1. Cont in rib working a buttonhole as on last 2 rows on every 17th and 18th row from previous buttonhole until 7 buttonholes in all have been worked. Work 2 rows. Cast off.

SECOND FRONT BAND

Omitting buttonholes, work to match first front band.

COLLAR (worked in C)

With No 6 needles, cast on 85/87 sts. Rep 1st and 2nd rows of ribbing as at start of fronts and back for 2 in. Change to No 4 needles and cont in rib until work measures $3\frac{1}{2}$ in from start. Cast off in rib.

TO MAKE UP

Observing general method on page 81, block and press.

Join shoulder and sleeve seams. Insert sleeves. Stitch on front bands (buttonholes on right for woman and left for man). Stitch collar in position from centre of right front band to centre of left front band, cast-on edge to neck. Stitch press-studs to top of front bands. Press seams. Sew on buttons.

Scandinavian Inspiration

The circular patterned yoke and the 'seeded' ground go to make up what Scandinavians call a bridal shirt

Materials: 10/11 (50g) balls Dark, 3/3 (50g) balls Light, 2/2 (50g) balls Medium, Patons Double Knitting. Pair each Nos 10 and 8 needles. 1 set of 4 No 10 and 2 sets of No 8 (12 in) needles for Yoke.

Measurements: To fit 38–39/40–42 in chest; length from top of shoulders, 25½/26 in; sleeve seam, 19/19 in.

Tension: 11 sts and 15 rows to 2 in over st st on No 8 needles.

Additional Abbreviations (see page 29): D=Dark; M=Medium; L=Light.

BACK AND FRONT (both alike)
** With No 10 needles and D, cast on 114/120 sts and work 8 rows K2, P2 rib. Change to L and K 1 row, then rib 1 row. Change to M and K 1 row, then rib 1 row. Change to L and K 1 row, then rib 1 row. Change to D and K 1 row, then rib 7 rows. Break M and L.**
Work colour motif as follows:
Next row: K10/3, * K twice in next st, K7/8; rep from * to end: 127/133 sts.

Next row: P.
Change to No 8 needles and Seeding patt as follows: 1st row: K, * 3D, 1L, 2D; rep from * to last st, 1D. 2nd to 5th row: St st in D, starting with a P row. 6th row: P, * 1L, 5D; rep from * to last st, 1L. 7th to 10th row: St st in D, starting with a K row. These 10 rows form Seeding patt. Cont straight in patt until work measures 16/16 in down centre, ending with a P row.

Shape armholes by casting off 6/7 sts at beg of next 2 rows, then K2tog at each end of next and every alt row until 105/105 sts rem. Patt back.

Divide for neck: Next row: K2tog, patt 20, turn and leave rem sts on a spare needle. Next row: P2tog, patt to end.

Cont in patt dec 1 st at armhole edge on next and every alt row and at the same time dec 1 st at neck edge on every row until 3 sts rem. P3tog and fasten off. With right side facing, slip centre 61/61 sts on a spare needle, rejoin yarn to rem 22/22 sts, patt to last 2 sts, K2tog. Finish to correspond with first side.

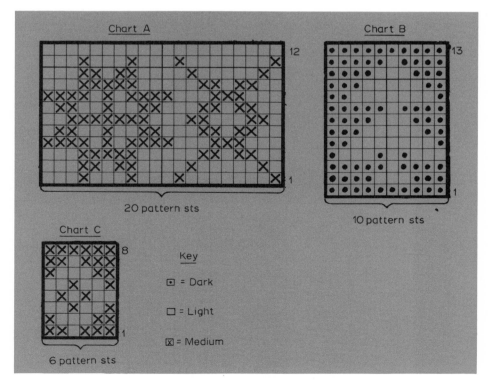

Chart A

12

1

20 pattern sts

Chart B

13

1

10 pattern sts

Chart C

8

1

6 pattern sts

Key

⊡ = Dark

☐ = Light

☒ = Medium

SLEEVES

With No 10 needles and D, cast on 56/56 sts and work as for welt on back from ** to **. Next row: K, inc 5/5 sts evenly across: 61/61 sts. Next row: P. Change to No 8 needles and Snowflake patt as for back, shaping sides by inc 1 st at each end of 11th and every foll 6th row until there are 87/89 sts, taking inc sts into patt.

Work straight until sleeve seam measures 19/19 in, ending with a P row. With right side facing shape top by casting off 5 sts at beg of next 2 rows. Next row: K2tog, patt to last 2 sts, K2tog. Work 1/3 rows straight. Rep last 2/4 rows once more. Now dec 1 st at each end of next and every alt row for both sizes until 55/55 sts rem. Patt back. Leave sts on a spare needle.

YOKE

Divide sts for back on to 2 needles, 30 sts on left side and 31 sts on right side.

With double pointed No 8 needles, D yarn and right side facing, start at centre back and K 30 sts from left back, knit up 13 sts up left side of Back, K 55 sleeve sts dec 1 st in centre, knit up 13 sts down left side of front, K 61 sts across centre front dec 1 st in centre, knit up 13 sts up right side of neck, K 55 sleeve sts dec 1 st in centre, knit up 13 sts down right side of back, then K rem 31 sts dec 1 st at beg: 280 sts.

Place a marker thread at centre back and work in rnds as follows: Next rnd: K, * 2D, 2L; rep from * all round. Rep this rnd twice more. Next rnd: K in L. Break D. Join in M and work the 12 rnds from Chart A, rep the 20 patt sts all round. Break M.

Next rnd: In L, * K2tog, K2; rep from * all rnd: 210 sts. Join in D and work the 13 rnds from Chart B repeating 10 patt sts all round. Break L and D yarns. Join in M. Next rnd: * K2tog, K3; rep from * all round: 168 sts. Join in L and work the 8 rnds from Chart C repeating 6 patt sts all round. Break M and L yarns.

Join in D. Next rnd: K8, * K3, K2tog; rep from * all round: 136 sts. Change to set of No 10 needles and work 5 rnds K2, P2 rib. Cast off in rib.

TO MAKE UP

Observing general method on page 81, block and press. Join raglan seams, then join side and sleeve seams. Press seams.

Fair Isle Scarf and Beret

Tradition traces some of the Fair Isle colour motifs back to wrecked sailors from the Spanish Armada of 1588

Materials: 5 (50g) balls Natural and oddments (approx. quarter ball each) of Red, Green, Blue, Yellow, White and Brown Patons Purple Heather 4-ply.

Beret: Set of 4 No 9 needles. **Scarf:** Set of 4 No 10 needles with points at both ends.

Measurements: Beret: Headband, 19 in. **Scarf:** Length (excluding fringes), 55 in.

Tension: 12 sts to 2 in over st st on No 9 needles. 14 sts to 2 in over st st on No 10 needles.

Additional Abbreviations (see page 29): N=Natural; R=Red; G=Green; B=Blue; Y=Yellow; W=White; Br=Brown.

BERET

With set of No 9 needles and N, cast on 108 sts. Work 10 rnds in K1, P1 rib. Next rnd: * Inc once in each of next 2 sts, K1; rep from * to end of rnd: 180 sts. Next rnd: K.

Work Fair Isle patt (every rnd K) joining in and breaking off colours as required:

1st rnd: * 1Br, 3N; rep from * to end of rnd. 2nd rnd: * 2Br, 1N, 1Br; rep from * to end of rnd. 3rd rnd: * 2N, 1Br, 1N; rep from * to end of rnd. 4th rnd: * 1N, 1Br; rep from * to end of rnd. 5th rnd: * 2B, 2Y, 1B, 3Y, 1B, 2Y, 1B; rep from * to end of rnd. 6th rnd: * 2B, 3Y, 1B, 1Y, 1B, 3Y, 1B; rep from * to end of rnd.

7th rnd: * 1W, 2R, 3W, 1R, 3W, 2R; rep from * to end of rnd. 8th to 13th rnd: As rnds 6 to 1 incl in backward rotation. 14th and 15th rnds: With N, K. 16th rnd: * 2N, 1G, 1N; rep from * to end of rnd. 17th rnd: * 1N, 1G; rep from * to end of rnd. 18th rnd: * 1G, 3N; rep from * to end of rnd. 19th and 20th rnds: As 14th and 15th. 21st to 33rd rnd: As 1st to 13th rnd incl. 34th rnd: With N, K. 35th rnd: With N, (K2tog, K2, K2tog, K3) 20 times: 140 sts.

Work crown: 1st rnd: * 1Br, 4N; rep from * to end of rnd. 2nd rnd: * 1N, 1Br, 7N, 3Br, 7N, 1Br; rep from * to end of rnd. 3rd rnd: * 1Br, 1W, 1Br, 5W, 1Br, 3W, 1Br, 5W, 1Br, 1W; rep from * to end of rnd.

4th rnd: * (1W, 1Br) twice, 3W, 1Br, 5W, 1Br, 3W, 1Br, 1W, 1Br; rep from * to end of rnd. 5th rnd: * (1G, 1W) 3 times, 1G, 2W, K3togtbl G, 2W, (1G, 1W) 3 times; rep from * to end of rnd. 6th rnd: * (1Y, 1G) 3 times, 3Y, 1G, 3Y, (1G, 1Y) twice, 1G; rep from * to end of rnd.

7th rnd: * (1G, 1Y) twice, 1G, 3Y, K3togtbl G, 3Y, (1G, 1Y) twice; rep from * to end of rnd. 8th rnd: * (1Y, 1B) twice, (4Y, 1B) twice, 1Y, 1B; rep from * to end of rnd. 9th rnd: * 1B, 1Y, 1B, 4Y, K3togtbl B, 4Y, 1B, 1Y; rep from * to end of rnd. 10th rnd: * 1W, 1B, (5W, 1B) twice; rep from * to end of rnd. 11th rnd: * 1B, 5W, K3togtbl B, 5W; rep from * to end of rnd. 12th rnd: * 1R, 4W, K3togtbl R, 4W; rep from * to end of rnd.

13th rnd: * 1R, 3W, K3togtbl R, 3W; rep from * to end of rnd. 14th rnd: * 1R, 2W, K3togtbl R, 2W; rep from * to end of rnd. 15th rnd: * 1R, 1W, K3togtbl R, 1W; rep from * to end of rnd. Break yarn. Thread through rem sts and fasten off securely.

Cut a circle of cardboard, 10½-in diameter. Insert into beret and observing general method on page 81 press on wrong side. Remove cardboard.

SCARF

With set of No 10 needles and N, cast on 120 sts. K 2 rnds.

Work Fair Isle patt (every row K) joining in and breaking off colours as required:

1st rnd: * 1Br, 3N; rep from * to end of rnd. 2nd rnd: * 2Br, 1N, 1Br; rep from * to end of rnd. 3rd rnd: * 2N, 1Br, 1N; rep from * to end of rnd. 4th rnd: * 1N, 1Br; rep from * to end of rnd.

5th rnd: * 2B, 2Y, 1B, 3Y, 1B, 2Y, 1B; rep from * to end of rnd. 6th rnd: * 2B, 3Y, 1B, 1Y, 1B, 3Y, 1B; rep from * to end of rnd.

7th rnd: * 1W, 2R, 3W, 1R, 3W, 2R; rep from * to end of rnd. 8th to 13th rnd: As rnds 6 to 1 incl in backward rotation. 14th and 15th rnds: With N, K. 16th rnd: * 2N, 1G, 1N; rep from * to end of rnd. 17th rnd: * 1N, 1G; rep from * to end of rnd. 18th rnd: * 1G, 3N; rep from * to end of rnd. 19th and 20th rnd: As 14th and 15th. 21st to 33rd rnd: As 1st to 13th rnd incl. Break off all colours except N.

Next rnd: With N, K3, K2tog, * K6, K2tog; rep from * to last 3 sts, K3: 105 sts.

Work straight in N until scarf measures 52 in from cast-on edge. Next rnd: K3, M1, * K7, M1; rep from * to last 4 sts, K4: 120 sts.

Joining in colours as required, work rnds 1 to 33 of Fair Isle patt. Break off all colours except N. K 2 rnds in N. Cast off. Fringe ends in N, as described in Chapter 8. Press scarf lightly.

As Knitted in Guernsey

There are further details about fishermen's jerseys in Chapter 7

Materials: 11/13 (50g) balls Patons Double Knitting. Pair each Nos 10 and 8 needles. Set of 4 No 10 needles. Cable needle.

Measurements: To fit 34–37/39–42in bust/chest; length, 23/27 in; sleeve seam, 16/18 in.

Tension: 11 sts and 15 rows to 2 in over st st on No 8 needles.

Additional Abbreviations (see page 29):

C3F = cable front by slipping next 3 sts on to cable needle and leaving at front of work, K3, then K the 3 sts from cable needle.

C3B = as C3F, but leaving sts on cable needle at back instead of front of work.

DIAMOND PANEL (worked over 13 sts)

1st row: K6, P1, K6. 2nd and every alt row: K all K sts and P all P sts. 3rd row: K5, P1, K1, P1, K5. 5th row: K4, (P1, K1) twice, P1, K4. 7th row: K3, (P1, K1) 3 times, P1, K3. 9th row: K2, (P1, K1) 4 times, P1, K2. 11th row: K1, (P1, K1) 6 times. 13th row: K2, (P1, K1) 4 times, P1, K2. 15th row: K3, (P1, K1) 3 times, P1, K3. 17th row: K4, (P1, K1) twice, P1, K4. 19th row: K5, P1, K1, P1, K5. 21st row: K6, P1, K6.

22nd row: As 2nd. 23rd row: K. 24th row: P. These 24 rows form diamond panel.

BACK AND FRONT (both alike)

With No 10 needles, cast on 96/108 sts and work in rib as follows: 1st row: K3, * P2, K2; rep from * to last st, K1. 2nd row: P3, * K2, P2; rep from * to last st, P1. Work 25/31 rows more in rib. Next row: Rib 2/4, (inc in next st, rib 9) 9/10 times, inc in next st, rib to end: 106/119 sts.

Change to No 8 needles and st st, starting with a K row until work measures $8\frac{1}{2}/12\frac{1}{2}$ in, ending with wrong side facing. Next row: P14, * (inc in next st, P1) 3 times, P13, (inc in next st, P1) 3 times *, P28/41, work from * to * once, P to end: 118/131 sts.

Work in rope and ladder patt with diamond panel as follows:

1st row: P3, K2, P7, K2, P2, * C3F, P2, work 1st row of diamond panel, P2, C3B, (P2, K2, P7, K2) * 2/3 times, P2; rep from * to * once, P3. 2nd and alt rows: K all K sts and P all P sts. 3rd row: P3, K2, P1, K5, P1, K2, P2, * K6, P2, work 3rd row of diamond panel, P2, K6, (P2, K2, P1, K5, P1, K2) * 2/3 times, P2; rep from * to * once, P3.

5th row: P3, K2, P7, K2, P2, * K6, P2, work 5th row of diamond panel, P2, K6, (P2, K2, P7, K2) * 2/3 times, P2; rep from * to * once, P3.

7th row: P3, K2, P1, K5, P1, K2, P2, * C3F, P2, work 7th row of diamond panel, P2, C3B, (P2, K2, P1, K5, P1, K2) * 2/3 times, P2; rep from * to *

once, P3. 9th row: P3, K2, P7, K2, P2, * K6, P2, work 9th row of diamond panel, P2, K6, (P2, K2, P7, K2) * 2/3 times, P2; rep from * to * once, P3. 11th row: P3, K2, P1, K5, P1, K2, P2, * K6, P2, work 11th row of diamond panel, P2, K6, (P2, K2, P1, K5, P1, K2) * 2/3 times, P2; rep from * to * once, P3. 12th row: As 2nd.

13th to 24th row: Rep rows 1 to 12 of Guernsey patt once, but working rows 13 to 24 of diamond panel. Rep these 24 rows twice more, then rows 1 to 23 again.

Next 2 rows: Cast off 42/47 sts in patt, work to end. Slip rem 34/37 sts on to a length of yarn.

SLEEVES

With No 10 needles, cast on 48/56 sts. Work in rib as on welt for 3 in, ending with a 1st row. Next row: Rib 1/5, (inc in next st, rib 3/4) 11/9 times, inc in next st, rib to end: 60/66 sts.

Change to No 8 needles and work 8 rows in st st. Cont in st st, inc 1 st at each end of next and every foll 6th row until there are 74/78 sts, then each end of every foll 4th row until there are 82/92 sts. Work 3 rows.

Work in Guernsey ladder patt as follows: 1st row: Inc in first st, K0/5, (P2, K2, P7, K2) 6 times, P2, K0/5, inc in last st. 2nd row: P2/7, (K2, P2, K7, P2) 6 times, K2, P2/7. 3rd row: K2/7, (P2, K2, P1, K5, P1, K2) 6 times, P2, K2/7. 4th row: P2/7, (K2, P2, K7, P2) 6 times, K2, P2/7.

Keeping ladder patt correct as on last 4 rows and working extra sts into st st, cont in patt inc 1 st at each end of next and every foll 4th row until there are 92/104 sts, each end of every alt row until there are 102/118 sts, then each end of every row until there are 116/132 sts.

Work 1 row. 1st and 2nd rows: Cast off 44/52 sts in patt, work to end. Cont straight in patt on rem 28 sts until strip fits along shoulder edge when slightly stretched. Cast off.

NECKBAND

Join saddle shoulders. With right side of work facing and set of No 10 needles, K across group of 34/37 sts on length of yarn, knit up 23 sts from saddle, K across 34/37 sts on length of yarn, finally knit up 23 sts from saddle: 114/120 sts. Work K1, P1 rib for 2½/3 in. Cast off in rib.

TO MAKE UP

Observing general method on page 81, block and press.

Stitch cast-off edges of sleeves to side edge of back and front. Join side and sleeve seams. Fold neckband in half to wrong side and slip-stitch neatly in position. Press seams.

Norwegian Cap and Ski-mitts

Another folk knitting style from Scandinavia

Materials: Woman's Set: 2 (50g) balls Dark, 1 (50g) ball Light Patons Purple Heather 4-ply. Two No 9 and two No 8 needles.

Man's Set: 2 (50g) balls Dark, 2 (50g) ball Light, Patons Double Knitting. Two No 8 and two No 7 needles.

Measurements: To fit average sizes.

Additional Abbreviations (see page 29): D=Dark; L=Light.

CAP

With No 9/8 needles and D, cast on 120 sts loosely and work K1, P1 rib for 1 in. Next row: Rib 10, (M1, rib 5) 20 times, M1, rib 10: 141 sts.

Change to No 8/7 needles and join in C, work rows 1 to 25 from Chart A repeating 28 patt sts 5 times across and last st on K rows and first st on P rows as indicated. Read odd rows K from right to left and even rows P from left to right.

Work 3 rows straight in D, dec 1 st at end of last row: 140 sts.

Work rows 1 to 5 from Chart D repeating 5 patt sts 28 times across rows. Break C. Cont in D as follows: 1st and every alt row: P.

2nd row: (K5, K2tog) 20 times: 120 sts. 4th row: (K6, K2tog) 15 times: 105 sts.

6th row: (K5, K2tog) 15 times: 90 sts. 8th row: (K4, K2tog) 15 times: 75 sts. 10th row: (K3, K2tog) 15 times: 60 sts. 12th row: (K2, K2tog) 15 times: 45 sts.

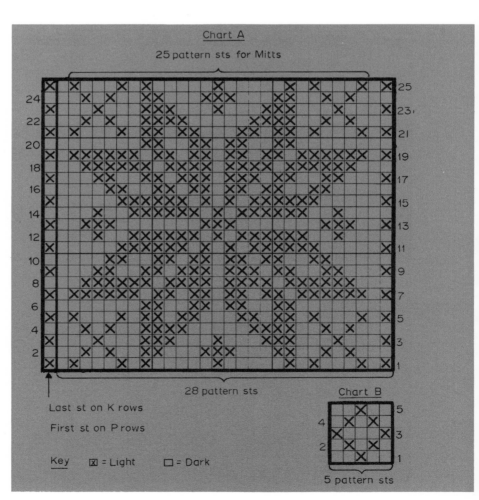

14th row: (K1, K2tog) 15 times: 30 sts.
16th row: (K2tog) 15 times: 15 sts.
18th row: (K3tog) 5 times: 5 sts.
Break yarn, thread through remaining sts, draw up tightly and fasten off securely.

TO MAKE UP

Observing general method on page 81, block and press. Join back seam. Press seam.

MITTS

Right Mitt: With No 9/8 needles and D, cast on 38 sts loosely and work K1, P1 rib for 2½ in.
Next row: Rib 3, (M1, rib 6) twice, M1, rib 4, (M1, rib 2) 8 times, M1, rib 3: 50 sts.
Change to No 8/7 needles, and work 10 rows in st st. 1st row: (right side), K all across.
Place thumb: Next row: Join in C, patt 25 from 1st row of Chart A for Mitts, slip next 7 sts on a safety-pin, cast on 7 sts, K to end. Next row: P25 in D, patt 25 from 2nd row of Chart A for Mitts. Cont as before until 25 patt rows have been worked. Break C.
Next row: P26, (P2tog, P5) 3 times, P2tog, P1: 46 sts.
** Work 8 rows st st.
Shape top: 1st row: K1, K2togtbl, K17, K2tog, K2, K2togtbl, K17, K2tog, K1.
2nd row: P1, P2tog, P15, P2togtbl, P2, P2tog, P15, P2togtbl, P1. Cont dec in this way until 18 sts rem.
Divide sts on 2 needles and graft together.**

Thumb: With right side facing and No 8/7 needles, K7 sts from safety-pin on to needle, cast on 7 sts: 14 sts.
Work 19 rows st st starting with a P row.
Shape top: 1st row: (K1, K2togtbl, K1, K2tog, K1) twice: 10 sts.
2nd row: P. 3rd row: (K1, K3tog, K1) twice: 6 sts. Break yarn, thread through rem sts, draw up tightly and fasten off securely.
Left Mitt: With No 9/8 needles and D, cast on 38 sts loosely and work K1, P1 rib for 2½ in.
Next row: Rib 3, (M1, rib 2) 8 times, M1, rib 4, (M1, rib 6) twice, M1, rib 3: 50 sts.
Change to No 8/7 needles and work 10 rows in st st.
Place thumb: Next row: Join in C, K18, slip next 7 sts on a safety-pin, cast on 7 sts, patt 25 from 1st row of Chart A for Mitts. Next row: Patt 25 from 2nd row of Chart A for mitts, P to end in D. Cont as before until 25 patt rows have been worked. Break C.
Next row: P1, (P2tog, P5) 3 times, P2tog, P26: 46 sts. Work as for right mitt from ** to **.
Thumb: With right side facing and No 8/7 needles, cast on 7 sts then K7 sts from safety-pin: 14 sts.
Finish as for right thumb.

TO MAKE UP

Observing general method on page 81, block and press.
Join side and thumb seams. Join base of thumb to main part. Press seams.

Chapter 17

'Of Your Charity . . . .'

It is a curious reflection on present-day living that the last few years have seen a marked renewal of interest in the attractive knitted and crocheted bits and pieces of which the Victorians were so very fond. The wheel has come full circle; making ingenious oddments for bazaars, coffee-mornings, and charitable causes has never been so popular. Dominated by computers, budgets, and management experts, women fly to the making of dolls' clothes, tea-cosies, neckties, and bottle covers. Little girls scorn their dolls at an earlier age, but grown-up girls love their mascots. Accordingly, the last group in the collection comprises a number of designs suitable for making and giving. Unashamedly sentimental, some of them represent new versions of long-loved objects from the happy days of childhood.

Doll's Knitted Outfit

Materials: 2/2 (25g) balls each Light and Medium Patons Purple Heather 4-ply. Pair each Nos 10 and 12 needles. 6 buttons. Ribbon for Coat and Bonnet. Elastic for Pants. No 3·00 mm crochet hook.

Measurements: To fit 12/14 in doll.

Tension: 14 sts and 18 rows to 2 in over st st on No 10 needles.

Additional Abbreviations (see page 29): L=Light; M=Medium.

DRESS
(Worked in one piece to underarm)
With No 11 needles and M, cast on 85/97 sts and work 3 rows garter st (every row K). Break M.
Change to No 9 needles, join in L and work in patt as follows: 1st row: (right side), * K1, yf, sl 1, K1, psso, K1, K2tog, yf; rep from * to last st, K1. 2nd row: P. 3rd row: * K2, yf, sl 1, K2tog, psso, yf, K1; rep from * to last st, K1. 4th row: P. These 4 rows form patt.
Rep them 6/7 times more, then rows 1 to 3 again. Next row: * P2tog, P1; rep from * to last 4 sts, (P2tog) twice: 56/64 sts. Next row: K.
Divide for armholes: Next row: P11/12, sl these sts on a safety-pin, cast off next 6/8 sts (1 st on needle), P21/23, sl these sts on a spare needle, cast off 6/8, P to end.
Cont on last 11/12 sts for left half of back and work in st st until back measures 1¾/2 in from dec row, ending with right side facing.
Shape neck by casting off 7/8 sts at beg of next row. Work 4 rows on rem 4 sts. Cast off. With right side facing, rejoin yarn to centre 22/24 sts and work in st st until front measures 1¼/1½ in from dec row, ending with right side facing.
Shape neck: Next row: K4, cast off 14/16, K to end.
Work on each set of 4 sts until front matches back at armhole edge. Cast off. With right side facing, rejoin yarn to rem 11/12 sts, work to match left half.

SLEEVES
With No 11 needles and M, cast on 22/24 sts and work 2 rows garter st. Next row: (inc in next st) 3/4 times, * K1, (inc in next st) 2/3 times; rep from *, ending K1/0: 37/43 sts. Break M. Change to No 9 needles, join in L and work 8 rows in patt as for main part. Cast off.

COAT
BACK
With No 11 needles and M, cast on 37/43 sts and work 3 rows garter st.
** Change to No 9 needles and work 17/21 rows patt as for dress. Dec 1 st at each end of next and foll 3 alt rows.** Leave rem 29/35 sts on a spare needle.

LEFT FRONT
With No 11 needles and M, cast on 19 sts and work as for back to start of armhole shaping, then dec 1 st at end of next and foll 3 alt rows. Leave rem 15 sts on a safety-pin.

RIGHT FRONT
Work to match left front.

SLEEVES
With No 11 needles and M, cast on 25 sts and work 3 rows garter st, then work as for back from ** to **: 17 sts.

YOKE
With right side facing, No 9 needles and M, K across right front, 1st sleeve, back, 2nd sleeve and left front: 93/99 sts. Next row: K.
Cont in garter st, shaping as follows: Next row: K7/8, K2tog, * K9/7, K2tog; rep from * to last 7/8 sts, K7/8: 85/89 sts. Work 1/2 rows.

Next row: K7/8, K2tog, * K8/6, K2tog; rep from * to last 6/7 sts, K6/7: 77/79 sts. Work 1/2 rows. Next row: K6/7, K2tog, * K7/5, K2tog; rep from * to last 6/7 sts, K6/7: 69/69 sts. Work 1/2 rows. Next row: K6/7, K2tog, * K6/4, K2tog; rep from * to last 5/6 sts, K5/6: 61/59 sts. Work 1 row.

Next row: K5/6, K2tog, * K5/3, K2tog; rep from * to last 5/6 sts, K5/6: 53/49 sts. Work 1 row. Next row: K5/6, K2tog, * K4/2, K2tog; rep from * to last 4/5 sts, K4/5: 45/39 sts.

1st size: Next row: K4, K2tog, * K3, K2tog; rep from * to last 4 sts. K4: 37 sts.

Both sizes: Change to No 11 needles and work 3 more rows garter st. Cast off.

BONNET

With No 11 needles and L, cast on 61/67 sts, and work 3 rows garter st.

Change to No 9 needles and work 4 rows in patt as for dress. Next 2 rows: P. Next row: P inc 3/5 sts evenly across: 64/72 sts.

Break L. Join in M and work in st st, starting with P row, until bonnet measures 2/2½ in, ending with right side facing. Shape back by casting off 25/27 sts at beg of next 2 rows. Work in garter st over centre 15/18 sts, inc 1 st at each end of next and every alt row until there are 30/36 sts. Work 5 rows, then dec 1 st at each end of next and every alt row until 14/18 sts rem. Cast off.

BOOTEES

With No 11 needles and L, cast on 25 sts and work 3 rows garter st. Change to No 9 needles and work 4 rows in patt as for dress, then P 3 rows, inc 4 sts evenly across on last row on 2nd size only: 25/29 sts. Break L. Join in M and work 3 rows st st, starting with a P row.

Divide for instep: K17/20, turn, P9/11, turn. Work 6/10 rows st st on these 9/11 sts. Break M.

With right side facing, rejoin M to inside edge of 8/9 sts left, knit up 5/7 sts down side of instep, K9/11 instep sts, knit up 5/7 sts from other side, K rem 8/9 sts: 35/43 sts. Work 3/5 rows garter

st. Next row: K2tog, K10/13, K2tog, K7/9, K2tog, K10/13, K2tog. Next row: K2tog, K9/12, K2tog, K5/7, K2tog, K9/12, K2tog. Cast off. Join leg and foot seams.

VEST
BACK AND FRONT (both alike)

With No 11 needles and L, cast on 28/34 sts and work 4 rows K1, P1 rib.

Change to No 9 needles and cont in rib until work measures 1¼/1½ in.

Shape armholes by casting off 4/5 sts at beg of next 2 rows: 20/24 sts. Work 4 rows.

Shape neck: Next row: K4, cast off 12/16 sts in rib, K to end. Work 10 rows garter st on each set of 4 sts. Cast off. Join shoulder and side seams.

PANTS
BACK AND FRONT (both alike)

With No 11 needles and L, cast on 28/34 sts and work 2 rows K1, P1 rib.

Next row: K1, * yf, work 2tog, rib 2; rep from * to last 3/1 sts, yf, work 2tog, rib 1/1. Rib 1 row.

Change to No 9 needles and cont in rib until work measures 1½/1¾ in, ending with right side facing. Shape legs by casting off 4 sts at beg of next 2 rows, then dec 1 st at each end of next and every alt row until 6/8 sts rem. Cast off.

TO MAKE UP

Observing general method on page 81, press.

Dress: Join shoulder and sleeve seams. Gather up cast-off edge of sleeve until top fits armhole; sew in position. Work 2 rows dc in M round neck. Work 2 rows dc in L along right side of back, making 6 buttonloops evenly spaced in 2nd row. To make a buttonloop, work 2ch, miss 2 sts. Work 2 rows dc in L along left side. Sew on buttons.

Coat: Join armhole, side and sleeve seams. Work 2 rows dc in M along each front edge. Sew ribbon to each front at neck.

Bonnet: Sew shaped back to side edges, then work 2 rows dc in M along neck edge. Sew ribbon to corners.

Pants: Join crutch and side seams. Thread elastic through holes in rib.

Doll's Crocheted Outfit

Materials: 4 (25g) balls Patons Baby 4-ply Courtelle. No 3·00 mm crochet hook; 5 small buttons; length of ribbon.

Measurements: To fit a 16 in doll; length of Dress, $7\frac{1}{2}$ in; length of Coat, 6 in (approx).

Tension: In width $13\frac{1}{2}$ trebles to 2 in.

Additional Abbreviations (see page 29): Dec 1 = decrease 1 stitch thus: yrh, insert hook into st, draw yarn through, now insert hook into next stitch, drawn yarn through, yrh and draw through first 3 loops on hook, yrh and draw through last 2 loops on hook.

Note: On plain fabric, the turning ch counts as a st. The first st of every row should be missed and the turning ch at the end of the row worked into unless otherwise stated.

COAT
RIGHT FRONT
Make 24ch. Foundation row: (right side), 1dtr into 5th ch from hook, 1dtr into foll ch, * 4ch, miss 1ch, ss into next ch, 4ch, miss 1ch, 1dtr into each of next 3ch; rep from * to end, turn with 4ch.
Now work in patt: 1st row: Miss 3dtr, ss into ch sp, * 4ch, ss into next ch sp, 4ch, miss 3dtr, ss into ch sp; rep from * to end, but working last ss into top of turning ch, turn with 8ch. 2nd row: Ss into first ch sp, * 4ch, 3dtr into next ch sp, 4ch, ss into foll ch sp; rep from *, ending 4ch, 1dtr into 1st ch, turn with 4ch.
3rd row: Miss 1ch sp, ss into next ch sp, * 4ch, miss 3dtr, ss into ch sp, 4ch, ss into next ch sp; rep from * to end, working last ss into 4th of 8 ch, turn with 4ch. 4th row: 2dtr into first ch sp, * 4ch, ss into next ch sp, 4ch, 3dtr into next ch sp; rep from * to end, turn with 4ch. These 4 rows form the patt.**
Cont in patt until front measures approx 4 in, ending with a 1st or 3rd row of patt, turning with 3ch.
Shape Yoke: 1st row: 2tr into first sp, 2tr into each of next 5 sps, turn with 3ch leaving 1 sp unworked. 2nd row: Miss first st, then 1tr into each st to end, turn with 3ch: 13 sts. *** Rep the last

row 3 times more (omitting turning ch at end of last row of left front).
Shape neck: 1st row: Miss first st, then 1tr into each of next 6 sts, dec 1, turn with 3ch. Work 2 rows, dec 1 st at neck edge on 1st of these rows. Fasten off.

LEFT FRONT
Work as right front to start of yoke shaping, turning with 2ch at end of last row.
Shape Yoke: 1st row: Ss into 1st sp, 2ch, ss into foll sp, 3ch, 1tr into same sp, 2tr into each sp to end, 1tr into last ch.
*** Complete to match right front, noting that 1st row of neck shaping will be: Ss into each of first 5 sts, 3ch, do not miss a st, dec 1, work to end.

BACK
Make 48ch and work as for right front to start of Yoke shaping, turning with 2ch at end of last row.
**** Shape Yoke: 1st row: Ss into first sp, 2ch, ss into foll sp, 3ch, 1tr into same sp, 2tr into each sp to last sp, turn with 3ch leaving last sp unworked.
**** Work 7 rows straight in tr. Fasten off.

SLEEVES
Work as right front until ** is reached. Cont in patt until sleeve seam measures approx $4\frac{1}{2}$ in, ending with a 1st or 3rd row and omitting turning ch at end of last row. Fasten off.

TO MAKE UP
Observing general method on page 81, press. Join side and shoulder seams. Join sleeve seams, leaving $\frac{3}{4}$ of an inch free at top. Insert sleeves, stitching top $\frac{3}{4}$ of an inch to armholes. With right side facing, work 2 rnds of dc all round front and neck edges, working 2 buttonholes on right front yoke on 2nd of these rows thus: 2ch, miss 2dc. Work 1 row more. Fasten off. Press seams. Sew on buttons.

DRESS
LEFT BACK
Work as right front of coat to ***, but working approx 6 in instead of 4 in.

Rep the last row 5 times more. Fasten off.

RIGHT BACK
Work as left front of coat to ***, but working approx 6 in instead of 4 in. Work 6 rows straight. Fasten off.

FRONT
Make 48ch. Work as right front of coat to start of yoke shaping, but working approx 6 in in place of 4 in, turn with 2ch at end of last row. Work as given for back of coat from **** to ****. Work 6 rows straight in tr. Fasten off.

TO MAKE UP
Leaving centre 12 sts free, join shoulders. Join centre back seam, leaving 3 in free at top. Join side seams. With right side of work facing, work 1 rnd of dc round neck and back opening leaving spaces for 3 buttonholes on right back opening. Now work 1 rnd dc round armholes. Sew on buttons.

BONNET
Crown: Make 5ch, join into a ring with ss. 1st rnd: 3ch, work 13tr into ring. Join with ss into first sp between 3ch and 1dtr. 2nd rnd: 3ch, 1tr into same sp as ss, (1tr into next sp, 2tr into foll sp) 6 times, 1tr into last sp, join with ss into first sp. 3rd rnd: 3ch, 1tr into same sp as ss, (1tr into each of next 2 sp, 2tr into foll sp) 6 times, 1tr into last 2 sps, join with ss into first sp. 4th to 7th rnd: Work 4 more rnds in this manner, working 2tr into sp between each 2tr of previous rnd and working 1tr into all other sps. Fasten off.
Lace Portion: Make 60ch, work as right front of coat to **. Cont in patt until work measures approx 3 in, ending with a 1st or 3rd row of patt. Fasten off.

TO MAKE UP
Stitch foundation ch of lace portion to last row of tr on crown. Sew on ribbon.

VEST
BACK AND FRONT (both alike)
Make 29ch. Foundation row: 1tr into 4th ch from hook, then 1tr into each ch to end, turn with 4ch. Next row: Miss first 2 sts, 1tr into next st, * 1ch, miss a st, 1tr into next st; rep from * to end, turn with 3ch. Next row: * 1tr into ch sp, 1tr into tr; rep from *, ending 1tr in last sp, 1tr in 3rd of 4ch, turn with 4ch**. Rep the last 2 rows 5 times more, turn with 3ch at end of last row.
Shape armholes: Next row: Miss first st, (dec 1) twice, 1tr into each st to last 4 sts, (dec 1) twice, turn with 3ch. Rep the last row twice more, omitting turning ch at end of last row. Fasten off.
Straps (make 2): Make 17ch. Work foundation row as on back and front, omitting turning ch. Fasten off.

TO MAKE UP
Join side seams. Stitch straps to top row of back and front.

PILCH
BACK AND FRONT (both alike)
Work as for vest until ** is reached. Rep the last 2 rows once more, turn with 3ch at end of last row.
Shape legs: Next row: Miss first st, (dec 1) twice, 1tr into each st to last 4 sts, (dec 1) twice, turn with 3ch. Rep the last row 4 times more. Work 3 rows without shaping. Fasten off.

TO MAKE UP
Join side seams and final row of tr of back and front. Work 1 rnd dc round legs. Using yarn double, crochet a length of ch 22 in long and slot through top of pilch.

Faithful Teddy

Materials: Teddy: 5 (50g) balls in Light and oddment of Black; **Dungarees:** 1 (50g) ball each Dark and Medium Patons Doublet. Pair No 8 needles. Two buttons. Kapok for stuffing.

Measurement: Height 16 in.

Tension: 9 sts to 2 in over garter stitch.

Additional Abbreviations (see page 29): L=Light; D=Dark; M=Medium.

Note: The Teddy Bear is knitted in garter st throughout (every row K). When making up, join all seams neatly on right side. If fluffy effect is desired, brush Teddy Bear. Work Dungarees in stripes of 4 rows D, 4 rows M.

LEGS AND BODY

With L, cast on 11 sts and K 44 rows. Break off yarn and push sts to end of needle. On same needle, cast on 11 sts and make another piece the same, but do not break off yarn.

Work across both sets of 11 sts as follows: K 4 rows. Next row: K, dec 1 st at each end. K 3 rows. Next row: (K2tog, K6, K2tog) twice: 16 sts. K 8 rows. Next row: K, inc 1 st at each end. K 10 rows. Next row: K, inc 1 st at each end. K 5 rows. Next row: K, inc 1 st at each end: 22 sts. K 3 rows.

Shape shoulders by casting off 3 sts at beg of next 4 rows. Cast off.

Make another piece the same then sew halves together leaving neck and legs open for stuffing. Stuff firmly and gather up openings.

FEET

With L, cast on 6 sts, K 1 row. Next row: K, inc 1 st at each end. K 3 rows. Rep last 4 rows twice more. Cast off. Make 3 more pieces the same. Sew each pair tog, leaving cast-off edges open. Stuff firmly and sew to leg ends as in photograph.

HEAD

With L, cast on 14 sts, K 1 row. Inc 1 st at each end of next 4 rows: 22 sts. K 31 rows. Dec 1 st at each end of next 4 rows. Cast off. Make another piece the same. Sew halves tog, leaving cast-off edges open. Stuff firmly and sew up opening. Sew head to body.

MUZZLE

With L, cast on 11 sts, K 3 rows. Next row: K, dec 1 st at each end. Rep these 4 rows twice more. Cast off. Make another piece the same. Sew halves tog, leaving cast-on edges open. Stuff firmly and sew open end to Head. With Black, embroider eyes, nose and mouth in stem and straight sts, then embroider a straight st in L at eyes as in photograph.

ARMS

With L, cast on 7 sts and K 1 row. Next 2 rows: K, inc 1 st at each end. K 5 rows. Next row: K2tog, K to end. K 3 rows. Rep last 4 rows once. Next row: K2tog, K to end. Next row: Inc in 1st st, K to end. K 1 row.

Shape as follows: 1st row: K5, turn. 2nd and alt rows: K to end. 3rd row: K4, turn. 5th row: K3, turn. 7th row: K2, turn. 8th row: K to end. K 17 rows across all sts. Next row: Inc in 1st st, K to end. K 3 rows. Next 2 rows: K, dec 1 st at each end. Cast off. Make another 3 pieces the same.

Sew each pair tog, placing short edges tog and leaving cast-off edges open. Stuff firmly, close opening and sew to Body.

EARS

With L, cast on 7 sts and K 1 row. Next 3 rows: K, inc 1 st at each end. K 4 rows. Next 3 rows: K, dec 1 st at each end. Cast off. Make another 3 pieces the same. Sew each pair tog. Fold one end of ears in half and stitch to head so that they curl forward.

DUNGAREES

Back: With D, cast on 14 sts and K 36 rows. Break off yarn and push sts to end of needle. On same needle, cast on 14 sts and K 36 rows. Next row: K across both sets of sts: 28 sts. Next row: K, dec 1 st at each end. K 3 rows. Rep last 4 rows twice more. K 2 rows.** Cast off. Front: Work as back to **.

*** Next row: Cast off 4 sts, K to last 4 sts, cast off 4. Break yarn. Rejoin yarn to remaining 14 sts and K 14 rows.

Next row: K2, yf, K2tog, K to last 4 sts, K2tog, yf, K2. K 2 rows. Cast off. Straps (2): Cast on 3 sts and work in garter st until sufficient has been worked to go over shoulders and cross at back. Join side and leg seams. Stitch straps in position and sew a button on each strap.

Miss 1920 Doll, Big-Big Bunny, and Ball

Instructions for the woolly ball are given on page 282

MISS 1920 DOLL

Materials: 2 (50g) balls Deep Pink and 1 (50g) ball each Blue, Yellow, and Fawn Patons Doublet. Scraps of Patons Double Knitting in Blue, Red, and White for features. Pair No 8 needles. Kapok for stuffing.

Measurement: Height 18 in.

Additional Abbreviations (see page 29): M=Deep Pink; B=Blue; Y=Yellow; F=Fawn.

Note: Doll is knitted in garter stitch (every row K), unless otherwise stated. When making up join all seams neatly on right side.

FEET AND LEGS

With M, cast on 10 sts and K 1 row. Next row: Inc 1 st at each end. K 3 rows. Next row: Dec 1 st at each end. Next row: Cast off 3, K to end. K 1 row. Break yarn and make another piece the same. Slip both sets of sts on to same needle with toes (i.e. cast-off sts) pointing towards the centre. K 2 rows. Break M. Join in F. Change to st st, starting with a K row, and work 7 rows. Next row: Inc 1 st at each end. Work 17 rows. Next row: Inc 1 st at each end. Work 6 rows. Break F. Join in B. K 4 rows. Cast off. Make another piece the same.
Fold each piece in half lengthways and sew tog, leaving cast-off edge open for stuffing. Stuff firmly and join inner top edges of legs together for 1 in.
Embroider laces of shoes with cross stitch in B, then tie in bows at top of each shoe as illustrated.

BODY

With B, cast on 20 sts and K 15 rows. Next row: Dec 1 st at each end. K 15 rows. Next row: Inc 1 st at each end. K 4 rows. Cast off 3 sts at beg of next 4 rows. Cast off. Make another piece the same, then sew halves tog, leaving cast-off edges open. Stuff firmly and sew legs to body at cast-on edge.

HEAD (work in st st in F)

Cast on 11 sts and K 1 row. Next row: Inc 1 st at each end. Rep last row 3 times more. Work 12 rows straight. Next row: Inc 1 st at each end. Work 6 rows straight. Dec 1 st at each end of next 2 rows. Cast off. Make another piece the same. Sew halves together leaving cast-off edge open. Stuff firmly and sew up opening.
Embroider features as shown in diagram and rouge cheeks. Sew head to body.

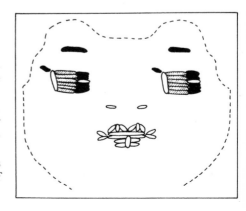

HAIR

With Y, cast on 7 sts. K 3 rows. Cast on 9 sts at beg of next 2 rows. K 2 rows. Cast on 3 sts at beg of next 2 rows. K 9 rows. Cast on 5 sts at beg of next 2 rows. K 8 rows. Next row: K19, K3tog, K19. K 3 rows. Next 2 rows: K20, turn and K back. Next 2 rows: K18, K2tog, turn and K back. Next 2 rows: K17, K2tog, turn and K back. Next 2 rows: K16, K2tog, turn and K back.
Next 2 rows: K15, K2tog, turn and K back. Next row: K14, K2tog, turn. Next row: K2tog, K to end. Cast off. Rejoin yarn to inside edge of rem sts. K 1 row. Next row: K to last 2 sts, K2tog. Rep last 2 rows 5 times more. Cast off. Fold in half and join cast-off edges and rem of seam tog. Pad with a little stuffing and sew hair to head with seam at back. Brush to give a fluffy effect.

HANDS AND ARMS (hands are worked in st st in F)

Cast on 18 sts and work 2 rows. Next row: K twice in first st, K7, (K twice in next st) twice, K7, K twice in last st: 22 sts. Work 5 rows.
Next row: K2tog, K7, (K2tog) twice, K7, K2tog. Next row: Dec 1 st at each end. Break F and join in M. K 2 rows M. Join in B. K 2 rows B, 4 rows M, 2 rows B, 2 rows M. Break M. K 20 rows. Cast off. Make another piece the same. Fold each piece in half lengthways and sew tog, leaving cast-off edge open.
Stuff firmly and sew arms to body. In F, make a large french knot on each hand for thumb. Outline armholes and yoke with a band of ch st in M.

SKIRT (work in st st in M)

Cast on 40 sts and work 2 rows straight. Next row: * K3, K twice in next st; rep from * to end. Next row: P. Next row: * K4, K twice in next st; rep from * to end. Next row: P. Next row: * K5, K twice in next st; rep from * to end. Work 5 rows straight. K 2 rows. Cast off. Join centre back seam. Fit on doll and sew in position.

HAT

With M, cast on 17 sts for crown and K 5 rows. Next row: Dec 1 st at each end. Rep last 6 rows once more. K 3 rows. Next row: Dec 1 st at each end. Rep last 4 rows until 5 sts rem. Next row: Dec 1 st at each end. Cast off firmly.
Make another 3 pieces the same; join sections tog, leaving cast-on edges open. With M, cast on 7 sts for brim and K 2 rows. Next 2 rows: K5, turn and K back. Rep last 4 rows until shorter edge fits along edge of crown. Cast off. Join ends neatly, then sew brim to hat. Fit hat on doll.

SCARF

With M, cast on 5 sts and K 100 rows. Cast off. Tie round neck with knot at front as illustrated, then catch in position.

BIG-BIG BUNNY

Materials: 3(50g) balls Patons Double Knitting in Grey; small ball Contrast shade for Tie; oddments of Black and Green for features. Pair No 8 needles. Kapok for stuffing.

Measurement: Height to tip of ears, 16 in.

Rabbit is knitted in garter st throughout (every row K). Join all seams neatly on right side.

BODY

Cast on 86 sts and K 1 row. Next row: K, inc 1 st at each end: 88 sts. K 33 rows. Next row: * K9, K2tog; rep from * to end. K 9 rows. Next row: * K8, K2tog; rep from * to end. K 9 rows. Next row: * K7, K2tog; rep from * to end. K 9 rows. Next row: * K6, K2tog; rep from * to end. K 11 rows. Next row: * K5, K2tog; rep from * to end. K 2 rows. Cast off. Fold in half lengthways and join seam (front). Leave ends open.

BASE

Cast on 11 sts and K 1 row. Now inc 1 st at each end of every row until there are 21 sts. K 24 rows. Now dec 1 st at each end of every row until 11 sts remain. Cast off. Sew base in position to cast-on edge of body. Stuff body firmly to shape, then gather up neck edge.

HEAD
Start at neck edge. Cast on 17 sts and K 3 rows. Next row: K to last st, K twice in last st. Next row: K twice in 1st st, K to end. Next row: K, inc 1 st at each end. Next row: K twice in 1st st, K to end. Rep last 4 rows once more. K 11 rows straight. Next row: K2tog, K to end. Next row: K to last 2 sts, K2tog. Rep last 2 rows 3 times more. Next row: K2tog, K to last 2 sts, K2tog. Next row: K to last 2 sts, K2tog. Rep last 2 rows twice more. Cast off.
Make another piece the same. Sew halves tog, leaving cast-on edge open. Stuff firmly, pushing head out to shape. Sew open end of head round top of Body, adding extra stuffing as you do so to keep neck firm.

EARS
Cast on 3 sts and K 1 row. Next row: K, inc 1 st at each end. K 3 rows. Rep last 4 rows until there are 23 sts. K 4 rows. Next row: K2tog, K to last 2 sts, K2tog. Next row: K9, K3tog, K9. Next row: K8, K3tog, K8. Next row: K7, K3tog, K7. Next row: K2tog, K to last 2 sts, K2tog. Cast off. Make 3 more pieces the same. Sew each pair tog and sew to head, folding cast-off edge in half so that ears curl forward.

TAIL
Cast on 7 sts and K 1 row, then inc 1

st at each end of foll 4 rows, K 15 rows straight, then dec 1 st at each end of next 4 rows. Cast off. Make another piece the same. Sew halves tog, leaving one end open for stuffing. Stuff firmly, then sew open end to body in line with base.

ARMS (make 2)
** Cast on 19 sts and K 3 rows. Next row: K9, K twice in next st, K9. K 3 rows. Next row: K9, (inc in next st) twice, K9. K 3 rows. Next row: K, inc 1 st at each end. K 3 rows. Rep last 4 rows once more. K 8 rows. Next row: K, inc 1 st at each end. K 2 rows **. Cast off. Fold in half lengthways and join, leaving cast-off end open. Stuff firmly, then sew open end of arms firmly in position to body.

BACK LEGS (make 2)
Work as for arms from ** to **, then K 5 rows. Next row: K, inc 1 st at each end. K 4 rows. Cast off. Stuff and sew in position as for arms.

FEATURES
Eyes: outlined black stem-st filled with green and black satin-st; eyebrows: black straight st; nose: black satin-st; mouth, black straight-st with vertical straight-st in centre; whiskers and paw markings: black straight-sts.

TIE
With Contrast, cast on 6 sts and work straight for 25 in. Cast off. Tie round neck with bow at front.

Knitted Humpty and Pig in Crochet

KNITTED HUMPTY
Materials: 1 (50g) ball each White and Red, and oddment in Black Patons Double Knitting. Pair No 8 needles. Kapok for stuffing.
Measurement: Height, 10½ in.
Additional Abbreviations (see page 29): W=White; R=Red; B=Black. Work in garter st unless otherwise stated.

BODY
With R, cast on 9 sts, K 1 row. Working in garter st (every row K), inc 1 st

at each end of every row until there are 41 sts. Work 29 rows straight. Break R. Join in W and change to st st, starting with a K row, and work 24 rows straight. Now dec 1 st at each end of every row until 19 sts rem. Cast off.

Make another piece the same. Join cast-on edges and side seams. Stuff firmly and sew up opening.

ARMS (2)

With W, cast on 11 sts, K 34 rows. Dec 1 st at each end of next 2 rows. Cast off. Join seam, leaving cast-on edge open. Stuff firmly and sew to body. Wind 2 strands of W round arms 1 in up from lower edge.

LEGS (2)

With R, cast on 15 sts, K 12 rows. Dec 1 st at each end of next and every foll 14th row until 9 sts rem. Work 1 row straight. Break R. Join in B, and K 2 rows. Now inc 1 st at each end of next and every alt row, until there are 15 sts. Work 7 rows straight. Now dec 1 st at each end of every row until 7 sts rem. Cast off. Join seam, leaving cast-on edge open. Stuff firmly and sew to body.

CAP

First Piece: With L, cast on 1 st and K into back and front of it: 2 sts. Cont in st st, starting with a P row, inc 1 st at each end of next 2 rows, then on foll 2 alt rows, then on foll 3rd rows twice: 14 sts. Work 3 rows straight. Next row: Inc 1 st at each end: 16 sts. Work 3 rows. Cast off. Work another 3 pieces the same (2 dark, 1 light).

Peak: With L, cast on 1 st and K into back and front of it: 2 sts. Next row: K1, inc in last st. Next row: Inc in first st, K to end. Rep last 2 rows 3 times: 10 sts. K 20 rows. Next row: K to last 2 sts, K2tog. Next row: Dec 1 st, K to end. Rep last 2 rows until 2 sts rem. K2tog. Fasten off.

Make tassel in B and sew to top of head for hair. Join 4 sections tog, stuff with kapok and stitch in position with hair showing, as in photograph. Sew peak to front of cap.

TIE

Joining in and breaking colours as required, cast on 10 sts, K 2 rows. Starting with a P row, work 3 rows st st. * Cont in st st thus: Work 4 rows L, 4 rows D.* Rep from * to * twice. With D, next row K. Next row: P. Cast off. Sew tie to front of body where two colours meet. Mark features as in photograph, using black for eyes, red for nose and mouth.

PIG IN CROCHET

Materials: 3(50g) balls Patons Double Knitting. Small amounts of White and Black yarn for Eyes and Flowers, length of Green yarn for embroidery. No 3·50 mm crochet hook. Kapok for stuffing.

Measurements: Height 10 in; Width 11 in.

Note: '1ch' worked at end of every row becomes first st on foll row.

LEGS AND BODY

Make 10ch. Foundation row: 1dc in 2nd ch from hook, 1dc in next 8ch, 1ch, turn. 1st and 2nd rows: Miss first dc, 1dc in next 8dc, 1ch, turn. 3rd row: (inc row), 1dc in next 8dc, 2dc in last st, 1ch, turn: 11 sts.

4th and 5th rows: Miss first dc, 1dc in next 10dc, 1ch, turn. 6th row: 1dc in next 10dc, 2dc in last st, 1ch, turn: 13 sts. 7th and 8th rows: Miss first dc, 1dc in next 12dc, 1ch, turn. 9th row: 1dc in next 12dc, 2dc in last st, 1ch, turn: 15 sts. 10th and 11th rows: Miss first dc, 1dc in next 14dc, 1ch, turn. 12th row: 1dc in next 14dc, 2dc in last st, 1ch, turn: 17 sts. Fasten off.

Make another leg to match but do not fasten off. Next row: Work across 17 sts of leg just worked, make 9ch for lower edge of body, work across 17 sts of first leg: 43 sts.**

Work 1 row, then inc 1 st at each end of next and every foll 3rd row until there are 53 sts. Cont shaping front edge only by inc 1 st at end of next and every alt row until there are 56 sts, make 3ch for snout, turn. Next row: 1dc in 2nd ch from hook, 1dc in next ch, work in dc to end: 58 sts. Work 7 rows without shaping, thus ending at front edge.

Shape top of body: 1st row: Miss first dc, 1ss in next dc, work in dc to end, 1ch, turn: 56dc. 2nd row: (Dec row), Miss 2dc, 1dc in next 52dc, 1ch, turn. 3rd row: Miss first dc, 1ss in next dc, work in dc to end. 1ch, turn.

4th row: Miss 2dc, 1dc in next 47dc, 1ch, turn. 5th row: As 3rd: 46dc. 6th row: Miss 2dc, 1dc in each dc to last 2 sts, miss 1dc, 1dc in last st, 1ch, turn. Cont dec 1 st at each end of every row as on 6th row until 18 sts rem. Fasten off. Work another piece to match.

GUSSET

Work as legs and body until ** is reached: 43 sts. Work 1 row, then inc 1 st at each end of next and every foll 3rd row until there are 49 sts. Fasten off. Work another piece to match.

EARS (make 2)

Make 12ch. Foundation row: 1dc in 2nd ch from hook, 1dc in next 10ch, 1ch, turn. Work 3 rows in dc, then dec 1 st at each end of next and every alt row until 1 st rem. Fasten off.

TAIL

Using yarn double, make 15ch, work 1ss into 12th ch from hook, thus making a loop. Fasten off.

FLOWERS (make 6)

With white, make 4ch, join into ring with ss. 1st rnd: Work 8dc into ring. 2nd rnd: (4ch, 1ss into 2nd ch from hook, 2ch, 1ss into next dc) 8 times. Fasten off.

EYES (make 2)

With white, make 4ch, join into ring with ss. 1st rnd: Work 8dc into ring. 2nd rnd: (1dc, 2dc in next dc) 4 times: 12 sts. 3rd rnd: (1dc, 2dc in next dc) 6 times: 18 sts. Fasten off.

PUPILS (make 2)

With black, work as eye to end of 1st rnd. Fasten off.

TO MAKE UP

Observing general method on page 81, block and press.

Place the two body pieces tog, matching front and back shapings. Stitch a gusset inside each body piece at lower edge (top edge of gusset is indicated by dotted line on diagram 1), stitching tog down sides, legs and under side of body and leaving top edge of gusset open. Now stitch the two body pieces tog all around top edge from X to X on diagram 1. Stuff body and legs firmly through gusset opening. Stitch up opening. Stitch a black pupil to each eye and referring to diagram 1, stitch eyes and ears into position, gathering lower edge of each ear. Work eyelashes in black straight stitches and mouth in stem stitch. Stitch tail in position and attach 3 flowers to each side of body as indicated by 3 crosses on diagram. Using green, work radiating straight stitches between each petal, as shown on diagram 2.

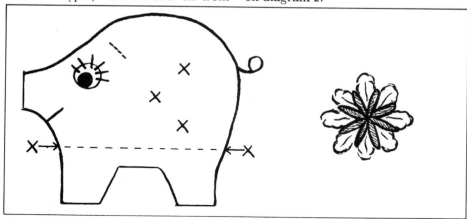

Trendy Trudy

Materials: 2 (50g) balls Royal Blue and 1 (50g) ball each of Red, White, Yellow, Pink, and Pale Yellow; oddment each of Beige, Black, Blue, and Red Patons Double Knitting. Kapok for stuffing. Pair each Nos 8 and 11 needles.

Measurement: Height to top of hat, 28 in.

Tension: 11 sts and 15 rows to 2 in over st st on No 8 needles.

Note: Doll is knitted in garter-stitch (every row K) unless otherwise stated. When making up join all seams neatly on right side.

LEGS AND BODY

With No 8 needles and Blue, cast on 14 sts and K 88 rows. Break yarn and push sts to end of needle. On to same needle cast on 14 sts and make another piece the same. Join legs tog by knitting across both sets of sts and K a further 26 rows. Break yarn.

Join in Red and K 2 rows, then join in White and K 2 rows. Rep the last 4 rows 8 times more. Cont in stripes and shape shoulders by casting off 4 sts at beg of next 4 rows. Cast off.

Make another piece the same, then sew halves tog leaving neck and legs open for stuffing. Stuff firmly keeping body and legs a good shape. Gather up openings.

ARMS AND HANDS

With No 11 needles and Pink, cast on 12 sts. 1st row: K. 2nd row: P, inc 1 st at each end. Work 13 rows straight in st st, then dec 1 st at each end of foll row. Break yarn.

Push sts to end of needle and on same needle make another piece the same. Break yarn.

Change to No 8 needles and using Red and White work 52 rows in stripes of 2 rows Red, 2 rows White over both sets of sts. K1 row Red. Cast off.

Make another piece the same. Fold each piece in half lengthways and join arm and all round hand, leaving top of arm open for stuffing. Stuff firmly; sew up opening and sew in position to body.

SHOES

With No 11 needles and Beige, cast on 11 sts.

Next 3 rows: K. Next row: K, inc 1 s at each end. Rep the last 4 rows onc more. K 28 rows straight. Next row K2tog, K to last 2 sts, K2tog. Next row K. Rep the last 2 rows 3 times more Cast off.

Make 3 more pieces the same. Sew eac pair tog, leaving an opening for stuffing Stuff firmly and sew up opening. Sew t legs. Lace up shoes with White yarn a illustrated.

HEAD

With No 11 needles and Pink, cast o 23 sts and work in st st, inc 1 st at eac end of every P row until there are 3 sts. Next row: Inc in 1st st, K6, twice into each of next 5 sts, K9, twice into each of next 5 sts, K6, inc i last st: 45 sts.

Work 9 rows straight. Next row: K (K2tog) 6 times, K7, (K2tog) 6 time K7: 33 sts. Work 27 rows straight, the dec 1 st at each end of foll 4 rows. Ca off.

With Pale Yellow, make another pie the same for back of Head. Join halv tog, leaving cast-off end open (top head). Stuff very firmly pushing o cheeks to give shape to face.

GUSSET AT TOP OF HEAD

With No 11 needles and Pale Yello cast on 9 sts and work in st st as follow K 1 row, then inc 1 st at each end next 5 rows. Work 16 rows straigh then dec 1 st at each end of foll 5 row Cast off. Sew gusset into open top Head, adding extra stuffing as you so.

HAIR

For fringe, cut thirty-six 4 in lengths Yellow, fold in half and sew across t of face. Cut rem yarn into 18 in lengt for long hair. Fold each length in ha and sew cut ends of loops evenly alo sides and back of head gusset.

HAT

With No 8 needles and White, cast 21 sts.

Work straight in moss st for 12 in, i.e. every row K1, P1 to last st, K1. Cast off. Join back seam.

HAT GUSSET
With No 8 needles and White, cast on 9 sts and work in garter-st as follows: K 1 row, then inc 1 st at each end of next 3 rows. K 30 rows straight, then dec 1 st at each end of foll 3 rows. Cast off.
Sew Gusset into top of Hat. Stuff top, then arrange Hat on Head as illustrated, sew in position. Pouch Hat over at back of Head and catch down.

SCARF
With No 8 needles and Red, cast on 3 sts, and work in garter-st: 1st row: K. 2nd row: K, inc 1 st at end. 3rd row: K, inc 1 st at beg. Rep the last 2 rows twice more: 9 sts.
Work 122 rows straight. Next row: K, dec 1 st at end. Next row: K, dec 1 st at

beg. Rep the last 2 rows twice more Cast off.

DOLL'S FEATURES
Using scraps of Black, Red, White and Blue, embroider features from diagram thus: Eyes: Black and White with pupils in Blue. Eyelashes and Eyebrows: Black. Mouth and Nose marking: Red. Colour cheeks with a little rouge.

Knitted and Crocheted Tea Cosies: Knitted Egg Cosies

KNITTED TEA COSY
Materials: 1 (50g) ball each of Dark, Medium and Light Patons Double Knitting. Pair No 9 needles. Plastic foam for pad.

Measurements: Width all round, 24 in; height, 10 in.

Note: Cosy is worked in 3 sections, 1 Dark, 1 Medium, and 1 Light.

SECTION
Cast on 47 sts. K 2 rows. Work in patt thus: 1st row: * K1, P1; rep from * to last st, K1. 2nd row: K1, * K1, P1; rep from * to last 2 sts, K2. 3rd and 4th rows: K. These 4 rows form patt.
Cont in patt until work measures 5 in from start, ending with a 2nd or 4th row of patt. Keeping patt correct, dec 1 st at each end of next and every alt row until 3 sts rem. Work 1 row. Next row: K3tog. Fasten off.

TO MAKE UP
Observing general method on page 81, press.
With wrong side facing, stitch the side edges of 3 sections tog. Turn right side out. Make 6 lengths of cord (see Chapter 8), 2 cords in each colour. Stitch a cord at each side of the 3 seams, Light cords on Dark sections; Dark cords on Medium and Medium cords on Light. Bind round each cord at top of cosy with matching yarn to make secure and trim away surplus cord to within 1 in of binding. Fringe top ends, see photograph. Cut 3 sections of plastic foam to match knitted sections and over-sew edges tog to make pad.

CROCHETED TEA COSY
Materials: 2 (50g) balls each Dark and Light Patons Double Knitting. No 4·00 mm crochet hook.

Measurement: To fit an average size Teapot.

Additional Abbreviations (see page 29): 1trB=one treble below as follows: Yarn over hook, insert hook into next st 2 rows below, yarn over hook, draw a loop through this st and draw loop up in front of last 2 rows, yarn over hook, draw through first 2 loops on hook, yarn over hook and draw through rem 2 loops on hook; D=Dark; L=Light.

Note: '1ch' at end of every row becomes first st on foll row.

With D, make 34ch.
Foundation row: 1dc in 2nd ch from hook, 1dc in next 32ch, 1ch, turn: 33 sts. Next row: Miss first dc, 1dc in next 32dc, 1ch, turn. Do not break off D. Join in L and work 2 rows in dc as on last row.
Work in patt: 1st row: With D, miss

268

first dc, * 1dc in back loop only of next dc, 1trB; rep from * to last 2 sts, 1dc into back loop only of each dc, 1ch, turn. 2nd row: With D, miss first dc, 1dc in every st to end of row, 1ch, turn. 3rd row: With L, miss 1dc, * 1trB, 1dc into back loop only of next dc; rep from * to end, 1ch, turn. 4th row: With L, as 2nd row. These 4 rows form patt. Rep 1st to 4th row 3 times more. Break off L. Cont in D, dec for top as follows: Next row: Miss 2dc, * 1dc in next 2dc, miss 1dc; rep from * to last st, 1dc, 1ch, turn: 22 sts. Work 3 rows dc. Next row: Miss 2dc, * 1dc in next 2dc, miss 1dc; rep from * to last 2 sts, 2dc, 1ch, turn: 15 sts. Work 1 row dc.

Ridge row: Make ridge by working dc into back loops only all across, 1ch, turn. Next row: Miss 2dc, * 1dc, miss 1dc; rep from * to last st, 1dc, 1ch, turn: 8 sts. Work 1 row dc. Next row: * Miss 1dc, 1dc in next dc; rep from * to end. Fasten off. Work another piece to match.

TO MAKE UP
Observing general method on page 81, block and press.
Leaving openings for spout and handle, join side seams, taking care to match ends of ridge row at top of cosy. Turn right side out and work collar thus: Starting at one side edge, using L, work 30dc into 30 loops of ridge row, 1ch, turn. Work 1 row dc, 1ch, turn. Work 1st to 4th row of patt. Fasten off. Join side edge of collar. Work 1 row dc in W round opening for spout and handle.

KNITTED EGG COSIES
Materials: Oddments of Patons Double Knitting. Pair No 8 needles.

Cast on 29 sts.
1st and 2nd rows: K. 3rd row: * P1, K3; rep from * to last st, P1. 4th row: P. 5th row: As 3rd. 6th row: K. 7th to 22nd row: Rep last 4 rows 4 times more. Break yarn, thread through sts, draw up and fasten off securely.

THE LOOP
Cast on 14 sts. Cast off.

TO MAKE UP
Join seam. Stitch loop in place at top of cosy.

Bertie Bottleguard

Materials: 1 (50g) ball each Royal Blue, Red, and Black; oddments of Pink and Yellow Patons Double Knitting. Small amount of cotton wool or kapok for stuffing. No 4·00 mm crochet hook.

Additional Abbreviations (see page 29): RB=Royal Blue; R=Red; B= Black; Pk=Pink; Y=Yellow.

BASE
With RB, make 4ch. Join with ss into ring. 1st rnd: Work 8dc into ring. 2nd rnd: (1dc, inc in next dc) 4 times: 12 sts. 3rd rnd: (1dc, inc in next dc) 6 times: 18 sts. 4th rnd: (1dc, inc in next dc) 9 times: 27 sts.
5th rnd: (2dc, inc in next dc) 9 times: 36 sts. 6th rnd: (3dc, inc in next dc) 9 times: 45 sts. 7th rnd: (2dc, inc in next dc, 2dc) 9 times: 54 sts. Fasten off.

BODY
Note: '1ch' at end of every row becomes first st on foll row.
Starting with trousers, with RB, make 46ch.
Foundation row: 1dc in 2nd ch from hook, 1dc in next 44ch, 1ch, turn: 45 sts. Next row: Miss 1dc, 1dc in next 44dc, 1ch, turn. Rep last row until work measures 5½ in from start. Fasten off.
With R, make 54ch for Tunic.
Foundation row: 1dc in 2nd ch from

hook, 1dc in next 52ch, 1ch, turn: 53 sts. Cont in dc until work measures 1 in from start. Dec row: * Miss 1dc, 5dc; rep from * to end of row, 1ch, turn: 45 sts.

Place last row of R in front of last row of RB and using R work a row of dc, taking an R and corresponding RB st tog all across row: 45 sts.

Work 1 row R. Do not break off R. Join in Y and work 2 rows for Belt. Break off Y. Cont working in R until work measures 8 in from start.

Make holes for cord: Next row: Miss 1dc, 1dc in next dc, * 2ch, miss 2dc, 1dc in next dc; rep from * to last st, 1dc. Work 1 row, working 2dc into each '2ch' space and 1dc into each 1dc. Fasten off. With R, make 12 inch ch and and thread through holes at top.

TOP (worked in 2 pieces)

With R, make 25ch. Foundation row: 1dc in 2nd ch from hook, 1dc in next 23ch, 1ch, turn: 24 sts. Work 1 row dc. Next row: * Miss 1dc, 2dc; rep from * to end of row, 1ch, turn: 17 sts. Work 1 row dc. Next row: Miss 1dc, 1dc, * miss 1dc, 2dc; rep from * to end of row, 1ch, turn: 12 sts. Work 4 rows dc. Break off R. Join in Pk and work 8 rows dc for face. Break off Pk. Join in B. Work 2 rows dc.

Next row: Miss 1dc, 1dc, * inc in next dc, 3dc; rep from * to last 2 sts, inc in next st, 1dc, 1ch, turn: 15 sts. Work 3 rows dc. Next row: Miss 1dc, * inc in next dc, 3dc; rep from * to last 2 sts, inc in next dc, 1dc, 1ch, turn: 19 sts. Work 11 rows dc. Next row: Miss 2dc, * 2dc, miss 1dc; rep from * to last 2 sts, 2dc, 1ch, turn: 13 sts. Work 1 row.

Next row: Miss 2dc, * 1dc, miss 1dc; rep from * to last st, 1dc, 1ch, turn: 7 sts. Work 1 row. Next row: Miss 2dc, * 1dc, miss 1dc; rep from * to last st, 1dc: 4 sts. Fasten off. Work another piece to match.

ARMS (make 4 pieces)

With Pk, make 4ch. Foundation row: 1dc in 2nd ch from hook, 1dc in next 2ch, 1ch, turn: 3 sts.

Inc row: 1dc in first dc, 2dc in next dc,

1dc, 1ch, turn: 5 sts. Inc row: 1dc in first dc, 2dc, 2dc in next dc, 1dc, 1ch, turn: 7 sts. Work 1 row.

Break off Pk. Join in R. Work 16 rows. Next row: Miss 2dc, 1dc in 3dc, miss 1dc, 1dc in last dc, 1ch, turn: 5 sts. Work 1 row. Next row: Miss 2dc, 1dc, miss 1dc, 1dc in last dc, 1ch, turn. Fasten off.

FEET (make 4 pieces)

With B, make 4ch and work as arms until first inc row has been worked: 5 sts. Work 7 rows. Fasten off.

TO MAKE UP

Observing general method on page 81, block and press.

With wrong side facing, stitch the 2 side edges of body together but noting that edges of tunic 'skirt' are left open. Pin lower edge of body to base and stitch. Slip body over bottle, draw up ch and tie. Pin arms into position on each side of body and stitch at top edge only. Slip body off bottle.

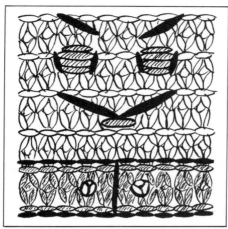

Take one piece of 'top' for front and embroider face as shown in diagram, using Blue for Eyes, Red for Mouth, and Black for Moustache and Brows.

Taking care to match rows, stitch th 2 Top pieces together up side edges an round top. Using a half strand (Black, work 2 lines of back-stitc round neck to outline Collar, one lin between Red and Pink rows and 2n line 2 rows down.

Work a centre upright st, then work Yellow french knot for buttons on eac side of centre line (see diagram). Wor 2 more buttons below and 4 buttons o Body part of Tunic. Work Buckle in Black straight sts. Using a half stran of Black, work a line of back-stitc down centre front of trousers, workin over seam. Make Feet by stitching Foot pieces together, stuff slightly an stitch into position at lower edge. Mak 4 inch Yellow ch and stitch round Fac to form strap. Pad hat with stuffing.

Golf Club Covers

Materials for 2 covers: 1 (50g) ball Dark and oddment of Light Patons Double Knitting. Pair each Nos 10 and 8 needles.

Measurement: Length 8 in.

Tension: 12 sts and 21 rows to 2 in over patt on No 8 needles.

Additional Abbreviations (see page 29): A=Dark; B=Light.

With No 10 needles and A, cast on 48 sts and work 24 rows K2, P2 rib.
Next row: * K2tog; rep from * to end: 24 sts. Work 5 rows K1, P1 rib. Next row: * Inc in next st; rep from * to last st, K into front, back, then front again of last st: 49 sts.
Join in B, change to No 8 needles and patt as follows: 1st row: (wrong side) in A, P. 2nd row: In B, K1, sl 1 with yarn at back, * K1, sl 3 with yarn at back; rep from * to last 3 sts, K1, sl 1, K1. 3rd row: In B, K1, * P3, sl 1 with yarn at front; rep from * to last 4 sts, P3, K1.

4th row: In A, K2, * sl 1 with yarn a back, K3; rep from * to last 3 sts, sl 1 K2. 5th row: In A, P. 6th row: In B K1, * sl 3 with yarn at back, K1; rep from * to end.
7th row: In B, K1, P1, * sl 1 with yarn at front, P3; rep from * to last 3 sts, sl 1 P1, K1. 8th row: In A, K4, * sl 1 with yarn at back, K3; rep from * to last st K1. Rows 1 to 8 form patt. Cont straight in patt until work measure 7½ in, ending with 1st or 5th row Break B.
Cont in A, shaping top: 1st row: K1 * K2tog, K1; rep from * to end: 33 sts 2nd row: P. 3rd row: K1, * K2tog; rep from * to end: 17 sts. 4th row: P Break yarn, thread through rem sts and fasten off securely.

TO MAKE UP
Observing general method on page 81 press.
Join side seams. With A, make a pom pon and sew to top of cover.

Neckties in Knitting and Crochet

KNITTED

Materials: 1 (50g) ball each of Medium, 1st Contrast, and 2nd Contrast Patons Purple Heather 4-ply. Pair No 10 needles. No 2·50 mm crochet hook.

Measurements: Length, 46½ in; width at widest point, 4 in.

Tension: 18 sts and 28 rows to 2 in over patt on No 10 needles.

Additional Abbreviations (see page 29): M=Medium, 1st C=1st Contrast, 2nd C=2nd Contrast.

With No 10 needles and M, cast on 18 sts and breaking off and joining in colours as required, work in stripe patt as follows:

1st row: (right side), * K1, yft, sl 1, yb; rep from * to end. 2nd row: P1, yb, sl 1, yft; rep from * to end. 3rd to 14th row: In M, as 1st and 2nd rows 6 times. 15th to 24th row: In 1st C, as 1st and 2nd rows 5 times.

25th to 28th row: In M, as 1st and 2nd rows twice. 29th to 38th row: In 2nd C, as 1st and 2nd rows 5 times. 39th to 42nd row: In 1st C, as 1st and 2nd rows twice. 43rd to 46th row: In 2nd C, as 1st and 2nd rows twice.

These 46 rows form stripe patt. Work straight in patt until tie measures 11 in, ending with right side facing.

Keeping continuity of stripe patt, shape tie by dec 1 st at each end of next and every foll 8th row until 12 sts rem. Work straight in stripe patt until 7 complete stripe patts have been worked from start, thus ending with a 46th row. Place marker at each end of last row. Now reverse stripe patt: 1st to 4th row: In 2nd C, as 43rd to 46th. 5th to 8th row: In 1st C, as 39th to 42nd. 9th to 18th row: In 2nd C, as 29th to 38th. 19th to 22nd row: In M, as 25th to 28th. 23rd to 32nd row: In 1st C, as 15th to 24th. 33rd to 46th row: In M, as 1st to 14th.

Now continue in stripe patt, shaping sides by inc 1 st at each end of next and every foll 20th row until there are 36 sts. Work straight in stripe patt until tie measures 44 in, ending with right side facing. Shape sides by dec 1 st at each end of next and every alt row until 7 complete stripe patts have been worked from marker. Cont in M, and dec as before until 2 sts rem. Next row: In M, work 2 tog and fasten off.

With right side facing, No 2·50 hook and M, start at centre back of neck and work 1 row dc all round edge, working 3dc into each corner, join with ss in first st. Fasten off.

Observing general method on page 81, press.

CROCHETED

Materials: 1 (50g) ball Patons Purple Heather 4-ply. No 3·00 mm crochet hook.

Measurements: Length, 52 in; width at widest part, 2¼ in.

Tension: 6½ sts and 5 rows to 1 in.

Note: Turning ch does not count as st.

Make 17ch, turn: 1st row: 1tr in 3rd ch from hook, * 1dc in next ch, 1tr in next ch; rep from * to end, turn with 1ch: 15 sts. 2nd row: 1dc in first tr, * 1tr in next st, 1dc in next st; rep from * to end, turn with 2ch. 3rd row: 1tr in first dc, * 1dc in next st, 1tr in next st; rep from * to end, turn with 1ch.

2nd and 3rd rows form patt. Rep 2nd and 3rd rows until 74 rows in all have been worked, turning with 1ch on last row.

Shape as follows: Next row: Miss first st, * 1dc in next st, 1tr in next st; rep from * to last 2 sts, miss 1 st, 1dc in last st, turn with 2ch: 13 sts.

Starting with 3rd patt row, rep the 2 patt rows 4 times. Rep last 9 rows until 9 sts rem. Cont straight in patt until tie measures 52 in.

Fasten off. Observing general method on page 81, press.

Crochet Shoulder Bag: Knitted Work Bag

CROCHET SHOULDER BAG

Materials: 4 (50g) balls Patons Double Knitting. No 4·00 mm crochet hook. Petersham ribbon for facing gusset and strap. Press stud.

Measurements: Width, 10 in; depth, 7½ in.

Tension: 10 sts and 12 rows to 2 in over dc.

Additional Abbreviations (see page 29): gr=group worked over 5 sts thus: (yoh, draw loop through next st, yoh, draw loop through first 2 loops on hook) 5 times, yoh, draw loop through all loops on hook, 1ch.

Turning ch of previous row counts as 1 st and the first st is missed on every row.

FRONT

** Make 52ch, turn. 1st row: 1dc in 2nd ch from hook, 1dc in each ch to end, turn with 1ch: 51 sts. 2nd row: 1dc in each st to end, turn with 1ch. Rep last row until front measures 7½ in.**
Fasten off.

BACK AND FLAP

Work as for front from ** to **.
Place marker at each end of last row. Work in dc for a further 2 in, omitting turning ch at end of last row.
Work flap: 1st row: (wrong side), 3ch, 2tr in first st, * miss 4 sts, 5tr in next st; rep from * to last 5 sts, miss 4 sts, 3tr in last st, turn with 3ch.
2nd row: (Yoh, draw loop through next st, yoh, draw loop through first 2 loops on hook) twice, yoh, draw loop through all loops on hook, * 4ch, 1gr; rep from * to last 3 sts, 4ch, (yoh, draw loop through next st, yoh, draw loop through first 2 loops on hook) 3 times, yoh, draw loop through all loops on hook, turn with 5ch.

3rd row: Miss first gr of 3tr, 3tr in top of next gr, * 5tr in top of next gr; rep from * to last gr of 5tr, 2tr in top of last gr of 5tr, yoh, draw loop through same st, yoh, draw loop through first 2 loops on hook, 1dtr in top of last gr of 3tr, yoh, draw loop through all loops on hook, turn with 3ch.
Rep last 2 rows 3 times more, then 2nd row again, turning with 4ch on last row.
Next row: 5tr in centre gr of 5tr, 1dtr in top of last gr of 3tr, turn with 3ch. Next row: (Yoh, draw loop through next st, yoh, draw loop through first 2 loops on hook) 4 times, yoh, draw loop through all loops on hook. Fasten off.

GUSSET AND STRAP

Make 11ch, turn. 1st row: 1dc in 2nd ch from hook, 1dc in each ch to end, turn with 1ch: 10 sts. 2nd row: 1dc in each st to end, turn with 1ch. Rep last row until work measures 54 in.

TO MAKE UP

Observing general method on page 81, block and press.
Back gusset and strap with petersham and join in a ring.
Sew lower edge and sides of front to one edge of strap placing join at centre of base. Now sew back in the same way to other edge of strap from marker to marker. Fold flap to front. Cut 6 lengths of yarn, 8 in long, and knot in point of flap to form tassel. Sew press stud on flap.

KNITTED WORK BAG

Materials: 1 (50g) ball each Main Shade and 2nd and 3rd Contrasts and 2 (50g) balls 1st Contrast Patons Doublet. Pair No 4 needles; 1 set of handles with 11 in slit; ⅜ yd of 48 in wide plastic lining.

Measurements: 11 in wide × 10 in deep without gusset.

Tension: 8 sts and 10 rows to 2 in over st st.

Additional Abbreviations (see page 29): MS=Main Shade; 1st C=1st Contrast; 2nd C=2nd Contrast; 3rd C =3rd Contrast.

FRONT AND BACK (both alike)

With MS, cast on 42 sts. 1st row: K. 2nd row: P. 3rd row: With 1st C, K. 4th row: With 1st C, * K1, P1; rep from * to end. 5th row: With 1st C, * P1, K1; rep from * to end. 6th and 7th rows: As 4th and 5th. 8th row: With 1st C, P. 9th and 10th rows: As 1st and 2nd. 11th to 16th row: As 3rd to 8th, with 3rd C in place of 1st C. 17th and 18th rows: As 1st and 2nd.

19th to 24th row: As 3rd to 8th, with 2nd C in place of 1st C. 25th to 32nd row: As 1st to 8th. 33rd to 40th row: As 17th to 24th. 41st to 48th row: As 9th to 16th. 49th to 56th row: As 1st to 8th. 57th and 58th rows: As 1st and 2nd. Cast off.

GUSSET

With 1st C, cast on 9 sts. Work in moss st (every row * K1, P1; rep from * to last st, K1) for 31 in. Cast off.

TO MAKE UP

Observing general method on page 81, block and press. Stitch gusset in position leaving 1¼ in at top of back and front for fixing into handles. Thread top of back and front through slits in handles, stitch in position. Cut piece of plastic for lining 11¼ × 22 in, then 2 strips 2½ × 10¼ in. Machine side gussets to lining. Fold in ⅛ in hem at top, machine round hem and stitch lining in position.

Belt in Crochet

Materials (sufficient for 2 belts): 1 (50g) ball each Brown, Yellow, and Dark Red Patons Double Knitting. No 4·00 mm crochet hook. 5 hooks and eyes.

Measurement: To fit 24–26 in waist.

Tension: 1 motif measures 4 in square.

Additional Abbreviations (see page 29): Y=Yellow; B=Brown; R=Dark Red.
Note: Carry yarn not in use loosely along back of work.

MOTIF 1

With Y, make 4ch, join into ring with ss.
1st rnd: 3ch, 11tr into ring, join with ss to top of ch. 2nd rnd: * 4ch, miss 2 sts, 1dc in next st; rep from * to end, but working last loop of last dc in R. 3rd rnd: In R, * (1dc, 1htr, 1tr, 3dtr, 1tr, 1htr, 1dc) all in next ch sp, 1ch; rep from * to end, using Y join with ss to 1st dc.
4th rnd: In Y, 3ch, 4tr, in last ch sp of previous rnd, * (3htr, 2ch, 3htr) all in centre of next 3dtr, 5tr in next ch sp; rep from * twice more, (3htr, 2ch, 3htr) in centre of next 3dtr, using R, join with ss to top of ch.
5th rnd: In R, 2ch, 1htr, in each st, 3htr in each ch sp, using B, join with ss to top of ch. Break R and Y. 6th rnd: In B, 2ch, 1htr in each st, but working 3htr in each corner st, join with ss to top of ch. Fasten off.

MOTIF 2

As Motif 1, but reading R for Y and Y for R.
Work 3 each of Motifs 1 and 2 (6 in all).

TO MAKE UP

Observing general method on page 81,

press. Alternating motifs, join 3 motifs into a long strip. Make another strip in the same manner.

Border: With B, work 1 rnd dc all round each strip working 3dc into each corner.

Sew hooks to wrong side of short edge of 1 strip, then sew eyes to other strip to correspond for back opening.

Lacing: With right side facing, rejoin B to corner of short edge of front, 1dc in corner st, * 2ch, miss 1 st, 1dc in next st; rep from * to next corner st. Fasten off. Work along other short edge in the same manner.

Cord: Using 1 strand Y and 1 strand R tog, make crochet chain 40 in long. Fasten off. Lace cord through holes. Using Y and R, make small tassels and sew to ends.

Knitted Cushion

Materials: 7 (50g) balls Patons Double Knitting. Pair No 8 needles.

Measurements: 18 × 18 in (excluding borders).

Tension: 16 sts and 18 rows to 3 in over patt.

Additional Abbreviations (see page 29): Trellis 8=sl next 8 sts on to right needle dropping extra loops to form long sts, place point of left needle through 5th, 6th, 7th and 8th sts and cross them over 1st, 2nd, 3rd and 4th sts and on to left needle, then sl first 4 sts back on to left needle and K8 in this position.

FRONT AND BACK (both alike)
Cast on 96 sts, K 1 row, now work in patt as follows: 1st and 2nd rows: K. 3rd row: K1, * K1 winding yarn 4 times round needle; rep from * to last st, K1. 4th row: * Trellis 8; rep from * to end. 5th and 6th rows: K.
These 6 rows form patt. Rep them until work measures 18 in, ending with a 6th patt row. Cast off.

TO MAKE UP
Observing general method on page 81, press.
With right sides facing, join 3 sides. Turn inside out and insert pad. Join 4th seam.

BORDER
Cast on 10 sts and patt as follows: 1st row: Sl 1, K2, yf, K2tog, K1, (yf, yrn,

K2tog) twice. 2nd row: Sl 1, * K1 into yrn and P1 into yf of previous row, K1; rep from * once, K to last 3 sts, yf, K2tog, K1. 3rd row: Sl 1, K2, yf, K2tog, K3, (yf, yrn, K2tog) twice. 4th row: As 2nd. 5th row: Sl 1, K2, yf, K2tog, K5, (yf, yrn, K2tog) twice. 6th row: As 2nd. 7th row: Sl 1, K2, yf, K2tog, K11. 8th row: Cast off 6, K to last 3 sts, yf, K2tog, K1.

These 8 rows form patt. Work straight in patt until border fits along one side of cushion, ending with an 8th patt row. Turn corner thus: Next row: As 1st patt row. Next row: Sl 1, * K1 into yrn and P1 into yf of previous row, K1; rep from * once, K to last 3 sts, turn. Next row: K to last 4 sts, (yf, yrn, K2tog) twice. Rep last 2 rows once more. Next row: Sl 1, * K1 into yrn and P1 into yf, K1; rep from * once, K to last 3 sts, turn. Next row: K to end. Next row: As 8th patt row.

Rep last 8 rows once more. Now cont in patt (from 1st patt row) until border fits along 2nd side, ending with an 8th patt row. Turn 2nd corner as before. Cont thus until 4th corner has been turned. Cast off.

Sew in position all round. Join cast-on and cast-off edges. Press seams.

Crocheted Cushion

Materials: 2 (50g) balls each Dark and Light Patons Double Knitting. No 4·00 mm crochet hook.

Measurements: 16 × 16 in.

Additional Abbreviations (see page 29): D=Dark; L=Light.

FRONT

With D, make 6ch. Join with ss into ring.

1st rnd: Work 16htr into ring and join with ss. Break off D, join in L. 2nd rnd: Make 3ch, 1tr into previous st (thus forming the first crossed treble), 1ch, miss 1 st, 1tr into next st, 1tr into previous st, 3ch, * miss 1 st, 1tr into next st, 1tr into previous st, 1ch, miss 1 st, 1tr into next st, 1tr into previous st, 3ch; rep from * to end of rnd, join with ss to top of first tr. 3rd rnd: 3ch, 1tr into previous '3ch sp', miss 2 sts, 1tr into next st (first st of second crossed tr), miss previous '1ch', 1tr into 2nd st of first crossed tr, 1ch, miss next tr, 1tr into '3ch sp', 1tr into previous tr, 3ch, * 1tr into first tr after '3ch sp', 1tr into previous '3ch sp', 1ch, miss 2 sts, 1tr into next tr, miss previous '1ch', 1tr into 2nd st of last crossed tr, 1ch, miss next tr, 1tr into '3ch sp', 1tr into previous tr, 3ch; rep from * to end of rnd, join with ss to top of first tr.

4th rnd: 3ch, 1tr into previous '3ch sp', 1ch, (miss 2 sts, 1tr in next tr, miss previous '1ch', 1tr into 2nd st of last crossed tr, 1ch) twice, miss next tr, 1tr into '3ch sp', 1tr into previous tr, 3ch, * 1tr into next tr, 1tr into previous '3ch sp', 1ch, (miss 2 sts, 1tr into next tr, miss previous '1ch' *, 1tr into 2nd st of last crossed tr, 1ch) twice, miss next tr, 1tr into '3ch sp', 1tr into previous tr, 3ch; rep from * to end of rnd, join with ss to top of first tr.

5th rnd: As 4th rnd, but working the bracketed portion 3 times instead of twice, thus giving 1 more crossed tr on each side of square. Break off L, join in D. 6th rnd: Work 1htr into every st all rnd, working 5htr into '3ch sp' at each corner. Work 8 more squares in same manner.

BACK

Work 9 squares as for Front but reversing colours, using L in place of D, and D in place of L.

TO MAKE UP

Observing general method on page 81, block and press.

Take the 9 squares for front and stitch tog on wrong side. With right side of work facing, using D, work a row of htr all round edge, working 3htr into each corner st. Join 9 squares tog for back and using L work a row of htr all round edge in same way. Press lightly and join tog round 3 sides, insert pad and stitch up 4th side.

Knitted and Crocheted Balls

See illustrations in Chapter 11, page 142, and Chapter 17, page 259

KNITTED BALL

Materials: 1 (50g) ball each Light and Medium Patons Double Knitting. Pair No 10 needles. Kapok for stuffing.

Tension: 12 sts and 16 rows to 2 in.

Additional Abbreviations (see page 29): L=Light; M=Medium.

ONE SECTION

With L, cast on 1 st. 1st row: K1. 2nd row: P into front and back of st. 3rd row: Inc in first st, K1, inc in last st.

Cont in st st with L, working duckling motif in M from chart (next row, 4th row), noting that each square across represents a st and each row of square represents a row; also one square extra

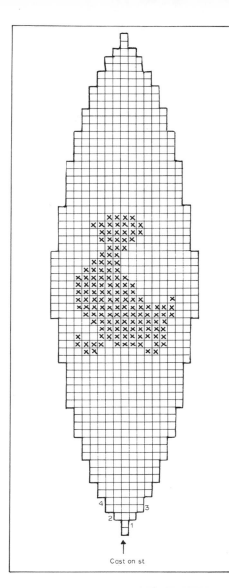

Cast on st

at each end of row equals an increase and one square less equals a decrease. Make 5 sections more (6 in all), 2 in L with motif in M and 3 in M with motif in L.

TO MAKE UP
Observing general method on page 81, block and press. Join sections tog neatly leaving an opening for stuffing. Stuff and sew up opening.

CROCHETED BALL
Materials: 1 (50g) ball Patons Double Knitting. No 4·50 mm crochet hook. Kapok for stuffing.

Make 4 ch, join into ring with ss.
1st rnd: 1ch, work 10dc into circle, join with ss in 1st ch. 2nd rnd: Work in dc, working twice into every alt st.
3rd, 4th, 5th and 6th rnds: 2ch, work in tr working twice into every alt st. Work 6 rnds in tr. Note: Join all rnds with ss.
Next rnd: 2ch, work in tr dec by missing every 3rd st to end of rnd. Next rnd: 2ch, work in tr dec by missing every 3rd st to end of rnd. Join with ss. Next 2 rnds: As last rnd.
Now draw loop on hook up a few in, remove hook and stuff ball firmly with kapok. Insert hook again in loop, draw up tightly and cont thus: Next rnd: As last rnd.
Next rnd: 2 ch, work in tr, dec by missing every alt st, join with ss. Next rnd: 1ch, work in dc dec as on last rnd. Break thread, run through rem sts, draw up and fasten off.

Chapter 18

Postscript—The Way Ahead

A successful book, like a good meal, should leave its readers avid for more. It would give the authors the greatest possible satisfaction to feel that the methods explained in this book and the collection of designs had given readers the urge to become adventurous and to try their hands at original designing. By way of inspiration we end with a collection of stitches – nine each in knitting and crochet. They provide a variety of effects and can be made the foundations for fashion and sports wear, shawls, afghans, baby things and a host of other uses. There is no satisfaction like the thrill of having created something which is one's very own!

Knitting Stitches

EYELET STITCH
Multiple of 4.

Knit the crochet look with this simple open-work stitch.

1st row: * K2, yf, yrn, K2; rep from * to end. 2nd row: * P2tog, (K1, P1) in made sts of previous row, P2tog; rep from * to end. 3rd row * yf (to make 1), K1; rep from * to end. 4th row: * P1, (P2tog) twice, K1; rep from * to end. These 4 rows form patt.

PEBBLE STITCH
Multiple of 2.

This neat all-over textured effect is excellent for children's garments.

1st and 2nd rows: K. 3rd row: * K2tog; rep from * to end. 4th row: * K1, pick up horizontal thread before next st and K it; rep from * to end. These 4 rows form patt.

MESH RIB
Multiple of 2.

An easy one-row stitch forms a very attractive lacy fabric when worked on big needles.

1st and every row: K1, * yf, K2tog; rep from * to last st, K1. This row forms patt.

TWIN CABLES
Multiple of 11 + 2.

Pairs of cables give an interesting Aran variation suitable for family sports garments.

1st row: * P2, K4, P1, K4; rep from * to last 2 sts, P2. 2nd row: * K2, P4, K1, P4; rep from * to last 2 sts, K2. 3rd and 4th rows: As 1st and 2nd. 5th row: * P2, slip next 2 sts on cable needle to front of work, K2, then K sts from cable needle, P1, slip next 2 sts on cable needle to back of work, K2, then K sts from cable needle; rep from * to last 2 sts, P2. 6th row: As 2nd. These 6 rows form patt.

OPEN HONEYCOMB
Multiple of 6.

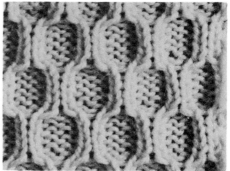

Good example of an interesting textured fabric which can be used for both casual and fashion designs.

1st row: * P2, K2, P2; rep from * to end. 2nd row: * K2, P2, K2; rep from * to end. 3rd and 4th rows: as 1st and 2nd. 5th row: * slip 2 sts on cable needle to back of work, K1, then P2 from cable needle, slip 1 st on cable needle to front of work, P2, then K st from cable needle; rep from * to end. 6th row: * P1, K4, P1; rep from * to end. 7th row: * K1, P4, K1; rep from * to end. 8th to 10th row: rep 6th and 7th rows once, then 7th row again. 11th row: * slip 1 st on cable needle to front of work, P2, then K st from cable needle, slip next 2 sts on cable needle to back of work, K1, then P2 from cable needle; rep from * to end. 12th row: As 2nd. These 12 rows form patt.

CROSSED INSERTION
Multiple of 6.

Patterning with a difference looks equally attractive as a chunky fabric or worked finely for baby garments.

1st row: (right side) * K1 wrapping yarn twice round needle; rep from * to end. 2nd row: * slip next 3 sts on cable needle to front of work dropping off extra loops, K3 dropping off extra loops, now K3 from cable needle; rep from * to end. These 2 rows form patt.

ALTERNATING BOBBLES
Multiple of 10 + 5.

These are used to give a bold embossed effect: they can be large or small.

1st row: K. 2nd row: P. 3rd row: K7, * make bobble (MB) thus: (K into front and back of same st) twice, then K into front of same st again, turn, work 4 rows stocking st on these 5 sts, then with left-hand needle slip 2nd, 3rd, 4th and 5th sts over first st (1 bobble made), K9; rep from * to last 8 sts, make bobble, K7. 4th row: P. 5th and 6th rows: As 1st and 2nd. 7th row: K2, * MB, K9; rep from * to last 3 sts, MB, K2. 8th row: P. These 8 rows form patt.

DIAGONAL LACE
Multiple of 4 + 1.

A pretty patterning which is very suitable for baby clothes and summer tops.

1st row: * K1, yf, sl1, K2tog, psso, yf; rep from * to last st, K1. 2nd and alt rows: P. 3rd row: * K2, yf, K2togtbl; rep from * to last st, K1. 5th row: K2 tog, * yf, K1, yf, sl1, K2tog, psso; rep from * to last 3 sts, yf, K1, yf, K2togtbl. 7th row: K4, * yf, K2togtbl, K2; rep from * to last st, K1. 8th row: P. These 8 rows form patt.

SLIP STITCH STRIPES
Multiple of 3.

One of the easiest ways of working in colour giving a Fair Isle effect but using only one colour on a row. Our version uses 3 colours.

Note: P1W means purl 1 wrapping yarn round needle twice. 1st row: In L, * K2, sl1 P; rep from * to last 3 sts, K3. 2nd row: In L, P3, * sl1 P, P2; rep from * to end. 3rd row: In L, K. 4th row: In L, P2, * P1W, P2; rep from * to last st, P1. 5th row: In D, K3, * sl1 P, K2; rep from * to end. 6th row: In D, * P2, sl1 P; rep from * to last 3 sts, P3. 7th row: In D, K. 8th row: In D, P1, * P1W, P2; rep from * to last 2 sts, P1W, P1. 9th row: In M, K1, * sl1 P, K2; rep from * to last 2 sts, sl 1P, K1. 10th row: In M, P1, * sl1P, P1; rep from * to last 2 sts, sl1P, P1. 11th row: In M, K. 12th row: In M, P3, * P1W, P2; rep from * to end. These 12 rows form patt.

Crochet Stitches

PICOT LACE
Foundation ch. Multiple of 4+10.

An open-work lace which is ideal for shawls and stoles.

1st row: 1dc in 10th ch from hook, 3ch, 1dc in same ch, * 5ch, miss 3ch, (1dc 3ch 1dc) in next ch; rep from * ending 5ch, miss 3 ch, 1dc in last ch, turn. 2nd row: 6ch, * (1dc, 3ch, 1dc) in 9ch loop of previous row, 5ch; rep from * ending 1dc in 5th of 10ch loop, turn. 2nd row forms patt.

TREBLE ARCHES
Foundation ch. Multiple of 3+2.

Rows of trebles and chain loops make this firm open fabric – suitable for rugs and accessories.

1st row: 1dc in 2nd ch from hook, * 5ch, miss 2ch, 1dc in next ch; rep from * to end, turn. 2nd row: 3ch, * 3tr in next ch loop, miss 1dc; rep from * ending 3tr in ch loop, 1tr in last dc, turn. 3rd row: 1ch, 1dc in 1st tr, * 5ch, miss 2 tr, 1dc in next tr; rep from * to end, turn. 2nd and 3rd rows form patt.

SMALL MOTIF

Simple motif for the beginner – is often linked with larger motifs in a patchwork of colours for Afghans.

Make 8ch, join in a ring with ss. 1st rnd: 12dc into ring, ss to 1st dc. 2nd rnd: (6ch, miss 2dc, ss in next dc) 4 times. 3rd rnd: In each 6ch loop, work (1dc, 9tr, 1dc), ss to 1st dc. Fasten off.

SOLOMONS LACE
Foundation ch. Multiple of 6+2.

A very popular open fabric which is worked quickly and is suitable for using in a variety of ways.

1st row: 1dc in 2nd ch from hook, * draw loop on hook up to ½ in in height, yoh, and draw through loop on hook, insert hook between loop and single thread of this ch and complete as dc (knot st made), work another knot the same (solomons knot completed), miss 5ch, 1dc in next ch; rep from * ending with 1½ solomons knots, turn. 2nd row: * 1dc over double loop at right of centre of next knot, 1dc over double knot at left of same knot, work 1 solomons knot; rep from * omitting 1 solomons knot at end of last rep, work 1½ solomons knots, turn. 2nd row forms patt.

FLOWER MOTIF

Circular motifs look attractive worked in planned colour schemes and joined together for rugs and Afghans.

Make 4ch, join in a ring with ss. 1st rnd: 12dc into ring, join with ss. 2nd rnd: 2dc in each dc all round inserting hook in back thread of each st. 3rd rnd: * 1dc (inserting hook in back thread only) 2ch, miss 1 st; rep from * all round. 4th rnd: (1dc, 1tr, 2dtr, 1tr, 1dc) in each 2ch sp all round. Fasten off.

DOUBLE TREBLE LATTICE
Foundation ch. Multiple of 10+7.

A clever use of double treble and double crochet to give a bold diagonal patterning.

1st row: 1dc in 7th ch from hook, * 7ch, miss 5ch, 1dc in next ch, 3ch, miss 3ch, 1dc in next ch; rep from * to end, turn. 2nd row: 4ch, 3dtr in 3ch sp, * 2ch, 1dc in 7ch loop, 2ch, 4dtr in 3ch sp; rep from * ending 4dtr in 6ch sp, turn. 3rd row: * 7ch, 1dc in 2ch sp, 3ch, 1dc in next 2ch sp; rep from * ending 7ch, 1dc in top of turning ch, turn. 4th row: 7ch, 1dc in 7ch loop, * 2ch, 4dtr in 3ch sp, 2ch, 1dc in 7ch loop; rep from * to end, turn. 5th row: 6ch, * 1dc in 2ch sp, 7ch, 1dc in next 2ch sp, 3ch; rep from * ending 1dc in 7ch loop, turn. 2nd to 5th row forms patt.

288

POPCORN BANDS
Foundation ch. Multiple of 6+3.

Bobbles are effective in crochet and are easily worked in treble and chain.

1st row: 1tr in 4th ch from hook, 1tr in each ch to end, 5ch, turn. 2nd row: Miss 3tr, * 4tr in next tr, remove hook from loop, insert in 1st tr of tr group then in dropped loop and draw it through (a popcorn stitch made), 2ch, miss 2tr, 1tr in next tr, 2ch, miss 2 tr; rep from * omitting 2ch at end of last rep and working last tr in 3rd of 3ch, 3ch, turn. 3rd row: * 2tr in next sp, 1tr in next popcorn stitch, 2tr in next sp, 1tr in next tr; rep from * working last tr in 3rd of 5ch, 5ch, turn. 2nd and 3rd rows form patt.

TREBLE ROUND TREBLE
Foundation ch (any number).

Bold ridged effect used when a firm solid fabric is required.

1st row: Work 1tr in 2nd ch from hook, 1tr in each ch all across, turn. 2nd row: 3ch, yoh, insert hook from right to left behind top of 2nd tr of previous row, pull loop through, yoh, complete tr in usual way; cont working thus in every tr all across row, turn. 2nd row forms patt.

HALF TREBLE TRELLIS
Foundation ch (any number)

Neat open fabric, popular for suits and jackets.

1st row: 1dc in 2nd ch from hook, 1dc in each ch to end, turn. 2nd row: 1ch, * 1htr in 2nd st, miss 1 st, 1htr in next st, 1htr inserting hook in sp between the 2 previous htr; rep from * ending miss 1 st, 1htr in last st. 3rd row: 1ch, then work in dc all across, inserting hook in the front thread at the head of each st of previous row. 2nd and 3rd rows form patt.

Book List

Books and publications consulted include:

E.M.C. *The Lady's Work-Book* (First Series. London: Hatchards 1876)

CLAPHAM, J. H. *An Economic History of Modern Britain* (Cambridge: University Press 1967)

CLEVERLY, DORIS A. *Fishermen's Ganseys* (The Dalesman July 1949) pp 141–4

DEFOE, DANIEL *A Tour Through the Whole Island of Great Britain* (London: J. M. Dent & Sons Ltd 1962)

DEFOE, DANIEL *The Life, Adventures & Piracies of the Famous Captain Singleton* (London: J. M. Dent & Sons Ltd 1911)

FELKIN, WILLIAM *A History of the Machine-wrought Hosiery and Lace Manufacturers* (W. Metcalfe 1867)

FIENNES, CELIA *The Journeys of Celia Fiennes* ed. Christopher Morris (London: Cresset Press 1947)

FISHER, F. J. ed. *Essays in the Economic and Social History of Tudor and Stuart England* (Cambridge: University Press 1961)

GAUGAIN, MRS. J. *The Knitters' Friend* (Edinburgh: I. J. Gaugain 1846)

GAUGAIN, MRS. J. *The Lady's Assistant* (Vols 1 & 2. Edinburgh: I. J. Gaugain 1844)

GAUGAIN, MRS. J. *The Accompaniment to Second Volume of Mrs. Gaugain's Work* (Edinburgh: I. J. Gaugain 1844)

GRASS, MILTON AND ANNA *Stockings for a Queen; the Life of the Rev. William Lee, the Elizabethan Inventor* (London: Heinemann 1967).

DE LA HAMELIN, RIGOLETTE *The Royal Magazine of Knitting, Netting, Crochet and Fancy Needlework* (Vol II. London: Sherwood & Co.)

HARTLEY, MARIE and INGILBY, JOAN *The Old Hand-knitters of the Dales* (Clapham: The Dalesman Publishing Company 1951)

LAMBERT, MISS *My Knitting Book* (First Series. London: John Murray 1846)

LEWIS, E. *Directions for Knitting Socks and Stockings* (London: Society for Promoting Christian Knowledge 1883)

LEWIS, E. *Wools and How to Use Them* (Strood: Sweet & Sons 1884)

LIPSON, E. *The Economic History of England* (London: Adam & Charles Black 1962)

MEE, CORNELIA *Exercises in Knitting* (London: David Bogue 1846)

NICOLLE, EDMUND TOULMIN *The Town of St. Helier* (Jersey C.I.: J. T. Bigwood Ltd)

NORBURY, JAMES A Note on Knitting and Knitted Fabrics in *A History of Technology* (Vol III. Oxford: University Press 1957)

POTTER, ESTHER *English Knitting and Crochet Books of the Nineteenth Century* (London: The Bibliographical Society 1955)

SCRIVENOR, M. ELLIOT *Knitting & Crocheting Book* (Alloa: John Paton Son & Co. Ltd. Editions of 1896, 1899 & 1908)

THOMSON, C. & W. *The Knitting and Crochet Work Book* (First and Second Series. Kilmarnock: M. & C. Laughland)

THOMSON, C. & W. *The Knitted Lace Pattern Book* (Kilmarnock: M. & C. Laughland)

UTTLEY, JOHN *The Story of the Channel Islands* (London: Faber & Faber 1966)

General Index

Design Index

Detailed instructions are given in this book for all the items
in the Design Index. Those in crochet are clearly indicated;
the remainder are in knitting.